Dictionary of Radio and Television Terms

German - English

Fachwörterbuch Hörfunk und Fernsehen

Deutsch - Englisch

Lists of abbreviations used in this dictionary and in the general field of broadcasting will be found on pages XI and XIII respectively.

Im Wörterbuch verwendete Abkürzungen und fachsprachliche Abkürzungen siehe Seite XI und XIII.

A

ab! (F, Band) cue! roll! go ahead! run...!

A/B Kopierverfahren *n* A and B printing

Abbau *m* dismantling *n*; ~ *m* (Dekoration) strike *n*

abbauen *v* dismantle *v*; ~ *v* (Dekoration) to strike a set, pull down *v*, to kill a set (US)

abbestellen *v* cancel *v*

Abbildunggröße *f* image size

Abbildungsebene *f* image plane

Abbildungsfehler *m* image defect, picture fault, aberration *n*

Abbildungsgüte *f* definition of image, picture quality

Abbildungslinse *f* image lens, objective lens

Abblende *f* (F) fade-out (FO) *n*, fading-down *n*; ~ *f* (Objektiv) stopping-down *n*; ~ *f* (Licht) dimming *n*; ~ *f* (Ton) sound fade

abblenden *v* fade down *v*; ~ *v* (F) fade out *v*, blend out *v*; ~ *v* (Objektiv) iris out *v*, stop down *v*; ~ *v* (Licht) dim *v*; ~ *v* (Ton) to dip the sound

Abblendung *f s.* Abblende

Abdeckblech *n* cover plate, cover sheet, back of receiver

abdecken *v* (Nachrichten) to ensure full coverage of; ~ *v* (Objektiv) cap *v*

Abdeckrahmen *m* masking frame

Abdeckung *f* (Blende) covering *n*, masking *n*; ~ *f* (Schutz) cover *n*; ~ *f* (Objektiv) cap *n*

abdrehen *v* finish *v*, complete *v*

Abdruck *m* reprint *n*

abdrucken *v* reprint *v*

abdrücken *v* (Räuspertaste) push *v*

Abendausgabe *f* evening edition

Abendprogramm *n* evening programme

Abendvorstellung *f* evening performance

Abenteuerfilm *m* adventure film

abfahren *v* (F, Band) run *v*, roll *v*

abfahren! (Kommando) go ahead!, roll!

Abfall *m* (Reste) waste *n*, junk *n*, scrap *n*

Abfallzeit *f* fall time

abfassen *v* (Text) word *v*, formulate *v*

Abfindung *f* compensation *n*

abfotografieren *v* (Thea.) to record a theatre production

abfragen *v* interrogate *v*; ~ *v* (EDV) query *v*

Abgang *m* (Darsteller) exit *n*

abgeben *v* (an) (bei Sendung) hand over *v* (to), go over *v* (to)

abgedreht *adj* dead *adj*

abgedroschen *adj* hackneyed *adj*

abgehackt *adv* (sprechen) staccato *adv*

Abgleichanweisung *f* line-up instructions *n pl*

abgleichen *v* align *v*, match *v*, adjust *v*; ~ (Brücke) balance *v*

Abgleichgenauigkeit *f* calibration accuracy

Abgleichung *f* alignment *n*, adjustment *n*; ~ *f* (Brücke) balancing *n*

Abgleichwiderstand *m* (Brücke) balancing resistor, calibration resistor

abheben *v* (Video) lift *v*

Abhebung *f* (Video) lift *n*

Abhörbericht *m* listening report, monitoring report

Abhörbox *f* sound booth, control cubicle, listening cubicle

Abhördienst *m* monitoring service

abhören *v* listen *v*, monitor *v*

Abhören *n* monitoring *n*

Abhörer *m* monitor *n*, monitoring loudspeaker

Abhörkabine *f* sound booth, control cubicle, listening cubicle
Abhörkontrolle *f* monitoring *n*
Abhörlautsprecher *m* monitoring loudspeaker, control loudspeaker
Abhörraum *m* monitoring room, listening room
Abhörverstärker *m* monitoring amplifier
abhusten *v* (Mikro) to clear the throat
Abisolierzange *f* stripping pliers *n pl*, wire strippers *n pl*
abklammern *v* paper up *v*, to assemble rush copy
Abklatschen *n* slash duping, direct printing
abklingen *v* fade *v*; ~ **lassen** fade out *v*, fade down *v*
Ablauf *m* run *n*, flow *n*; ~ *m* (Sendung) presentation continuity ~ **machen** to make the running order, to fix the running order; **szenischer** ~ scenic progression
Ablaufplan *m* story-board *n*; ~ *m* (Sendung) running order; ~ **machen** to make the running order, to fix the running order; **vorläufiger** ~ (Prod.) provisional running order, production outline
Ablaufregie *f* (R) continuity suite, presentation suite
Ablaufregisseur *m* network director, presentation director, continuity director
abläuten *v* to give the red
Ablenkeinheit *f* (FS-Empfänger) deflecting unit, sweep unit
ablenken *v* deflect *v*, sweep *v*
Ablenkgenerator *m* scanning generator, time-base generator, sweep generator
Ablenkgerät *n* scan generator
Ablenkschaltung *f* deflection circuit, sweep circuit
Ablenkspannung *f* (EDV) deflecting voltage
Ablenkspule *f* sweeping coil, deflection coil
Ablenkung *f* deflection *n*, scanning *n*, sweep *n*
Ablenkzeit *f* deflection time, scanning time, sweep time
ablesen *v* read *v*, read off *v*
Abluft *f* exhaust air
abmelden *v* (Leitung) cancel *v*
Abmessungen *f pl* dimensions *n pl*
Abnahme *f* acceptance *n*; ~ *f* (R) scrutiny *n*; ~ *f* (Minderung, Licht) reduction *n*, decrease *n*, fall-off *n*; ~ *f* (TV) preview *n*; ~ *f* (Minderung, Beleuchtung) dimming *n*; ~ *f* (Minderung, Schärfe) decrease *n*; ~ *f* (Minderung, Signal) loss *n*
Abnahmebericht *m* acceptance report, test certificate
abnahmefertig *adj* (TV) ready for preview; ~ *adj* (R) ready for scrutiny
abnahmeklar *adj s.* abnahmefertig
Abnahmekopie *f* transmission copy, transmission print, transmission tape
Abnahmeprotokoll *n* acceptance report, test certificate
Abnahmevorführung *f* preview screening, preview *n*
abnehmbar *adj* removable *adj*, detachable *adj*
abnehmen *v* accept *v*; ~ *v* (R) scrutinise *v*; ~ *v* (TV) preview *v*, shotgun *v* (US); ~ *v* (mindern) decrease *v*, lessen *v*, diminish *v*
Abrechnung *f* liquidation *n*, settlement *n*
Abrechnungsstelle *f* accounting department
abreißen *v* (Oszillator) break off *v*, to be interrupted
Abreißzeit *f* break-off time
Abrieb *m* abrasion *n*
abrufen *v* call *v*
Absage *f* closing announcement; **kurze** ~ back cue
absagen *v* to close a programme,

sign off *v* (US)
abschalten *v* switch off *v*; ~ *v*
(trennen) disconnect *v*, break *v*
Abschaltung *f* switching-off *n*; ~ *f*
(Trennung) disconnection *n*
abschirmen *v* screen *v*, shield *v*
Abschirmung *f* screening *n*, screen
n, shielding *n*, shield *n*
abschließen *v* close *v*, finish *v*; ~ *v*
(tech.) terminate *v*
Abschluß *m* closing *n*, conclusion *n*;
~ *m* (tech.) termination *n*
Abschlußbefehl *m* (EDV) close
statement
Abschlußbericht *m* (Dreh)
completion report
Abschlußwiderstand *m* terminating
resistance
abschminken, sich etwas (fam.) to
be disenchanted with s.th.
Abschminkpapier *n* tissues *n pl*
abschneiden *v* (begrenzen) clip *v*,
cut off *v*
Abschneiden *n* (Begrenzen)
clipping *n*, limiting *n*
Abschneidestufe *f* (TV) clipper *n*,
clipping circuit; **symmetrische** ~
symmetrical clipper
abschwächen *v* weaken *v*; ~ *v* (Text)
water down *v*; ~ *v* (Ton) attenuate
v; ~ *v* (Bild) reduce *v*; ~ *v* (sich)
(Bild) to grow blurred
Abschwächer *m* attenuator *n*, fader
n; ~ *m* (Bild) reducer *n*; **geeichter**
~ calibrated fader, calibrated
attenuator
Abschwächung *f* attenuation *n*; ~ *f*
(Bild) reduction *n*
Absenkung *f* (Tonwiedergabe) de-
emphasis *n*
absetzen *v* (Progr.) drop *v*; ~ *v*
(Agenturmeldung) run *v*, put out *v*
Absorption *f* absorption *n*
Absorptionsgrad *m* absorption
factor, absorption coefficient
Abspann *m* (fam.) end titles *n pl*
abspannen *v* (Mast) guy *v*, stay *v*
Abspannseil *n* guy rope, guy wire,

stay *n*
Abspanntitel *m* end titles *n pl*
Abspieldauer *f* duration of tape,
playback duration
abspielen *v* play *v*, play back *v*
Abspielerchassis *n* tape deck
Abspielfehler *m* reproducing loss,
playback loss
Abspielgerät *n* (Ton) replay
machine; ~ *n* (MAZ) reproducer *n*
Abspielgeschwindigkeit *f* replay
speed
Abspielnadel *f* reproducing stylus,
stylus *n*
Abspielung *f* reproduction *n*, replay
n, playback *n*
Absprache *f* (journalistisch) talk-up
n
abspulen *v* unspool *v*, unwind *v*,
uncoil *v*, reel off *v*
Abstandsisolator *m* stand-off
insulator
abstauben *v* dust *v*
Abstaubpinsel *m* lens brush
Abstellraum *m* store *n*
Abstimmbereich *m* tuning range
abstimmen *v* (Sender, Empfänger)
tune *v*, tune to *v*, tune in *v*; ~ *v*
(Farbe) adjust *v*
Abstimmkreis *m* tuning circuit
Abstimmton *m* tuning note, tone *n*,
line-up tone
Abstimmung *f* tuning-in *n*, tuning *n*
Abstimmvariometer *n* tuner *n*,
tuning variometer
Abstimmvorrichtung *f* tuning
device
abstoppen *v* (Zeit) time *v*
Abstrahlebene *f* radiating surface,
phase plane
abstrahlen *v* (Ant.) radiate *v*; ~ *v*
(Progr.) transmit *v*
Abstrahlung *f* (Ant.) radiation *n*; ~ *f*
(Progr.) transmission *n*
abstufen *v* (opt.) grade *v*, graduate *v*;
~ *v* (Farbe) shade *v*, tone *v*, alter *v*
Abstufung *f* graduation *n*,
gradation *n*

Abtastbreite *f* (Kamera, Filmgeber) track width

Abtastdose *f* (Platte) pick-up cartridge, pick-up *n*; **elektrodynamische ~** electrodynamic pick-up; **elektromagnetische ~** electromagnetic pick-up

Abtasteinrichtung *f* scanning device

abtasten *v* scan *v*, sample *v*

Abtaster *m* scanner *n*, analyser *n*; **optischer ~** (EDV) photoelectric reader

Abtastkopf *m* (Platte) pick-up head

Abtastlinearität *f* scanning linearity

Abtastnadel *f* (Platte) reproducing stylus tip, stylus tip

Abtastpunkt *m* (TV) scanning spot

Abtastraum *m* scanner area, telecine area, scanning room

Abtastsignal *n* scanning signal, scanning waveform

Abtastspalt *m* scanning gap, gap *n*

Abtaststrahl *m* scanning beam

Abtastung *f* scanning *n*, sweep *n*; **zeilensprungartige ~** interlaced scanning

Abtastwinkel *m* scanning angle

Abtastzeile *f* scanning line

Abtastzeit *f* scanning time

Abteilung *f* department *n*, section *n*, unit *n*

Abteilungsleiter *m* head of department

abtrennen *v* separate *v*, disconnect *v*, cut off *v*

abtrommeln *v* unwind *v*, spool off *v*

Abwärtsfrequenz *f* (Sat.) down-link frequency

Abwärtsverbindung *f* (Sat.) down-link *n*

Abweichung *f* deflection *n*, deviation *n*, divergence *n*, aberration *n*, drift *n*

Abwickelkassette *f* feed magazine

abwickeln *v* (Kabel) pay out *v*; ~ *v* (F) feed *v*

Abwickelspule *f* feed reel, feed

spool, supply spool, supply reel; ~ *f* (Proj.) upper spool

Abwickelsystem *n* spooling system

Abwickeltrommel *f* feed reel, feed spool, supply spool, supply reel; ~ *f* (Proj.) upper spool

Abwicklung *f* settlement *n*, liquidation *n*, disposal *n*; ~ *f* (Dekoration) extended elevation; ~ *f* (tech.) operation *n*; ~ *f* (F) feed *n*, feeding *n*; ~ *f* (Kabel) winding-off *n*, unwinding *n*

abziehen *v* (Negativ) print *v*

Abzug *m* (F, Foto) copy *n*; ~ *m* (Foto) print *n*

Abzweigdose *f* junction box, conduit box, connector box, distribution box

Abzweigkasten *m s.* Abzweigdose

Abzweigung *f* bifurcation *n*; ~ *f* branching-off *n*

achromatisch *adj* achromatic *adj*

Achse *f* axis *n* (pl. axes); ~ *f* (Bild) line of vision; **Bewegung auf der ~** movement about the axis; **optische ~** optical axis, principal axis; **über die ~ springen** to cross the line of vision

Achsensprung *m* reverse angle

Achter *m* (fam.) *s.* Achtermikrofon

Achtermikrofon *n* bidirectional microphone, figure-of-eight microphone

Achtspur-Lochstreifen *m* (EDV) eight-track punched tape

Achtung! Aufnahme! (Kamera) camera!, stand by!

Achtungszeichen *n* warning sign

Adapter *m* adapter *n*

Adaption *f* adaptation *n*; ~ *f* (elek.) adaption *n*

additiv *adj* additive *adj*

Adresse *f* (EDV) address *n*; **binär codierte ~** (EDV) binary-coded address; **indirekte ~** *f* (EDV) indirect address, second level address

Adressenansteuerung *f* (EDV)

address selection
Adressenauswahl f (EDV) address selection
Adressen-Code m (EDV) address code
Agentur f agency n
Agenturbericht m agency story, agency report
Agenturberichterstattung f agency coverage, agency reporting
Aggregat n power unit, power plant, generating set; ~ n (Gerätegruppe) set n
Aizes m pl (fam.) tip n, lead n
Akkumulatorenzelle f accumulator cell, secondary cell
Akkuraum m battery room
Akquisiteur m (F) film salesman
Akt m (Thea.) act n; ~ m (Spule) spool n, reel n
Aktivspeicher m (EDV) active store
Aktrolle f (Spule) spool n, reel n
aktualisieren v up-date v
Aktualitäten f pl topical events
Aktüberblendzeichen n pl change-over cues, cue dots
aktuell adj topical, of topical interest, in the news
Aktuelles n current affairs n pl, current affairs programmes n pl, news and current affairs n pl
Akustik f acoustics n
akustisch adj acoustic adj
Alarmeingabe f (EDV) alarm signal input device; **dynamische** ~ (EDV) dynamic alarm signal input device; **statische** ~ (EDV) static alarm signal input device
Alkali n alkali n
Allbereichantenne f wide-band aerial
Allbereichverstärker m wide-band amplifier
Alligatorklammer f alligator clip
Alligatorklemme f s. Alligatorklammer
Allonge f (F) protection leader, identification leader

Allstromgerät n AC/DC equipment
Allwetterlampe f all-weather lamp
Allwetterschutz m all-weather protection
alphamerisch adj s. alphanumerisch
alphanumerisch adj (EDV) alphanumeric adj, alphameric adj
Alterung f aging n
Altes Werk pre-classical music
Amateurband n amateur frequency band
Amateurband f (Mus.) amateur band
Amateurfilm m amateur film
Amperezange f clip-on probe, current probe
Ampex f s. MAZ
Amplitude f amplitude n
Amplitudenbegrenzung f amplitude limitation, clipping n
Amplitudenfehler m amplitude error
Amplituden-Frequenzgang m amplitude frequency characteristic, frequency response, amplitude frequency response
Amplitudengang m s. Amplituden-Frequenzgang
Amplitudenmodulation (AM) f amplitude modulation (AM) n; ~ **mit unterdrücktem Träger** suppressed-carrier modulation
Amplitudenmodulator m amplitude modulator
Amplitudensieb n amplitude filter
Amplitudenverzerrung f amplitude distortion
Amt, betriebsführendes directing station, control station
Amtsdauer f term of office
Analogausgabe f (EDV) analog output, analog output device
Analog-Digital-Umsetzer (ADU) m (EDV) analog-to-digital converter (ADC), digitiser n, quantiser n
Analogeingabe f (EDV) analog

Analogeingabe 6

input, analog input device
Analyse *f* analysis *n*
Anamorphose *f* anamorphosis *n*
Anamorphot *m* anamorphic lens,
distorting lens
anamorphotisch *adj* anamorphic
adj
Anastigmat *m* anastigmatic lens
anastigmatisch *adj* anastigmatic
adj
Anastigmatismus *m* anastigmatism
n
Anbaudose *f* female socket
anbelichten *v* (Filmmaterial) to
expose thin
Änderungsblatt *n* amendment
sheet, correction sheet
Andruckkufe *f* pressure pad, skid *n*;
seitliche ~ edge guide
Andruckmagnet *m* pressure
solenoid
Andruckplatte *f* pressure plate
Andruckrolle *f* pressure roller,
pinch roller, capstan idler, lay-on
roller
Aneinanderhängen *n* (F) butt-join *n*
anfallen *v* (Nachrichten) break *v*
anfangen *v* (mit) (Sendung) lead *v*
(with), open *v* (with)
Anfangskapazität *f* minimum
capacitance
Anfangstitel *m* opening titles *n pl*
Anfangszeit *f* (Übertragung)
starting time
anfeuchten *v* moisten *v*, wet *v*,
damp *v*
anflanschen *v* flange to *v*, flange-
mount *v*, screw on *v*
Anfrage *f* (EDV) query *n*, inquiry *n*
Angel *f* (Ton) boom arm
angeschlossen *adj* (Sender) relayed
adj, linked *adj* (with); ~ **waren** ...
joint broadcast by ...
Angestellter *m* employee *n*,
member of staff
angleichen *v* match *v*
Angleichung *f* matching *n*
anheben *v* accentuate *v*; ~ *v* (Ton,

Licht) bring up *v*; ~ *v*
(Tonwiedergabe) pre-emphasise *v*;
~ *v* (tech.) boost *v*
Anhebung *f* accentuation *n*; ~ *f*
(Tonwiedergabe) pre-emphasis *n*;
~ *f* (tech.) boost *n*
Ankleidekabine *f* dressing cubicle
Ankleider *m* dresser *n*
Ankleideraum *m* dressing-room *n*
ankommen *v* (Progr.) come off *v*;
nicht ~ flop *v* (coll.)
ankommend *adj* (Leitung) incoming
adj
ankoppeln *v* couple to *v*
Ankopplung *f* coupling *n*
ankündigen *v* trail *v*, promote *v*
Anlage *f* installation *n*, plant *n*; ~ *f*
(Gerät) equipment *n*, set *n*
Anlagekante *f* reference edge
Anlagenausstattung *f* (EDV) system
configuration
Anlaßwiderstand *m* starter resistor,
starter rheostat
anlaufen *v* (F) open *v*; ~ *v* (Motor)
start up *v*, run up *v*
Anlaufmoment *m* starting torque
Anlaufstrom *m* (Masch.) initial-
velocity current, starting current;
~ *m* (Röhre) residual current
anlegen *v* dub *v*, to put in sync,
sync up *v*
annullieren *v* cancel *v*
Anode *f* anode *n*, plate *n* (US)
Anodenbasisschaltung *f* cathode
follower, cathode-coupled circuit,
grounded anode amplifier
Anodenbatterie *f* anode battery,
high-tension battery
Anodengleichrichter *m* anode
detector, anode bend detector
Anodenkreisabstimmung *f* anode
circuit tuning, anode tuning
Anodenmodulation *f* anode
modulation
Anodenspannung *f* anode voltage
Anodenspannungsdiagramm *n*
anode voltage current
characteristic

Anodenstrom *m* anode current
anpassen *v* adapt *v*, fit *v*, match *v*
Anpaßglied *n* adapter *n*, matching section
Anpassung *f* adaption *n*, matching *n*
Anpassungseinrichtung *f* (EDV) adapter *n*
Anpassungselement *n* matching element
Anpassungsglied *n* matching device
Anpassungsimpedanz *f* matching impedance
Anpassungskreis *m* matching circuit
Anpassungsnetzwerk *n* matching network
Anpassungsübertrager *m* matching transformer
Anpassungsvorrichtung *f* matching device
Anpassungswiderstand *m* matching resistance, matching resistor
anpeilen *v* to take a bearing on
Anpeilung *f* bearing *n*
Ansage *f* announcement *n*, opening announcement, presentation *n*, billboard *n* (US)
ansagen *v* announce *v*
Ansageplatz *m* presenter's position
Ansager *m* announcer *n*, presenter *n*
Ansagestudio *n* continuity studio, presentation studio, announcer booth, announcer studio
Ansagetext *m* continuity script, programme notes *n pl*
ansaugen *v* (F) take in *v*
Anschauungsmaterial *n* visual aids *n pl*
anschließen *v* (Sender) connect *v*, connect up *v*, join *v* (to), hook up *v*; ~ *v* (sich) join *v*, opt in *v*
Anschluß *m* (elek.) connection *n*, junction *n*, mains lead; ~ *m* (Telefon) connection *n*; ~ *m* (F) continuity *n*, cueing *n*
Anschlußdose *f* junction box

Anschlußgebühr *f* connection charge
Anschlußkabel *n* supply cable, mains lead
Anschlußkasten *m* terminal box, outlet box, conduit box
Anschlußklemme *f* terminal *n*, connecting clip
Anschlußleiste *f* terminal strip
Anschlußleitung *f* junction circuit
Anschlußplatte *f* terminal board
Anschlußpunkt *m* junction point
Anschlußrosette *f* connection rose
Anschlußspannung *f* mains voltage
Anschlußwert *m* connected load
anschneiden *v* cut *v*
Anschnitt *m* cut *n*; ~ **in der Bewegung** cut into a movement; **im** ~ in the cut
Anschnittsteuerung *f* phase-shift control
ansehen *v* view *v*, screen *v*
ansetzen *v* (F) prepare *v*; ~ *v* (auf ein Thema) assign *v*, put on *v*
Ansprechempfindlichkeit *f* response sensitivity
Ansprechen *n* response *n*; ~ *n* (Relais) pick-up *n*
Ansprechschwelle *f* response threshold, minimum operating value
Ansprechwert *m* (Relais) pick-up value
Ansprechzeit *f* operating time, transit time, attack time, reacting time; ~ *f* (Relais) pick-up time
Anstalt *f* station *n*, organisation *n*; **abspielende** ~ originating station; **federführende** ~ originating station, organisation in charge; **übernehmende** ~ relaying station
Anstaltsbereich *m* broadcasting area, service area, transmission range, service range, coverage area, area covered, transmission area, area served
Ansteckmikrofon *n* lapel microphone

anstellen 8

anstellen v (Gerät) turn on v
Ansteuerlogik f (EDV) control logic
ansteuern v (Meßtechnik) trigger v;
~ v (Sender) drive v, excite v
Ansteuerung f (Sender) excitation n
Ansteuerungssignal n drive signal
Anstiegzeit f build-up time; ~ f
(Impuls) rise time; ~ f (Verstärker)
attack time
anstoßen v trigger v
Anteilvertrag m contract on sharing
terms
Antenne f aerial n, antenna n (US);
abgeschirmte ~ screened aerial;
ausziehbare ~ telescopic aerial;
eingebaute ~ built-in aerial;
künstliche ~ artificial aerial,
dummy aerial; **logarithmische** ~
log-periodic aerial; **ungerichtete** ~
non-directional aerial,
omnidirectional aerial;
zusammenklappbare ~ collapsible
aerial
Antennenabzweigdose f aerial
junction box, aerial spur box
Antennenanlage f aerial system,
aerial installation, aerial
equipment
Antennenanpassung f aerial
coupling, aerial matching
Antennenanpassungsfilter m aerial
matching filter, aerial coupling
filter
Antennenanschlußdose f aerial
junction box, aerial connection
box
Antennendiagramm n aerial polar
diagram, aerial radiation pattern
Antennenebene f aerial stack
Antennenelement n aerial element
Antennengewinn m aerial gain;
~ **einer Richtantenne** directional
gain
Antennengruppe f aerial array
Antennenkabel n aerial cable,
aerial feeder
Antennenkopplung f aerial
coupling

Antennenleitung f aerial feeder,
aerial lead; ~ f (Sender)
transmission line
Antennenmast m (Träger) aerial
mast, support mast; ~ m (Strahler)
mast radiator
Antennenmastverstärker m mast-
head amplifier
Antennenniederführung f aerial
down lead
Antennenschwerpunkt m centre of
gravity of aerial
Antennenspeiseleitung f feeder line
Antennenspiegel m parabolic aerial
Antennenstab m aerial rod
Antennenstandrohr n aerial pole
Antennensteckdose f aerial outlet,
aerial socket
Antennenstecker m aerial plug
Antennenstrahler m aerial radiator,
radiating element of aerial
Antennenumschalter m aerial
switch, aerial change-over switch
Antennenverteilerdose f aerial
distribution box
Antennenwart m rigger n
Antennenweiche f aerial diplexer,
aerial combining unit
Antennenzuleitung f feeder n,
aerial lead-in
Antext m (fam.) (FS-Nachrichten)
introduction n, intro n (coll.), cue
n, lead-in n
antexten v to provide with a cue, to
write the lead-in
Antireflexbelag m blooming n,
coating n
Antrieb m drive n
Antriebsachse f drive shaft
Antriebsmotor m drive motor
Antriebsriemen m drive belt
Antriebsritzel n drive pinion
Antriebsrolle f drive roller
Antriebswelle f drive capstan
Antriebszahnrad n drive gear
antuckern v (fam.) staple v
Anweisung f (EDV) statement n
Anwenderprogramm n (EDV) user

Arrangement

programme
Anzapfspeisung *f* shunt feed, feed of tapping point
Anzapfung *f* tapping *n*, tap *n*; **hochohmige** ~ high-impedance tap; **niederohmige** ~ low-impedance tap
Anzeige *f* (tech.) indication *n*, reading *n*
Anzeigeeinheit *f* (EDV) indicating element
Anzeigefeld *n* (EDV) indicator panel
Anzeigefrequenz *f* indicated frequency
Anzeigegerät *n* indicator *n*, meter *n*
anzeigen *v* announce *v*; ~ *v* (Werbung) advertise *v*; ~ *v* (tech.) indicate *v*
Anzeigenwerbung *f* advertising *n*
Anzeigeverstärker *m* detector amplifier
aperiodisch *adj* aperiodic *adj*, dead-beat *adj*
Aperturkorrektur *f* aperture correction
Apogäum *n* apogee *n*
Apparat *m* apparatus *n*, equipment *n*, device *n*, appliance *n*, set *n*
Äquatorialbahn *f* equatorial orbit
äquipotential *adj* equipotential *adj*
Arbeitsfolge *f* sequence of operations
Arbeitsfoto *n* photo blow-up (PBU), working plan
Arbeitsgang *m* working process
Arbeitsgemeinschaft der öffentlich-rechtlichen Rundfunkanstalten der Bundesrepublik Deutschland (ARD) Association of public-service broadcasting organisations of the Federal Republic of Germany
Arbeitsgericht *n* labour court
Arbeitskennlinie *f* working characteristic
Arbeitskleidung *f* working clothes *n pl*
Arbeitskopie *f* work print, cutting-copy print, rush print
Arbeitsprogramm *n* (EDV) working programme
Arbeitspunkt *m* working point, bias *n*; ~ *m* (Röhre, Transistor) operating point
Arbeitspunktverschiebung *f* shift of working point; ~ *f* (Röhre, Transistor) shift of operating point
Arbeitsspeicher *m* (EDV) computing store, main memory, working store, working memory, general store
Arbeitsspeicherkapazität *f* (EDV) main-memory capacity
Arbeitstag *m* working day
Arbeitstitel *m* (Prod.) working title; ~ *m* (Nachrichten) slug *n*
Arbeitsverhältnis *n* terms of employment
Arbeitsweise *f* (Gerät) mode of operation
Arbeitswiderstand *m* working resistance, working resistor
Arbeitszeit *f* working hours *n pl*
Arbeitszyklus *m* (EDV) operation cycle
Architektenbüro *n* designer's office
Archiv *n* archives *n pl*, library *n*
Archivar *m* archivist *n*, librarian *n*
Archivaufnahme *f* (F) stock shot, library film, library shot; ~ *f* (Foto) library picture, library still
Archivfilm *m* library film, file copy
Archivgehilfe *m* library assistant
archivieren *v* file *v*, to put in the library
Archivierung *f* storage *n*, filing system
Archivleiter *m* chief librarian
Archivmaterial *n* library material
Armatur *f* (elek.) fitting *n*, mounting *n*
Armaturenbrett *n* dash-board *n*, instrument panel
A-Rolle *f* A roll
Arrangement *n* arrangement *n*

Arrangeur *m* arranger *n*
Arretierung *f* locking device
Artikel *m* article *n*, piece *n*
Artist *m* circus performer
Asbest *m* asbestos *n*
A-Schaltung *f* (Sender) class A circuit
A-Seite *f* (Platte) A side
Assembler *m* (EDV) assembly programme, assembly routine
Assistent *m* assistant *n*, helper *n*
Astigmatismus *m* astigmatism *n*
asynchron *adj* asynchronous *adj*, non-synchronous *adj*, out-of-sync *adj*
Asynchronbetrieb *m* (EDV) asynchronous working, variable cycle operation
Asynchronität *f* asynchronism *n*
Atelier *n* studio *n*; **ins ~ gehen** to start studio work, to begin the interiors
Atelierarbeiter *m* stage hand, grip *n* (US)
Atelieraufnahme *f* studio shot
Atelierbetrieb *m* film studios *n pl*
Atelierbetrieb* *m* film operations and services*
Atelierdisposition *f* studio allocation
Atelierdrehtag *m* day in the studio, day on the stage
Atelierfundus *m* properties *n pl*, property department, props *n pl* (coll.)
Ateliergebäude *n* studios *n pl*, studio buildings *n pl*
Ateliergelände *n* lot *n*, studio area
Atelierkamera *f* studio camera
Atelierleitung *f* studio management
Ateliermiete *f* studio rent
Ateliersekretärin *f* script-girl *n*, continuity girl
atmen *v* (tech.) breathe *v*
Atmen *n* (tech.) breathing *n*
Atmo *f s.* Atmosphäre
Atmosphäre *f* atmosphere *n*, wild track effects

audio-visuell (AV) *adj* audio-visual (AV) *adj*
Aufbau *m* construction *n*, assembly *n*; ~ *m* (Bericht) layout *n*, outline *n*, shape *n*
aufbauen *v* set up *v*, build up *v*
Aufbauten *m pl* set *n*, built set
Aufbereitung *f* (Signal) processing *n*
aufblasen *v* blow up *v*
Aufblende *f* (F) fade-in *n*; ~ *f* (TV) fade-up *n*, fading-up *n*; ~ *f* (Objektiv) opening of aperture, opening of diaphragm
aufblenden *v* (Bild, Ton) fade up *v*, fade in *v*; ~ *v* (Objektiv) to open diaphragm, iris out *v*
Aufblendung *f* (F) fade-in *n*; ~ *f* (TV) fade-up *n*, fading-up *n*; ~ *f* (Objektiv) opening of aperture, opening of diaphragm
auffangen *v* (Funkspruch) pick up *v*
Auffangwinkel *m* angle of acceptance
Aufführung *f* performance *n*
Aufführungslizenz *f* performing licence
Aufführungsrecht *n* performing rights *n pl*
Aufhänger *m* news peg, peg *n*
Aufhängung *f* suspension *n*
Aufhellblende *f* silvered reflector, silver foil reflector
aufhellen *v* brighten up *v*
Aufheller *m* filler *n*, fill light, fill-in light
Aufhellicht *n s.* Aufheller
Aufhellschirm *m* reflector screen, reflector *n*
Aufhellung *f* filler lighting
aufklappen *v* open *v*, unfold *v*, flap up *v*
Aufklebekarton *m* stick-on cardboard, adhesive cardboard
aufkreisen *v* (Objektiv) iris out *v*
Aufladung, statische (F) static charge
Auflageflansch *m* supporting flange
Auflagegewicht *n* (Tonarm) weight

of pick-up head
Auflagekraft f (Tonarm) stylus force
Auflagemaß n (opt.) back focal distance
auflösen v resolve v, dissolve v
Auflösung f (chem.) dissolution n, solution n; ~ f (opt.) resolution n, dissolution n, definition n; **szenische** ~ scenic realisation
Auflösungsgrenze f limit of resolution
Auflösungskeil m resolution wedge
Auflösungstestbild n test chart
Auflösungsvermögen n (opt.) resolving power, resolution n; ~ n (Filmmaterial) fineness of grain; ~ n (chem.) dissolving power, solvent power
aufmachen v (mit) lead v (with), open v (with)
Aufmacher m lead story, lead n
aufmöbeln v (Text, Bild) pep up v, liven up v, to find a new angle
Aufnahme f (Foto) photograph n, picture n, still n, exposure n; ~ f (F, TV) shot n, take n, recording n ~ f (Ton) recording n, take n; ~ **wiederholen** retake v, to do a retake; ~ **wiederholen** (Bild) reshoot v; ~ **wiederholen** (Ton) re-record v; **schlechte** ~ dud take, NG take (coll.), NG n (coll.); **schlechte** ~ (Ton) unsatisfactory recording; **stumme** ~ mute shot, mute take
Aufnahmebericht m dope-sheet n, camera sheet
Aufnahmeeinheit f recording unit
Aufnahmegegenstand m subject n, photographic subject
Aufnahmegelände n location n, lot n
Aufnahmegenehmigung f filming permission, filming permit
Aufnahmegerät n (Ton) recording equipment, recorder n; ~ n (F, TV) camera equipment
Aufnahmegeschwindigkeit f

absorption rate; ~ f (Kamera) camera speed, running speed of film; ~ f (Ton) recording speed
Aufnahmegruppe f (F, nur Bild) camera unit; ~ f (Bild, Ton) film crew; ~ f (Bild, Ton, Beleuchtung) film unit; ~ f (R) OB unit; ~ f (Ton) sound crew
Aufnahmekamera f cine camera, movie camera, film camera
Aufnahmekanal m recording channel
Aufnahmekette f recording chain
Aufnahmekopf m recording head
Aufnahmeleiter m (TV) floor manager, studio manager (SM), stage manager (SM); ~ m (R) studio manager, programme operations assistant (POA)
Aufnahmeleitung f studio management
Aufnahmemaschine f recorder n
Aufnahmematerial n (F) camera stock, raw stock; ~ n (Ton) recording material
Aufnahmeobjektiv n taking lens, camera objective, shooting lens
Aufnahmeort m location n, lot n
Aufnahmepegel, maximaler maximum recording level
Aufnahmeplan m shooting schedule, film schedule
Aufnahmeraum m recording room, recording theatre
Aufnahmeröhre f camera tube, pick-up tube
Aufnahmestab m production team
Aufnahmesystem n recording system
Aufnahmetaste mit Sperre recording key with safety-lock
Aufnahmeteam n production team
Aufnahmetonband n master tape, original n
Aufnahmewagen m (TV) television car; ~ m (R) recording van, recording car
Aufnahme-Wiedergabegerät n

Aufnahme-Wiedergabegerät   12

recording-reproducing unit,
record-replay equipment
Aufnahme-Wiedergabekopf,
kombinierter combined
recording/reproducing head,
record/replay head
Aufnahme-Wiedergabemaschine *f*
recording-reproducing unit,
record-replay equipment
Aufnahmewinkel *m* taking angle,
camera angle, shooting angle; ~ *m*
(Objektiv) lens angle
aufnehmen *v* (Ton) record *v*, take *v*;
~ *v* (F, TV) shoot *v*, film *v*, tape *v*,
record *v*; ~ *v* (Foto) photograph *v*;
~ *v* (Nachrichten) take down *v*
Aufpro *f s.* Aufprojektion
Aufprojektion *f* front projection
Aufputzdose *f* surface socket
aufquellen *v* (Kopierwerk) soak *v*
Aufquellen *n* (Kopierwerk) soaking
n
Aufsatz *m* article *n*, piece *n*
aufschalten *v* offer *v*; **1000 Hz-Ton** ~
to put on 1000 Hz; **Meßton** ~ to
send reference tone, to send tone;
sich ~ auf (elektron.) to lock on to;
Testbild ~ to put out test card
Aufschaltung, harte cut *n*
Aufsichtsgremium *n* supervisory
body
Aufsichtsingenieur *m* engineer-in-
charge *n*
Aufsprechstrom *m* recording
current
aufspulen *v* spool (up) *v*, wind (up) *v*,
coil (up) *v*, reel (up) *v*, take up *v*
aufstecken *v* slip on *v*, clip on *v*,
push on *v*
Aufsteckfilter *m* (elek.)
interchangeable filter; ~ *m* (opt.)
push-on filter, slip-on type filter
auftasten *v* gate *v*
Auftastimpuls *m* gate pulse
Auftastschaltung *f* gate circuit
Auftastung *f* gating *n*
Auftrag *m* commission *n*, order *n*; ~
m (Berichterstattung) assignment

n, job *n*
Auftragsarbeit *f* commissioned
work
Auftragsdienst *m* (Telefon)
telephone answering service
Auftragsfilm *m* commissioned film
Auftragskomposition *f* commission
n
Auftragsproduktion *f* commissioned
production
Auftragswerk *n* commissioned work
Auftrennung, elektrische electrical
separation
auftreten *v* (Darsteller) enter *v*,
appear *v*; **vor der Kamera** ~ to
perform on-camera, to be on the
spot
Auftritt *m* (Darsteller) appearance *n*
Auftritt! you're on!
auftrommeln *v* spool *v*, reel (up) *v*
Aufwärmzeit *f* warming-up time
Aufwärtsfrequenz *f* (Sat.) up-link
frequency
Aufwärtsverbindung *f* (Sat.) up-link
n
Aufwickelgeschwindigkeit *f* take-up
speed
Aufwickelkassette *f* take-up
magazine
aufwickeln *v* spool (up) *v*, wind (up)
v, coil (up) *v*, reel (up) *v*, take up *v*
Aufwickelspule *f* take-up spool,
take-up reel; ~ *f* (Proj.) lower
spool
Aufwickelsystem *n* take-up system
Aufwickelteller *m* take-up plate
aufzeichnen *v* record *v*, tape *v*;
Band ~ tape *v*; **FAZ** ~ to record on
film, kine *v*, film-record *v*; **Film** ~
to record on film, kine *v*, film-
record *v*; **MAZ** ~ VTR *v*, VT *v*, tape
v; **über Leitung** ~ to record over a
circuit, to record down the line
Aufzeichnung *f* (s. a. Film-,
Fernseh-, Magnetbildaufzeichnung)
recording *n*; ~ **an Ort und Stelle**
on-the-spot recording; ~ **über**
Strecke recording from line;

magnetische ~ magnetic
recording; **mechanische ~**
mechanical recording
Aufzeichnungsanlage *f* recording
equipment, recording system;
magnetische ~ magnetic recorder
Aufzeichnungsgeschwindigkeit *f*
recording speed
Aufzeichnungskette *f* recording
chain
Aufzeichnungskopf *m* recording
head
Aufzeichnungspegelanzeiger *m*
recording level indicator
Aufzeichnungsprotokoll *n*
continuity log
Aufzeichnungsstrom *m* recording
current
Aufzeichnungsverfahren *n* (EDV)
recording mode, recording
technique
Aufzeichnungsverluste *m pl*
recording loss
Aufzeichnungswagen *m* (R)
recording van, recording car; ~ *m*
(TV) mobile VTR (MVTR)
aufziehen *v* (kleben) mount *v*, paste
(on) *v*; ~ *v* (Regler) turn up *v*; ~ *v*
(Bild, Ton) fade in *v*, fade up *v*; ~ *v*
(Bericht) treat *v*, handle *v*; ~ *v*
(Zoom) open out *v*, zoom out *v*,
widen out *v*
Augenblickswert *m* instantaneous
value
Augenempfindlichkeit *f* sensitivity
of the eye
Augenempfindlichkeitskurve *f*
relative sensitivity curve
Augenhöhe *f* eye level, eye line
Augenlicht *n* (Beleuchtung) catch
light, eye light
Augenmuschelkissen *n* eye guard
Augenzeugenbericht *m* eye-witness
account, on-the-spot report,
running commentary
aus off; ~ ! cut!; ~ ! (Gerät) stop!
Ausbildungswesen *n* staff training
ausbleichen *v* (Farbe) fade *v*, bleach

out *v*; ~ *v* (Kopierwerk) bleach *v*
Ausblende *f* (F) fade-out (FO) *n*,
fading-down *n*; ~ *f* (Objektiv)
stopping-down *n*; ~ *f* (Licht)
dimming *n*; ~ *f* (Ton) sound fade
ausblenden *v* fade out (FO) *v*, fade
down *v*; ~ *v* (Störsender) tune out
v; ~ *v* (sich) (Sender) opt out *v*,
cut away *v* (US); ~ *v* (EDV) mask *v*
Ausblenden *n* fading-out *n*; ~ *n*
(Sender) opting-out *n*, opt-out *n*; ~
n (Störsender) tuning-out *n*
Ausblendung *f s.* Ausblenden
Ausbreitung *f* propagation *n*
Ausbreitungszone *f* coverage area
Ausdruck *m* (EDV) expression *n*
auseinandernehmen *v* dismantle *v*,
detach *v*, dismount *v*, to take
apart
Ausfall *m* breakdown *n*, drop-out *n*;
~ *m* (Röhre) failure *n*; ~ *m*
(Sender) outage *n*; ~ *m* (EDV)
failure *n*, outage *n*; ~ **des**
Bildgleichlaufs frame-pulling *n*;
~ **des Zeilengleichlaufs** line-
pulling *n*, line-tearing *n*
ausfallen *v* (Progr.) to be cancelled,
to be dropped; ~ *v* (tech.) fail *v*
Ausfallgage *f* cancellation fee, pay-
off fee
Ausfallquote *f* (EDV) failure rate
Ausfallrate *f* (EDV) failure rate
Ausfallversicherung *f* contingency
insurance
Ausfallzeit *f* (EDV) down time, fault
time
Ausführender *m* performer *n*,
player *n*, actor *n*
Ausgabe *f* (EDV) output *n*
Ausgang *m* exit *n*; ~ *m* (elek.) outlet
n, output *n*; ~ *m* (EDV) exit *n*,
outlet *n*
Ausgangsanpassung *f* output
matching
Ausgangsbild *n* output picture
Ausgangsimpedanz *f* output
impedance
Ausgangsimpuls *m* output pulse

Ausgangskreuzschiene f output switching matrix, output selector
Ausgangsleistung f output power
Ausgangsleitung f output connection, outgoing circuit
Ausgangsmonitor m output monitor
Ausgangspegel m output level
Ausgangsposition! stand by!
Ausgangssignal n output signal
Ausgangstransformator m output transformer
Ausgangsübertrager m output transformer
Ausgangsverstärker m output amplifier
Ausgangswiderstand m output resistance
Ausgleich m balance n, equalising n, equalisation n, balancing n, compensation n
ausgleichen v balance v, equalise v, compensate v
Ausgleichsentwickler m compensating developer
Ausgleichsimpuls m equalising pulse
Aushilfskraft f supernumerary n, holiday relief
Auskoppelwiderstand m (Sender) load resistance
Auskopplung f coupling-out n, output coupling
Auslandsabteilung f overseas and foreign relations (BBC)
Auslandsberichterstattung f foreign coverage
Auslandsdienst m (Progr.) external broadcasting service
Auslandskorrespondent m foreign correspondent
Auslandsreferat n overseas and foreign relations*
Auslandsstudio n overseas office (BBC), premises in foreign country
Auslandsstudioleiter m overseas representative (BBC), head of overseas office (BBC),

representative in foreign country
Auslauf m finish n
Auslaufrille f (Platte) lead-out groove, run-out groove
auslegen v (Proj.) unlace v; ~ v (Kamera) unload v, unthread v
Ausleger m jib arm, jib n
auslesen v (EDV) read out v, roll out v
ausleuchten v light v
Ausleuchten n lighting-up n
Ausleuchtung f lighting n; ~ mit Schlagschatteneffekt lighting with hard-shadow effect; **flache** ~ flat lighting
Ausleuchtungszone f lit area
auslochen v (EDV) erase v
Auslöschung f (Band) erasure n; ~ f (Licht) extinction n
Auslöseknopf m release button
auslösen v press v, release v, trip v; ~ v (Blitz) fire v
Auslöser m release n, shutter release, release gear, shutter button
Auslösetaste f trip button, operational key
Auslösezeichen n release signal, starting blip
Auslöten n unsoldering n
ausmustern v reject v, select v
Ausmustern n daily selection
ausrasten v release v
Ausrüstung f equipment n
Ausrüstung*, technische engineering equipment*
ausschalten v switch off v, turn off v, cut out v, disconnect v
Ausschalten n switching-off n, turning-off n, cutting-out n, disconnection n
Ausschalter m circuit-breaker n, cut-out n, disconnecting switch
Ausschaltung f switching-off n, turning-off n, cutting-out n, disconnection n
Ausschließlichkeitsrecht n exclusive rights n pl

Ausschnitt *m* (R, TV, F, Text) cut *n*
ausschreiben *v* (Text) transcribe *v*
Ausschuß *m* (Schnitt) junk *n*, scrap
  n, waste *n*
Außen- (in Zus.) exterior *adj*,
  outside *adj*, outdoor *adj*
Außenantenne *f* outdoor aerial
Außenaufnahme *f* (R, TV) outside
  broadcast (OB), OB recording,
  remote broadcast (US); ~ *f* (TV)
  field pick-up (US); ~ *f* (R) nemo *n*
  (US); ~ *f* (F, TV) exterior shot,
  exterior shooting, exterior *n*,
  location shot, location shooting,
  outdoor shot, outdoor shooting
Außenaufnahmetag *m* day on
  location
Außenaufzeichnung *f* OB recording
Außenbau *m* location set, exterior
  set
Außenbetriebstechnik* *f* outside
  broadcasts* (OBs)
Außenbetriebstechnik *f* outside
  broadcast operations *n pl*
Außenbote *m* dispatch rider
Außendekor, realer original
  location, outdoor location
Außendienst haben to be away
  from base, to be on an outside job
  (coll.)
Außenpolitik *f* (R, TV) diplomatic
  desk, foreign news *n pl* (US)
Außenpolitik* *f* diplomatic unit*
Außenproduktion *f* OB production
Außenreportage *f* OB commentary
Außenrequisiteur *m* property buyer
Außenstudio *n* regional studio
Außenübertragung (AÜ) *f* outside
  broadcast (OB), remote broadcast
  (US), field pick-up (US), nemo *n*
  (US coll.)
Außenübertragungsdienst* *m*
  outside broadcasts* (OBs)
Außenübertragungsort *m* OB point,
  OB location
Außenwiderstand *m* (Röhre) anode
  load resistance; ~ *m* (Transistor)
  collector-load resistance

Außerbetriebnahme *f* (Sender)
  taking out of service
aussieben *v* filter out *v*, screen out
  v
ausspiegeln *v* reflect out *v*
Ausstatter *m* furnisher *n*, set
  dresser, designer *n*
Ausstattung *f* (Bühne) furnishing *n*,
  dressing *n*, setting *n*, decor *n*; ~ *f*
  (tech.) equipment *n*
Ausstattungsabteilung *f* design
  department
Ausstattungsbesprechung *f* design
  planning meeting
Ausstattungsfilm *m* spectacular *n*
Ausstattungsingenieur *m*
  installation engineer
Ausstattungskosten *plt* design costs
Ausstattungsleiter *m* head of design
Ausstattungsstab *m* design team
Ausstattungstechnik* *f* planning
  and installation*
Ausstellungsrecht *n* exhibition
  rights *n pl*
aussteuern *v* modulate *v*, deviate *v*
Aussteuerung *f* modulation *n*
Aussteuerungsbereich *m*
  modulation range
Aussteuerungsmesser *m*
  programme meter, volume
  indicator, level indicator,
  programme-volume indicator
ausstrahlen *v* broadcast *v*, transmit
  v, to put on the air; ~ *v* (nach)
  beam *v* (to); ~ *v* (tech.) radiate *v*,
  emit *v*
Ausstrahlung *f* transmission *n*,
  broadcasting *n*; ~ *f* (tech.)
  radiation *n*, emission *n*
austasten *v* blank *v*, gate *v*
Austasten *n* blanking *n*, black-out *n*
  (US)
Austastgemisch *n* mixed blanking
  pulses, mixed blanking signal
Austastimpuls (A-Impuls) *m*
  blanking pulse
Austastlücke *f* blanking interval
Austastniveau *n* blanking level

Austastpegel *m* blanking level
Austastpegelfesthaltung *f* blanking
level stability
Austastsignal (A-Signal) *n* blanking
signal
Austastung *f* blanking *n*,
suppression *n*, gating *n*, black-out
n (US)
Austastverstärker *m* blanking
amplifier
Austastwert *m* blanking level
austimen *v* time *v*
Austrittsebene *f* emergence plane,
rear element
Austrittslinse *f* exit pupil,
emergence lens
Austrittswinkel *m* angle of
emergence
ausverkauft *adj* sold out; ~ *adj*
(Plakat) full house
Auswahl *f* selection *n*, choice *n*
auswählen *v* select *v*, choose *v*
auswechselbar *adj* interchangeable
adj, replaceable *adj*
Ausweisleser *m* (EDV) badge reader
auswerten *v* evaluate *v*, interpret *v*,
exploit *v*
Auswertung *f* exploitation *n*,
interpretation *n*, evaluation *n*
Auswertungsrecht *n* right of
exploitation
Auswuchten *n* removal of mass by
flywheel-drilling
Auswuchtung *f* counterbalance *n*,
balancing *n*
ausziehbar *adj* extensible *adj*, pull-
out *adj*, removable *adj*, telescopic
adj
Auszug *m* compendium *n*, excerpt *n*,
extract *n*; ~ *m* (Drehbuch) abstract
n; ~ *m* (Kamera) extension *n*;
doppelter ~ double extension
Auszugspositiv *n* separation
positive
Autochroma *n* (MAZ) automatic
chroma control
Autoempfänger *m* car radio
Autokino *n* drive-in cinema

Automat *m* automaton *n*
Automation *f* automation *n*
**automatische Lautstärkeregelung
(ALR)** automatic volume control
(AVC)
Autor *m* author *n*, writer *n*
Autoradio *n* car radio
Autorenfilm *m* writer's own film
Autorenrechte *n pl* author's rights
Autotransformator *m*
autotransformer *n*

B

Babyspot *m* babyspot *n*, pup *n*
Babystativ *n* pup stand, small
lighting stand, turtle *n* (coll.)
Background *m* background *n*
Bad *n* (F) bath *n*; ~ **ansetzen** (F) to
prepare a bath
Bädertank *m* developing tank,
processing tank
Bajonettfassung *f* bayonet fitting
Bajonettsockel *m* bayonet socket; ~
m (Röhre) bayonet cap (BC)
Bajonettverschluß *m* bayonet
connection
Bakenfrequenz *f* (Sat.) beacon
frequency
Balanceregelung *f* balance
adjustment
Balgen *m* bellows *n*
Balken *m* bar *n*
Balkengeber *m* bar generator
Ball, am ~ **sein** to be on a story
Ballaströhre *f* ballast tube
Ballasttriode *f* ballast triode
Ballempfang *m* rebroadcasting
reception (RBR), rebroadcast *n*
Ballempfänger *m* rebroadcast
receiver, repeater receiver
Ballettkorps *n* corps de ballet,
ballet company
Ballettmeister *m* ballet-master *n*
Balletttruppe *f* corps de ballet,

ballet company
Bananenbuchse *f* banana jack
Bananenstecker *m* banana plug
Band *f* (Mus.) band *n*, group *n*; ~ *n*
tape *n*, track *n*; ~ *n* (Welle) band *n*
~ **abfahren** to play a tape;
~ **aufzeichnen** tape *v*;
~ **randnumerieren** to mark a tape;
~ **trennen** to cut a tape; **Abhören**
hinter ~ separate head monitoring
Abhören vor ~ pre-record
listening, pre-listening *n*;
bespieltes ~ recorded tape;
endloses ~ endless tape, tape loop;
magisches ~ magic band valve;
perforiertes ~ perforated tape;
statisches ~ separator *n*;
unbespieltes ~ unrecorded tape;
unperforiertes ~ unperforated
tape
Bandabheber *m* tape lifter
Bandandruck *m* (MAZ) tape
pressure
Bandandruckfehler *m* (MAZ) tape
pressure fault
Bandantriebswelle *f* drive capstan,
drive shaft
Bandarchiv *n* tape library
Bandaufnahme *f* tape recording
Bandaufzeichnung *f* tape recording
Bandauszug *m* (EDV) tape edit
Bandbearbeitung *f* tape editing
Bandbegleitkarte *f* VT log
Bandbeitrag *m* tape insert; ~ *m*
(Bild) VT insert
Bandbeschichtung *f* tape coating
Bandbewegung *f* (EDV) tape feed,
tape transport
Bandbreite *f* (Frequenz) bandwidth
n, frequency range; ~ *f*
(Magnetband) tape width
Bändchenmikrofon *n* ribbon
microphone
Bandfehler *m* tape error
Bandfehlstelle *f* drop-out *n*
Bandfilter *m* band pass, band-pass
filter, waveband filter
Bandfluß *m* tape flux

Bandführung *f* tape guide, tape
guiding
Bandführungsfehler *m* (MAZ)
incorrect head position
Bandführungsschuh *m* vacuum
tape guide
Bandführungsvorrichtung *f* tape
guides *n pl*
Bandgerät *n* tape machine
Bandgeschwindigkeit *f* tape speed
Bandgeschwindigkeitsumschalter
m speed selector
Bandkassette *f* tape cassette, tape
cartridge
Bandkontrollkarte *f* VT log
Bandkopie *f* tape copy
Bandlauf *m* tape run
Bandlaufrichtung *f* tape travel
direction, travel direction
Bandleitung *f* twin lead, ribbon
feeder
Bandlöschkabine *f* bulk erasure
cubicle
Bandmaschine *f* tape machine
Bandmusik *f* grams *n pl* (coll.)
Bandpaß *m s.* Bandpaßfilter
Bandpaßfilter *m* band pass, band-
pass filter, waveband filter
Bandrauschen *n* tape noise
Bandreportage *f* recorded report
Bandriß *m* tape break
Bandschnitt *m* tape edit, tape
editing
Bandsendung *f* pre-recorded
broadcast, pre-recorded
programme, transmission of pre-
recorded material
Bandspeicher *m* (EDV) magnetic
tape store
Bandsperre *f* band-stop filter, band-
rejection filter
Bandspieler *m* tape recorder
Bandspule *f* tape reel, tape spool
Bandteller *m* tape plate
Bandtransport *m* tape transport
Bandtransportrolle *f* capstan *n*
Bandtrieb *m* tape drive capstan
Bandverdehnung *f* tape curvature

Bandverformung *f* tape curling, tape deformation
Bandwickelfehler *m* cinch *n*
Bandzählwerk *n* position indicator
Bandzug *m* tape tension
Bandzugregelung *f* regulation of tape tension
Bandzugschalter *m* tape tension cut-out switch
Bandzugwaage *f* tension measuring device
Bank, optische aerial-image printer, optical bench
BA-Regler *m* variable video attenuator
Bärenführer *m* (fam.) EID guide
Bartschatten *m* beard line
Basis *f* base *n*; ~ *f* (Stereo) sound stage
Basisbreite *f* (Stereo) sound-stage width
Basiseinspeisung *f* base-feeding *n*
Basisgrundschaltung *f* grounded-base connection
Basisschaltung *f* grounded-base connection
Baßanhebung *f* bass boost
Baßlautsprecher *m* low-frequency loudspeaker unit, woofer *n* (coll.)
Baßregelung *f* bass control
Batterie *f* battery *n*
Batteriebetrieb *m* battery operation
Batteriedienst *m* battery service
Batteriegerät *n* battery-operated device
Batterieladegerät *n* battery charger
Batterieleuchte *f* battery light, battery lamp
Batteriespeisung *f* battery operation
Batterietonbandgerät *n* battery tape recorder
Batteriewart *m* battery attendant
Batteriewartung *f* battery service
Bau und Ausstattung scenery and furnishing
Bauabteilung *f* architectural and civil-engineering department

Baubesprechung *f* design planning meeting
Baubühne* *f* scenic services
Baubühne *f* (Raum) scenic dock; ~ *f* (Gruppe) scenery operatives *n pl*, scene hands *n pl*
Baubühnenarbeiter *m* scene hand
Baueinheit *f* (Dekoration) built piece, solid piece, scenic unit
Bauelement *n* component *n*; ~ *n* (Dekoration) stage flat, piece *n*; **elektronisches** ~ electronic component
Baufundus *m* scenery stock
Bauhöhe *f* limiting height
Bauingenieur *m* civil engineer, structural engineer
Baukolonne *f* building team
Bauleiter *m* site supervisor
Baulicht *n* working light, house light
Bauplan *m* working drawing
Bauschaltplan *m* wiring diagram of building
Baustab *m* building team
Baustein *m* module *n*; **integrierter** ~ integrated circuit (IC)
Bausteintechnik *f* modular construction
Bautag *m* studio building day
Bauteil *n* component *n*, element *n*
Bauten *m pl* setting *n*, scenery *n*; ~ *m pl* (Filmtitel) art direction
Bauzeichner *m* draughtsman *n*
BCD-Darstellung *f* (EDV) binary-coded decimal representation, binary-coded decimal notation
Beanspruchung *f* (elek.) load *n*, loading *n*; ~ *f* (mech.) stress *n*, strain *n*; **maximale** ~ maximum load
bearbeiten *v* (Text) adapt *v*, edit *v*; ~ *v* (Mus.) arrange *v*; ~ *v* (tech.) process *v*; ~ *v* (F) work on *v*, treat *v*
Bearbeiter *m* (Text) adaptor *n*; ~ *m* (Mus.) arranger *n*

Bearbeitung f (Text) adaptation n; ~ f (Mus.) arrangement n; ~ f (F) treatment n; ~ f (tech.) processing n

Bearbeitungshonorar n (Buch) adaptation fee; ~ n (Mus.) arranging fee

Bedämpfung f damping n

Bediengerät n control panel

Bedienpult n control desk

Bedienung f operation n, maintenance n; **örtliche** ~ local operation

Bedienungsanleitung f operating instruction, service instruction

Bedienungsblattschreiber m (EDV) console typewriter, operator console typewriter

Bedienungsfeld n control panel; ~ n (EDV) console n, control panel, operator's console

Bedienungsknopf m control knob

Bedienungsplatz m operator's position

Bedienungsraum m control room, operations area, maintenance area

Bedienungsvorschrift f operating instruction, service instruction

Bedienungswanne f studio console

Beeinträchtigung f degradation n, impairment n

Befehl m (EDV) instruction n, command n

Befehlscode m (EDV) instruction code

Befehlsfolge f (EDV) sequence of instructions

Befehlswort n (EDV) instruction word

Befestigungskette f suspension chain, fixing chain

Befestigungsleine f suspension cord

Begleitmusik f incidental music

Begleitmusiker m accompanist n

Begleittext m narration n, accompanying script; ~ m (Nachrichten) dope-sheet n

Begleitton m ambient sound

Begleittonleitung f international sound circuit, effects circuit

Begleitung f (Mus.) accompaniment n

Begrenzer m limiter n, clipper n

Begrenzung f limiting n, clipping n

Beifilm m supporting film

Beiprogramm n supporting programme, programme filler

Beirat m advisory council

Beitrag m contribution n; ~ m (Nachrichten) item n, story n; ~ m (Text) report n, copy n, piece n (coll.)

Belastung f (elek.) load n, loading n; ~ f (mech.) stress n, strain n; **ohmsche** ~ resistive loading

Belastungsimpedanz f load impedance

Belastungswiderstand m load resistance, bleeder n

Belegschaft f staff n

beleuchten v illuminate v, light v

Beleuchter m studio electrician n, lighting electrician, lighting man, spark n (coll.)

Beleuchterbrücke f lighting bridge, gantry n

Beleuchterbühne f s. Beleuchterbrücke

Beleuchterfahrzeug n lamp trolley

Beleuchtergalerie f lighting gallery

Beleuchtergang m catwalk n, gallery n

Beleuchtertrupp m lighting crew, sparks n pl (coll.)

Beleuchtung f lighting n; ~ f (Stärke) brightness n; ~ **mit Schlagschatteneffekt** lighting with hard-shadow effect; **flache** ~ flat lighting; **indirekte** ~ indirect lighting

Beleuchtungsanlage f lighting installation, lighting equipment

Beleuchtungsdienst m lighting department

Beleuchtungseinrichtung f lighting

Beleuchtungseinrichtung 20

installation, lighting equipment
Beleuchtungsfeuer *n* beacon *n*
Beleuchtungsgeräte *n pl* lighting
equipment
Beleuchtungskontrast *m* lighting
contrast
Beleuchtungskörper *m* lighting unit
Beleuchtungsmaterial *n* lighting
equipment
Beleuchtungsmeister *m* lighting
supervisor
Beleuchtungsoptik *f* (Proj.) optical
system of projector
Beleuchtungspult *n* lighting-control
console
Beleuchtungsrampe *f* footlight *n*,
float *n*
Beleuchtungsraum *m* lighting
control room
Beleuchtungsstärke *f* lighting level
Beleuchtungsstärkemessung *f*
measurement of light level
Beleuchtungsstärkeumfang *m*
range of light level
Beleuchtungssteuerfeld *n* console-
dimmer lever bank, lever bank,
dimmer bank
Beleuchtungssteuerung *f* lighting
control
Beleuchtungsstromkreis *m* lighting
circuit
Beleuchtungsumfang *m* lighting-
level range
Beleuchtungsverhältnis *n* lighting
contrast ratio
Beleuchtungswerkstatt *f* lighting
workshop
Beleuchtungswesen *n* lighting *n*
belichten *v* expose *v*
Belichtung *f* exposure *n*
Belichtungsindex *m* exposure index
Belichtungskeil *m* sensitometric
step wedge, step wedge
Belichtungsmesser *m* exposure
meter, light meter, photometer *n*
Belichtungsmessung *f*
measurement of exposure
Belichtungsprobe *f* exposure
test

Belichtungsschablone *f* punched
tape
Belichtungsspielraum *m* range of
exposure; ~ *m* (Filmmaterial)
exposure latitude
Belichtungstabelle *f* exposure
chart, exposure guide, exposure
table, exposure scale
Belichtungsuhr *f* exposure timer,
darkroom timer, timer *n*
Belichtungszeit *f* exposure period,
exposure time
Belüftungsanlage *f* ventilation
system
Bemusterung *f* sample *n*, sampling
n
Benennung *f* designation *n*
Benutzerprogramm *n* (EDV) user
programme
Benutzerzeit, verfügbare (EDV)
available machine time
Benutzungsgebühr *f* usage fee
berechnen *v* calculate *v*, compute *v*
Berechnung *f* calculation *n*,
computation *n*
Bereich *m* area *n*, region *n*, zone *n*;
~ *m* (Skala) range *n*; ~ *m*
(Frequenz) band *n*, range *n*;
achromatischer ~ achromatic
region, achromatic zone
Bereichsantenne *f* band aerial
Bereichssperrkreis *m* band-stop
filter
Bereichsverstärker *m* band
amplifier
Bereichsweiche *f* band diplexer
Bereitschaft *f* readiness *n*, stand-by
n; **in** ~ at stand-by
Bereitschaftsdienst *m* stand-by
service; ~ *m* (Personal) skeleton
staff
Bericht *m* report *n*; ~ *m* (Sport)
commentary *n*; ~ *m* (aktuell)
dispatch *n*, report *n*, story *n*, piece
n; ~ *m* (R) talk *n*; ~ *m* (Agentur)
message *n*; **aktuelle** ~**e** news
coverage
berichten *v* report *v*, cover *v*
Berichterstatter *m* reporter *n*,

correspondent *n*, commentator *n*, newsman *n* (US)

Berichterstattung *f* reporting *n*, coverage *n*; ~ **Ausland** foreign news; ~ **Inland** home news, national news (US); ~ **wahrnehmen** report *v*, cover *v*; **ausführliche** ~ full coverage, wide coverage; **laufende** ~ coverage of running story; **regionale** ~ regional news, local news (US), area coverage (US)

Berichtigung *f* correction *n*

berufsmäßig *adj* professional *adj*

Berufsschauspieler *m* professional actor

besaften *v* (fam.) to put on the juice (coll.)

beschallen *v* to equip with public address

Beschallung *f* public address (PA)

Beschallungsanlage *f* public address system, PA system

Beschaltung *f* wiring *n*

Beschichtung *f* (F) coating *n*, emulsion layer

Beschleuniger *m* accelerator *n*

Beschleunigungsspannung *f* acceleration voltage

Beschreibung *f* description *n*

Beschriftungsbild *n* label *n*

Besenkeil *m* wedge *n*, resolution wedge; ~ *m* (Testbild) test wedge *n*

besetzen *v* (Darsteller) cast *v*

Besetztzeichen *n* busy signal, engaged tone

Besetzung *f* (Darsteller) cast *n*, casting *n*

Besetzungsbüro *n* booking section, artists' bookings

Besetzungskartei *f* artists' index

Besetzungsliste *f* cast list

bespielen *v* record *v*

Bespurung *f* striping process, laminating process

Bespurungsverfahren *n* (F) striping *n*

bestellen *v* order *v*, book *v*

Bestimmungsland *n* country of destination

bestücken *v* equip *v*

Bestückung *f* equipment *n*, component parts *n pl*

Besuch *m* attendance *n*, audience *n*

Besucher *m* visitor *n*; ~ *m* (F) cinema-goer *n*; ~ *m* (Thea.) theatre-goer *n*

Besucherrückgang *m* audience fall-off

betätigen *v* operate *v*, actuate *v*

betiteln *v* title *v*; ~ *v* (Agentur) slug *v*

Betrachter *m* viewer *n*

Betrachtungsschirm *m* viewing screen, oscilloscope screen

betreiben *v* operate *v*

Betrieb *m* operation *n*; ~ *m* (eigen) internal operation; ~ *m* (fremd) external operation; ~ **mit Schaltuhr** operation by timing switch; ~ **mit Zeitschaltuhr** operation by time switch; **außer** ~ **sein** (Sender) to be off the air; **autarker** ~ independent operation **in** ~ in operation, in service; **in** ~ **nehmen** to put into operation, to put into service, start up *v*; **in** ~ **sein** (Sender) to be on the air; **in** ~ **setzen** to put into operation, to put into service, start up *v*; **stabiler** ~ stable operation, good working order

Betriebsabwicklung *f* operating procedure

Betriebsabwicklung* *f* technical operations*

Betriebsanleitung *f* operating instruction, code of practice

Betriebsanweisung *f* s. Betriebsanleitung

Betriebsart *f* mode of operation; ~ *f* (EDV) mode *n*

Betriebsartenschalter *m* function selector switch, selector switch, mode selector

Betriebsartenwahl *f* function selection

Betriebsarzt *m* staff medical adviser, staff medical officer

betriebsärztliche Dienststelle medical unit, surgery *n*

Betriebsaufsicht *f* monitoring *n*

betriebsbereit *adj* ready for operation

Betriebsbereitschaft *f* (Dienst) staff on call; ~ *f* (Gerät) readiness for operation

Betriebsbüro *n* supervisor's office

Betriebseinrichtung *f* plant *n*, technical equipment

Betriebserde *f* service earth, operational earth

Betriebsfernsehen *n* closed-circuit television (CCTV)

Betriebsfrequenz *f* operating frequency, nominal frequency, working frequency

Betriebshandwerker *m* staff maintenance worker

Betriebshelfer *m* unskilled staff

Betriebsingenieur *m* operations engineer, senior engineer

Betriebskosten *plt* operating expenses, working costs, running costs

Betriebsleiter *m* technical superintendent, senior engineer

Betriebsoszillograf *m* service oscilloscope

Betriebsrat *m* works council

Betriebsraum *m* operations room

Betriebsschwester *f* staff nursing sister

Betriebssicherheit *f* service reliability, operational reliability

Betriebsspannung *f* operating voltage

Betriebsstörung *f* breakdown *n*

Betriebssystem (BS) *n* (EDV) operating system (OS)

Betriebstechnik *f* engineering operations and maintenance; ~ **Fernsehen** television

engineering operations; ~ **Film** film operations

Betriebstechniker *m* staff engineer

Betriebstelefon *n* internal telephone

Betriebstemperatur *f* working temperature

Betriebsüberwachung *f* operational supervision, monitoring of operations

Betriebsverstärkung *f* effective transmission gain

Betriebsverwaltung* *f* central services group*

Betriebswartung *f* maintenance *n*

Betriebszeit *f* operating time; ~ *f* (Personal) working hours *n pl*

Betriebszentrale *f* technical operations*

Betriebszustand *m* working order, working condition; ~ *m* (Röhre) working point

beweglich *adj* movable *adj*, mobile *adj*

Bewegung *f* movement *n*, motion *n*

Bewegungsunschärfe *f* motion unsharpness, unsharpness due to movement

bewertet *adj* (tech.) evaluated *adj*, weighted *adj*

Bewertungsfilter *m* weighting network

Bewertungstabelle *f* (UER) table of subjective grades

Bezeichnung *f* designation *n*

Bezug *m* reference *n*

Bezugsband *n* calibration tape, standard tape, standard magnetic tape, test tape, reference tape, line-up tape

Bezugsgenerator *m* reference generator, standard signal generator

Bezugshelligkeit *f* reference luminosity

Bezugsimpuls *m* reference pulse

Bezugskante *f* reference edge

Bezugslinie *f* reference axis,

reference line, datum line
Bezugsoszillator *m* reference oscillator
Bezugspegel *m* reference level
Bezugsphase *f* reference phase
Bezugspunkt *m* reference point, fiducial mark
Bezugsschwarz *n* reference black
Bezugsspannung *f* reference voltage
Bezugsweiß *n* reference white
Bezugswert *m* reference value
Bibliothek *f* library *n*
Bibliothekar *m* librarian *n*
bifilar *adj* bifilar *adj*
bilateral *adj* bilateral *adj*
Bild *n* (s. a. Foto) image *n*, picture *n*, vision *n*; ~ *n* (Vollbild) frame *n*; ~ *n* (Drehbuch) sequence *n*, scene *n* ~ *n* (Einstellung) framing *n*, shot *n*
Bild- (in Zus.) visual *adj*, vision (compp.), video *adj*
Bild ab! run!; ~ **aufziehen** fade in *v*, fade up *v*; ~ **einstellen** centre *v*, frame *v*; ~ **grau in grau** sooty picture; ~ **halten** to hold the picture; **aus dem** ~ **gehen** to go out of shot, to get out of shot; **einfarbiges** ~ monochrome picture, black-and-white picture; **eingebranntes** ~ sticking *n*; **flaches** ~ flat picture, picture without contrast; **Fremdkörper im** ~ extraneous object in picture; **gegen das** ~ **texten** to write against the picture; **geteiltes** ~ split screen; **im** ~ **sein** (TV) to be in vision, to be in shot, to be on-camera; **ins** ~ **kommen** to come into shot; **kalkiges** ~ burnt-out picture; **kopfstehendes** ~ inverted image, upside-down image; **latentes** ~ latent image; **matschiges** ~ misty picture; **mehrfarbiges** ~ polychrome picture; **monochromes** ~ monochrome picture, black-and-white picture; **negatives** ~

negative picture; **nicht aufs** ~ **kommen** to miss the shot; **polychromes** ~ polychrome picture; **rollendes** ~ rolling picture synchrones ~ synchronous picture **umgesetztes** ~ converted image; **unbrauchbares** ~ unusable picture **unsichtbares** ~ latent image; **verschleiertes** ~ blurred image, soft picture, fogged picture, hazy picture; **verwackeltes** ~ unstable picture; **verzerrtes** ~ distorted picture; **weiches** ~ uncontrasty picture, soft picture; **Ziehen des** ~**es** frame rolling, picture slip
Bildablenktransformator *m* frame-scan transformer
Bildablenkung *f* frame scan, picture scan, vertical sweep
Bildabtaster *m* television scanning device, scanner *n*, scanning device
Bildabtastung *f* picture scanning, image scanning
Bildabzug *m* paper print
Bildamplitude *f* picture amplitude
Bildanpaßmonitor *m* picture matching monitor
Bildarchiv *n* picture library
Bildarchivar *m* picture librarian *n*
Bildaufbau *m* picture synthesis, build-up of picture, picture composition
Bildauflösung *f* picture definition, picture resolution
Bildaufnahme *f* picture recording, visual recording, shot *n*, take *n*
Bildaufnahmeröhre *f* camera tube, pick-up tube, iconoscope *n*, vidicon *n*, Plumbicon *n*, orthicon *n*, image orthicon
Bildaufnahmewagen *m* mobile control room (MCR), television car, OB scanner (coll.)
Bildaufzeichnung *f* vision recording, visual recording, picture recording; **elektronische** ~ electronic video recording (EVR);

Bildaufzeichnung 24

magnetische ~ (MAZ) video tape
recording (VTR)
Bildaufzeichnungsgerät *n* television
recording equipment, telerecorder
n
Bildausfall *m* image drop-out,
vision break
Bildausgangssignal *n* picture
output signal
Bildauskippen *n* line-tearing *n*, line-
pulling *n*
Bildausreißen *n* picture break-up
Bildausschnitt *m* image area,
picture area
Bildausschnittsucher *m* director's
finder, gonoscope *n*
Bildaussteuerung *f* picture control
Bildaustastimpuls *m* blanking
pulse
Bildaustastsignal (BA-Signal) *n*
picture and blanking signal,
blanked picture signal, video
signal without sync pulse
**Bildaustastsynchronsignal (BAS-
Signal)** *n* composite signal,
composite video signal, composite
picture signal; ~ **mit Prüfzeile
(BASP-Signal)** composite video
signal with insertion test signal,
composite signal with test line
(coll.)
Bildband *n* video tape; ~ *n* (F) film
strip; ~ *n* (Kopierwerk) grading
strip; ~ **und Tonband auf gleiche
Länge ziehen** sync up *v*, to bring
into lip sync, lip-sync *v*
Bildbandarchiv *n* video tape
library, tape store
Bildbandbreite *f* video tape
bandwidth, picture bandwidth
Bildbandgerät *n* video tape
recorder (VTR), video tape
machine
Bildbandkassette *f* video tape
cassette, video tape cartridge
Bildbandkassettengerät *n* cassette
video tape recorder
Bildbegrenzung *f* (F) framing *n*; ~ *f*

(TV) frame-limiting *n*
Bildberichterstatter *m* press
photographer, stills man (coll.)
Bildbetrachter *m* film viewer, slide
viewer, editola *n* (US)
Bildbreitenregler *m* width control
Bildbrumm *m* picture hum
Bilddauer *f* picture duration, frame
duration
Bilddauerleitungsnetz *n* permanent
vision network
Bilddetail *n* image detail, picture
detail
Bilddiagonale *f* diagonal of picture
Bilddramaturgie *f* dramatic
composition of picture
Bilddup *n* dupe *n*
Bilddurchlauf *m* picture roll,
picture slip, frame roll
Bildebene *f* (Kamera) image plane;
~ *f* (Objektiv) focal plane
Bildeinstellung *f* centring-up *n*,
framing *n*; **fehlerhafte ~** bad
framing, bad centring; **fehlerhafte
~** (Empfänger) mistuning *n*
Bildeinzelheit *f* image detail,
picture detail
Bildendkontrolle *f* final picture
quality check, quality check
Bilder pro Sekunde frames per
second (fps), pictures per second
(pps)
Bildfalle *f* trap circuit
Bildfang *m* s. Bildfangregler
Bildfangregler *m* hold control,
framing control, frame hold,
vertical hold, vertical lock
Bildfehlschaltung *f* picture
switching error
Bildfeld *n* image field, picture area,
image area, field of vision, frame
n
Bildfenster *n* film gate, picture gate,
gate *n*; ~ *n* (Kamera) camera
aperture; ~ *n* (Proj.) projection
aperture, projection gate
Bildfensterabdeckung *f* film-gate
mask; ~ *f* (Kamera) taking mask

Bildfenstereinsatz *m s.*
Bildfensterabdeckung
Bildfensterplatte *f* aperture plate
Bildfilm *m* picture film; ~ **mit**
Cordband Sepmag *n*; ~ **mit**
Magnetrandspur Commag *n*
Bildfolge *f* sequence of pictures
Bildfolgefrequenz *f* picture
repetition frequency, scanning
rate, number of frames per
second
Bildformat *n* dimension of picture,
picture size, image size, frame
size, aspect ratio (AR), picture
ratio, picture shape
Bildfortschaltzeit *f* film sequencing
time, film pulldown time,
pulldown period
Bildfrequenz *f* (Vollbild) picture
frequency (25 or 30 Hz); ~ *f*
(Teilbild) vertical frequency (50 or
60 Hz), field frequency (50 or 60
Hz); ~ *f* (F) frame frequency
Bildführung *f* direction *n*; ~ **hatte ...**
(im Titel) directed by ...
bildfüllend *adj* full-frame *adj*
Bildfunk *m* picture telegraphy,
facsimile broadcasting, facsimile
transmission, picture
transmission
Bildfunkempfänger *m* picture
receiver, facsimile receiver
Bildfunksender *m* picture
transmitter, facsimile transmitter
Bildfunkstrecke *f* vision radio link
Bildgeber *m* picture transmitter,
facsimile transmitter
Bildgeometrie *f* picture geometry
Bildgestaltung *f* picture
composition, pictorial
composition
Bildgleichlaufimpuls *m* picture
synchronising pulse, vertical
synchronising pulse
Bildgüte *f* picture quality
Bildhelligkeit *f* picture brightness,
brightness of image
Bildhintergrund *m* picture

background
Bildhöhe *f* picture height, image
height, frame height
Bildhöhenregler *m* height control
Bildimpuls *m* picture synchronising
pulse
Bildinformation *f* picture
information
Bildingenieur *m* vision control
engineer, senior television
engineer
Bildinhalt *m* picture content
Bildintermodulation *f* crossview *n*
Bildkante *f* picture edge, frame
edge
Bildkassette *f* video tape cassette,
video tape cartridge
Bildkennung *f* picture
identification, vision
identification, identification
caption
Bildkippen *n* loss of picture lock,
picture roll, frame roll
Bildkippgerät *n* frame sweep unit
Bildkomposition *f* picture
composition, pictorial
composition
Bildkontrast *m* image contrast,
picture contrast
Bildkontrolle *f* picture control
Bildkontrolleitung *f* vision control
circuit, video monitoring circuit
Bildkontrollempfänger *m* vision
check receiver, picture monitor,
monitor *n*, picture monitoring
receiver, television monitor
Bildkontrollgerät *n* picture and
waveform monitor
Bildkontrollraum *m* vision control
room
Bildkontur *f* picture contour
Bildkopie *f* copy *n*, print *n*
Bildlage *f* picture position, frame
position
Bildleitung (BL) *f* vision circuit,
video circuit
Bildleitungsnetz *n* vision network,
vision circuit network

Bildmaske *f* framing mask, film-gate mask

Bildmaterial *n* picture material

Bildmischeinrichtung *f* vision-mixing apparatus, vision-mixing panel

Bildmischer *m* (Gerät) video mixer, vision mixer; ~ *m* (Person) vision mixer, vision switcher; ~ **am Trickpult** video effects mixer, vision effects mixer

Bildmischpult *n* video mixer, vision mixer, video monitoring and mixing desk, video mixing desk

Bildmischung *f* video mixing, vision mixing

Bildmitte *f* (TV) centre of picture; ~ *f* (F) centre of frame; **aus der ~ setzen** to off-centre the picture, to compose off-centre; **in die ~ setzen** frame *v*, centre on *v*

Bildmittelpunkt *m s.* Bildmitte

Bildmonitor *m* vision check receiver, picture monitor, monitor *n*, picture monitoring receiver, television monitor

Bildmuster *n pl* picture rushes, rushes *n pl*

Bildnegativ *n* picture negative

Bildnegativbericht *m* negative report

Bildoperateur *m* camera control operator

Bildoriginal *n* picture original

Bildpegel *m* picture level

Bildpegeländerung *f* change of picture level

Bildpegelschwankung *f* fluctuation of picture level

Bildpegelsprung *m* sudden picture-level change

Bildperiode *f* picture period

Bildplastik *f* plastic effect, relief effect

Bildplatte *f* video disc

Bildpositiv *n* positive picture, picture positive

Bildprojektor *m* still projector

Bildpunkt *m* image point; ~ *m* (TV) picture element

Bildqualität *f* picture quality

Bildrand *m* margin of image

Bildrandverschärfer *m* contour correction unit

Bildraster *m* picture raster, raster *n*

Bildrauschen *n* picture noise, video noise

Bildregie *f* vision control, video control

Bildregiepult *n* vision control desk

Bildregieraum *m* vision control room

Bildregisseur *m* director *n*

Bildregler *m* fader *n*, vision fader, video attenuator

Bildreportage *f* picture feature

Bildreporter *m* press photographer, stills man (coll.); ~ *m* (TV) TV reporter

Bildröhre *f* picture tube, kinescope *n* (US)

Bildröhrenspeicher *m* (EDV) flying-spot store

Bildrücklauf *m* picture flyback, frame flyback

Bildschallplatte *f* video disc

Bildschaltraum *m* vision switching centre

Bildschärfe *f* picture sharpness, image sharpness, picture definition, image definition

Bildschirm *m* (FS-Empfänger) picture screen, television screen; ~ *m* (Aufnahmeröhre) target *n*; ~ *m* (EDV) screen *n*

Bildschirmformat *n* screen size

Bildschirmübertragung *f* television transmission

Bildschnitt *m* (F) picture editing, cutting *n*; ~ *m* (TV) vision switching

Bildschramme *f* scratch *n*

Bildschritt *m* frame gauge

Bildschwarz *n* picture black

Bildscript *n* camera script

Bildseitenverhältnis *n* aspect ratio

Bild- und

(AR), picture aspect ratio
Bildsender *m* (Bildfunk) facsimile transmitter, picture transmitter; ~ *m* (TV) vision transmitter
bildsequent *adj* frame-sequential *adj*
Bildsignal (B-Signal) *n* vision signal, modulation signal, video signal, picture signal; ~ **mit Austastung** picture and blanking signal, blanked picture signal, video signal without sync pulse; **zusammengesetztes** ~ composite video waveform, composite video signal
Bildsignalabgleich *m* video adjustment
Bildsignalverstärkung *f* picture signal gain, video gain
Bildspeicherröhre *f* storage-type camera tube
Bildsprung *m* break of picture sequence; ~ *m* (tech.) rollover *n*; ~ *m* (Schnitt) jump cut
Bildspur *f* video track
Bildstand *m* picture steadiness
Bildstandfehler *m* picture instability
Bildstandschwankung *f* picture jitter
Bildstandschwankungen, horizontale horizontal jitter
Bildstart *m* picture start
Bildstartmarke *f* picture start mark, sync cross, envelope *n* (coll.)
Bildsteg *m* (TV) frame bar; ~ *m* (F) frame line, rack line
Bildstern *m* vision switching centre
Bildsternpunkt *m* s. Bildstern
Bildsteuersender *m* vision pilot frequency
Bildstörung *f* picture interference, picture breakdown, vision breakdown
Bildstrich *m* frame line
Bildstricheinstellung *f* framing *n*
Bildstruktur *f* picture structure, picture grain

Bildsucher *m* viewfinder *n*
bildsynchron *adj* picture-phased *adj*
Bildsynchronimpuls *m* frame sync, frame synchronising pulse, vertical synchronising pulse, vertical sync pulse
Bildsynchronisation *f* frame synchronisation, picture synchronisation, vertical hold
Bildtechnik *f* video engineering
Bildtechniker *m* vision controller
Bildtelefon *n* picture telephone, visphone *n*
Bildtelefonie *f* picture telephony
Bildtelegrafie *f* picture telegraphy, picture transmission, facsimile transmission
Bild-Ton- (in Zus.) picture-and-sound (compp.), audio-visual *adj*
Bild-Ton-Kamera *f* double-headed camera
Bild-Ton-Platte *f* picture-and-sound disc
Bild-Ton-Versatz *m* (ungewollt) slippage of sound to picture; ~ *m* (gewollt) sound track advance, sound advance, sync advance
Bild-Ton-Versatzvorrichtung *f* picture/sound offset unit
Bild-Ton-Weiche *f* vision/sound diplexer, vision/sound combining unit
Bildträger *m* vision carrier; ~ *m* (Vertrag) visual recording
Bildträgerfrequenz *f* vision frequency
Bildüberblendung *f* cross-fading *n*, dissolve *n*, lap dissolve, mix *n*, mix-through *n*
Bildüberblendzeichen *n pl* change-over cues, cue dots, cue marks
Bildübersprechen *n* crossview *n*
Bildübertragung *f* (TV) picture transmission
Bildüberwachung *f* picture control, picture monitoring
Bild- und Tonschaltraum *m* vision

and sound switching area, central apparatus room (CAR)

Bildung* *f* educational broadcasting*

Bildungsfernsehen *n* educational television (ETV)

Bildungsfunk *m* educational broadcasting, educational radio

Bildungsprogramm *n* educational programme

Bildunterkleber *m* perforated transparent tape, tape join

Bildunterschrift *f* caption *n*

Bildverdrängung *f* picture displacement

Bildverschiebung *f* image shift

Bildverstellung *f* (Proj.) picture framing

Bildverzerrung *f* image distortion, picture distortion

Bildwand *f* projection screen, screen *n*, cinema screen, theatre screen

Bildwandhelligkeit *f* screen brightness, screen luminance

Bildwandler *m* image converter

Bildwandlerschärfe *f* image converter sharpness

Bildwechsel *m* (Vollbild) picture frequency (25 or 30 Hz); ~ *m* (elektron.) vision switching, camera cut; ~ *m* (dramaturgisch) change of scene

Bildwechselfrequenz *f* (Vollbild) picture frequency (25 or 30 Hz); ~ *f* (EDV) frame frequency

Bildwechselimpuls *m* frame sync, frame synchronising pulse, vertical synchronising pulse, vertical sync pulse

Bildweiß *n* picture white

Bildwerfer *m* (Dia) slide projector, still projector

Bildwiedergabe *f* image reproduction, picture reproduction

Bildwiedergaberöhre *f* picture tube, pick-up tube, television tube,

kinescope *n* (US)

Bildwinkel *m* angle of image, picture angle, angular field of lens, shooting angle

Bildwinkelanzeige *f* zoom angle indication

Bildwinkelanzeiger *m* zoom indicator

Bildzahl *f* (Vollbild) picture frequency (25 or 30 Hz); ~ *f* (F) number of frames

Bildzähler *m* frame counter

Bildzeile *f* scanning line, picture line

Bimetallkontakt *m* bimetallic contact

binär *adj* (EDV) binary *adj*; ~ **codierte Adresse** (EDV) binary-coded address

Binärcode *m* (EDV) binary code; **reiner** ~ (EDV) pure binary code

Binärmuster *n* (EDV) bit configuration, bit pattern

Binärstelle *f* (EDV) binary digit, bit *n*

Binärzahl *f* (EDV) binary number

Binärzähler *m* (EDV) binary counter

Binärziffer *f* (EDV) binary digit, bit *n*

binaural *adj* binaural *adj*

Bipack *n* bipack *n*

Birne *f* light-bulb *n*, bulb *n*

bistabil *adj* (EDV) bistable *adj*

Bit *n* (EDV) binary digit, bit *n*

Blankfilm *m* blank film, clear film, spacing *n*; ~ *m* (Start) clear leader; ~ **mit Bildstrich** clear film with frame line

blankieren *v* (F) polish *v*

Blankiermaschine *f* polishing machine

Blankschramme *f* celluloid scratch, scratch on base side

Blankseite *f* (F) base side

Blasmusik *f* brass band music

Blasorchester *n* brass band, wind band

Blaustanzverfahren *n* colour separation overlay, chroma key, blue screen
Bleichbad *n* bleach bath
bleichen *v* bleach *v*
Bleichen *n* bleaching *n*
Bleichung *f* bleaching *n*
Blende *f* (Objektiv) aperture *n*, diaphragm *n*, stop *n*, lens stop, iris *n*; ~ *f* (Proj., Kamera) shutter *n*; ~ *f* (Scheinwerfer) lantern *n*, douser *n*, diffuser *n*, barndoor *n*; ~ *f* (Trick) dissolve *n*, optical *n*, wipe *n*; ~ *f* (Licht) gobo *n*, flag *n*, nigger *n*, target *n*, blade *n*, dot *n*, frenchman *n*, barndoor *n*; ~ *f* (Bühne) flat *n*; ~ **öffnen** to open aperture, to open diaphragm, open up *v*; ~ **schließen** to close aperture, to close diaphragm, stop down *v*; **chemische** ~ chemical fade; **fotometrische** ~ photometric aperture; **geometrische** ~ geometric aperture; **kritische** ~ critical aperture; **ziehende** ~ travel ghost, ghosting *n*
blenden *v* fade *v*, wipe *v*
Blendenband *n* (Kamera) exposure control band, exposure control strip; ~ *n* (Kopierung) printing control band, printing control strip
Blendenbandkopiermaschine *f* control band printer
Blendeneinstellung *f* diaphragm setting, aperture setting, stop setting, iris setting
Blendenflügel *m* shutter blade, mirror shutter
Blendenklammer *f* cleat *n*, flat clamp
Blendennachdrehvorrichtung *f* shutter-phasing device, inching knob
Blendenöffnung *f* lens aperture, shutter aperture, working aperture, aperture of diaphragm, iris aperture, aperture *n*, shooting

aperture
Blendenraste *f* click setting
Blendenregulierung *f* iris adjustment
Blendenring *m* diaphragm ring
Blendenschablone *f* camera matte, effects matte
Blendenskala *f* diaphragm scale
Blendenstrebe *f* s. Blendenstütze
Blendenstütze *f* brace *n*, stay *n*
Blickfeld *n* field of vision, field of view; **im** ~ **sein** to be in shot, to be in frame
Blickwinkel *m* angle of view
Blimp *m* blimp *n*
Blimp-Kamera *f* blimped camera
Blindanteil *m* reactive component
Blindbuchen *n* blind booking
Blindfilm *m* blacking *n*, black spacing, spacing *n*
Blindleistung *f* reactive power, wattless power
Blindleitwert *m* susceptance *n*
Blindröhre *f* reactance valve
Blindwiderstand *m* reactance *n*, reactive impedance
Blindwiderstände, verteilte distributed reactance
Blinkgeber *m* blinker unit
Blitz *m* flash *n*
Blitzgerät *n* flash unit, flash gun
Blitzlicht *n* flashlight *n*
Blitzmeldung *f* news flash, snap *n*
Blitznachrichten *f pl* flash news
Blitzprogramm *n* flash programme
Blitzschaltung *f* switching flash
Blitzschutz *m* lightning protection
Blitzumschaltung *m* s. Blitzschaltung
Blitzzange *f* lightning stick
Blockbuchen *n* block booking
Blockdiagramm *n* (EDV) block diagram
Blockierung *f* blocking *n*, locking *n*
Blockschaltbild *n* (EDV) block diagram
Blockschaltplan *m* block diagram
Blooming *n* pulling on whites,

Blooming 30

blooming *n*
Blubbern *n* (tech.) bubbling *n*,
motor-boating *n*
Bobby *m* (fam.) bobbin *n*, core *n*,
hub *n*, centre *n*
Bodenfunkstelle *f* terrestrial radio
station
Bodenleitfähigkeit *f* ground
conductivity
Bodenleitungsverbindung *f* land-
line connection
Bodenplatte *f* base plate
Bodenstation *f* earth station
Bodenstativ *n* floor stand
Bodenwelle *f* ground wave, surface
wave, direct wave
Bodenwellenausbreitung *f* ground-
wave propagation
Bogenlampe *f* HI arc-lamp, arc *n*
Bohle *f* plank *n*
Bolzen *m* bolt *n*
Bolzensetzwerkzeug *n* stud driver
Boolesche Algebra (EDV) Boolean
algebra
Boosterspannung *f* booster voltage
Bote *m* messenger *n*; ~ *m*
(Außendienst) dispatch rider
Botenmeister *m* messenger
supervisor
Botenmeisterei *f* messenger service
Boulevardstück *n* light comedy
Branchenwerbung *f* collective
product advertising, product-
group advertising
Brandmeister *m* head fireman
Brechung *f* refraction *n*
Breitband *n* broad band, wide band
Breitbandantenne *f* wide-band
aerial
Breitbandkreis *m* wide-band circuit
Breitbandmikrofon *n* wide-
response microphone
Breitbandtechnik *f* wide-band
technique
Breitbandtechniker *m* (fam.) all-
round engineer
Breitbandverstärker *m* wide-band
amplifier

Breitbildfilm *m* wide-screen picture
n, wide-screen film
Breitenwinkel *m* azimuth *n*, wide
angle
Breitfilm *m* (70 mm) wide-gauge
film
Breitwand *f* wide screen
Bremsfeld *n* braking field,
retarding field
Bremsgitter *n* suppressor grid
Bremsrelais *n* braking relay
Brennpunkt *m* focus *n*, focal point
Brennpunktebene *f* focal plane
Brennstoffzelle *f* fuel cell
Brennweite *f* focal distance, focal
length; **doppelte** ~ double focal
length; **große** ~ long focal length,
long focus; **kurze** ~ short focal
length, short focus; **lange** ~ long
focal length, long focus
Brennweitenänderung *f* change of
focal length
Brennweitenband *n* focus
calibration tape
Brennweitenbereich *m* range of
focus
Brennweitenbügel *m* zoom handle
Brennweitenring *m* focus ring
Brennweitenverlängerer *m* range
extender
Brett *n* plank *n*
Brettschaltung *f* (EDV) breadboard
circuit
Brillantsucher *m* reflector
viewfinder
Brillanz *f* brilliance *n*
B-Rolle *f* B roll
Brücke *f* bridge *n*
Brückengleichrichter *m* bridge-
connected rectifier, bridge
rectifier
Brückenglied *n* bridge network
Brückenmeßgerät *n* measuring
bridge
Brückenschaltung *f* bridge circuit,
bridge connection
Brumm *m* hum *n*, ripple *n*, buzz *n*,
humming noise

brummen v hum v, buzz v
Brummer m buzzer n
Brummspannung f ripple voltage, hum voltage, ripple n
Brummstör-Amplitudenmodulation f hum amplitude modulation
Brummstreifen m hum bar
Brummton n hum n, ripple n, buzz n, humming noise
Brummüberlagerung f hum bars n pl, hum superimposition
Brummunterdrückung f hum suppression
Brüstung f guard-rail n, hand-rail n, railing n, parapet n, balustrade n
Brut n (fam.) brut n
B-Schaltung f class B circuit
Buch n (F) scenario n, script n, shooting script
Buchabnahme f acceptance of script
Buchbesprechung f book review; ~ f (F) script discussion, script conference
Buchentwicklung f run-up period
Buchhalter m book-keeper n
Buchnummer f shot number
Buchse f (elek.) jack n, socket n; ~ f (mech.) bush n
Buchsenleiste f socket cleat
Buchstabencode m (EDV) mnemonic code
Bühne f stage n, set n, scene n; ~ f (fam.) stage hands n pl; **versenkbare ~** tank n
Bühnenarbeiter m stage hand, scene shifter, grip n (US); ~ m (Baubühne) scene hand; ~ m (Drehbühne) scenic service man
Bühnenbau m setting construction
Bühnenbauten m pl settings n pl
Bühnenbild n set n, decor n, scenery n, setting n, set design; ~ n (im Filmtitel) art direction
Bühnenbildentwurf m set design, set sketch
Bühnenbildner m designer n, set designer, scenery designer, scenic

designer, art director
Bühnenbildnerei f set designing, scenery designing
Bühnenbildnerei* f scenic design*
Bühnendekoration f stage decorations n pl, set dressing
bühnenlinks adv stage left, prompt side
Bühnenmaler m scenic painter
Bühnenmaschinerie f stage machinery
Bühnenmeister m construction manager
Bühnenpersonal n stage hands n pl
bühnenrechts adv stage right, off-prompt side
Bühnenschlosser m studio fitter, studio metalworker
Bühnenschreiner m scenic carpenter
Bühnenschreinerei f scenic carpenter's shop
Bühnentischler m scenic carpenter
Bühnentischlerei f scenic carpenter's shop
Bühnenvorarbeiter m stage hands' foreman
Bühnenwache f stand-by stage team
Bühnenwagen m scenic truck, boat-truck n, stage waggon
Bühnenwerkstatt f scenic workshop
Bündelung f focusing n
Buntsendung f colour programme
Burst m (Farbsynchronsignal) colour burst
Burst-Auftastimpuls m burst keying pulse
Bürsten f pl (elek. Motor) brushes n pl
Bürstenhalter m (elek. Motor) brush-holder n
Byte n (EDV) byte n

Chanson 32

C

Chanson *n* popular song
Charakterdarsteller *m* character actor
Charakterrolle *f* character part
Charge *f* batch *n*; ~ *f* (Darsteller) (fam.) bit actor, bit-part actor
Chargennummer *f* (Filmmaterial) batch number
Chargenspieler *m* bit actor, bit-part actor
checken *v* (Information) check *v*
Chef vom Dienst (CvD) (R) senior duty editor; ~ **vom Dienst (CvD)** (TV) editor for the day
Chefansager *m* chief announcer
Chefarchitekt *m* chief architect
Chefcutter *m* senior film editor
Chefdirigent *m* chief conductor
Chefdramaturg *m* head of scripts
Chefkameramann *m* director of photography, lighting cameraman
Chefredakteur *m* editor *n*, editor-in-chief *n*, head of news, news director (US)
Chefreporter *m* chief reporter
Chefsprecher *m* chief announcer
Chor *m* chorus *n*, choir *n*
Choreograf *m* choreographer *n*
Choreografie *f* choreography *n*
Chorinspektor *m* chorus supervisor
Chorist *m* chorus singer, member of a chorus
Chorleiter *m* chorus master, chorus director
Chormusik *f* choral music
Chorsänger *m* chorus singer, member of a chorus
Chorwart *m* chorus manager
Chrominanz *f* chrominance *n*
Chrominanzkanal *m* chrominance channel

Chrominanzkomponente *f* chrominance component
Chrominanzmodulator *m* chrominance modulator
Chrominanzsignal *n* chrominance signal, chrom. sig. (coll.)
Chronist *m* writer *n*; ~ *m* (TV, R) talks-writer *n*
Cineast *m* film-maker *n*
Clamp *m* clamping circuit, clamp *n*
clippen *v* (abschneiden) clip *v*
Clipperstufe *f* (TV) clipper *n*, clipping circuit
Code *m* code *n*
Colorkiller *m* colour killer
Colortranlampe *f* colortran lamp
Colortranlicht *n* colortran light
Compiler *m* (EDV) compiling programme, compiler *n*
Compurverschluß *m* compur shutter
Computer *m* computer *n*
Conferencier *m* compère *n*
Coplanarkassette *f* coplanar cassette, coplanar cartridge
Copyright *n* copyright *n*
Cord *n* s. Cordband
Cordband *n* magnetic film, perforated magnetic film, perforated magnetic tape
Cordmaschine *f* magnetic film recording machine
Cordspieler *m* s. Cordmaschine
Cosinus *m* cosine *n*
Cosinus-Entzerrer *m* cosine aperture corrector
Cosinus-Entzerrung *f* cosine correction
C-Schaltung *f* class C circuit
Cut *m* cut *n*
cutten *v* edit *v*, cut *v*
Cutter *m* editor *n*; ~ *m* (F) cutter *n*, film editor; ~ *m* (Band) tape editor
Cutterassistent *m* assistant film editor
Cutterbericht *m* editor's report (ER), film editor's report (FER)
Cutterin *f* editor *n*; ~ *f* (F) cutter *n*,

film editor; ~ *f* (Band) tape editor
Cutterzettel *m s.* Cutterbericht

D

Dachantenne *f* roof aerial
Dachrinnenantenne *f* eaves aerial
Dachschräge *f* (Impuls) bar tilt,
pulse tilt; **prozentuale** ~
percentage tilt
Damenschneiderin *f* tailoress *n*,
dressmaker *n*
dämpfen *v* attenuate *v*, damp *v*; ~ *v*
(Licht) soften *v*
Dämpfung *f* damping *n*, attenuation
n; **frequenzabhängige** ~
dependence of attenuation upon
frequency
Dämpfungsentzerrer *m* attenuation
equaliser
Dämpfungsglied *n* attenuator *n*,
attenuator pad
Dämpfungskreis *m* attenuator
circuit
Dämpfungsperle *f* ferrite bead
Dämpfungsregler *m* variable
attenuator
Dämpfungsverlust *m* attenuation
loss
Dämpfungswiderstand *m* loss
resistance, attenuator resistance
Darbietung *f* performance *n*
darstellen *v* (Rolle) play *v*
Darsteller *m* actor *n*, player *n*,
performer *n*, artist *n*; **einen** ~
herausstellen to feature an actor
Darstellerbesetzung *f* casting *n*
Darstellergagen *f pl* performers'
fees, artists' fees
Darstellergarderobe *f* artist's
dressing-room
Darstellerliste *f* cast list
Darstellung *f* (Schauspieler)
interpretation *n*, performance *n*;
grafische ~ graph *n*, diagram *n*,

chart *n*, graphic *n*, visual aid
Datei *f* (EDV) data set, file *n*, data
file
Daten *n pl* data *n pl*, characteristics
n pl; ~ *n pl* (EDV) data *n pl*
Datenaufnahme *f* (EDV) data
acquisition, data collection
Datenbearbeitung *f* (EDV) data
handling
Datenblatt *n* data sheet
Dateneingabe *f* (EDV) data input
Datenfluß *m* (EDV) data flow
Datenflußplan *m* (EDV) data flow
chart, data flow diagram, dynamic
flow chart, dynamic flow diagram
Datenkanal *m* (EDV) data channel
Datensichtgerät *n* (EDV) data
display device, video data
terminal
Datenstation *f* (EDV) terminal *n*
Datenträger *m* (EDV) data carrier,
data medium
Datenverarbeitung *f* data
processing; **elektronische** ~ **(EDV)**
electronic data processing (EDP)
Datenverarbeitungsanlage *f* data
processing system
Dauer *f* duration *n*
Dauerleitung *f* permanent circuit
Dauerleitungsnetz *n* permanent
network
Dauermagnet *m* permanent magnet
Dauerstörung *f* continuous
interference
Deckung *f* (Raster) registration *n*,
convergence *n*; ~ *f* (Negativ)
density *n*
Deckungsfehler *m* (Raster)
convergence error, registration
error; ~ *m* (Negativ) error in
density
Deemphasis *f* de-emphasis (DE) *n*
dehnen *v* (schwarz) stretch *v*
dejustiert *adj* out of alignment
Deko *m* (fam.) decorator *n*,
upholsterer *n*, drapes *n pl* (coll.)
Dekoder *m* decoder *n*
Dekodiermatrix *f* decoder matrix

Dekodierung 34

Dekodierung *f* decoding *n*,
transcoding *n*
Dekoklammer *f* scenery clamp
Dekor *n* scenery *n*, set *n*, studio
scenery; **reales ~ (Innen)** natural
interior
Dekorateur *m* decorator *n*,
upholsterer *n*, drapes *n pl* (coll.)
Dekoration *f* design *n*, scenery *n*,
scenery set, decoration *n*, setting
and properties, setting and
upholstery, set *n*
Dekorationsabbau *m* set striking
Dekorationsaufbau *m* set erection
Dekorationslicht *n* set light,
background light
Dekorationsmaler *m* scene painter
Dekorationsmodell *n* set model
Dekorationsrequisiten *n pl* set
dressings
Dekorationsteil *n* piece *n*
Dekorationsversatzstück *n* special
n
Dekorationsvorfertigung *f* set
prefabrication
Dekorationswand *f* decorative flat,
decorative screen
Dekowerkstatt *f* drapes workshop
Dementi *n* denial *n*
Demodulator *m* demodulator *n*
Densitometer *n* densitometer *n*
Densitometrie *f* densitometry *n*
densitometrisch *adj* densitometric
adj
desensibilisieren *v* desensitise *v*
Desk *m* desk *n*
Detailaufnahme *f* macro-filming *n*,
very-short-distance shooting,
macrophotography *n*
Detailkontrast *m* detail contrast
Detailzeichnung *f* detail drawing
Detektor *m* detector *n*
Deutsches Fernsehen (DFS)
German Television ARD
Dezibel *n* decibel *n*
Dezibelmesser *m* decibel meter
Dezimeterwellen (UHF) *f pl*

decimetre waves, dm waves, ultra-
high frequencies (UHF)
Dezimeterwellenbereich *m* UHF
band, decimetre-wave band
Dezistrecke *f* microwave link
Dia *n* diapositive *n*, slide *n*,
transparency *n*
Diaabtaster *m* slide scanner; **~** *m*
(Titel) caption scanner
Diageber *m s.* Diaabtaster
Diagonalblende *f* diagonal wipe
Diagonalklebestelle *f* diagonal join,
diagonal splice
Diagramm *n* diagram *n*, graph *n*
Dialog *m* dialogue *n*
Dialogautor *m* dialoguist *n*, writer
of dialogue scripts
Dialogbuch *n* dialogue script
Dialogführung *f* dialogue direction
Dialogliste *f* dialogue script
Dialogregie *f* dialogue direction
Dialogregisseur *m* dialogue director
~ *m* (Synchronisation) dubbing
editor
Dialogsystem *n* (EDV) dialog
system
Dialogszene *f* dialogue scene
Diapositiv *n* diapositive *n*, slide *n*,
transparency *n*
Diapositiv-Wechselschlitten *m* slide
carrier, slide changer
Diaprojektor *m* slide projector
Diarahmen *m* slide mount,
transparency mount
Diäten *f pl* daily allowances
Diawerbung *f* slide publicity, slide
advertising
Diawerfer *m* slide projector
Dichte *f* (Schwärzung) density *n*
Dichtebereich *m* density range
Dichtefilter *m* neutral filter, neutral
density filter
Dichteschwankungen *f pl* neutral
density fluctuation, variations in
density
Dielektrizitätskonstante *f*
permittivity *n*, dielectric constant

Dienst *m* duty *n*, service *n*;
  empfangender ~ receiving service
Dienstgerät *n* staff set
Dienstgespräch *n* official telephone
  call
Dienstleiter *m* senior member of
  staff on duty; ~ *m* (aktuelle
  Redaktion) duty editor, senior
  duty editor
Dienstleitung *f* service circuit; ~ *f*
  (Telefon) service line
Dienstplan *m* duty roster, time-
  table *n*, staff duty sheet
Dienstreise *f* official journey
Dienstreiseantrag *m* application for
  travel authorisation
Dienstreiseauftrag *m* travel
  authorisation
Dienststelle *f* office *n*
Dienststellenleiter *m* office head
Dienstvertrag *m* employment
  contract, service contract
Differentialübertrager *m*
  differential transformer
Differenzfrequenz *f* difference
  frequency
differenzieren *v* differentiate *v*
Differenzierverstärker *m*
  differentiating amplifier
Differenzsignal *n* difference signal
Differenzton *m* beat note,
  difference frequency
Differenztonverfahren *n* difference
  frequency method
Differenzträger *m* intercarrier *n*
Differenzträgerverfahren *n*
  intercarrier system
Differenzverstärker *m* differential
  amplifier
diffus *adj* diffused *adj*, diffuse *adj*
Diffuserlinse *f* diffusing lens,
  diffuser lens, soft-focus lens
Diffusion *f* diffusion *n*
Diffusionsfilter *m* (opt.)
  romanticiser *n*, diffusing filter; ~
  m (Beleuchtung) scrim *n*
digital *adj* (EDV) digital *adj*
Digital-Analog-Umsetzer *m* (EDV)

digital-to-analog converter
Digitalanzeige *f* digital read-out
Digital-Baustein *m* (EDV) logic unit
digitale Anzeige (EDV) digital
  display
Digitalmeßinstrument *n* digital
  meter
Digital-Rechner *m* (EDV) digital
  computer
Digitalzähler *m* digital counter
DIN-Norm *f* entspricht British
  Standards Specification (BSS)
Diode *f* diode *n*
Diodenanschluß *m* diode terminal
Diodengleichrichter *m* diode
  rectifier
Dioptrie (dptr) *f* dioptre *n*
Dioptrieausgleich *m* dioptre
  correction
Dipol *m* dipole *n*, doublet *n* (US);
  gestreckter ~ plain dipole
Dipolantenne *f* dipole *n*, dipole
  aerial, doublet *n* (US)
Dipolebene *f* broadside array
Dipolfeld *n* dipole panel
Dipolgruppe *f* dipole array, group
  aerial
Dipolreihe *f* collinear array of
  dipoles
direkt *adj* direct *adj*, live *adj*;
  ~ **senden** to broadcast live
Direktempfang *m* direct reception
Direktion *f* directorate *n*;
  technische ~ engineering
  directorate
Direktor, technischer director of
  engineering, technical director
  (US)
Direktschaltung *f* direct relay,
  direct hook-up (coll.)
Direktsendung *f* live transmission,
  live broadcast; **eine** ~ **aus** ... live
  from ...
Direktsucher *m* optical viewfinder
Direktübertragung *f* live
  transmission, live broadcast; ~ *f*
  (tech.) direct transmission, direct
  relay, live relay

Direktverbindung   36

Direktverbindung zwischen zwei Punkten point-to-point circuit
Dirigent *m* conductor *n*
Disk-Jockey *m* disc-jockey *n*
Diskothek *f* discotheque *n*; ~ *f* (Archiv) gramophone library
Diskriminator *m* discriminator *n*
Diskussion *f* discussion *n*, debate *n*; **eine ~ leiten** to chair a discussion
Diskussionsleiter *m* chairman *n*, anchor man, discussion chairman, moderator *n* (US)
Diskussionssendung *f* discussion programme
Diskussionsteilnehmer *m* panellist *n*, participant *n*
Dispersion *f* dispersion *n*
Disponent *m* organiser *n*
Disposition *f* planning *n*, technical arrangements *n pl*; ~ *f* (Studio) studio allocation, studio bookings; ~ *f* (Prod.) shooting plan, schedule *n*; **technische ~** technical arrangement, technical planning
Dispositionsbüro *n* studio bookings*
Dispositionswünsche *m pl* production requirements
Distanzring *m* spacer ring
Divergenz *f* divergence *n*
Dokumentarbericht *m* documentary feature, documentary *n*
Dokumentarfeature *n* s. Dokumentarbericht
Dokumentarfilm *m* documentary film, documentary *n*, fact film (US)
Dokumentarsendung *f* documentary *n*
Dokumentarspiel *n* drama documentary, dramatised documentary
Dokumentation* *f* central research*
Dokumentation *f* documentation *n*; ~ *f* (Bericht) documentary feature; ~ *f* (F) documentary film,

documentary *n*, fact film (US); **szenische ~** drama documentary, dramatised documentary
Dokumentationen* *f pl* current affairs specials* *n pl*
Dokumentenabtaster *m* documents scanner
Dokumentenfilm *m* document film, high-contrast film, document-copying stock
Dolly *m* dolly *n*, camera dolly, doll buggy (US)
Dollyfahrer *m* tracker *n*, steerer *n*, helmsman *n*
Dopesheet *n* dope-sheet *n*
Doppel 16 *n* double 16 *n*
Doppelbelichtung *f* double exposure, superimposition *n*
Doppeldose *f* double socket
Doppelgänger *m* double *n*
Doppelkontur *f* ghosting *n*, echo effect
Doppelseitenbandmodulation *f* double-sideband modulation, dsb modulation
Doppelspielband *n* (Ton) double-play tape
Doppelspur *f* double track, twin track
Doppelspur-Tonbandgerät *n* dual-track recorder, two-track recorder, twin-track recorder
Doppelweggleichrichter *m* full-wave rectifier
Dosierung *f* (Regenerierung) dosage *n*, dosing *n*
Dosierungsgerät *n* dosimeter *n*, flowmeter *n*
Doubel *n* double *n*, stand-in *n*
doubeln *v* (synchronisieren) dub *v*; ~ *v* (Darsteller) stand in, double *v*
Doubeln *n* (Synchronisation) dubbing *n*, post-synching *n*, voice dubbing; ~ *n* (Kopierwerk) duping *n*
Doublette *f* double *n*
Drahtauslöser *m* cable release

Drahtfernsehen *n* cable television, wired television
Drahtfunk *m* wired broadcasting, wired radio
Drahtgazefilter *m* wired gauze filter
Drahtleitung *f* wire line, wiring *n*
drahtlos *adj* wireless *adj*
Drahtwiderstand *m* wire-wound resistor
Drama *n* drama *n*
Dramatiker *m* dramatist *n*, playwright *n*
Dramatisierung *f* dramatisation *n*
Dramaturg *m* (R, TV) script editor, scenario editor
Dramaturgie *f* dramaturgy *n*
Dramaturgie* *f* script department, script unit*
dran sein (fam.) (Bericht) to be on a story; ~ **sein** (fam.) (Auftritt) to be on
Draufsicht *f* (Kamera) tilt shot
Dreh *m* shooting *n*, filming *n*; **chronologischer** ~ chronological shooting
Dreharbeiten *f pl s.* Dreh
drehbar *adj* rotatable *adj*; ~ *adj* (F) suitable for filming
Drehbeginn *m* start of shooting
Drehbericht *m* dope-sheet *n*, shooting record
Drehbuch *n* scenario *n*, screenplay *n*, script *n*, shooting script; **technisches** ~ continuity *n*
Drehbuchautor *m* scenario-writer *n*, script-writer *n*, writer *n*, screenwriter *n*, scenarist *n*; ~ *m* (Einstellung) continuity writer
Drehbühne *f* revolving stage; ~ *f* (Studio) scenic service crew, show workers (coll.)
drehen *v* film *v*, shoot *v*; **aus der Hand** ~ to shoot with hand-held camera
Dreherlaubnis *f* filming permission
Drehfolge *f* shot list, shooting order
Drehkeil-Entfernungsmesser *m* rotating wedge range-finder

Drehknopf *m* knob *n*, control knob
Drehkondensator *m* rotary capacitor
Drehmoment *m* turning moment, torque *n*
Drehmomentbegrenzer *m* torque-limiter *n*
Drehort *m* location *n*
Drehplan *m* shooting plan, shooting schedule, schedule *n*
Drehpotentiometer *n* rotary potentiometer
Drehprobe *f* dry run, run-through *n*
Drehregler *m* knob-twist fader
Drehrichtung *f* direction of rotation
Drehschalter *m* rotary switch
Drehspiegel *m* tilting mirror
Drehspule *f* moving coil
Drehspulinstrument *n* moving coil instrument
Drehstab *m* production team
Drehstabilisierung *f* (Sat.) stabilisation of rotation
Drehstabliste *f* production list
Drehsteller *m* knob-twist fader
Drehstrom *m* three-phase current, polyphase current
Drehstrommotor *m* induction motor
Drehstromnetz *n* three-phase circuit
Drehstromsynchronmotor *m* three-phase synchronous motor
Drehtag *m* shooting day
Drehtransformator *m* phase shifter
Drehübersicht *f* shooting plan, shooting schedule, schedule *n*
Drehverhältnis *n* shooting ratio
Drehwähler *m* uniselector *n*, rotary switch
Drehzeit *f* shooting time, shooting period
Dreieckspannung *f* delta voltage, mesh voltage
Dreiecksystem *n* delta system
Dreifarbensystem *n* tricolour system, three-colour process
Dreifarbenverfahren *n* three-colour

Dreifarbenverfahren 38

process, trichromatic process, three-colour method
Dreifuß *m* tripod *n*; **ausziehbarer ~** extensible tripod, collapsible tripod
Dreiklang *m* triad *n*, common chord
Dreiphasennetz *n* (Dreileiter) three-phase three-wire network; **~** *n* (Vierleiter) three-phase four-wire network
dreipolig *adj* three-pole *adj*
Dreipunktoszillatorschaltung *f* Hartley oscillator, Hartley circuit
Dreistrahlröhre *f* three-gun colour tube
Dreiviertel-KW *n* 750 Watt pup
Drift *f* (MAZ) drift *n*
Driftfehler *m* (EDV) drift error
Dröhnen *n* boominess *n*; **~** *n* (akust.) booming drone
Drop-out *m* (F) scratch *n*; **~** *m* (Ton) drop-out *n*
Drop-out-Unterdrückung *f* (F) anti-scratch treatment; **~** *f* (Ton) drop-out suppression
Drossel *f* inductance *n*, inductance coil, retard coil, reactance coil, choke *n*
Drosselspule *f s.* Drossel
Drucker *m* (EDV) printer *n*
Druckerei *f* printing-office *n*, printing-house *n*
Druckgradientenmikrofon *n* pressure-gradient microphone
Druckluft *f* compressed air
Druckluftleitung *f* pressure-air duct, compressed-air line
Druckmikrofon *n* pressure microphone
Druckschalter *m* push switch
Drucktaste *f* push button
dual *adj* (EDV) binary *adj*
Dualcode, reiner (EDV) pure binary code
Dualzahl *f* (EDV) binary number
Dunkelkammer *f* darkroom *n*
Dunkelphase *f* dark period
Dunkelraum *m* darkroom *n*

Dunkelsack *m* changing bag
Dunkelstrom *m* dark current
Dünnfilmbaustein *m* thin-film component
Dünnfilmspeicher *m* (EDV) thin-film memory, thin-film store
Dünnfilmtechnik *f* thin-film technique
Dünnschichtfilm *m* thin-emulsion film, polyester film
Dup *n* (fam.) duplicate *n*, dupe *n*
Duplex-Cordanlage *f* mechanically coupled tape recorder
Duplexleitung *f* duplex circuit
Duplexmaschine *f* mechanically coupled tape recorder
Duplikat *n* duplicate *n*, dupe *n*
duplikatfähig *adj* suitable for duping
Duplikatfilm *m* (Rohfilm) duplicating film, duplicating stock **~** *m* (entwickelt) duplicated film
Duplikatnegativ *n* (Rohfilm) duplicating negative; **~** *n* (entwickelt) duplicated negative, dupe negative
Duplikatpositiv *n* (Rohfilm) duplicating positive; **~** *n* (entwickelt) duplicated positive, dupe positive
Duplikatprozeß *m* duplicating process, duping process, duping *n*
Duplikatumkehrfilm *m* (Rohfilm) duplicate reversal stock; **~** *m* (entwickelt) duplicate reversal, dupe reversal
Dupnegativ *n* (entwickelt) duplicated negative, dupe negative
duppen *v* duplicate *v*, dupe *v*
Duppositiv *n* (Rohfilm) duplicating positive; **~** *n* (entwickelt) duplicated positive, dupe positive
durchblenden *v* superimpose *v*, dissolve *v*, mix *v*
Durchblendung *f* superimposition *n*, dissolve *n*, lap dissolve, mix *n*, super *n* (coll.)

durchbrennen v (Kopierwerk) burn out v; ~ v (Sicherung) blow v, fuse v

Durchbruchspannung f breakdown voltage, avalanche voltage

durchdrehen v to shoot in sequence

durchfallen v (Bild) break up v, to become unlocked

Durchführung f execution n, performance n

Durchführungsbuchse f feed-through sleeve

Durchführungskondensator m feed-through capacitor

Durchgangsdämpfung f transmission loss

Durchgangsdose f (Ant.) through-connection junction box

durchgebrannt adj (Kopierwerk) burnt-out adj; ~ adj (Sicherung) blown adj

Durchgriff m (Röhre) reciprocal of amplification factor, inverse of amplification factor

Durchklatschen n print-through n

Durchlaßbandbreite f filter pass-band

Durchlässigkeit f transmittance n, transmission n

Durchlässigkeitsbereich m pass-band n

Durchlaßkurve f transmission characteristic

Durchlaßspannung f forward voltage

Durchlauf m (Probe) run-through n; ~ m (Kopierwerk) run n, clear run ~ m (Wobbler) sweep n

durchlaufen v (Bild) roll v; ~ v (elek.) traverse v, sweep v

Durchlaufgeschwindigkeit f (Band) tape speed; ~ f (Wobbler) sweep n

Durchlaufkopiermaschine f continuous film-printer, continuous rotary printer, continuous printer

Durchlaufzeit f transit time; ~ f (Band) playing time

Durchprojektion f rear projection, back projection (BP)

Durchsage f announcement n, message n; ~ f (Reklame) spot n

durchsagen v broadcast v

durchschlagen v break down v; ~ v (Sicherung) blow v, fuse v

Durchschlagspannung f disruptive voltage, breakdown voltage

durchschleifen v connect through v; ~ v (Kabel) loop through v

Durchschleiffilter m bridging-type filter

Durchsichtigkeit f transparency n

durchspielen v (Szene) run through v

durchstellen v (Szene) block v

durchstoppen v time v

Durchstoßen des Schwarzwertes signal above black level

Durchwahl f (Telefon) through-dialling n

Dynamik f dynamics n

Dynamikbereich m dynamic range

Dynamikkompression f compression of dynamic range

Dynamikumfang m s. Dynamikbereich

dynamisch adj dynamic adj

Dynode f dynode n

Dynodenfleck m dynode spot, first dynode spot

E

Ebene f plane n; **horizontale ~** horizontal plane; **senkrechte ~** vertical plane

EC-Anlage f (E-CAM) video-film equipment

Echo n echo n

Echomaschine f artificial reverberation device

Echomikrofon n echo microphone

Echoraum m reverberation

Echoraum 40

chamber, echo room
Echtzeit- (in Zus.) (EDV) real-time
adj
Echtzeitbetrieb *m* (EDV) real-time
operation, real-time working
Echtzeit-Datenverarbeitung *f* (EDV)
real-time processing
EC-Kamera *f* video-film camera
ECO-Schaltung *f* ECO circuit
Editec *f* editec *n*
Effekt *m* effect *n*; **stroboskopischer**
~ stroboscopic effect, stroboscopic
interference, strobing *n*
Effektbeleuchtung *f* effects lighting,
special effects lighting, decorative
lighting
Effektfarbe *f* coloured lighting
effektive Strahlungsleistung (ERP)
effective radiated power (ERP)
Effektivwert *m* root-mean-square
value (RMS value)
Effektlicht *n* effect lighting, effect
light
Effektmikrofon *n* effect microphone
Effektmusik *f* effect music, mood
music
Effektscheinwerfer *m* effects spot,
profile spot
Effektspitze *n* effect lighting, effect
light
eichen *v* standardise *v*, calibrate *v*
Eichmarke *f* calibration mark
Eichpegel für Monitor (PEM)
monitor calibration level
Eichung *f* calibration *n*;
fotometrische ~ photometric
calibration
Eidophor *m* eidophor *n*
Eigenfrequenz *f* (akust.)
eigenfrequency *n*, natural
frequency, characteristic
frequency
Eigengeräusch *n* residual noise,
inherent noise; ~ *n*
(Plattenspieler) surface noise; ~ *n*
(F) inherent film noise
Eigenkapazität *f* self-capacitance *n*
Eigenmodulation *f* self-modula-

tion *n*
Eigenproduktion *f* own production
Eigenprogramm *n* own programme
Eigenrauschen *n* ground noise; ~ *n*
(Verstärker) internal noise
Eigenresonanz *f* self-resonance *n*,
natural resonance
Eigenschwingung *f* natural
oscillation, characteristic
oscillation
Eigenspur *f* home track
Eigensynchronisation *f* self-
synchronisation *n*
Eigenversorgung *f* local supply
Eigenverzerrung *f* inherent
distortion
ein on; ~ (Gerät) start
Ein-Ausgabebefehl *m* (EDV)
peripheral control instruction,
input-output statement
einblenden *v* fade in *v*, dub in *v*; ~ *v*
(Zweitbild) superimpose *v*; ~ *v*
(sich) cut in *v*
Einblender *m* (Person) vision mixer
Einblendtitel *m* caption *n*
Einblendung *f* cross-fade *n*, fade-in
n; ~ *f* (Zweitbild) superposition *n*,
super *n*; ~ *f* (Beitrag) insert *n*,
inject *n*
einblocken *v* (fam.) insert *v*, inject *v*
Einbrennen *n* sticking *n*; ~ *n*
(Röhre) warm-up *n*
Einbrennfleck *m* ion spot
Einbrennschutz *f* ion trap
Eindruck, visueller visual
impression
Einergang *m* stop motion, frame-by-
frame display
einfädeln *v* lace up *v*
Einfädelschlitz *m* ridge *n*
Einfallswinkel *m* angle of
incidence, arrival angle
Einfangwinkel *m* angle of
acceptance
Einfarbenkopie *f* monochrome
copy, monochrome print
Einfärbgerät *n* tinting equipment
einfarbig *adj* monochrome *adj*

Einfärbung f tinting n
einfügen v insert v
Einfügungsdämpfung f insertion loss
einführen v introduce v, present v
Einführung f introduction n, lead-in n, intro n (coll.)
Eingabe f (EDV) input n
Eingabegerät n (EDV) input device, input equipment
Eingang m (tech.) input n; **symmetrischer** ~ balanced input
Eingangsbelastung f input loading
Eingangsbild n input picture
Eingangsempfindlichkeit f input sensitivity
Eingangsenergie f input energy, input power
Eingangsfehlspannung f input offset voltage
Eingangsimpedanz f input impedance
Eingangskapazität f input capacitance
Eingangskreuzschiene f input switching matrix, input selector
Eingangspegel m input level
Eingangsschaltung f input circuit
Eingangssignal n input signal
Eingangsspannung f input voltage
Eingangsstufe f input stage
Eingangsübertrager m input transformer
Eingangswiderstand m input resistance
eingelassen adj (Schalter) locked adj
eingeschaltet, nicht unconnected adj
eingrenzen, einen Fehler to localise a fault
Einheit f unit n; **austauschbare** ~ interchangeable unit; **periphere** ~ (EDV) peripheral unit; **steckbare** ~ plug-in unit
einkanalig adj single-channel adj; ~ adj (Tonaufnahme) monophonic adj, mono adj (coll.)

Einkanalverstärker m single-channel amplifier
Einkauf* m buying* n
Einknopfbedienung f single-knob control
einkopieren v superimpose v, overprint v
Einkopierung f superimposing n, overprinting n
Einlaufrille f (Platte) run-in groove, lead-in groove
Einlaufzeit f warm-up time, running-up time
Einlegemarke f start mark
einlegen v (Proj.) lace up v; ~ v (Kamera) load v, thread up v; ~ v (Band) lace up v
einleiten v (Sendung) introduce v
Einleitung f introduction n, lead-in n, intro n (coll.)
einleuchten v to set the lighting
Einleuchtung f lighting setting
Einleuchtzeit f lighting setting time
Einlichtkopie f one-light print
Einlichtkopierung f one-light printing
Ein-Mann-Bedienung f one-man operation
Einmessen der Köpfe alignment of heads
Einmischer m fader n
Einnahmen f pl revenue n, income n
Einnorm- (in Zus.) single-standard adj
einpegeln v line up v
Einpegeln n line-up n, level adjustment
einpfeifen v to tune to zero beat frequency
Einphasennetz n single-phase power supply
einpolig adj single-pole adj; ~ adj (Transistor) unipolar adj
einrasten v lock v, engage v
Einrastkontakt m snap contact
Einregelzeit f (Übertragung) line-up period

einrichten *v* establish *v*, set up *v*; ~ *v* (Buch) arrange *v*

Einrichtung *f* equipment *n*, installation *n*

Einsatz *m* (F) release *n*; ~ *m* (Stichwort) cue *n*

einsatzbereit *adj* (F) ready for release

einsatzfähig *adj* usable *adj*, in good working order

Einsatzsignal *n* cue *n*

Einsatzzeit *f* period of use

Einschaltbrumm *m* starting hum

einschalten *v* switch on *v*; ~ *v* (Kamera) start *v*; ~ *v* (Spannung) switch in *v*

Einschaltfeld *n* starting panel

Einschaltpreis *m* advertising tariff

Einschaltquote *f* audience rating

Einschaltung *f* switching-on *n*; ~ *f* (Progr.) insert *n*

einschieben *v* insert *v*, interpose *v*

einschlagen *v* succeed *v*, catch on *v*, to be a hit

einschleifen *v* connect *v* (into a line), bridge across *v*; ~ *v* (Durchschleiffilter) insert *v*

Einschub *m* slide-in unit, plug-in unit

Einschwingen *n* build-up *n*

Einschwingvorgang *m* initial transient, ringing *n*

Einschwingzeit *f* build-up time, rise time

Einseitenband (ESB) *n* single sideband (SSB)

einsetzen *v* (Prog.) insert *v*

Einsichtsrecht *n* right of inspection

einspielen *v* (Platte, Band) record *v*; ~ *v* (zuspielen) inject *v*, feed *v*, insert *v*, play in *v*; ~ *v* (Gewinn) bring in *v*, make *v*

Einspielleitung *f* contribution circuit

Einspielung *f* (Platte, Band) recording *n*; ~ *f* (Zuspielung) insert *n*, inject *n*

Einspringbereich *m* lock-in range

einspringen *v* (Oszillator) lock in *v*; ~ *v* (Titel) jump on *v*; ~ *v* (Darsteller) understudy *v*

Einspur *f* single track

einstarten *v* cue in *v*, to make start marks, to place cue marks

einstecken *v* plug in *v*

Einsteckleiterplatte *f* plug-in panel

einstellen *v* (regulieren) adjust *v*, regulate *v*, set *v*; ~ *v* (R-, TV-Progr.) tune in *v*; ~ *v* (opt.) focus *v*; ~ *v* (Kamera) point *v*, aim *v*, set up *v*; ~ *v* (Bild) frame *v*; ~ *v* (Personal) engage *v*, take on *v*, hire *v* (US)

Einstellen der Bildfrequenz picture-frequency setting, picture-frequency adjustment; ~ **der Zeilenfrequenz** line-frequency adjustment, line-frequency setting

Einstelltestbild *n* (TV-Kamera) test card; ~ *n* (TV-Gerät) test pattern

Einstellung *f* adjustment *n*, setting *n*, position *n*; ~ *f* (opt.) focusing *n*, angle *n*, framing *n*; ~ *f* (Personal) engagement *n*; ~ *f* (Drehbuch) shot *n*, set-up *n*; **feste ~** fixed angle

Einstellungsfolge *f* sequence of shots; **schnelle ~** cross-cutting *n*

Einstellungswechsel *m* (Drehbuch) change of angle; ~ *m* (opt.) change of focus

Einstrahlungsgebiet *n* irradiated area

einstreichen *v* (Text) tighten up *v*

Einstreifenverfahren *n* Commag system

Einstreuung *f* crosstalk *n*

einstudieren *v* (Rolle) get up *v*, rehearse *v*; ~ *v* (Szene) rehearse *v*

Eintaktstufe *f* single-ended stage

eintasten *v* key in *v*, punch up *v*, inlay *v*

Eintastung *f* keying *n*, inlay *n*

Eintaumeln des Kopfes head adjustment

Eintrittsebene *f* entry plane, entry

level

Eintrittslinse *f* front lens element

Einweggleichrichter *m* half-wave rectifier

Einweichung *f* (F) soaking *n*

Einzelaufhängung *f* (Scheinwerfer) single suspension unit, single-lamp suspension unit

Einzelbild *n* frame *n*, single frame; **weiterkopiertes** ~ stop frame, hold frame, freeze frame, still copy, frozen picture, suspended animation

Einzelbildaufnahme *f* single-frame shooting, frame-by-frame exposure, single-frame exposure, stop-frame shooting

Einzelbildmotor *m* stop-frame motor, single-frame motor, animation motor

Einzelbildschaltung *f* single-frame mechanism, stop-frame mechanism

Einzeldose *f* single socket

Einzelempfang *m* (R) individual listening; ~ *m* (TV) individual viewing

Einzelgarderobe *f* private dressing-room

Einzelsteuerung *f* individual control

Einzelvertrag *m* individual contract

Einzugsgebiet *n* licence-fee collection area

Eisenverlust *m* iron loss

E-Kameramann *m* television cameraman

Elatechnik (Ela) *f* electro-acoustics *n*

Electronic-Cam (E-Cam) *f* electronicam *n*, VFR equipment, video film camera

Elektriker *m* electrician *n*, wireman *n*

elektrisch *adj* electric *adj*, electrical *adj*

Elektrizität *f* electricity *n*, juice *n* (coll.)

Elektroakustik (Ela) *f* electro-

acoustics *n*

Elektrode *f* electrode *n*

elektrodynamisch *adj* electrodynamic *adj*

Elektrolyse *f* electrolysis *n*

Elektrolytkondensator *m* electrolytic capacitor

Elektromagnet *m* electromagnet *n*

elektromagnetisch *adj* electromagnetic *adj*

Elektromechaniker *m* electrician *n*

Elektromeister *m* head electrician

Elektron *n* electron *n*

Elektronenkanone *f* electron gun

Elektronenoptik *f* electron optics

Elektronenstrahl *m* electron beam

Elektronenstrahlaufzeichnung *f* electron beam recording

Elektronenvervielfacher *m* electron multiplier, photocell multiplier

Elektronik *f* electronics *n*

elektronisch *adj* electronic *adj*

Elko *m* (fam.) electrolytic capacitor

eloxiert *adj* anodised *adj*

Emitter *m* emitter *n*

Emitterbasisschaltung *f* grounded-emitter configuration

Emitterfolger *m* emitter follower

Emitterschaltung *f s.* Emitterbasisschaltung

Emitterverstärker *m* emitter follower

Empfang *m* reception *n*; **individueller** ~ (Sat.) individual reception

empfangen *v* (Sender) receive *v*

Empfänger *m* receiver *n*, receiving set

Empfängerprimärvalenzen *f pl* (Farbe) display primaries, receiver primaries

Empfängerröhre *f* receiving valve

Empfängerseite *f* receiving end

Empfängerweiche *f* receiver diplexer

Empfangsantenne *f* receiving aerial

Empfangsbereich *m* service area; ~ *m* (phys.) tuning range, frequency

Empfangsbereich 44

range
Empfangsdame *f* receptionist *n*,
hostess *n*
Empfangsdienst* *m* visitors
service
Empfangsdienst *m* (tech.) technical
monitoring service
Empfangsfrequenz *f* received
frequency, incoming frequency
Empfangsgebiet *n* service area; ~ *n*
(phys.) tuning range, frequency
range
Empfangsgerät *n* receiver *n*,
receiving set
Empfangsgüte *f* reception quality
Empfangskreis *m* receiving circuit
Empfangsleitung *f* incoming circuit
Empfangsrichtung *f* direction of
reception
Empfangsspannung *f* received
voltage
Empfangsstation *f* receiving station
Empfangsverhältnisse *n pl*
reception conditions
empfindlich *adj* sensitive *adj*; ~ *adj*
(Kopierwerk) high-speed *adj*
Empfindlichkeit *f* sensitivity *n*; ~ *f*
(F) speed *n*, emulsion speed;
differentielle ~ differential
sensitivity; **hohe** ~ high
sensitivity, high speed; **niedrige** ~
low sensitivity, low speed
Empfindlichkeitsgrenze *f* limit of
sensitivity
Empfindlichkeitsmesser *m*
sensitometer *n*
Empfindlichkeitsregelung *f*
sensitivity control; **automatische**
~ automatic sensitivity control
(ASC)
Empfindung *f* sensation *n*
Emulsion *f* emulsion *n*;
orthochromatische ~
orthochromatic emulsion;
panchromatische ~ panchromatic
emulsion
Emulsionschargennummer *f*
emulsion batch number

Emulsionsebene *f* sensitised side,
sensitised face, emulsion side
Emulsionsschicht *f* emulsion
coating, emulsion layer
E-Musik *f* (=Ernste Musik) serious
music
Endabhörkontrolle *f* (Sender)
output monitoring
Endabnahme *f* final viewing,
acceptance *n*
Endabschaltung *f* closing-down *n*
Endanweisung *f* (EDV) trailer
statement
Endband *n* identification trailer,
trailer *n*, trailer tape; ~ **kleben** to
attach trailer tape
Endbild *n* (Regie) outgoing picture
Enddose *f* termination box
Ende des Ablaufs (EDV) end of job
(EOJ)
Endezeichen *n* (EDV) end mark
Endfassung *f* final version
Endfertigung *f* finishing *n*
Endkonfektionierung *f* s.
Endfertigung
Endkontrolle *f* main control (MC),
master control (MC), broadcast
operations control (US) (BOC); ~ *f*
(Raum) central control room,
master control room (MCR), main
control room (MCR)
Endlos-Bandkassette *f* tape loop
cassette, tape loop cartridge
Endpunkt *m* (Leitung) terminal *n*,
terminating point, terminal point;
internationaler ~ international
terminal
Endschwärzung *f* maximum density
Endstelle *f* (Leitung) terminal *n*,
terminating point, terminal point
Endstufe *f* output stage, final stage
Endtitel *m* end titles *n pl*, closing
titles *n pl*
Endverstärker *m* final amplifier,
output amplifier
Endverstärkerstufe *f* final amplifier
stage, output amplifier stage
Endzeit *f* finishing time, end time,

out time
Energieleitung *f* aerial feeder,
feeder *n*
Energieversorgung *f* power supply
Energieverteilung *f* energy
distribution
Engagement *n* engagement *n*
engagieren *v* engage *v*, book *v*
Enkoder *m* encoder *n*, coder *n*
Ensemble *n* ensemble *n*, group *n*,
company *n*, troop *n*
Entbrummer *m* anti-hum
potentiometer
Ente *f* (Falschmeldung) canard *n*
Entfernung *f* distance *n*; ~ **schätzen**
to estimate distance; **endliche** ~
finite distance; **kürzeste scharf**
einstellbare ~ minimum focusing
distance, minimum range of
focus, minimum focus
Entfernungseinstellung *f* focus
setting, distance setting
Entfernungsmesser *m* range-finder
n; **gekoppelter** ~ coupled range-
finder
Entfernungsskala *f* distance scale,
focusing scale
entkoppeln *v* (Meßtechnik) balance
out *v*, decouple *v*; ~ *v*
(Funktechnik) isolate *v*, tune out
v
Entkopplung *f* (Meßtechnik)
balancing-out *n*, decoupling *n*; ~ *f*
(Funktechnik) tuning-out *n*,
isolation *n*
Entkopplungsfilter *m* decoupling
filter
entkuppeln *v* (mech.) uncouple *v*,
declutch *v*; ~ *v* (elek.) disengage *v*,
disconnect *v*
Entkupplung *f* (mech.) uncoupling *n*,
declutching *n*; ~ *f* (elek.)
disengaging *n*, disconnection *n*
Entladewiderstand *m* (Bauteil)
discharging resistor; ~ *m* (phys.)
discharge resistance
Entladung *f* discharge *n*; **statische** ~
static discharge

Entlötgerät *n* unsoldering set
Entlötpistole *f s.* Entlötgerät
Entlüfter *m* exhauster *n*
Entlüftungsanlage *f* ventilation
system
Entmagnetisierung *f*
demagnetisation *n*, degaussing *n*
Entmagnetisierungsdrossel *f*
demagnetiser *n*, demagnetising
coil, degausser *n*
Entriegelung *f* (eines Schaltkreises)
unlocking *n* (of a circuit)
entsättigen *v* desaturate *v*, pale out
v
Entsättigung *f* paling-out *n*,
desaturation *n*
Entschichtung *f* (F) emulsion
stripping
Entschlüsselung *f* deciphering *n*
Entschlüsselungsmatrix *f* (EDV)
decoder matrix
Entspiegeln *n* (Linse) reduction of
reflection
entstören *v* to clear interference, to
eliminate jamming, to suppress
noise
Entstörfilter *m* interference
suppressor
Entstörung *f* interference
elimination, interference
suppression, anti-jamming *n*, anti-
interference *n*, noise suppression,
static suppression; ~ *f* (EDV)
debugging *n*
entwickeln *v* develop *v*, process *v*
Entwickler *m* (Kopierwerk)
developer *n*
Entwicklerbad *n* developing bath
Entwicklerdose *f* developing tank
Entwicklerregenerierung *f*
replenishment *n*
Entwicklertank *m* developing tank
Entwicklung *f* development *n*; ~ *f*
(F) developing *n*
Entwicklungsabteilung *f*
(Kopierwerk) film-processing
department; ~ *f* (Planung)
research department

Entwicklungsanlage 46

Entwicklungsanlage *f* developing
equipment, developing plant
Entwicklungsanstalt *f* film
laboratory
Entwicklungsingenieur *m*
development engineer, research
engineer
Entwicklungskonstanz *f*
maintenance of development
standard
Entwicklungskontrast *m*
development contrast
Entwicklungskosten *plt*
development costs
Entwicklungsmaschine *f*
developing machine, processing
machine
Entwicklungsprozeß *m* developing
process
Entwicklungsschleier *m* darkroom
fog
Entwicklungssubstanz *f* developing
agent
Entwurf *m* design *n*
entzerren *v* (Bild, Ton) correct *v*,
equalise *v*; ~ *v* (Kopierwerk) grade
v, time *v* (US)
Entzerrer *m* (Bild, Ton) equaliser *n*,
corrector *n*; ~ *m* (Kopierwerk)
grader *n*, timer *n* (US)
Entzerrerverstärker *m* equalising
amplifier
Entzerrung *f* (Bild, Ton)
equalisation *n*, correction *n*; ~ *f*
(Kopierwerk) grading *n*, timing *n*
(US)
Epidiaskop *n* epidiascope *n*
Episkop *n* episcope *n*
Episodenfilm *m* serial film
Episodenreihe *f* series *n*
Episodenserie *f s.* Episodenreihe
Erdanschluß *m* earth connection,
earth *n*
Erdantenne *f* buried aerial
Erde *f* earth *n*, ground *n* (US)
Erdefunkstelle *f* ground signal
station, earth station, ground
station

erden *v* earth *v*, ground *v* (US)
Erdfeld *n* (Ant.) earth mat
erdfrei *adj* floating *adj*, ungrounded
adj
Erdkabel *n* underground cable
Erdleitung *f* earth connection, earth
wire
Erdmagnetfeld *n* terrestrial
magnetic field, earth's magnetic
field
Erdschattenzone *f* earth's shadow
area
Erdspieß *m* earth rod, earth spike
Erdtrabant *m* earth satellite
Erdumlaufbahn *f* earth orbit
Erdung *f* earthing *n*, earth *n*,
grounding *n* (US), ground *n* (US)
Erdungsleitung *f* earth connection,
earth wire
Erdungsschutz *m* protective
earthing
Erdungstrenner *m* earthing isolator
Ereignisablauf *m* sequence of
events
Erhebungswinkel *m* elevation angle
Erkennungsmelodie *f* signature
tune
Erkennungszeichen *n* station
identification signal
Erregerstrom *m* exciting current,
induction current, energising
current
errichten *v* (Bühne) set up *v*, build
up *v*
Ersatzbatterie *f* spare battery,
replacement battery
Ersatzbesetzung *f* understudy *n*
Ersatzgerät *n* spare set
Ersatzleitung *f* reserve circuit
Ersatzschaltbild *n* equivalent
circuit diagram
Ersatzsender *m* stand-by
transmitter
Ersatzsendung *f* stand-by
programme, substitute
programme
Ersatzteil *n* spare part, spare *n*,
replacement *n*

Erstaufführung *f* first night, première *n*, first run
Erstaufführungskino *n* first-run theatre
Erstaufführungstheater *n* first-run theatre
Erstausstrahlung *f* first broadcast
Erstentwicklung *f* primary development
Erstkopie *f* answer print
Erstsendung *f* first broadcast; ~ *f* (TV) first showing
Erwachsenenbildung *f* adult education, further education
Erzähler *m* narrator *n*
Erziehung* *f* educational broadcasting*
Erziehungsfilm *m* training film, instructional film
Etikett *n* label *n*; **nichtstandardisiertes** ~ (EDV) non-standard label
Euro *f* (fam.) Eurovision *n*
Eurovision *f* Eurovision *n*
Eurovisionsabwicklung *f* Eurovision operations *n pl*, Eurovision procedure
Eurovisionsaustausch *m* Eurovision exchange
Eurovisionsfanfare *f* Eurovision tune
Eurovisionskennung *f* Eurovision identification
Eurovisionskontrollzentrum *n* Eurovision control centre (EVC)
Eurovisionsnachrichtenaustausch *m* Eurovision news exchange
Eurovisionsnetz *n* Eurovision network
Eurovisionssendung *f* Eurovision transmission, Eurovision hook-up
Eurovisionsübertragung *f* Eurovision relay
Eurovisionszeichen *n* Eurovision caption
Exklusiv- (in Zus.) exclusive *adj*
Expander *m* (Ton) volume expander
Expedition* *f* shipping office,

shipping* *n*
Experimentalfilm *m* experimental film
Experte *m* expert *n*
Explosion *f* explosion *n*
Explosionsblende *f* explosion shutter
Exposé *n* synopsis *n*

F

Fach *n* (Darsteller) line *n*
Facharbeiter *m* craftsman *n*, skilled worker
Fächerblende *f* fan wipe
Fachgebiet *n* speciality *n*, field *n*
Fachjournalist *m* specialist correspondent
Fachmann *m* expert *n*, specialist *n*
Fachredakteur *m* specialist correspondent
Fadenkreuz *n* crosshairs *n pl*, reticule *n*
Fading *n* fading *n*
Fahne *f* (Bild) smear *n*, streak *n*
Fahnenziehen *n* streaking *n*, afterglow *n*
Fahraufnahme *f* tracking shot, travelling shot, truck shot, track *n*
fahrbar *adj* mobile *adj*
Fahrbereitschaft* *f* motor pool*, transport* *n*
Fahrbereitschaftsleiter *m* transport officer
Fahrdienstleiter *m* transport manager
fahren *v* (Kamera) to be on the camera; ~ *v* (Linse) zoom *v*; ~ *v* (Sendung) to put on the air; **rückwärts** ~ (Kamera) dolly out *v*, track out *v*; **seitwärts** ~ (Kamera) crab *v*; **vorwärts** ~ (Kamera) dolly in *v*, track in *v*
Fahrplan *m* (Ablauf) running order
Fahrspinne *f* castored base

Fahrstativ 48

Fahrstativ *n* rolling tripod
Fahrt *f* tracking shot, travelling
shot, truck shot, track *n*; **optische**
~ zoom *n*
Falle *f* trap *n*
Fallenfilter *m* reflection filter,
notch filter
Fallenkreis *m* notch-filter circuit
Fälschung *f* fake *n*
Faltdipol *m* folded dipole
Familienprogramm *n* family
programme, general audience
programme
Familienserie *f* comedy show,
family series
Fangbereich *m* lock-in range, pull-
in range
Farb- (in Zus.) chromatic *adj*, colour
(compp.), chroma (compp.)(coll.)
Farbabgleich *m* colour balance
Farbabschalter *m* colour killer
Farbabstimmung *f* colour balance
Farbabweichung *f* colour deviation,
colour distortion, hue error; ~ *f*
(opt.) chromatic aberration
Farbabzug *m* colour print
Farbanalyse *f* colour analysis
Farbanpassung *f* colour matching,
colour matrixing
Farbart *f* chromaticity *n*
Farbartflimmern *n* colour flicker,
chromatic flicker
Farbartkanal *m* chromatic chain,
chromatic channel
Farbartsignal (F-Signal) *n*
chrominance signal
Farbaufbrechen *n* colour break-up
Farbauflösung *f* chrominance
resolution
Farbauflösungsvermögen *n* power
of chromatic resolution, acuity of
colour image
Farbaufteilung *f* chromatic
separation, chromatic splitting
Farbausgleichfilter *m* colour
balance filter, colour
compensating filter
Farbauszug *m* colour separation,

chromatic component
Farbauszugsbild *n* primary colour
image
Farbauszugsraster *m* primary
colour raster
Farbauszugssignal *n* primary
colour signal, colour separation
signal
Farbbalance *f* colour balance
Farbbalken *m* colour bar
Farbbalkentestbild *n* colour bar
pattern
Farbbänder *n pl* colour banding
Farbberater *m* colour adviser
Farbbereich *m* colour range
Farbbestimmungsprobe *f* colour
cinex test
Farbbezugspunkt *m* colour
reference
Farbbild *n* colour picture, colour
frame
Farbbildaustastsignal (FBA-Signal)
n colour picture signal
**Farbbildaustastsynchronsignal
(FBAS-Signal)** *n* composite colour
video signal (comp. sig.), colour
video signal, composite colour
signal
Farbbilddeckung *f* convergence *n*
Farbbildkontrollgerät *n* colour
picture and waveform monitor
Farbbildröhre *f* chromoscope *n*,
colour picture tube, colour tube,
colour kinescope (US)
Farbbildsignal *n* colour picture
signal
Farbbildsignalgemisch *n* composite
colour video signal (comp. sig.),
colour video signal, composite
colour signal
Farbdeckung *f* registration *n*
Farbdekoder *m* decoder *n*, colour
decoder
Farbdemodulator *m* colour
demodulator, chrominance
demodulator
Farbdia *n* colour slide
Farbdichte *f* colour density,

colorimetric purity

Farbdifferenz *f* colour difference, chromatic difference

Farbdifferenzsignal *n* colour difference signal

Farbdramaturgie *f* colour composition within picture

Farbdreieck *n* colour triangle

Farbduplikatnegativ *n* colour duplicate negative, colour dupe neg (coll.), internegative (interneg) *n*

Farbe *f* colour *n*, dye *n*, hue *n*, paint *n*; **blasse** ~ pale colour; **gedämpfte** ~ muted colour, subdued colour; **reine** ~ pure colour; **schreiende** ~ loud colour, garish colour; **unreine** ~ impure colour; **verwaschene** ~ washed-out colour, desaturated colour

Farbeindruck *m* colour effect

Farbelektronik *f* colour electronics

Farbempfang *m* colour reception

Farbempfänger *m* colour television receiver, colour receiver

Farbempfindlichkeit *f* colour sensitivity, spectral response, chromatic sensitivity

Farbenblindheit *f* colour blindness, achromatopsy *n*

Farbenspiel *n* (Scheinwerfer) effects with colour lighting; **rotierendes** ~ revolving colour disc

Farbentwicklung *f* colour developing

Farberinnerungsvermögen *n* colour memory

Farbfehler *m* colour defect, chromatic defect, colour error

farbfehlsichtig *adj* red-green blind

Farbfehlsichtigkeit *f* daltonism *n*, red-green blindness

Farbfernsehempfänger *m* colour television receiver, colour receiver

Farbfernsehen *n* colour television, colour broadcasting

Farbfernsehkamera *f* colour television camera

Farbfilm *m* colour film

Farbfilmmaterial *n* colour stock

Farbfilmverfahren *n* colour film system; **additives** ~ technicolor *n*

Farbfilter *m* colour filter, coloured filter

Farbflimmern *n* colour flicker

Farbgebung *f* colouring *n*, coloration *n*

Farbgleichgewicht *n* colour balance

Farbgrauwerttafel *f* colour grey-scale chart

Farbhilfsträger *m* colour subcarrier (CSC), colour carrier (coll.)

Farbigkeit *f* chromaticity *n*

Farbinformation *f* colour information, chrominance information

Farbkanalentzerrer *m* chrominance equaliser

Farbkanalübersprechen *n* cross-colour *n*

Farbkennung *f* colour identification

Farbkoder *m* colour coder, colour encoder

Farbkoeffizient *m* chromatic coefficient

Farbkoeffizienten, trichromatische chromatic tristimuli

Farbkompensationsfilter *m* colour compensation filter

Farbkomponente *f* colour component

Farbkontrast *m* colour contrast

Farbkonturschärfe *f* chromatic resolution

Farbkoordinate *f* chromatic coordinate

Farbkopie *f* colour print

Farbkorrektureinrichtung *f* paint box (coll.); ~ **für stichige Filme** television apparatus for the rectification of indifferent film (TARIF)

Farbkorrekturmaske *f* colour correction mask

Farbkreis *m* colour circle
Farbkuppler *m* colour matcher
Farblavendel *n* colour lavender
Farblehre *f* chromatics *n*,
colorimetry *n*
Farblichtbestimmer *m* colour
temperature meter, colour grader
farblos *adj* colourless *adj*,
achromatic *adj*
Farblosigkeit *f* colourlessness *n*,
achromatism *n*, absence of colour
Farbmatrix *f* (Technicolor) colour
matrix
Farbmatrixschaltung *f* colour
matrix unit, colour matrix circuit
Farb-MAZ-Wagen *m* colour mobile
video tape recorder (CMVTR)
Farbmessung *f* colorimetry *n*
Farbmetrik *f* colorimetry *n*
farbmetrisch *adj* colorimetric *adj*
Farbmischkurven *f pl* trichromatic
response
Farbmischung *f* colour mixing,
colour blending, colour mixture
Farbmodulator *m* colour modulator,
chrominance modulator
Farbnachlauffilm *m* colour tail
leader, colour run-out leader
Farbnegativfilm *m* colour negative
film
Farbnormalsichtigkeit *f* normal
colour sight
Farbnormwandler *m* transcoder *n*
Farbort *m* point on colour triangle
Farbortmessung *f* measurement of
colour coordinates
Farbpositivfilm *m* colour positive
film
Farbproduktion *f* colour production
Farbqualität *f* colour quality
Farbrasterfilm *m* mosaic screen
film, lenticulated film
Farbrauschen *n* coloured noise
Farbreinheit *f* colour purity
Farbreinheitsgrad *m* excitation
purity
Farbreinheitsmagnet *m* purity
correction magnet

Farbreiz *m* colour stimulus
Farbsättigung *f* saturation *n*, colour
saturation
Farbsättigungsregelung *f* colour
saturation adjustment
Farbsättigungsregler *m* colour
saturation control
Farbsättigungsstreifigkeit *f*
saturation banding
Farbsaum *m* colour fringing
Farbschablonentrick *m* chroma
key, blue screen
Farbschwelle *f* colour threshold
farbselektiv *adj* colour-selective *adj*
Farbsendung *f* colour transmission,
colour programme
Farbservicegenerator *m* colour-
servicing signal generator
Farbsignal *n* colour signal
Farbsperre *f* colour killer
Farbstärkeregler *m* colour intensity
control
Farbstich *m* colour cast, colour
tinge; **kippender** ~ predominance
of one colour
Farbstoff *m* dye *n*, colouring matter,
pigment *n*
Farbsynchronimpuls *m*
chrominance sync pulse
Farbsynchronsignal *n* colour burst,
colour synchronising burst, colour
synchronising signal
Farbsynthese *f* colour synthesis;
additive ~ additive colour
synthesis; **subtraktive** ~
subtractive colour synthesis
Farbtafel *f* colour chart,
chromaticity diagram
Farbteiler *m* colour separator
Farbteilung *f* colour splitting,
colour separation
Farbtemperatur *f* colour
temperature (CT)
Farbtemperaturmesser *m* colour
temperature meter, Kelvin meter
Farbton *m* colour shade, tone *n*,
shade *n*, hue *n*, tint *n*
Farbtonknopf *m* colour intensity

control
Farbtonstreifigkeit *f* colour hue banding
Farbtonverfälschung *f* colour shading
Farbträger *m* colour subcarrier (CSC), colour carrier (coll.); **verkoppelter ~** *m* locked colour carrier
Farbträgermoiré *n* patterning *n*
Farbträgerschwingung *f* colour subcarrier oscillation
Farbtreue *f* colour fidelity, colour rendering, colour reproduction
Farbtripel *m* colour triad
farbtüchtig *adj* polychromatic *adj*, colour-capable *adj*
Farbübergang *m* colour transition
Farbübersprechen *n* colour contamination
Farbübertragung *f* colour transmission
Farbumkehrduplikat *n* colour reversal print
Farbumkehrfilm *m* colour reversal film
Farbumkodierer *m* transcoder *n*
Farbunterscheidungsschwelle *f* colour difference threshold
Farbunterscheidungsvermögen *n* colour difference sensitivity
Farbunterschied *m* colour difference
Farb-Ü-Wagen *m* colour OB vehicle, colour mobile control room (CMCR)
Farbvalenz *f* colour stimulus specification
Farbvalenzflimmern *n* colour flicker
Farbverfahren *n* colour process; **additives ~** additive colour process, additive colour system; **subtraktives ~** subtractive colour system, subtractive colour process
Farbverschiebung *f* colour distortion
Farbvorlauffilm *m* colour film

leader, colour head leader
Farbwert *m* chromaticity *n*, hue *n*, colour value
Farbwertbild *n* chrominance component
Farbwerte *m pl* tristimulus values
Farbwertkontrollgerät *n* tristimulus values monitor, RGB waveform monitor
Farbwertkoordinaten *f pl* chromaticity co-ordinates
Farbwertoszillograf *m s.* Farbwertkontrollgerät
Farbwertoszilloskop *n s.* Farbwertkontrollgerät
Farbwertsignal *n* chrominance signal
Farbwiedergabe *f* colour rendition, colour reproduction, colour rendering
Farbzerlegungssystem *n* colour splitting system
Farbzwischenpositiv *n* colour intermediate positive
Faseroptik *f* fibre optics
Fassung *f* version *n*; **~** *f* (elek.) fitting *n*, socket *n*; **synchronisierte ~** dubbed version
FAZ aufzeichnen to record on film, kine *v*, film-record *v*
FAZ-Anlage (FAZ) *f* film recorder, telerecording equipment, kinescope *n* (US)
fazen *v* (fam.) to record on film, telerecord *v*, kine *v* (coll.)
Feature *n* feature *n*, documentary *n*
Feature* *n* documentary and talks programmes*
federführende Anstalt originating station, organisation in charge
Federleiste *f* female multi-point connector, spring strip
Federspannung *f* spring tension
Federwerk *n* spring mechanism, clockwork *n*
Feeder *m* feeder *n*, aerial feeder
fehlanpassen *v* mismatch *v*
Fehlanpassung *f* mismatch *n*,

Fehlanpassung 52

mismatching *n*
Fehlbelichtung *f* faulty exposure
Fehlbesetzung *f* miscasting *n*
Fehler *m* error *n*, fault *n*,
impairment *n*, defect *n*, failure *n*,
mistake *n*; ~ *m* (Linse) flaw *n*,
aberration *n*; ~ *m* (EDV) error *n*;
chromatischer ~ chromatic
aberration, colour defect; **deutlich
störender** ~ definitely
objectionable impairment; **einen
~ eingrenzen** to localise a fault;
gerade wahrnehmbarer ~ just
perceptible impairment; **gut
wahrnehmbarer aber nicht
störender** ~ definitely perceptible
but not disturbing impairment;
leicht störender ~ somewhat
objectionable impairment; **nicht
wahrnehmbarer** ~ imperceptible
impairment
Fehlerbeseitigung *f* (EDV)
debugging *n*
Fehlereingrenzung *f* fault location
Fehlererkennung *f* (EDV) error
detection
fehlerhaft *adj* faulty *adj*, defective
adj, incorrect *adj*
Fehlerhäufigkeit *f* (EDV) error rate
Fehlermeldung *f* (EDV) error
message, alarm message, fault
message, fault report
Fehlerprüfung *f* (EDV) error
checking
Fehlerspannung *f* error voltage
(EV)
**Fehlerspannungsrelais (FU-
Schalter)** *n* error voltage relay
Fehlerstrom *m* fault current,
leakage current
Fehlerstromrelais (FI-Schalter) *n*
leakage current relay, fault
current relay
Fehlersuche *f* trouble-hunting *n*,
trouble-shooting *n*, fault-locating
n
Fehlerwahrscheinlichkeit *f* (EDV)
error probability

Fehlschaltung *f* faulty switching,
switching error
Feineinstellung *f* fine adjustment,
fine setting, fine control,
trimming *n*
Feinkorn *n* fine grain
Feinkornentwickler *m* fine-grain
developer
Feinkornfilm *m* fine-grain stock,
fine-grain film
feinkörnig *adj* fine-grain *adj*
Feinkornkopie *f* fine-grain print
Feinmechaniker *m* precision tool
maker, precision tool worker
Feinschnitt *m* final cut, fine cut
Feld *n* field *n*; ~ *n* (Bild) frame *n*;
optisches ~ optical field
Feldeffekttransistor (FET) *m* field
effect transistor (FET)
Feldlinse *f* field lens, field flattener
Feldnetz *n* field mesh
Feldspule *f* field coil
Feldstärke *f* field strength; ~ *f*
(phys.) power flux intensity
Feldstärkemessung *f* field-strength
measuring
Feldwicklung *f* field winding, field
coil
Fensterantenne *f* window-frame
aerial, window-mounted aerial
Fensterbefestigung *f* (Ant.) window-
mounting *n*
Ferienprogramm *n* programme for
holiday-makers
Fernanzeige *f* (EDV) remote
indication
Fernaufnahme *f* (Foto) telephoto
picture; ~ *f* (F) long shot (LS), long-
distance shot, vista shot (US)
Fernauge *n* closed-circuit TV
camera
Fernauslöser *m* remote release
fernbedienen *v* to operate by
remote control
Fernbediengerät *n* remote-control
unit, remote-control equipment
Fernbedienung *f* remote control
Fernbetätigung *f* s. Fernbedienung

Fernsehbetriebstechnik

Fernbildlinse *f* telephoto lens
Fernempfangsgebiet *n* secondary
service area, sky-wave service
area
ferngesteuert *adj* remote-controlled
adj
fernleiten *v* radio-control *v*
Fernleitung *f* long-distance line,
trunk line, long-distance circuit
Fernleitungsnetz *n* trunk network,
trunk-line system, long-distance
network
Fernmeldeamt *n*
telecommunications office
Fernmeldesatellit *m*
communications satellite,
telecommunications satellite
Fernmeldetechnik *f*
telecommunications *n pl*,
telecommunications engineering
Fernmeldetechnik* *f*
communications* *n pl*
Fernmeldetechniker *m*
telecommunications engineer
Fernmeldewesen *n*
telecommunications *n pl*
Fernmeldezentrum *n*
telecommunications centre
Fernmeßdaten *n pl* telemetrical
data
Fernpunkt *m* (Sat.) apogee *n*
Fernschaltung *f* remote control,
distant control, remote switching,
remote-controlled switching
Fernschreiben *n* teleprinter
message, telex message, telex *n*,
teleprint *n*
Fernschreiber *m* (Gerät) teleprinter
n, telex *n*, ticker *n* (coll.), teletype
n, teletyper *n*, teletypewriter *n*; ~
m (EDV) teleprinter *n*, teletype *n*,
teletyper *n*, teletypewriter *n*; ~ *m*
(Person) teleprinter operator,
telex operator; **über den ~ laufen
lassen** teleprint *v*, to put on telex
Fernschreibnetz *n* teleprinter
network
Fernschreibstelle *f* teleprinter

service
Fernseh- (in Zus.) television
(compp.) (TV), video *adj* (US)
Fernsehanlage *f* television
installation
Fernsehansager *m* television
announcer
Fernsehansprache *f* television
address
Fernsehanstalt *f* television station,
television corporation
Fernsehantenne *f* television aerial
Fernsehapparat *m* television
receiver, television set, television
n (coll.)
Fernseharchiv *n* television archives
n pl
Fernsehaufnahme *f* television
recording, telerecording *n*, vision
pick-up (US)
Fernsehaufnahmekamera *f*
television camera
Fernsehaufnahmewagen *m*
television OB van, television car,
mobile video tape recorder
(MVTR), television camera truck
(US), video bus (US), pick-up
truck (US)
Fernsehaufzeichnung *f*
telerecording (TR) *n*
Fernsehausstrahlung *f* television
transmission
Fernsehaustauschleitung *f*
television programme exchange
circuit
Fernsehbearbeitung *f* television
adaptation
Fernsehbeirat *m* television advisory
council
Fernsehbericht *m* television report
Fernsehberichterstattung *f*
television coverage
Fernsehbetrieb Bild* video
operations* *n pl*; ~ **Ton***
television sound operations* *n pl*
Fernsehbetriebstechnik* *f*
television operations and
maintenance*

Fernsehbild *n* television image,
television picture
Fernsehbildprojektor *m* television
picture projector
Fernsehbildsender *m* vision
transmitter
Fernsehdienst *m* television service
Fernsehdirektion *f* television
directorate
Fernsehdirektor *m* director of
television, managing director of
television (BBC)
Fernsehdirektübertragung *f* live
television broadcast, live
television relay
Fernsehdiskussion *f* television
panel discussion, television
debate
Fernsehdramaturgie* *f* television
scripts unit
Fernsehempfang *m* television
reception
Fernsehempfänger *m* television
receiver, television set, television
n (coll.)
Fernsehempfangsgerät *n* television
receiver, television set, television
n (coll.)
fernsehen *v* to watch television
Fernsehen (FS) *n* television (TV) *n*,
video *n* (US); **industrielles ~**
closed-circuit television (CCTV);
kommerzielles ~ commercial
television, independent television
(GB); **über ~ ausstrahlen** televise
v
Fernseher *m* (Gerät) (fam.)
television receiver, television set,
television *n* (coll.); **~** *m* (Person)
viewer *n*, video viewer (US)
Fernsehfassung *f* television version
Fernsehfilm *m* television film,
telefilm *n* (US)
Fernsehfilmkassette *f* television
film cassette, television film
cartridge
**Fernsehfilmkassettenwiedergabe-
gerät** *n* television cassette player,

teleplayer *n*
Fernsehgebühr *f* television licence
fee
Fernsehgenehmigung *f* television
licence
Fernsehgerät *n* television receiver,
television set, television *n* (coll.)
Fernsehgesellschaft *f* television
station, television corporation
Fernsehgroßbildprojektion *f* large-
screen television projection
Fernsehgroßbildprojektor *m* large-
screen television projector,
eidophor *n*
Fernsehhaushalt *m* television
budget; **~** *m* (Zuschauerforschung)
television home
Fernsehinszenierung *f* television
production
Fernsehjournalist *m* television
journalist
Fernsehkamera *f* television camera
tragbare ~ hand-held TV camera,
creepie-peepie *n* (US)
Fernsehkanal *m* television channel;
~ mit normaler Lage der Träger
television channel using upper
sideband; **~ mit spiegelbildlicher
Lage der Träger** television
channel using lower sideband
Fernsehkanäle, spiegelbildliche
channels in tête-bêche
Fernsehkanalumsetzer *m* television
transposer, television translator
Fernsehkasch *m* television
graticule
Fernsehkassette *f* television
cassette, television cartridge
Fernsehkofferempfänger *m*
portable TV receiver
Fernsehkomplex *m* television
centre
Fernsehkritik *f* (Presse) television
column
Fernsehkursus *m* television course
Fernsehlehrer *m* television teacher
Fernsehleitung *f* television circuit
Fernsehlektion *f* televised lesson

Fernsehleute *plt* broadcasters *n pl*
Fernsehlivesendung *f* live
television transmission
Fernsehlizenz *f* television franchise
Fernsehmodulationsleitung *f*
television distribution circuit
Fernsehmusical *n* television
musical
Fernsehnachrichten *f pl* television
news
Fernsehnetz *n* television network
Fernsehnorm *f* television standard
Fernsehoper *f* television opera
Fernsehpreis *m* television prize
Fernsehproduktion *f* television
production, television output
Fernsehproduzent *m* television
producer
Fernsehprogramm *n* television
programme
Fernsehprogrammkommission *f*
(ARD) television programme
directors' committee
Fernsehpublikum *n* television
audience
Fernsehpublizist *m* television news
commentator, television pundit
(coll.)
Fernsehrat *m* (ARD) television
programme committee; ~ *m*
(ZDF) television council
Fernsehrechte *n pl* television rights
Fernsehregisseur *m* television
director
Fernsehreklame *f* television
advertising; ~ *f* (Spot) television
advertisement
Fernsehreporter *m* television
reporter
Fernsehröhre *f* television tube,
picture tube, kinescope *n* (US)
Fernsehrundfunk *m* television
broadcasting
Fernsehsatellit *m* television
satellite
Fernsehschaltraum *m* television
switching area
Fernsehschirm *m* (Empfänger)
television screen
Fernsehschüler *m* school viewer
Fernsehsender *m* television station;
~ *m* (tech.) television transmitter;
farbtüchtiger ~ colour-capable
transmitter; **tragbarer** ~ portable
television transmitter
Fernsehsendung *f* television
broadcast, television
transmission, television
programme
Fernsehsignal *n* television signal
Fernsehspiel *n* television play,
television drama
Fernsehspiel* *n* television
drama*
Fernsehspielarchiv *n* television
drama library
Fernsehspot *m* commercial *n*
Fernsehstation *f* television station;
~ *f* (tech.) television transmitter
Fernsehstrecke *f* television link,
television relay link
Fernsehstudio *n* television studio
Fernsehtaktgeberimpulse *m pl*
television synchronising signals
Fernsehtechnik *f* television
engineering, television technology
Fernsehteilnehmer *m* television
licence-holder
Fernsehtelefon *n* television
telephone, video telephone (US)
Fernsehtelefonie *f* video telephony
Fernsehtonsender *m* television
sound transmitter
Fernsehturm *m* television tower
Fernsehübertragung *f* television
transmission; ~ **über Satelliten**
satellite television transmission;
direkte ~ **vom Satelliten** live
television relay by satellite
Fernsehübertragungsanlage *f*
television installation
Fernsehübertragungsstrecke *f*
television transmission circuit,
television link
Fernsehübertragungswagen *m*
mobile control room (MCR)

Fernsehübertragungszug *m* mobile unit, mobile OB unit
Fernsehumsetzer *m* television translator
Fernsehunterhaltung *f* television light entertainment
Fernsehveranstaltung *f* television show, television event
Fernsehversorgung *f* television coverage
Fernsehverteilersatellit *m* television distribution satellite
Fernsehverteilleitung *f* television distribution circuit
Fernsehwerbung *f* television advertising
Fernsehwettbewerb *m* television contest
Fernsehzeitschrift *f* television magazine
Fernsehzentrum *n* television centre
Fernsehzubringerleitung *f* television OB link
Fernsehzuführungsleitung *f* incoming TV circuit (to a centre)
Fernsehzuschauer *m* viewer *n*, video viewer (US)
Fernsprech- (in Zus. s. Telefon-)
Fernsprechzeitanschluß *m* temporary telephone connection
Fernstart *m* remote start
fernsteuern *v* to operate by remote control
Fernsteuerung *f* remote control, telecontrol *n*
Fernüberwachung *f* remote monitoring
Fernwirkeinrichtung *f* remote-control system
Fernwirksystem *n* (EDV) remote-control system
Ferritantenne *f* ferrite aerial
Ferritkern *m* (EDV) ferrite core
Fertigmeldung *f* go-ahead signal
Fertigung *f* finish *n*, finishing *n*; ~ *f* (Beitrag) editing *n*
Fertigungszeit *f* production time
Festangestellte *pl* permanent staff

Festanschluß *m* permanent connection
Festeinstellung *f* (opt.) fixed angle; **schaltbare ~** (Empfänger) switchable preset tuning
Festkörper-Bauelement *n* (EDV) solid-state component, solid-state device
Festkörperschaltkreis *m* (EDV) solid-state circuit
Festobjektiv *n* fixed-angle lens, fixed lens
Festpreis *m* fixed price
Festspiele *n pl* festival *n*
feststehend *adj* fixed *adj*
feststellen *v* (Kamera) lock *v*
Feststellring *m* locking ring
Festwertspeicher *m* (EDV) read-only memory, read-only store, fixed store
Festwoche *f* festival *n*
Fettstift *m* chinagraph pencil, grease pencil
Feuchtabtastung *f* anti-static treatment, anti-static device
Feuchtigkeit *f* humidity *n*; **~ absaugen** to dry out by suction; **relative ~** relative humidity (RH)
Feuchtkopierung *f* immersion printing, wet printing
Feuerbeleuchtungseffekt *m* fire-light effect
feuerfest *adj* fire-proof *adj*, fire-resistant *adj*
Feuerlöscher *m* fire extinguisher
Feuerschutzklappe *f* (Proj.) safety shutter; **~** *f* (F) booth shutter, fire shutter, safety screen, douser *n*
Feuerschutztrommel *f* fire-proof magazine, safety magazine
Feuerwehrmann *m* fireman *n*
Feuilletonredakteur *m* cultural editor
Figurine *f* figurine *n*
Film *m* film *n*, picture *n*, motion-picture *n* (US), movie *n* (US); **~** *m* (Kunstgattung) cinematography *n* **~** *m* (Material) stock *n*, film *n*

Film- (in Zus.) cine (compp.), filmic *adj*, film (compp.)

Film ab! run telecine!, run TK!; **~ ansehen** to view a film, to screen a film; **~ aufzeichnen** to record on film, kine *v*, film-record *v*; **~ auslegen** (Proj.) to unlace a film; **~ auslegen** (Kamera) to unload a camera, to unlace a film; **~ drehen** to take a film, to shoot a film, film *v*; **~ einlegen** (Kamera) to load a camera, to thread a film; **~ einlegen** (Proj.) to lace up a film **~ einstarten** to make start marks; **~ für Erwachsene** film for adults; **~ herausbringen** to release a film, to bring out a film; **~ mit Magnetrandspur** film with magnetic edge sound track; **~ mit Magnetspur** film with magnetic sound track, film with magnetic track, magnetic sound stripe; **~ randnumerieren** to edge-number a film, to rubber-number a film; **~ vorführen** to screen a film; **abendfüllender ~** full-length film; **belichteter ~** exposed film; **der ~ schwimmt** it's in the bath (coll.), it's in soup (coll.); **doppelt perforierter ~** double-perforated film, double-perforated stock; **einseitig perforierter ~** single-perforated film; **geknickter ~** creased film; **geräderter ~** indented film; **gewachster ~** waxed film; **lackierter ~** lacquered film; **nicht freigegebener ~** banned film; **unbelichteter ~** unexposed film, non-exposed stock, raw stock; **verregneter ~** scratched film; **verschrammter ~** scratched film; **zweiseitig perforierter ~** double-perforated film, double-perforated stock; **zweiter ~** second film, second feature film

Filmabtaster *m* film scanner, telecine machine, telecine (TK) *n*

Filmabtasterraum *m* telecine area

Filmabtastung *f* film scanning

Filmamateur *m* amateur film-maker, amateur cinematographer

Filmandruckschiene *f* film pressure guide

Filmarchitekt *m* art director, set designer

Filmarchiv *n* film library, film archives *n pl*

Filmarchivar *m* film librarian

Filmatelier *n* film studio

Filmaufnahme *f* filming *n*, shooting *n*, film shot, film take

Filmaufnahmestudio *n* film studio

Filmaufzeichnung (FAZ) *f* electronic film recording (EFR), telerecording *n*, kinescope recording (US)

Filmaufzeichnungsgerät *n* film recorder, electronic film recorder, kinescope *n* (US)

Filmauslauf *m* film run-out

Filmausschnitt *m* film excerpt, film clip, clip *n*

Filmautor *m* film author, screenplay writer, screen author, screenwriter *n*, scenarist *n*

Filmbahn *f* film path

Filmband *n* film strip, film *n* (coll.)

Filmbearbeitung *f* film-processing *n*; **~ f** (Buch) film adaptation, screen adaptation

Filmbehandlung *f* film treatment

Filmbeitrag *m* film item, film inject, film sequence

Filmbericht *m* film report, film story (US); **aktueller ~** newsfilm *n* **zusammenfassender ~** film summary, compilation *n*

Filmbeschädigung *f* film mutilation

Filmbeschaffung* *f* purchased programmes* *n pl*

Filmbeschaffung *f* film-purchasing *n*

Filmbespurung *f* striping sound track

Filmbetrachter *m* (Gerät) film-

Filmbetrachter 58

viewer *n*
Filmbewertungsstelle *f* film
valuation board
Filmbild *n* film image; ~ *n*
(Einzelbild) frame *n*
Filmbranche *f* film business
Filmbreite *f* film width
Filmbüchse *f* film can
Filmbüro *n* film service
Filmclub *m* film society, film club
Filmcutter *m* film editor; ~ *m* (F)
film cutter, cutter *n*
Filmdichte *f* film density
Filmeinblendung *f* underlay *n*,
floater *n*
Filmeinfädelung *f* (Proj.) lacing-up
n
Filmeinlegen *n* (Kamera) loading *n*,
threading *n*; ~ *n* (Proj.) lacing-up
n
Filmeinspielung *f* film insert,
telecine insert
Filmeinzeichnung *f* cutting mark
Film/E-Kamera, kombinierte video
film camera
Filmemacher *m* film-maker *n*
filmen *v* film *v*, shoot *v*
Filmentwickler *m* developer *n*
Filmentwicklung *f* film-processing
n, film-developing *n*
Filmerzählung *f* film narrative
Filmfenster *n* film gate, picture
window, projection aperture
Filmfestspiele *n pl* film festival
Filmformat *n* film size, film gauge,
film format, aspect ratio (AR)
Filmfortschaltung *f* film feed,
intermittent movement,
intermittent mechanism,
pulldown movement
Filmfortschaltzeit *f* pulldown time
Filmführung *f* film guide
Filmgalgen *m* trims bin; **an den ~
hängen** to hang up trims
Filmgeber *m* film scanner, telecine
machine, telecine (TK) *n*
Filmgeberraum *m* telecine area
Filmgeberwagen *m* mobile telecine

Filmgelände *n* lot *n*
Filmgerätestelle *f* camera store
Filmhersteller *m* film producer
Filmherstellung *f* film production
Filmhobel *m* scraper *n*
Filmindustrie *f* film industry
Filminsert *m* underlay *n*, floater *n*
filmisch *adj* filmic *adj*, cinematic
adj
Filmkamera *f* film camera, motion
picture camera; ~ *f* (Schmalfilm)
cine camera
Filmkameramann *m* cameraman *n*,
camera operator
Filmkanal *m* film channel, film
track
Filmkassette *f* film cassette, film
magazine
Filmkern *m* film bobbin, hub *n*,
film core, centre *n*, core *n*
Filmkitt *m* film cement, splicing
cement, joining cement
Filmklebepresse *f* film splicer, film
joiner
Filmkleber *m* (Person) negative-
cutter *n*, neg cutter (coll.)
Filmkleberin *f* splicing girl
Filmkomödie *f* film comedy
Filmkomponist *m* composer of film
music
Filmkonservierung *f* protective
treatment
Filmkopie *f* copy *n*, print *n*
Filmkopienfertiger *m* film-printer
n
Filmkopierer *m* s.
Filmkopienfertiger
Filmkopiermaschine *f* s.
Filmkopienfertiger
Filmkopierung *f* film-printing *n*
Filmkorn *n* film grain
Filmkritik *f* film review
Filmkritiker *m* film critic
Filmkunde *f* filmology *n*
Filmkunst *f* cinematography *n*,
cinematics *n pl*
Filmkunsttheater *n* art cinema, art
house (US)

Filmlabor *n* film laboratory
Filmladekassette *f* film magazine, film cassette
Filmlager *n* film stock
Filmlagerung *f* film storage
Filmlänge *f* footage *n*; ~ *f* (Zeit) duration *n*, running time
Filmlängenmeßuhr *f* footage counter
Filmlauf *m* film run, film travel; **kontinuierlicher ~** continuous run
Filmleinwand *f* projection screen
Filmmagazin *n* film cassette, film magazine; ~ *n* (Zeitschrift) film magazine
Filmmanager *m* business manager
Filmmaß *n* film dimension
Filmmaterial *n* film stock, raw stock; ~ *n* (belichtet) film material **kontrastreiches ~** high-contrast film, hard film
Filmmattiermaschine *f* film-polishing machine
Filmmusik *f* film music
Filmnachrichten *f pl* newsreel *n*, newsfilm *n*
Filmologie *f* filmology *n*
Filmothek *f* film library, film archives *n pl*
Filmpack *m* film-pack *n*
Filmpoliermaschine *f* film-polishing machine
Filmpresse *f* film-trade press
Filmprobe *f* film test strip
Filmproduktion *f* film production
Filmproduktionsbetrieb* *m* (TV) television film studios* *n pl*
Filmprojektor *m* film projector
Filmprüfer *m* film examiner; ~ *m* (Zensur) film censor
Filmprüfstelle *f* film censorship office
Filmprüfung *f* film examination
Filmredakteur *m* film critic; ~ *m* (Realisator) producer/scriptwriter *n*
Filmredaktion* *f* film reviews department; ~ *f* (TV) purchased

programmes* *n pl*
Filmregisseur *m* film director
Filmreinigung *f* film-cleaning *n*
Filmriß *m* break *n*, tear *n*
Filmrolle *f* (Proj.) reel *n*; ~ *f* (Kamera) roll *n*
Filmsalat *m* (Kamera) film jam, pile-up *n* (coll.); ~ *m* (Proj.) rip-up *n* (coll.)
Filmschaltzeit *f* pulldown time
Filmschlaufe *f* (Proj.) film loop
Filmschleife *f* film loop, loop *n*
Filmschneidegerät *n* film-editing machine
Filmschnitt *m* film-editing *n*, film-cutting *n*
Filmschrank *m* film cabinet, film-storage cabinet
Filmschrumpfung *f* film shrinkage
Filmserie *f* series *n*
Filmspedition *f* film traffic
Filmsprecher *m* narrator *n*
Filmspule *f* film spool
Filmstar *m* film star
Filmsternchen *n* starlet *n*
Filmstreifen *m* film strip, film *n* (coll.)
Filmstudio *n* film studio
Filmtechnik *f* film technology
Filmtechniker *m* film technician
Filmtext *m* commentary *n*, narrative *n*, script *n*
Filmtheater *n* cinema *n*, picture house, pictures *n pl* (coll.), movie theater (US)
Filmtheaterleiter *m* cinema manager
Filmtitel *m* film title, film caption
Filmtitelanmeldung *f* registration of film title
Filmtitelregister *n* register of film titles
Filmton *m* sound on film (SOF), sound track
Filmträger *m* film support, film carrier, film base, backing film
Filmtransport *m* film transport, pulldown *n*, film travel, film

Filmtransport   60

advance, film drive
Filmtransportrolle *f* feed sprocket,
film-feed sprocket
Filmtresor *m* vault *n*
Filmtrupp *m* camera crew
Filmübertragungsanlage *f* telecine
(TK) *n*
Filmumroller *m* film rewind
Filmverbrauch *m* film consumption
Filmverleih *m* film distributors *n pl*,
film distribution
Filmverleiher *m* film distributor
Filmverzeichnis *n* general film
catalogue
Filmvorführer *m* projectionist *n*
Filmvorführraum *m* projection
booth
Filmvorführung *f* film projection,
film screening, viewing *n*
Filmvorschub *m* film feed
Filmvorspann *m* titles *n pl*, opening
titles *n pl*, opening credits *n pl*,
opening captions *n pl*; ~ *m*
(Startband) leader *n*, head leader
Filmwagen *m* camera car
Filmwirtschaft *f* film industry
Filmzeitschrift *f* film magazine
Filmzugschwankung *f* variation in
running speed
Filter *m oder n* filter *n*
Filterband *n* (Kopiermaschine)
printer charge-band
Filtereingang *m* filter input; ~ *m*
(Kamera) filter slot
Filterfaktor *m* filter factor, filter
coefficient
Filterfolie *f* filter foil
Filterhalter *m* filter holder
Filterhalterung *f s.* Filterhalter
Filterkreuzschiene *f* video matrix
filtern *v* filter *v*
Filternetz *n* filter network
Filterrad *n* filter wheel, filter turret
Filterrahmen *m* filter frame
Filterrand *m* filter border
Filterrevolver *m* filter wheel, filter
turret
Filterschicht *f* filter layer

Filzröllchen *n* felt roller
Filzscheibe *f* felt mat, felt washer
Finanzabteilung *f* finance
department
Finanzausgleich *m* financial
equalisation
Finanzbuchhaltung* *f* accounting
services *n pl*
Finanzdirektion *f* finance
directorate
Finanzdirektor *m* director of
finance
Firmenwerbung *f* brand advertising
Fischauge *n* fish-eye lens
Fixfokus *m* fixed focus
Fixierbad *n* fixing bath, hypobath *n*
fixieren *v* fix *v*
Fixieren *n* fixing *n*
Fixiernatron *n* sodium
thiosulphate, hypo *n*
Fixiertank *m* fixing tank
Flachbahnsteller *m* sliding
attenuator
Flachbauelement *n* flat pack
component
Fläche *f* (Licht) broad *n* (coll.);
geflutete ~ flooded broad
Flächenantenne *f* flat-top aerial
Flächendiode *f* junction diode
Flächenleuchte *f* bank of lamps,
soft source
Flachkabel *n* twin lead, ribbon
feeder
flackern *v* flicker *v*, flutter *v*, jitter *v*
Flackern *n* flicker *n*, flutter *n*, jitter
n
Flanke *f* (Impuls) edge *n*
Flankensteilheit *f* edge steepness
Flankenwiedergabe *f* transient
response
Flansch *m* flange *n*
Flanschdose *f* flange socket; ~ *f*
(Buchse) flange-type socket; ~ *f*
(Stecker) flange-type plug
Flaschenzug *m* block and tackle
flattern *v* flutter *v*
flau *adj* (Bild) flat *adj*, weak *adj*, low-
contrast *adj*

Fliege *f* (fam.) blooping patch
Fliehkraftschalter *m* centrifugal
switch
Flimmerkiste *f* (fam.) box *n* (coll.)
flimmern *v* flicker *v*, sparkle *v*
Flimmern *n* flicker *n*, flickering *n*
Flip-Flop *n* flip-flop *n*;
monostabiles ~ (EDV) one-shot
multivibrator, monostable circuit,
monostable trigger circuit,
monostable multivibrator,
monostable flip-flop
Flip-Flop-Register *n* (EDV) flip-flop
register
Flip-Flop-Schaltung *f* (EDV) flip-
flop circuit, bistable trigger
Flugbahn *f* trajectory *n*
Flügelblende *f* rotary disc shutter,
rotating shutter
Fluoreszenz *f* fluorescence *n*
Fluoreszenzlampe *f* fluorescent
lamp, fluorescent tube (US)
Fluß, magnetischer magnetic flux
Flüssigkeitsblende *f* fluid iris
Flüssigkeitsmengenmesser *m*
liquid meter, flowmeter *n*
Flüssigkeitsumwälzung *f*
recirculation *n*
Fluter *m* flood *n* (coll.)
Flutlicht *n* floodlight *n*, flood *n*
(coll.)
Flutlichtscheinwerfer *m* floodlight
projector
Fokus *m* focus *n*
Fokusdifferenz *f* depth of focus
fokussieren *v* focus *v*
Fokussierung *f* focusing *n*
Folge *f* series *n*; ~ *f* (einzelne)
continuation *n*, instalment *n*,
sequel *n*
Folgefrequenz *f* repetition
frequency
Folgerecht *n* consequential right,
droit de suite
Folgeschaltung *f* sequence control,
sequence operation
Folgesteuerung *f* (EDV) sequential
control
Folge-Umschaltkontakt *m* sequence

change-over contact
Folienblende *f* silver-foil reflector
Fön *m* hair dryer
Format *n* format *n*, size *n*, gauge *n*,
dimension *n*, aspect ratio (AR); ~ *n*
(EDV) format *n*;
abgetastetes ~ scanned format
Formatfehler *m* (EDV) format error
formatfüllend *adj* full-format *adj*
Formelsprache *f* (EDV) formula
language
formieren *v* form *v*
Formierung *f* forming *n*, formation
n
Forschung und Entwicklung*
research and development*
Fortbildungskurs *m* refresher
course
Fortpflanzungsgeschwindigkeit *f*
velocity of propagation
Fortsetzungsbericht *m* series *n*
Fortsetzungsreihe *f* serial *n*
Fortsetzungsserie *f* s.
Fortsetzungsreihe
Forum *n* round table, panel *n*
Foto *n* photograph *n*, photo *n*, still *n*
Fotoarchiv *n* stills library
Fotoatelier *n* photographic studio
Fotodiode *f* photodiode *n*
Fotoeffekt, äußerer photoelectric
emission; **innerer** ~ photo-
conductive effect
fotoelektrisch *adj* photoelectric *adj*
Fotoelektron *n* photoelectron *n*
Fotoelektronenvervielfacher *m*
photomultiplier *n*
Fotoelement *n* photovoltaic cell,
photoelectric cell
Fotoemission *f* photoemission *n*
fotogen *adj* photogenic *adj*
Fotograf *m* photographer *n*, stills
photographer
Fotografie *f* photograph *n*, photo *n*,
still *n*
Fotokathode *f* photocathode *n*
Fotolabor *n* photographic
laboratory
Fotolaborant *m* laboratory
technician

Fotoleitfähigkeit *f*
photoconductivity *n*
fotometrisch *adj* photometric *adj*
Fotomontage *f* photomontage *n*
Fotospotmeter *n* spot photometer,
spotmeter *n*
Fotostelle *f* stills library
Fototitel *m* photographic title
Fotowiderstand *m* photoresistance
n
Fotozelle *f* photocell *n*,
photoelectric cell (PEC)
Fotozellennetzgerät *n* photocell
power supply unit
Fotozellenvervielfacher *m*
photomultiplier *n*
Frage/Antwort-System *n* (EDV)
dialog system
Franzose *m* (Werkzeug) monkey
wrench; ~ *m* (fam.) (Beleuchtung)
flags *n pl*
Fräsmaschine *f* milling machine,
miller *n*, cutting machine
Frauenfunk* *m* programmes for
women
Freiakustik *f* free field, free
acoustics
freiberuflich *adj* free-lance *adj*
Freigabebescheid *m* projection
permit
freigeben *v* (Nachricht) release *v*
freilaufen *v* self-oscillate *v*
Freileitung *f* open-wire line
Freilicht- (in Zus.) open-air *adj*,
outdoor *adj*, exterior *adj*
Freilichtkino *n* open-air cinema
Freilichtvorführung *f* open-air
performance
freischwingen *v* self-oscillate *v*
Freistellung von Rechten clearance
of rights
Fremdansteuerung *f* external
excitation
Fremdbild *n* crossview *n*
Fremdeinstrahlung *f* (Empfang)
radiated interference
Fremderregung *f* separate
excitation
Fremdfeld *n* (elek.) interfering field

Fremdfilmmaterial *n* non-original
material, library material, stock
shots *n pl*
Fremdleistung *f* contract service
Fremdleuchter *m* secondary source
Fremdmodulation *f* external
modulation
Fremdproduktion *f* external
production
Fremdprogramm *n* external
programme
Fremdsignal *n* external signal
Fremdspannung *f* noise voltage,
interference voltage, disturbing
voltage
Fremdspannungsabstand *m*
unweighted signal-to-noise ratio
Fremdsteuerung *f* external control
Fremdsynchronisation *f* slaving *n*
Fremdsynchronisierungseinrichtung
f slaving unit
Frequenz *f* (s.a.Ton- und
Hochfrequenz) frequency *n*; **hohe**
~ high frequency; **sehr hohe** ~
very high frequency (VHF);
superhohe ~ super-high
frequency (SHF); **tiefe** ~ low
frequency (LF); **ultrahohe** ~ ultra-
high frequency (UHF); **~en
beschneiden** to cut off
frequencies
Frequenzabfall *m* frequency fall-off
frequenzabhängig *adj* frequency-
dependent *adj*; ~ *adj*
(Darstellung) as a function of
frequency
Frequenzabstimmung *f* frequency
tuning
Frequenzabweichung *f* frequency
drift
Frequenzänderung *f* frequency
variation; ~ *f* (gewollt) frequency
change
Frequenzauslöschung *f* signal
cancellation, mush area
Frequenzband *n* frequency band;
übertragenes ~ (Sender) occupied
bandwidth
Frequenzbandbreite *f* frequency

bandwidth

Frequenzbandverschachtelung *f* overlapping frequency bands *n pl*

Frequenzbereich *m* frequency range

Frequenzcharakteristik *f* frequency response characteristic

Frequenzdrift *f* frequency drift

Frequenzgang *m* frequency response, amplitude frequency response; ~ **über alles** overall amplitude frequency response; ~ **über alles** (magn. Aufzeichnung) recording/reproducing frequency response

Frequenzgangabsenkung *f* attenuation as a function of frequency

Frequenzgangabweichung *f* variation in amplitude-frequency response

Frequenzganganhebung *f* lift in frequency response

Frequenzgangbegradigung *f* frequency-response equalisation

Frequenzgangentzerrung *f* frequency-response equalisation

Frequenzgangnachentzerrung *f* de-emphasis *n*

Frequenzgangtestband *n* frequency magnetic tape

Frequenzgangverzerrung *f* frequency distortion

Frequenzgangvorverzerrung *f* pre-emphasis *n*

Frequenzgenerator *m* frequency generator

Frequenzgleichheit *f* frequency synchronisation

Frequenzgrenze *f* frequency limit, critical bandwidth

Frequenzhub *m* frequency deviation; ~ **eines Wobblers** sweep width, deviation *n*

Frequenzhubmesser *m* frequency deviation meter

Frequenzlinie *f* frequency spectral

line

Frequenzmarke *f* frequency mark, frequency marker

Frequenzmeßbrücke *f* frequency-measuring bridge

Frequenzmesser *m* frequency meter

Frequenzmodulation (FM) *f* frequency modulation (FM)

Frequenzmultiplex *m* (Stereo) frequency-division multiplex

Frequenznachsteuerkreis *m* frequency-correction circuit

Frequenznachsteuerung, automatische automatic frequency control (AFC)

Frequenzplan *m* frequency plan, frequency allocation plan

Frequenzraster *m* frequency raster

Frequenzreihe *f* frequency series

Frequenzschwankung *f* frequency fluctuation

frequenzselektiv *adj* frequency-selective *adj*

Frequenzspektrum *n* frequency spectrum

Frequenzteiler *m* frequency divider, sub-harmonic generator

Frequenztestbild *n* frequency test pattern

Frequenzüberwachungszentrale *f* receiving and measuring station (CEM)

Frequenzumschalter *m* frequency selector switch

Frequenzumsetzer *m* frequency translator, frequency changer

Frequenzumwandler *m* frequency converter, frequency changer

frequenzunabhängig *adj* independent of frequency

Frequenzverdoppler *m* frequency doubler

Frequenzversatz *m* frequency offset

Frequenzverschiebung *f* frequency shift

Frequenzverteilung *f* frequency

Frequenzverteilung   64

allocation
Frequenzverzerrung *f* frequency distortion
Frequenzweiche *f* frequency separator, separator *n*; ~ *f* (akust.) dividing network, cross-over network
Fresnelsche Linse Fresnel lens
Friktion *f* friction *n*
Friktionsantrieb *m* friction drive
Friktionskopf *m* friction head
Friktionskupplung *f* friction clutch
Friktionsschwenkkopf *m* oil-filled friction head
Frischband *n* virgin tape, raw tape, new tape
Frontallicht *n* front light
Frontfenster *n* front window
Frontlinse *f* front lens, front element
Frontplatte *f* front panel
Froschperspektive *f* worm's-eye view
FS- (in Zus., s. Fernseh-)
FS-Film /100 Perforationslöcher 100-perforation television film
Fühlhebel *m* sensing lever, lever *n*, tape-tension lever
Führung *f* (Licht) key lighting, key light, main light; ~ *f* (Spurhaltung) guide *n*
Führungsbolzen *m* guide pin
Führungsbuchse *f* guide sleeve, guide bushing
Führungslicht *n* key lighting, key light, main light
Führungsrolle *f* guide roller, guide pulley
Führungstift *m* guide pin
Füllgrad *m* (Platte) groove spacing ratio
Füllhaltermikrofon *n* pencil microphone
Füllicht *n* fill light, fill-in light, filler *n*
Füllprogramm *n* fill-up *n*
Füllschriftverfahren *n* microgroove system

Füllsender *m* low-power transmitter, stand-by transmitter
Fundus *m* stock *n*
Fundusbestand *m* properties in stock
Fundusteil *n* stock scenery part
Fundusverwalter *m* stock-keeper *n*
Funk *m* (fam. s. a. Rundfunk, Radio, Hörfunk) radio *n*
Funkamateur *m* radio amateur, ham *n* (coll.)
Funkausstellung *f* radio and television exhibition
Funkautor *m* radio writer
Funkbake *f* radio beacon
Funkbearbeitung *f* radio adaptation
Funkbild *n* radio-photogram *n*, radio picture
Funkdienst *m* radio service, radio-communication service; **fester ~ mit Satelliten** fixed-satellite service
Funke *m* spark *n*
Funkempfänger *m* radio receiver
funken *v* radio *v*
Funkenlöscher *m* spark extinguisher, spark arrester, spark absorber
Funkenschutzschirm *m* spark screen
Funkenstörung *f* sparking *n*; ~ *f* (Auto) ignition noise
Funkenstrecke *f* spark gap
Funkentstörfilter *m* interference filter, radio interference filter, radio frequency filter
Funker *m* radio operator
Funkfeld *n* radio link hop; **drehbares ~** steerable radio link; **umzündbares ~** reversible radio link
Funkfeuer *n* radio beacon
Funkform *f* type of broadcast, format *n*
Funkfoto *n* radio-photogram *n*, radio picture
Funkhaus *n* broadcasting house
funkisch *adj* radiophonic *adj*, radio

adj
Funkmeßdienst* *m* monitoring station
Funkoper *f* radio opera
Funkrelais *n* radio relay
Funkrufdienst *m* paging device, bleeper *n*
Funksendung *f* radio transmission
Funksprechgerät *n* radio telephone, walkie-talkie *n*, RT apparatus
Funksprechverkehr *m* radiotelephonic traffic (RT traffic)
Funkspruch *m* radio message
Funksteuerung *f* radio control
Funkstörmeßdienst* *m* radio interference service
Funkstrahl *m* radio beam
Funktionsablauf, festverdrahteter (EDV) hardware operation
Funktionsdiagramm *n* functional diagram; ~ *n* (EDV) function chart, action chart
Funktionsprüfung *f* function test, performance test, performance check; ~ *f* (EDV) checkout *n*, operation checkout
Funktionsschaltplan *m* functional diagram
Funktionstabelle *f* (EDV) function table, truth table, Boolean operation table
Funktionswahlschalter *m* function switch, selector switch
Funkverbindung *f* radio communication
Funkverkehr *m* radio traffic, radio communication; **terrestrischer ~** terrestrial radio communication
Funkwagen *m* radio car
Funkwelle *f* radio wave
Funkwerbung *f* radio advertising
Fußlängenzähler *m* footage counter
Fußleiste *f* skirting board
Fußnummer *f* footage number, edge number, key number
Fußpunkt *m* nadir *n*; ~ *m* (Ant.) base *n*; **geerdeter ~** earthed base; **isolierter ~** insulated base

Fußpunkteinspeisung *f* base feed
Fußpunktwiderstand *m* base impedance
Fußrampe *f* (Licht) footlights *n pl*, striplights *n pl*
Fußtaste *f* foot switch, foot control
Fußtitel *m* subtitle *n*
Fußtitelmaschine *f* subtitler *n*, subtitling machine

G

Gabelhalterung *f* forked bracket
Gabelschaltung *f* (Telefon) hybrid set, hybrid *n*
Gabelverstärker *m* hybrid amplifier
Gag *m* gag *n*
Gage *f* fee *n*, salary *n*
Gagenanspruch *m* fee entitlement, fee claim, fee demand
Gagman *m* gag-writer *n*, gag-man *n* (US)
Galerie *f* gallery *n*
Galgen *m* (Ton) microphone boom, sound boom, boom *n*; ~ *m* (Schneideraum) trims bin, cuts rack
Galgenschatten *m* boom shadow
Galvanometer *n* galvanometer *n*
Gamma *n* gamma *n*; **multiplikatives ~** multiple gamma, black stretch and white stretch; **über alles ~** overall gamma
Gammaentzerrung *f* gamma correction, log-masking *n* (US)
Gammaregelung *f* gamma control
Gammaschalter *m* gamma selector
Gammawert *m* gamma value
Gammazeitkurve *f* gamma characteristic, Hurter and Driffield curve
Gang *m* (Darsteller F) move *n*; ~ *m* (Darsteller Thea.) cross *n*
Gänsegurgel *f* swan neck, goose neck (US)

Garagenmeister *m* garage foreman

Garderobe *f* (Kleidung) wardrobe *n*; ~ *f* (Kleiderablage) cloakroom *n*; ~ *f* (Raum) dressing-room *n*

Garderobier *m* dresser *n*, costumier *n* (US)

Garderobiere *f* (Darsteller) dresser *n*; ~ *f* (Kleiderablage) cloakroom attendant, check-girl *n* (US)

Gasse *f* (Bühne) side wings *n pl*

Gastarbeiterprogramm *n* (approx.) immigrant programmes *n pl*

Gastspiel *n* guest performance

Gatter *n* gate circuit

Gaze *f* gauze *n*

Gazeschirm *m* scrim *n*

Geberseite *f* sending end, transmitting end

Gebläse *n* blower *n*, fan *n*

Gebrauchsgrafiker *m* (TV) graphic artist

Gebühr *f* fee *n*, charge *n*; ~ *f* (R, TV) licence fee

Gebührenaufkommen *n* licence revenue

Gebühreneinzugsgebiet *n* licence-fee collection area

Gebühreneinzugsstelle *f* licence-fee collection office

Gebührenentrichtung *f* payment of licence fee

Gebührenfernsehen *n* television financed from licence fees

gebührenfrei *adj* free of charge

Gebührenordnung *f* rate card

gebührenpflichtig *adj* chargeable *adj*, taxable *adj*

Gebührenrundfunk *m* radio financed from licence fees

Gebührenzahler *m* licence-holder *n*

gedruckte Schaltung printed circuit

Gefälligkeit *f* facility *n*

Gefälligkeitsaufnahme *f* facility recording

Gefäß *n* tank *n*

gefedert *adj* shock-mounted *adj*, sprung *adj*

Gegendarstellung *f* reply *n*; **Recht**

auf ~ right of reply; **von dem Recht auf ~ Gebrauch machen** to exercise right of reply

Gegeneinstellung *f* reaction shot, reverse angle, reverse shot

Gegenfarbe *f* complementary colour

Gegenkopplung *f* negative feedback, reverse feedback, antiphase feedback

Gegenlicht *n* reverse lighting, back lighting, contre-jour *n*, back light

Gegenlichtblende *f* lens hood, lens shade, sunshade *n*

Gegenmaske *f* reverse mask

Gegenphase *f* antiphase *n*, opposite phase

Gegenschnitt *m* cut-away *n*

Gegenschuß *m* reaction shot, reverse angle, reverse shot

Gegensprechanlage *f* two-way intercommunication system, talkback circuit, talkback *n*, intercom *n* (coll.)

Gegensprechmikrofon *n* talkback microphone

Gegensprechverbindung *f* duplex circuit

Gegenstandsfarbe *f* colour of object

Gegenstreiflicht *n* kicker light

Gegentaktaufzeichnung *f* push-pull recording

Gegentakt-Längsaufzeichnung *f* longitudinal recording

Gegentaktschaltung *f* push-pull circuit

Gegentaktstufe *f* push-pull stage

Gehalt *n* salary *n*

Gehaltsbüro *n* salaries department

Gehaltsempfänger *m* salary-earner *n*, salaried employee

Gehalts- und Lohnstelle *f* salaries office, salaries-and-wages office

Gehäuse *n* housing *n*, casing *n*

Gehäuseschluß *m* casing short-circuit

Gehilfe *m* helper *n*

Gehobener ... (Beruf) senior *adj*

Gehör *n* hearing *n*; **absolutes** ~

perfect pitch
gehörrichtig *adj* aurally
compensated
Geige, erste first violin, violinist of
first desk
Geisterbild *n* ghost image, ghost *n*,
echo *n*, double image, multi-path
effect
Gelände *n* (F) lot *n*, studio area,
studios *n pl*
Gelatine *f* gelatin *n*
Gelatinefilter *m* gelatin filter, jellies
n pl (coll.)
Gelatineschutzschicht *f* protective
gelatin layer, supercoat *n*
Gelbschleier *m* yellow fog
Gelenkarm *m* (Beleuchtung)
articulated arm, hinged arm
Gemeinschaftsantenne *f* communal
aerial, community aerial
Gemeinschaftsantennenanlage *f*
(TV) central aerial television
(CATV)
Gemeinschaftsempfang *m* (R)
community listening; ~ *m* (TV)
community viewing
Gemeinschaftsproduktion *f* co-
production *n*, joint production
Gemeinschaftsprogramm *n* joint
programme, national programme
Gemeinschaftssendung *f* joint
programme, multilateral
programme
Generalansage *f* (TV) presentation
preview of evening programmes
Generator *m* generator *n*
Genre *n* genre *n*
Genremusik *f* genre music
Geometriebrumm *m* positional hum
Geometriefehler *m* geometric error
Geometrietestbild *n* geometrical
test pattern, linearity test pattern
gepuffert *adj* (EDV) buffered *adj*
Geradeausempfänger *m* straight-
circuit receiver, straight receiver,
direct-detection receiver
Geradeausprojektion *f* straight-
forward projection

Geradeausverstärker *m* straight
amplifier
Gerät *n* apparatus *n*, set *n*,
instrument *n*, device *n*, unit *n*
Geräte *n pl* equipment *n*
Geräteraum *m* apparatus room
Gerätewerkstatt *f* apparatus
workshop
Geräusch *n* noise *n*
Geräuschabschwächer *m* (Störung)
noise suppressor
Geräuschabstand *m* weighted
signal-to-noise ratio
Geräucharchiv *n* sound effects
library
geräucharm *adj* low-noise *adj*
Geräuschatmosphäre *f* atmosphere
noise
Geräuschaufnahme *f* sound effects
recording
Geräuschband *n* effects track,
effects tape
Geräuschdämpfung *f* sound-
proofing *n*, silencing *n*, sound
attenuation, sound insulation
Geräusche *n pl* sound effects,
effects *n pl*
Geräuscheffekte *m pl* spot effects
Geräuschemacher *m* sound effects
technician, effects operator
Geräuschkulisse *f* sound effects *n
pl*, background sound effects *n pl*
geräuschlos *adj* noiseless *adj*
Geräuschmikrofon *n* effects
microphone, audience
microphone
Geräuschpegel *m* noise level
Geräuschspannung *f* noise voltage;
bewertete ~ weighted noise
voltage
Geräuschspannungsmesser *m*
psophometer *n*, noise meter
Geräuschsperre *f* squelch circuit
Geräuschstudio *n* effects studio
Geräuschsynchronisation *f* dubbing
of effects, sound sync
Geräuschtechniker *m* sound effects
technician, effects operator

Geräuschteppich *m* acoustic carpet

Geräuschunterdrückung *f* noise suppression

Geräuschwert *m* noise value

Gerichtsreporter *m* court correspondent, court reporter

Gerüst *n* scaffolding *n*

Gesamtaufhellung *f* general lighting, overall lighting, general ambient light, overall ambient light

Gesamtaufnahme *f* long shot (LS), establishing shot, master shot, vista shot (US)

Gesamtklirrfaktor *m* total harmonic distortion factor

Gesamtszenenbeleuchtung *f* production lighting

Gesangsbox *f* acoustic flat

Gesangsstimme *f* vocal *n*

Gesangssynchronisation *f* voice sync

Geschäftsleitung *f* board of management

Geschwindigkeit *f* speed *n*, velocity *n*; **mit zweierlei** ~ double-speed *adj*; **steuerbare** ~ controlled speed **veränderliche** ~ variable speed; **zu niedrige** ~ underspeed *n*

Geschwindigkeitsabweichung *f* speed variation

Geschwindigkeitsänderung *f* speed change; **stufenlose** ~ continuous speed variation

Geschwindigkeitsfehler *m* speed error

Geschwindigkeitsregler *m* speed controller, speed regulator, speed governor

Geschwindigkeitsschwankung *f* speed fluctuation

Gesichtsabdruck *m* face impression

Gesichtsfarbe *f* flesh tone

Gesichtsfeld *n* visual field, field of view

Gesichtsplastik *f* plastic face-piece

Gesichtswinkel *m* angle of view, camera angle, viewing angle

Gespräch *n* (R,TV) debate *n*, discussion *n*

Gesprächsleiter *m* chairman *n*, anchor man, discussion chairman, moderator *n* (US)

Gesprächspartner *m* interlocutor *n*, participant *n*

Gestell *n* rack *n*, frame *n*, stand *n*, support *n*

gestochen *adj* pin-sharp *adj*

gestorben *adj* (Meldung) dead *adj*

gestorben! (fam.) (Aufnahme) wrap it up!, that's all!, in the can!; ~ (Dekoration) strike!

gestört *adj* faulty *adj*, defective *adj*, out of order (o.o.o.); ~ *adj* (ungewollt) interfered with, disturbed *adj*; ~ *adj* (gewollt) jammed *adj*

gestrichen *adj* cancelled *adj*

getastet *adj* keyed *adj*

Getriebe *n* gear *n*, gears *n pl*, gear unit

Getterpille *f* getter *n*

Gewandmeister *m* wardrobe supervisor

Gewandmeisterei *f* wardrobe* *n*

Gewinde *n* thread *n*

Gewindesteigung *f* angle of pitch

Gewindestift *m* threaded stud, headless screw, grub screw

Gewinn *m* gain *n*

Gips *m* plaster *n*

Gitter *n* lattice *n*, grid *n*, grille *n*, grating *n*; ~ *n* (Orthikon) mesh *n*

Gitterableitwiderstand *m* grid leak resistance

Gitteranodenkapazität *f* anode-to-grid capacitance, grid-plate tube capacity, grid-plate capacitance

Gitterantenne *f* umbrella-type aerial

Gitterbasisschaltung *f* grounded-grid circuit

Gitterblende *f* venetian-blind shutter

Gitterdecke *f* (Beleuchtung) lighting grid

Gittergleichrichter *m* grid rectifier
Gitterkreis *m* grid circuit
Gitterkreisabstimmung *f* grid-circuit tuning
Gittermast *m* lattice mast
Gitterreflektor *m* (Ant.) reflector grid
Gitterrostdecke *f* lighting suspension grid, lighting grid, grid *n*
Gitterspannung *f* grid voltage, bias *n*
Gitterspannungsnetzgerät *n* grid bias supply
Gitterstrom *m* grid current
Gitterstruktur *f* mesh effect
Gittertestbild *n* grid test pattern
Gittervorspannung *f* grid bias voltage
Gitterwechselspannung *f* control-grid signal voltage
Gitterwiderstand *m* grid resistance, grid-leak *n* (coll.)
Glamourlicht *n* (Beleuchtung) glamour light
Glanzlicht *n* highlight *n*
Glanzseite *f* shiny side
Glaser *m* glazier *n*
Glashaut *f* (Orthikon) storage plate
Glasplatte *f* glass plate
Glättungsschaltung *f* smoothing circuit
Gleichenergiespektrum *n* equal energy spectrum
Gleichenergieweiß *n* equal energy white
Gleichkanalbetrieb *m* common-channel service, co-channel service
Gleichlauf *m* (Bewegung) ganging *n* ~ *m* (Platte) regular rotational movement, no flutter and wow; ~ *m* (synchron) synchronism *n*, tracking *n*
Gleichlaufschwankung *f* (Platte) irregular rotational movement, flutter and wow
Gleichlaufsignal *n* synchronising signal

Gleichrichter *m* rectifier *n*, detector *n*, straightener *n*
Gleichrichter-Kaskadenschaltung *f* cascaded rectifiers *n pl*
Gleichrichterröhre *f* rectifier valve, detector valve
Gleichspannung *f* direct current voltage
Gleichspannungsverstärker *m* direct current voltage amplifier
Gleichstrom *m* direct current (DC)
Gleichstromanteil *m* direct current component
Gleichstromkomponente *f* direct current component
Gleichstrommotor *m* direct current motor; **fliehkraftgeregelter ~** centrifugally-governed direct current motor
Gleichstromverstärker *m* direct current amplifier
Gleichstromweiche *f* DC-separating network
Gleichstromwiderstand *m* direct current resistance, ohmic resistance
Gleichwellenbetrieb *m* common-wave operation
Gleichwellensender *m* synchronised transmitter
gleichzeitig *adj* simultaneous *adj*, coincident *adj*
Gleitkomma *n* (EDV) floating point
Gleitkomma-Operation *f* (EDV) floating-point operation
Gleitrichtung *f* directional slip
Gleitschiene *f* slide-rail *n*
Glied *n* element *n*; ~ *n* (Kette) link *n*
Glimm-Entladung *f* glow-discharge *n*
Glimmlampe *f* glow-lamp *n*, glow-discharge lamp
Glimmröhre *f* glow-discharge tube
Glockenkreis *m* (Secam) gaussian filter circuit; **komplementärer ~** (Secam) complementary gaussian circuit

Gloriole 70

Gloriole f (Licht) rim light
Glosse f marginal comment, vignette n
Glühdraht m filament n
Glühelektrode f hot cathode
Glühlampe f incandescent lamp
Glühlampenfassung f lamp socket, lamp holder
Glühlicht n incandescent light
Glühlichtscheinwerfer m inky n
Grad m degree n
Gradation f gradation n; ~ **eines Fotopapiers** gradation of printing paper; **flache ~** flat gradation
Gradationsentzerrung f gamma correction
Gradationskurve f gamma characteristic, Hurter and Driffield curve
Gradationsregelung f gamma control
Gradationsverlauf m gamma characteristic, Hurter and Driffield curve
Gradationsverzerrung f gamma distortion
Gradientenmikrofon n pressure-gradient microphone
Graetzgleichrichter m bridge rectifier
Grafik f graph n, diagram n, chart n, graphic n, visual aid
Grafik* f graphic design*
Grafiker m graphic designer
Grafikständer m caption easel, caption stand
grafischer Zeichner m graphic artist
Grammofonplatte f gramophone record, disc n
grau adj grey adj; ~ **in grau sein** to be flat, to be grey
Grauentzerrung f grey-scale correction
Graukeil m grey scale, neutral wedge, step wedge
Graukeilsignal n staircase signal
Graukeiltestvorlage f staircase test chart

Grauskala f grey scale, neutral wedge, step wedge
Graustufe f grey step, shade of grey
Grauwert m grey value, tonal value, half-tone n
Grauwerttafel f grey-scale chart; **harmonisch abgestufte ~** calibrated grey-scale chart
Grauwertverzerrung f half-tone distortion
Grauwertwiedergabe f half-tone rendering
Gravurring m engraved ring
Greifer m claw n, gripper n, register pin, pilot pin, moving pin
Greiferarm m claw arm
Greifersystem n claw feed system
Grenzempfindlichkeit f cut-off sensitivity, limiting sensitivity
Grenzfrequenz f limit frequency, cut-off frequency
Grieß m (Bild) shot noise, random noise, Johnson noise, grass n (coll.)
Grobeinstellung f rough focusing, coarse setting, rough adjustment
grobkörnig adj coarse-grained adj
groß adj (Einstellung) close-up (CU) adj; **ganz ~** big close-up (BCU), very close shot (VCS), big close shot (BCS)
Großaufnahme f close-up (CU) n, close shot (CS), close-up view (US)
Großbildprojektion f large-screen projection
Größe f (Format) size n, dimension n, format n, gauge n, aspect ratio (AR)
Großflächensender m wide-coverage transmitter, main station
Großraumspeicher m (EDV) bulk memory, bulk store
Großsender m high-power transmitter, high-power station
Grunddämpfung f pass-band attenuation, insertion loss

Grundeinheit *f* (Maßsysteme) basic unit
Grundfrequenz *f* fundamental frequency
Grundgage *f* basic fee
Grundgeräusch *n* background noise
~ *n* (Platte) surface noise
Grundhelligkeit *f* background brightness
Grundierfarbe *f* background colour, primer *n*
Grundleuchtdichte *f* base-light intensity
Grundlicht *n* base light, foundation light
Grundrauschen *n* background noise
Grundrestspannung *f* residual voltage
Grundschleier *m* base veil, background fog
Grundton *m* keynote *n*, fundamental tone, fundamental *n*;
~ *m* (Geräusch) background noise, atmosphere *n*
Grundwelle *f* fundamental wave, fundamental *n*
Gruppeneinstellung *f* group shot, crowd shot
Gruppenlaufzeit *f* group delay, envelope delay
Gruppenlaufzeitdifferenz *f* group delay difference
Gruppenmischer *m* group mixer
Gruppensteuerung *f* group control
Gruppenvertrag *m* group contract
Guckkasten *m* (fam.) television receiver, television set, television *n* (coll.)
Guide-Leitung *f* guide circuit
Gummidichtung *f* rubber gasket, rubber packing, rubber washer
Gummifuß *m* rubber foot
Gummilinse *f* zoom lens;
~ **aufziehen** zoom out *v*; ~ **ziehen** zoom *v*; ~ **zuziehen** zoom in *v*
Gummimuschel *f* foam-rubber earpad
Gurt *m* girdle *n*, strap *n*, belt *n*

Guß *m* (F) coating *n*
Güteabfall *m* loss of quality, impairment *n*; ~ *m* (tech.) degradation *n*

H

Haarteil *n* hairpiece *n*, wig *n*
Halbbild *n* field *n*;
ineinandergeschriebene ~er interlaced fields
Halbbilddauer *f* field period, field duration
Halbbildfrequenz *f* field frequency
Halbbildimpuls *m* field pulse, vertical pulse (US)
halbfrontal *adj* semi-frontal *adj*;
~ **aufnehmen** to do a three-quarter shot
Halb-KW *n* 500 Watt pup
Halbleiter *m* semiconductor *n*
Halbleiterdiode *f* semiconductor diode
Halbnahe *f* (Einstellung) close-medium shot (CMS), medium close-up (MCU), semi-close-up (SCU) *n*, medium shot (MS), mid-shot (MS) *n*, bust shot
Halbprofil *n* semi-profile *n*
Halbschatten *m* half-shadow, half-shade *n*, penumbra *n*
Halbspur *f* (Amateurgerät) half-track *n*
Halbton *m* (akust.) semi-tone *n*; ~ *m* (opt.) half-tone *n*
Halbtonwiedergabe *f* half-tone reproduction
Halbtotale *f* medium long shot (MLS), full-length shot (FLS)
Halbwelle *f* half-wave *n*
Halbwertsbreite *f* 3-db bandwidth, bandwidth at 50 % down; ~ *f* (Ant.) lobe width
Halbzeilenimpuls *m* equalising

Halbzeilenimpuls   72

pulse

Hall *m* echo *n*, reverberation *n*;
~ **geben** to add reverberation, to
add echo; **überlagerter** ~
superimposed reverberation,
added reverberation

Hallanteil *m* degree of echo

Hallausgang *m* reverberation
output, echo go

Halleingang *m* reverberation input,
echo return

hallen *v* echo *v*, resound *v*,
reverberate *v*

Hallgenerator *m* reverberation
generator, echo source

hallig *adj* reverberant *adj*, live *adj*

Halligkeit *f* liveness *n*,
reverberation *n*

Hallplatte *f* reverberation plate,
echo plate

Hallraum *m* reverberation room,
reverberation chamber, echo
room

Haloeffekt *m* halo effect, halo *n*

Halogenlicht *n* halogen light

Haltbedingung *f* (EDV) stop
condition

Haltebereich *m* locking range

Haltebügel *m* handle *n*, supporting
strap

Halterung *f* bracket *n*, mounting *n*;
schwenkbare ~ swivel mounting

Haltestelle *f* (fam.) (Kopierwerk)
processing stop

Handfunksprechgerät *n* walkie-
talkie *n*

handgezeichnet *adj* hand-drawn
adj

Handkabel *n* hand cable

Handkamera *f* hand-held camera,
portable camera

Handlampe *f* hand lamp, inspection
lamp

Handleuchte *f s.* Handlampe

Handlungsablauf *m* plot *n*, story
line

Handmikrofon *n* hand-held
microphone

Handpuppenspieler *m* puppeteer *n*

Handregelmotor *m* manually
controlled motor

Handregelung *f* manual control,
hand control, manual operation

Handsteuerung *f s.* Handregelung

Handvermittlung *f* manual
telephone system

Handvermittlungsanlage *f* manual
exchange

Hängegitter *n* (Scheinwerfer)
hanging grid

Hänger *m* (Scheinwerfer) hanger *n*

Hängestück *n* suspension unit

Hardware *f* hardware *n*

Harmonische *f* (Frequenz)
harmonic *n*

hart *adj* (Ton) harsh *adj*; ~ *adj* (Bild)
hard *adj*; **zu** ~ too contrasty, soot
and whitewash

Hartley-Schaltung *f* Hartley
oscillator circuit

Hartschnittschalter *m* video switch

Härtung der Emulsion hardening of
emulsion

Hartzeichner *m* (Optik) sharp-focus
lens, high-definition lens

Haube *f* hood *n*

Haupt- (in Zus.) main *adj*

Hauptabteilung (HA) *f* department
n

Hauptabteilungsleiter *m* head of
department

Hauptansage *f* (TV) presentation
preview of evening programmes

Hauptbeleuchtung *f* key lighting,
main lighting

Hauptdarsteller *m* protagonist *n*,
star *n*

Hauptfilm *m* main feature film

Hauptgeräteraum *m* central
apparatus room (CAR)

Hauptleitung *f* mains *n pl*

Hauptlicht *n* key light, main light,
key *n*

Hauptmonitor *m* transmission
monitor

Hauptnachrichten *f pl* (Sendung)

main news transmission

Hauptphase *f* (Zeichentrick) key animation

Hauptphasenzeichner *m* key animator

Hauptprogramm *n* (EDV) main programme, master programme

Hauptrolle *f* leading part; **in der ~** starring ...

Hauptschalter *m* main switch; **~** *m* (EDV) master switch

Hauptschaltraum *m* central control room (CCR)

Hauptsendezeit *f* (TV) peak viewing time; **~** *f* (R) peak listening time

Hauptspeicher *m* (EDV) computing store, main memory, working store, working memory, general store

Hauptstrahlrichtung *f* direction of maximum radiation

Hauptstrommotor *m* series motor

Hauptstudio *n* main studio

Haupttitel *m* main title

Hauptträger *m* main carrier

Haupttrennschalter *m* main isolating switch

Hauptverteiler *m* main distributing frame (MDF), trunk distributing frame (US)

Haushaltswesen* *n* budgeting* *n*

Hausmeister *m* house foreman

Hauspianist *m* resident pianist

Hausverwalter *m* house manager

Hausverwaltung* *f* central services* *n pl*

Hauteffekt *m* skin effect

Hebebühne *f* stage lift

Hebelschaltung *f* lever switch, knife switch

Hebevorrichtung *f* lifting device

Heckantenne *f* rear aerial

Heimatfunk *m* regional cultural programme

Heimempfänger *m* domestic receiver, home receiver

Heimstudioanlage *f* domestic studio equipment

Heißleiter *m* NTC resistor

Heizautomatik *f* (Thermostat) oven control

Heizbatterie *f* filament battery, low-tension battery, A-battery *n*

Heizfaden *m* (indirekt) heater *n*; **~** *m* (direkt) filament *n*

Heizsonne *f* bowl-fire *n*, electric fire

Heizspannung *f* filament voltage, heater voltage

Heizsymmetrierung *f* hum buckling

Heizung *f* heating *n*; **~** *f* (Röhre) filament *n*; **symmetrierte ~** balanced filament

Heizungstechniker *m* heating engineer

Heldenfriedhof *m* (fam.) obituaries *n pl*, obits *n pl* (coll.)

Helicalscanverfahren *n* helical scan system

Hellempfindlichkeitskurve, spektrale relative luminosity factor, spectral sensitivity curve

Helligkeit *f* (Leuchtdichte) luminosity *n*, intensity *n*; **~** *f* (TV) brightness *n*, brilliance *n*

Helligkeitsabstufungen *f pl* shades *n pl*

Helligkeitsbereich *m* (TV) brightness range

Helligkeitseindruck *m* brightness impression, sensation of brightness

Helligkeitsflimmern *n* luminance flicker, brightness flicker

Helligkeitskontrast *m* brightness contrast

Helligkeitssignal *n* brightness signal, luminance signal

Helligkeitssprung *m* brightness step

Helligkeitssteuerung *f* intensity modulation, brightness control

Helligkeitsüberstrahlung *f* white crushing

Helligkeitsumfang *m* brightness range, contrast range

Helligkeitsverteilung *f* brightness
distribution
Helligkeitswert *m* brightness value,
density value
Hellphase *f* (Kamera) light period
Helltastimpuls *m* unblanking pulse
herauftransformieren *v* step up *v*
herausbringen *v* (F) release *v*,
launch *v*; ~ *v* (Thea.) stage *v*,
present *v*; **ein Stück** ~ to put on a
play
herauskommen *v* to be released
herausschneiden *v* cut out *v*, excise
v
herausstellen *v* (Darsteller) feature
v, star *v*
herausstreichen *v* edit out *v*, strike
out *v*, excise *v*
herstellen *v* produce *v*
Herstellung *f* production *n*,
manufacture *n*
Herstellungskosten *plt* production
costs
Herstellungsplan *m* production
schedule
Herstellungsvertrag *m* production
contract
Herstellungszeit *f* production time
Hertz (Hz) *n* Hertz (Hz) *n*, cycles
per second (cps)
herunterregeln *v* (Licht) dim *v*, take
down *v*
heruntertransformieren *v* step
down *v*
Hesselbach *m* (fam.) synchronising
unit, synchroniser *n*
heulen *v* howl *v*
Heuler *m* (Ton) wow *n*; ~ *m* (fam.)
hit *n*
hexadezimal *adj* (EDV) sedecimal
adj, hexadecimal *adj*, sexadecimal
adj
Hexadezimalzahl *f* (EDV) sedecimal
number, hexadecimal number,
sexadecimal number
HF- *s.* Hochfrequenz-
HF-Wagen *m* radio car
Hi-Fi *n* hi-fi *n*

Highband *n* high band
Highband-Norm *f* high-band
standards *n pl*
High-key *n* high key (HK)
Hilfe, technische technical facilities
n pl, technical assistance,
technical support
Hilfeleistung *f* assistance *n*, help *n*,
service *n*
Hilfsarbeiter *m* unskilled worker
Hilfscode *m* (EDV) auxiliary code
Hilfsgerät *n* auxiliary set, auxiliary
equipment
Hilfskanal *m* auxiliary channel; ~ *m*
(Sender) sub-channel *n*
Hilfskraft *f* temporary help, holiday
relief, relief *n*, temporary *n*
Hilfsphase *f* (Motor) split phase
Hilfsquelle *f* resource *n*, expedient
n
Hilfsredakteur *m* editorial assistant
Hilfsregisseur *m* second director
Hilfssender *m* auxiliary transmitter
Hilfssynchronsignal *n* equalising
pulse, blip *n*
Hilfstonspur *f* cue track, guide
track, pilot tone track
Hilfsträger *m* subcarrier *n*
Hinterbandkontrolle *f* separate
head monitoring
Hintereinanderschaltung *f* series
connection, tandem connection,
serial hookup (US)
Hintergrund *m* background *n*, back-
drop *n*, upstage *n*
Hintergrundaufbauten *m pl* built
background
Hintergrundausleuchtung *f*
background lighting, background
illumination
Hintergrunddekor *n* backing *n*
Hintergrunddekoration *f*
background set
Hintergrundlicht *n* background
light, background mood light
Hintergrundmusik *f* background
music
Hintergrundprojektion *f*

background projection
Hintergrundprojektor *m*
background projector
Hintergrundspeicher *m* (EDV)
backing store, auxiliary store
Hintergrund-Verarbeitung *f* (EDV)
background processing
Hinterlicht *n* back light
Hintersetzer *m* backing *n*, set-in *n*
Hinweis *m* tip *n*, tip-off *n*, pointer *n*,
clue *n* (US)
hinziehen *v* (Bild und Ton) sync up
v, to bring into lip sync, lip-sync *v*
HI-Scheinwerfer (HI) *m* arc *n*
Hit *m* hit *n*
Hochformat *n* upright size, upright
format
hochfrequent (HF) *adj* high-
frequency *adj*, radio-frequency
(RF) *adj*
Hochfrequenz (HF) *f* high
frequency (HF); ~ *f*
(Radiofrequenz) radio frequency
(RF)
Hochfrequenzabschlußwiderstand
m radio-frequency terminating
resistance
Hochfrequenzbild *n* radio-
frequency television signal
Hochfrequenzdrossel *f* radio-
frequency choke, radio-frequency
choke coil
Hochfrequenzgenerator *m* radio-
frequency generator
Hochfrequenzleitung *f* radio-
frequency circuit, high-frequency
circuit
Hochfrequenzlitze *f* litz wire
Hochfrequenzschutzabstand *m*
radio-frequency protection ratio
Hochfrequenzspule *f* radio-
frequency coil
Hochfrequenzstörabstand *m* radio-
frequency-wanted/interfering-
signal ratio
Hochfrequenzüberlagerung *f* radio-
frequency heterodyne
Hochfrequenzverstärker *m* radio-

frequency amplifier
Hochfrequenzwobbelsignal *n*
wobbulated RF signal
Hochintensität (HI) *f* high intensity
(HI)
Hochintensitätskohle *f* high-
intensity carbon
Hochintensitätslampe *f* high-
intensity arc lamp, high-power
arc lamp
Hochlauf, synchroner synchronous
run-up
hochlaufen *v* run up *v*
Hochlaufzeit *f* run-up time
hochohmig *adj* highly resistive *adj*;
~ *adj* (Anpassung) high-
impedance *adj*, high-resistance
adj
Hochpaß *m* *s.* Hochpaßfilter
Hochpaßfilter *m* high-pass filter
Hochrechnung *f* extrapolation *n*
Hochspannung *f* high tension (HT),
high voltage (HV)
Hochspannungsfreileitung *f* high-
voltage overhead line
Hochspannungsnetzgerät *n* high-
tension power unit
Hochspannungstransformator *m*
high-voltage transformer
Höchstbeanspruchung *f* maximum
permissible load, peak load
Hochton *m* high pitch, treble *n*
Hochtonlautsprecher *m* high-
frequency loudspeaker, treble
loudspeaker, tweeter *n* (coll.)
Höhen *f pl* treble *n*
Höhenabschwächung *f* treble cut,
treble attenuation, top cut
Höhenanhebung *f* treble boost,
high-frequency emphasis
Höheneinspeisung *f* top feed
Höhenentzerrung *f* treble
equalisation, treble correction
Höhensperre *f* top-cut filter
Hohlleiter *m* waveguide *n*
Hohlspiegel *m* reflector *n*, concave
reflector
Holmantenne *f* cantilever aerial

Hologramm *n* hologram *n*
Holzstativ *n* wooden tripod
Home-track *n* home track
Honorar *n* fee *n*
Honorarabteilung *f* fees
department; ~ *f* (TV) artists'
contracts*; ~ *f* (R) programme
contracts*
Honorarrahmen *m* fee scale
Honorarvertrag *m* artist's contract
honorieren *v* to pay a fee for,
remunerate *v*
hörbar *adj* audible *adj*
Hörbarkeit *f* audibility *n*
Hörbereich *m* audibility range
Hörbericht *m* running commentary
Hörbeteiligung *f* audience rating
Hörbild *n* sound picture; ~ *n* (R)
feature *n*
Höreindruck *m* auditory
impression
Hörer *m* listener *n*; ~ *m* (Telefon)
receiver *n*, earpiece *n*; ~ *m* (tech.)
headset *n*, cans *n pl* (coll.)
Höreranalyse *f* audience survey
Hörerauskunft* *f* duty office
Hörerbefragung *f* audience
research survey, audience survey
Hörerforschung *f* listener research,
audience research
Hörergemeinde *f* audience *n*
Hörerpost *f* listeners' letters *n pl*
Hörerpost* *f* correspondence
section
Hörerschaft *f* audience *n*
Hörerwünsche *m pl* listeners'
requests; ~ *m pl* (Progr.) requests
programme; ~ *m pl* (Platten)
record requests
Hörerzahl *f* audience figure, size of
audience
Hörfeld *n* auditory sensation area,
acoustic field
Hörfolge *f* feature series, radio
series
Hörfrequenz *f* audible frequency,
audio frequency *n*, acoustic
frequency

Hörfrequenzbereich *m* audio-
frequency range, audio range
Hörfunk *m* (s. a. Funk, Radio,
Rundfunk) sound broadcasting,
radio *n*, radio broadcasting
Hörfunk- (in Zus.) radio *adj*
Hörfunkaufnahme *f* radio recording
Hörfunkdienst *m* radio service
Hörfunkdirektion *f* radio
directorate
Hörfunkdirektor *m* director of
radio, managing director of radio
(BBC)
Hörfunkgebühr *f* radio licence fee
Hörfunkgenehmigung *f* radio
licence
Hörfunkhörer *m* listener *n*
Hörfunkinszenierung *f* radio
production
Hörfunkkomplex *m* radio centre
Hörfunkleitung *f* radio directorate;
~ *f* (tech.) radio circuit, radio
programme circuit, programme
line
Hörfunklivesendung *f* live radio
broadcast
Hörfunklizenz *f* radio franchise
Hörfunkmagazin *n* radio magazine
Hörfunknachrichten *f pl* radio
news, news bulletin
Hörfunknachrichten* *f pl* radio
news*
Hörfunknetz *n* radio network
Hörfunkproduktion *f* radio
production
Hörfunkprogramm *n* radio
programme
Hörfunkreihe *f* radio serial
Hörfunksendung *f* radio broadcast,
radio programme
Hörfunkspielleiter *m* radio drama
producer
Hörfunkstudio *n* radio studio
Hörfunkteilnehmer *m* radio licence-
holder
Hörfunkübertragung *f* radio
transmission, radio relay
Hörgerät *n* hearing aid

Horizontal- (H-) (in Zus.) horizontal (H) *adj*
Horizontalablenkspule *f* line deflection coil
Horizontalauflösung *f* horizontal definition
Horizontalaustastimpuls *m* horizontal blanking pulse
Horizontalbalken *m* horizontal bar, strobe line
Horizontalfrequenz *f* line frequency
Horizontalimpuls *m* horizontal synchronising pulse, line synchronising pulse, line pulse
Horizontalsägezahn *m* horizontal saw-tooth
Horizontalschwenk *m* horizontal pan
Horizontal-Synchronimpuls *m* horizontal synchronising pulse, line synchronising pulse, line pulse
Horizontalumroller *m* horizontal rewind
Hörkopf *m* reproducing head, playback head, pick-up head
Hornstrahler *m* horn radiator
Hörrundfunk *m* sound broadcasting, radio *n*
Hörsaal *m* auditorium *n*
Hörschärfe *f* auditory acuity, acuteness of hearing
Hörschwelle *f* aural threshold, audibility threshold
Hörspiel *n* radio play, radio drama
Hörspiel* *n s.* Hörspielabteilung
Hörspielabteilung *f* radio drama*
Hörspielarchiv *n* radio drama library
Hörspielautor *m* radio playwright
Hörspielbuch *n* anthology of radio plays
Hörspielinszenierung *f* radio drama production
Hörspielleiter *m* head of radio drama
Hörspielmanuskript *n* radio drama script

Hörspielmusik *f* incidental music for radio drama
Hörspielproduktion *f* radio drama production
Hörspielregisseur *m* radio drama producer
Hörspielstudio *n* drama studio
Hörweite *f* ear-shot *n*
Hospitant *m* unpaid trainee
Hub *m* (Frequenz) deviation *n*
Hubschrauberaufnahme *f* helicopter shot
Hubstapler *m* stacker truck
Hülle *f* (Kamera) case *n*, covering *n*; **schalldichte ~** sound-proof covering, blimp *n*
Hüllkurve *f* envelope curve
Hybridrechner *m* (EDV) hybrid computer
Hybridschaltung *f* hybrid circuit
hydraulisch *adj* hydraulic *adj*
Hysteresisschleife *f* hysteresis loop
Hysteresisverluste *m pl* hysteresis losses

I

IC-Fassung *f* IC socket
Igel *m* tag block
Ikonoskop *n* iconoscope *n*
Illustration *f* visual aid, illustration *n*
Image-Orthikon (IO) *n* image orthicon (IO)
Impedanz *f* impedance *n*
Impedanzanpasser *m* impedance matching device
Impedanzanpassung *f* impedance matching
Implosion *f* implosion *n*
implosionsgeschützt *adj* implosion-proof *adj*
Improvisierung *f* improvisation *n*,

ad-libbing *n*
Impuls *m* impulse *n*, pulse *n*; **2T-20T~** *m* pulse-and-bar test signal, sine-square and rectangular pulse
Impulsabfallzeit *f* pulse decay time, pulse fall time
Impulsabtrennstufe *f* pulse clipper
Impulsabtrennung *f* pulse clipping
Impulsamplitude *f* pulse amplitude
Impulsanstiegzeit *f* pulse rise time
Impulsboden *m* tip of synchronising pulses
Impulsbreite *f* pulse width, pulse length
Impulsdauer *f* pulse duration; ~ *f* (EDV) impulse duration, impulse length
Impulseinschaltvorgang *m* pulse switch-on transient
Impulserneuerung *f* pulse regeneration
Impulsflanke *f* pulse edge
Impulsfolge *f* (EDV) bit rate
Impulsfolgefrequenz *f* pulse repetition frequency (PRF), pulse recurrence frequency (PRF); ~ *f* (EDV) impulse repetition rate, impulse recurrence rate
Impulsform *f* pulse shape
Impulsformer *m* pulse shaper
Impulsformierung *f* pulse shaping, pulse forming
Impulsfrequenzmodulation (IFM) *f* pulse frequency modulation (PFM)
Impulsgeber *m* impulse generator, pulse generator (PG), pulser *n*; ~ *m* (Taktgeber) synchronising-signal generator, synchronising-pulse generator; ~ *m* (EDV) digit emitter
Impulsgenerator *m* impulse generator, pulse generator (PG), pulser *n*; ~ *m* (Taktgeber) synchronising-signal generator, synchronising-pulse generator
Impulsgleichrichter *m* pulse rectifier

Impulshaushalt *m* complete pulse chain
Impulslage *f* pulse position
Impulsmodulation *f* pulse modulation
Impulsperiodendauer *f* pulse repetition period
Impulsregenerator *m* pulse regenerator
Impulsregeneriergerät *n* sync regenerator
Impulsserie *f* pulse train
Impulssiebung *f* pulse filtration, pulse separation
Impulsspeicher *m* (EDV) cycle delay unit
Impulsspitzenleistung *f* pulse peak power
Impulsstörung *f* pulse interference
Impulstastverhältnis *n* pulse duty factor; ~ *n* (Pause) mark-to-space ratio
Impulstrennstufe *f* pulse clipper
Impulstrennung *f* synchronising-pulse separation, pulse separation
Impulsverbesserung *f* pulse restoration
Impulsverfahren *n* pulse operation
Impulsverformung *f* pulse distortion
Impulsverteiler *m* pulse distributor
Impulsverzögerung *f* pulse delay
Inbetriebnahme *f* (Gerät) putting into service, putting into operation; ~ *f* (Sender) start-up *n*
Inbusschlüssel *m* set-screw wrench, Allen-type wrench, Bristo wrench
Inbusschraube *f* socket-head screw
Indexröhre *f* index tube
Indikativ *n* station identification signal; ~ **einer Sendung** signature tune
Indizieren *n* (EDV) indexing *n*
Induktion *f* induction *n*
Induktionsschleife *f* induction loop
Induktionsspule *f* induction coil
induktiv *adj* inductive *adj*
Induktivität *f* inductivity *n*,

inductance *n*
Induktivitätsmeßbrücke *f*
inductance bridge
Industriefilm *m* industrial film
Industrieschallplatte *f* commercial
record
Influenz *f* static induction
Informant *m* informant *n*
Information *f* information *n*, news
material, item of information,
dope *n* (coll.); ~ **freigeben** to
release information
Informationsbit *n* (EDV)
information bit
Informationsdienst *m* newsletter *n*
Informationseinheit *f* (EDV)
information unit
Informationsfilm *m* information
film
Informationsfluß *m* (EDV)
information flow
Informationsprogramm *n* news and
current affairs programme,
informational programme
Informationssendung *f* news
broadcast
Informationsspeicher *m* computer
memory
Informationsspeicherung *f*
memorisation of data, data
storage
Informationsspur *f* (EDV)
information track
Informationsträger *m* (EDV)
information carrier
Informationsübermittler *m* medium
of information
infrarot *adj* infrared *adj*
Infrarotfilter *m* infrared filter
Infraschall *m* infrasound *n*
Infraschall- (in Zus.) infrasonic *adj*
Ingenieur *m* engineer *n*; ~ **vom**
Dienst (IvD) duty engineer,
technical operations manager
(TOM); **leitender** ~ chief engineer
Inhaltsangabe *f* statement of
contents; ~ *f* (F) story *n*, synopsis
n; ~ *f* (Bildbericht) shot list, dope-

sheet *n*
Inhibitimpuls *m* (EDV) inhibit
impulse
Inklusives-ODER-Schaltung *f*
(EDV) inclusive-OR circuit
Inky Dinky *n* (Beleuchtung) inky
dinky *n*
Inlay *n* inlay *n*
Innenantenne *f* internal aerial,
indoor aerial
Innenaufnahme *f* interior shooting,
indoor shot, studio shot, interior
shot; ~ *f* (Foto) interior *n*;
~ **drehen** to shoot indoors
Innenpolitik* *f* home political
news
Innenrequisiteur *m* property man
Innenverwaltung* *f* central
services* *n pl*
Innenwiderstand *m* internal
resistance
Insert *n* insert *n*; ~ *n* (Schriftbild)
caption *n*
Insertabtaster *m* caption scanner
Insertpult *n* caption desk, caption
easel, caption stand
Insertwechsler *m* caption changer
Inspizient *m* (Thea.) stage manager
(SM); ~ *m* (Hörspiel) studio
manager (SM)
Instandsetzung *f* restoration *n*,
repair *n*, reconditioning *n*
Instrumentalbox *f* acoustic flat
inszenieren *v* direct *v*, produce *v*; ~
v (Thea.) stage *v*
Inszenierung *f* direction *n*,
production *n*; ~ *f* (Thea.) staging *n*
Intendant *m* director-general *n*;
stellvertretender ~ deputy
director-general
Intendanz *f* director-general's office
Intensität *f* intensity *n*
Intensitäts- und Phasenstereofonie
f spaced-microphone stereo;
intensity and phase stereophony
Intensitätsstereofonie *f* intensity-
difference stereo, coincident-
microphone stereo, intensity

stereophony

Intercarrierbrumm *m* intercarrier hum

Intercarrierverfahren *n* intercarrier sound system

Interessentenvorführung *f* trade showing, pre-release *n*

Interferenz *f* interference *n*, beat *n*

Interferenzfilter *m* interference filter

Interferenzstörung *f* disturbance due to interference

Interlock *n* interlock *n*

Intermed-Negativ *n* internegative *n*, intermediate negative, interneg *n* (coll.)

Intermed-Positiv *n* interpositive *n*, intermediate positive, interpos *n* (coll.)

Intermodulation *f* intermodulation *n*

internationale Tonleitung (IT-Leitung) international sound circuit, effects circuit

internationaler Ton (IT) international sound

internationales Tonband (IT-Band) international sound track, music and effects track (M and E track), international sound (coll.)

Internegativ *n* internegative *n*, intermediate negative, interneg *n* (coll.)

Interpositiv *n* interpositive *n*, intermediate positive, interpos *n* (coll.)

Intersatellitenfunkdienst *m* inter-satellite service

Interview *n* interview *n*

interviewen *v* interview *v*

Interviewer *m* interviewer *n*

Interviewpartner *m* interviewee *n*

Intervision (IV) *f* Intervision (IV) *n*

Inventarverwaltung* *f* inventory audit*

Inversion *f* (EDV) NOT operation, Boolean complementation, inversion *n*, negation *n*

Ionenfalle *f* ion trap

Ionenfleck *m* ion spot, ion burn

Iris *f* iris *n*

Irisblende *f* iris diaphragm, iris fade; ~ *f* (Trick) iris wipe

Isolationsprüfung *f* insulation test

Isolationswiderstand *m* insulation resistance

Isolierband *n* insulating tape

Isolierschlauch *m* insulating sleeve, insulating tubing

Isolierung *f* insulation *n*

Istwert *m* true value

IT-Fassung *f* M and E version

IT-Leitung *f* international sound circuit, effects circuit

J

Jalousieblende *f* multi-flap shutter, venetian shutter

Jalousieeffekt *m* venetian blinds *n pl*

Jaulen *n* (Ton) howl *n*, howling *n*, wow *n*

Jazz *m* jazz *n*

Jazzsendung *f* jazz programme

Jitter *n* jitter *n*

Jodlampe *f* iodine lamp

Jodquarzlampe *f* quartz iodine lamp

Journalismus *m* journalism *n*

Journalist *m* journalist *n*, newsman *n* (US)

Jugendfilm *m* youth film

jugendfrei *adj* U-certificate *adj*; **nicht** ~ X-certificate *adj*

Jugendfunk* *m* youth programmes *n pl*, youth broadcasting, programme for young listeners

Jugendsendung *f* programme for young people

jugendungeeignet *adj* unsuitable for young people

Jugendvorstellung *f* children's

performance
Jury *f* jury *n*
justieren *v* adjust *v*, align *v*
Justierkeil *m* adjusting wedge
Justierstift *m* fixed pin
Justierung *f* adjustment *n*,
alignment *n*, setting *n*
Justitiar *m* legal adviser
Justitiariat *n* legal adviser's
department

K

Kabarett *n* cabaret *n*
Kabarettensemble *n* cabaret group
Kabarettsendung *f* cabaret
programme
Kabel *n* cable *n*, cord *n*, flex *n*;
~ **verlegen** to lay cable;
dreiadriges ~ three-core cable;
gewendeltes ~ twisted flex;
konzentrisches ~ coaxial cable;
vieradriges ~ four-core cable;
zweiadriges ~ two-core cable
Kabelabweiser *m* cable deflector
Kabelanschlußdose *f* (Ant.) cable
connecting box
Kabelanschlußkasten *m* cable
jointing box, cable jointing
cabinet
Kabelbaum *m* cable assembly,
cable harness, cable form
Kabelbefestigung *f* cable clamp,
cable fixing
Kabelbericht *m* cabled dispatch
Kabelbrücke *f* cable link
Kabeldurchgang *m* cable duct
Kabeleinführung *f* cable entry
Kabelende *n* cable termination
Kabelfernsehen *n* cable television,
wire distribution service, closed-
circuit television (CCTV)
Kabelhalter *m* cable support, cable
tray
Kabelhalterung *f* cable clamp

Kabelhilfe *f* cable man
Kabelkanal *m* cable duct
Kabelkasten *m* cable jointing box,
cable box, junction box
Kabelkern *m* cable core
Kabelkopf *m* cable head
Kabellängenentzerrer *m* cable-
length compensator, cable-length
equaliser
Kabellaufzeitausgleich *m* cable-
delay equalisation
Kabelleitung *f* cable circuit
Kabelmantel *m* cable serving, cable
jacket, cable sheath
Kabelmesser *n* cable-stripping
knife, electrician's knife
Kabelquerschnitt *m* cross-section
of cable
Kabelring *m* coil of cable
Kabelschelle *f* cable clamp, cable
clip
Kabelschlauch *m* cable sheath
Kabelschuh *m* cable socket, cable
thimble, cable terminal plug
Kabelseele *f* cable core
Kabelspleißstelle *f* cable splice,
cable joint
Kabelsteckvorrichtung *f* plug
assembly
Kabelstrecke *f* length of cable
Kabeltrommel *f* cable reel, cable
drum
Kabelüberspielung *f* (Foto, NF)
cable film
Kabelverbindung *f* cable
connection; ~ *f* (Leitung) cable
circuit, cable link
Kabelverbindungsmuffe *f* cable
connecting sleeve
Kabelverlegung *f* cable-laying *n*
Kabelverstärker *m* cable amplifier,
repeater *n*
Kabelverteiler *m* cable distributor
Kabelverteilerkasten *m* cable
distribution box
Kabelweg *m* cable run
Kabelzubringerleitung *f* cable
contribution circuit

Kabine f cabin n, booth n, cubicle n
Kabinenfenster n cabin window, booth window, lens port, projection port
Kader m (Bildfeld) frame n
Käfigläufer m squirrel-cage motor
Kalenderjahr n calendar year
Kalendertag m calendar day
Kalenderwoche f calendar week
kalibrieren v calibrate v
Kalibrieren n calibration n, calibrating n
Kalkulation f management accountancy, cost accountancy
Kalkulator m management accountant, cost accountant
Kaltleiter m PTC resistor, barretter n (US)
Kaltlicht n cold light
Kamera f camera n; ~ **ab!** turn over! ~ **fahren** to be on the camera; ~ **heben** to elevate the camera; ~ **kippen** to tilt the camera; ~ **klar!** (TV) finished with cameras!, clear cameras!; ~ **klar!** (F) o.k. for camera!; ~ **läuft!** camera running!; ~ **leicht von oben** high-angle shot; ~ **leicht von unten** low-angle shot; ~ **rückwärts fahren** dolly out v, track out v; ~ **seitwärts fahren** crab v; ~ **senken** to depress the camera; ~ **von oben** very high-angle shot; ~ **von unten** very low-angle shot; ~ **vorwärts fahren** dolly in v, track in v; **Ausswiegen der** ~ camera weight adjustment, camera balancing, camera levelling; **drahtlose** ~ radio camera; **elektronische** ~ (E-Cam) electronic camera; **fahrbare** ~ mobile camera; **ferngesteuerte** ~ remote-controlled camera; **fest eingestellte** ~ rigid camera, fixed camera; **für** ~ **in Ordnung** (Einstellung) fine for camera!; **mit zwei ~s aufnehmen** double-shoot v; **selbstgeblimpte** ~ blimped camera; **senkrechte** ~ vertical

camera; **stumme** ~ mute camera; **versteckte** ~ concealed camera; **vor der** ~ **auftreten** to perform on-camera, to be on the spot
Kameraabstellraum m camera store
Kameraachse f camera axis
Kameraarm m camera boom arm, pan bar
Kameraassistent m camera assistant, assistant cameraman, focus puller; **erster** ~ camera operator; **zweiter** ~ second cameraman, focus operator
Kameraaufnahme f camera shooting, camera shot; ~ f (TV) recording n
Kameraausrüstung f camera equipment
Kamerabericht m dope-sheet n, shot list, film report; ~ m (Kamerazustand) camera report
Kamerabewegung f camera movement
Kamerablende f camera fade n
Kameradeckel m camera cover, camera door
Kameraeinrichtung f camera set-up
Kameraeinstellung f (F) camera alignment; ~ f (TV) camera placing; ~ f (Aufnahme) shooting angle
Kamerafahrer m tracker n, steerer n, helmsman n, grip n
Kamerafahrgestell n camera dolly, pedestal n, camera truck, dolly n, rolling tripod
Kamerafahrplan m (MAZ) camera script
Kamerafahrt f camera tracking; ~ f (Aufnahme) travelling shot, dolly shot; ~ **rückwärts** tracking back, back-track n, tracking out; ~ **vorwärts** tracking in; **seitliche** ~ crabbing n
Kameraführung f camerawork n, photography n

Kameragehäuse *n* camera housing
kamerageil sein (fam.) to hog the
  camera
Kameragewichtsausgleich *m*
  camera weight adjustment,
  counterbalance weight
Kameragrundplatte *f* camera base-
  plate, camera mounting-plate
Kamerahaltegriff *m* pistol grip
Kameraheizung *f* camera heating
Kamerakabel *n* camera cable,
  camera lead
Kamerakette *f* camera chain
Kamerakoffer *m* camera case
Kamerakontrollbedienung *f*
  camera control operator
Kamerakontrolle *f* camera control
Kamerakontrollgerät (KKG) *n*
  camera monitor, camera control
  unit (CCU)
Kamerakontrollschrank *m* camera
  control desk
Kamerakontrollverstärker *m*
  camera control amplifier
Kamerakopf *m* camera head
Kamerakran *m* camera crane,
  camera boom
Kameraleute *plt* cameramen *n pl*
Kameralupe *f* eyepiece *n*
Kameramann *m* cameraman *n*,
  operator *n*, camera operator;
  ~ **und Regisseur in einer Person**
  director-cameraman *n*; **erster ~**
  (F) director of photography,
  lighting cameraman; **erster ~** (TV)
  senior cameraman
Kameranotiz *f* camera cue-card,
  camera card
Kameraprobe *f* camera rehearsal
Kameraprüfzeile *f* camera test line
Kameraröhre *f* camera tube
kamerascheu *adj* camera-shy *adj*
Kameraschwenk *m* camera pan,
  camera panning, pan shot
Kameraschwenkkopf *m* panning
  head, pan head; ~ **mit**
  Kreiselantrieb pan head with
  gyroscopic drive, gyroscopic

  mounting
Kamerascript *n* camera script,
  shooting script
Kamerasignal *n* camera signal,
  camera pulse
Kamerasignalüberwachung *f*
  camera signal control, vision
  control, pulse monitoring,
  racks *n pl* (coll.)
Kamerastand *m* camera stand,
  camera mounting
Kamerastandort *m* camera
  position, camera set-up
Kamerastativ *n* camera tripod
Kamerastecker *m* camera plug
Kamerastellprobe *f* camera
  rehearsal
Kameratage *m pl* camera days
Kamerateam *n* camera team,
  camera crew, film crew
Kameratechniker *m* (F) camera
  maintenance man; ~ *m* (TV)
  camera maintenance engineer,
  racks engineer, vision control
  operator, vision operator
Kameraverschluß *m* camera
  shutter
Kameraverstärker *m* camera
  amplifier
Kamerawagen *m* camera truck,
  camera car, dolly *n*, velocilator *n*
Kameraweg *m* tracking line
Kamerawerkstatt *f* camera
  workshop
Kamerazentralbedienung *f* central
  apparatus room (CAR), camera
  operations centre
Kamerazubehör *n* camera
  accessories *n pl*
Kamerazug *m* camera channel
Kammermusik *f* chamber music
Kammerorchester *n* chamber
  orchestra
Kanal *m* channel *n*; ~ *m* (Ton)
  sound channel; ~ *m* (Progr.)
  channel *n*, service *n*; **auf einen**
  anderen ~ schalten to change
  channels

Kanalanpassung f channel-balancing n
Kanalantenne f single-channel aerial
kanalbenachbart adj adjacent-channel adj
Kanalgruppe f group of channels
Kanalmeßsender m channel signal generator
Kanalschalter m channel selector switch, channel selector
Kanalsperrkreis m channel rejector circuit
Kanaltrennung f channel separation
Kanalverstärker m channel amplifier
Kanalwähler m channel selector
Kanalweiche f channel diplexer, channel combining unit
Kante f edge n; ~ f (Licht) rim light
Kantenanhebung f edge correction
Kanteneffekt m edge effect
Kantenlicht n rim light
Kantenschärfe f edge sharpness, definition n, contour sharpness
Kantine f canteen n
Kapazität f capacity n, capacitance n
Kapazitätsdiode f silicon capacitor, varicap n (coll.), capacitance diode
Kapazitätseichung f capacitance calibration
Kapazitätsmeßbrücke f capacitance bridge
Kapazitätsregelung f capacitance regulation
Kapazitätsvariationsdiode f silicon capacitor, varicap n (coll.), capacitance diode
kapazitiv adj capacitive adj
Kapellmeister m musical director, conductor n, bandmaster n
Kappe f cap n
Kardioide f cardioid n
Kartei f card index
Kartenleser m (EDV) card reader
Kartenlocher m (EDV) card punch

Kasch m matte n, mask n, vignette n, cover n; **äußerer** ~ cut-off area; **innerer** ~ distortion area
Kascheur m plasterer n
Kaschgeber m electronic outline generator
Kaschhalter m matte box, matte holder
Kaschierband n magnetic laminating tape
Kaskadeur m stuntman n
Kaskodeschaltung f cascode circuit
Kasse f cash office
Kassenschlager m box-office hit
Kassette f magazine n, cartridge n, cassette n; ~ f (Platte) album n
Kassettendeckel m magazine lid
Kassettenkoffer m cassette case
Kassettenmotor m cassette motor
Kassettenrahmenträger m slide cassette, transparency cassette
Kassettenrecorder m cassette recorder, cartridge recorder
Kassettenverstärker m cassette amplifier, plug-in amplifier
Kassettenwechselsack m changing bag
Kassierer m cashier n
Kasten m box n; **im ~ sein** to be in the can
Kathode f cathode n; **direkt geheizte** ~ directly-heated cathode, filament-type cathode; **indirekt geheizte** ~ indirectly-heated cathode
Kathodenbasis (KB) f earthed cathode circuit, grounded cathode circuit
Kathodenbasisschaltung f s. Kathodenbasis
Kathodenfolgeschaltung f cathode follower
Kathodenpotential n cathode potential
Kathodenstrahloszilloskop n cathode ray oscilloscope (CRO)
Kathodenstrahlröhre f cathode ray tube (CRT)

Kathodenstrahlspeicherröhre *f* (EDV) cathode-ray store
Kathodenstrom *m* cathode current
Kathodenverfolger *m* cathode follower
Kathodenverstärker *m* cathode-coupled circuit
Kathodenwiderstand *m* cathode resistor
Kathodynschaltung *f* cathodyne circuit
Kegelrad *n* bevel wheel, cone wheel, bevel pinion, bevel gear
Kehlkopfmikrofon *n* throat microphone
Keil *m* (Kopierwerk) optical wedge
Keilentfernungsmesser *m* wedge range-finder
Keilplatte *f* wedge plate
Keilvorlage *f* density wedge, sensitometric wedge, step wedge
Kelvin-Grade *m pl* Kelvin degrees (K)
Kenndaten *n pl* characteristics *n pl*
Kennimpuls *m* (Band) blip *n*; ~ *m* (F) sync plop, sync pip
Kennlinie *f* characteristic curve; **fallende** ~ falling characteristic; **linearer Teil einer** ~ linear part of characteristic; **steigende** ~ rising characteristic
Kennlinienschar *f* family of characteristics
Kennmelodie *f* signature tune
Kennung *f* identification *n*, identifiable signal, ident *n* (coll.); ~ *f* (Grafik) caption *n*; ~ *f* (Progr.) jingle *n* (coll.); ~ *f* (Mus.) musical caption; ~ **geben** to give identification; ~ **wegnehmen** to cut identification *v*, to take away identification
Kennungsband *n* identification tape, tape ident (coll.)
Kennungsgeber *m* identification generator; ~ *m* (Quelle) identification source
Kennungssignal *n* identification

signal
Kennzeichen *n* (Grafik) caption *n*
keramisch *adj* ceramic *adj*
Kernmatrix *f* (EDV) core array, core matrix
Kernschatten *m* complete shadow, deep shadow
Kernspeicher *m* (EDV) core store, magnetic core store
Kette *f* chain *n*
Kettenleiter *m* recurrent network, iterative network
Kettenüberwachung *f* chain control
Kettenverstärker *m* chain amplifier
Kettenzug *m* chain hoist
Keule *f* lobe *n*
Kinderfernsehen *n* children's television
Kinderfilm *m* children's film
Kinderfunk *m* children's broadcasts *n pl*
Kindernachrichten *f pl* children's news programme
Kinderprogramm *n* children's programme
Kinderstunde *f* children's hour
Kinefilm /96 Perforationslöcher 96-perforation cinema film
Kinemathek *f* film library
Kinematografie *f* cinematography *n*
Kino *n* cinema *n*, picture house, pictures *n pl* (coll.), movie theater (US)
Kinofilm *m* cinema film; ~ *m* (Material) cinefilm *n*
Kinomobil *n* mobile-cinema van
Kinoreklame *f* screen publicity, cinema publicity
Kintopp *m* (fam.) flicks *n pl* (coll.), vintage movies *n pl*; ~ *m* (Filmwesen) screen *n*
kippen *v* (Bild) tilt *v*
Kippgerät *n* sweep generator, relaxation generator
Kippschalter *m* toggle switch, tumbler switch
Kippschaltung *f* (EDV) trigger circuit, multivibrator *n;* **bistabile** ~

Kippschaltung 86

(EDV) flip-flop circuit, bistable trigger; **monostabile ~** (EDV) one-shot multivibrator, monostable circuit, monostable trigger circuit, monostable multivibrator, monostable flip-flop

Kippspannung f sweep voltage

Kippspannungserzeuger m relaxation oscillator

Kipptransformator m sweep transformer

Kippumschalter m toggle change-over switch

Kippunkt m (elek.) transition point, change-over point

Kirchenfunk* m religious broadcasting*

Kissenentzerrung f pin-cushion equaliser

Kissenverzerrung f pin-cushion distortion, negative distortion

Klammerteil m (Kopierwerk) paper-to-paper

Klammerteile fahren, ~ kopieren to print papered section, to print paper-to-paper

Klammerzange f (F) film stapler

Klamotte f (fam.) slapstick n

Klang m sound n, tone n

Klangbestimmung f sound definition

Klangbild n sound pattern, acoustic pattern

Klangblende f tone control

Klangeindruck m sound impression

Klangentzerrerstufe f frequency response correction stage

Klangfarbe f tone colour, tone quality, tonality n, timbre n

Klangfarbenkorrektur f tone correction

Klangfarbenregelung f tone control

Klangfilter m sound filter

Klangfülle f sound volume; ~ f (Mus.) fullness of tone, richness of tone

Klanggemisch n sound spectrum

klanggetreu adj high-fidelity adj,

orthophonic adj

Klangkörper m orchestra n, music ensemble

Klangquelle f sound source

Klangregler m tone control

Klangübertragung f sound transmission

Klappdeckel m hinged lid

Klappe f clapper n, clapper board

Klappenliste f camera sheet, camera notes n pl, magazine card, rushes log

Klappenschläger m clapper boy

Klappstativ n folding tripod

Klapptitel m flip caption, flip titles n pl

Klappwand f flipper n

Klärbad n clearing bath

Klären n clearing n

Klarschriftleser m (EDV) optical character reader

Klassenempfang m classroom reception

Klatschkopie f direct print, slash print, slash dupe

Klebeband n (F, Ton) splicing tape, joining tape, adhesive tape; ~ n (MAZ) strip of foil, foil n

Klebelade f joiner n, jointer n, splicer n, splicing press

kleben v splice v, join v

Kleben n splicing n, joining n

Klebepresse f joiner n, jointer n, splicer n, splicing press

Kleber m (Person) negative-cutter n, neg cutter (coll.); ~ m (Material) film cement

Kleberin f splicing girl

Klebestelle f splice n, join n; **fehlerhafte ~** faulty join, bad join, faulty splice; **mechanische ~** manual splice

Klebestellen abdecken bloop v

Klebestellenlack m blooping ink

Klebetisch m splicing table, splicing bench

Kleeblattschauzeichen n star indicator

Kleidungslicht n cloth light
Kleindarsteller m bit player, small-part actor
Kleinsender m low-power transmitter
Kleinstativ n baby-legs n pl
Klemme f clamp n; ~ f (elek.) terminal n
klemmen v clamp v; ~ v (mech.) jam v
Klemmhalterung f clamp n
Klemmimpuls m clamping pulse, clamp pulse
Klemmkasten m terminal box
Klemmlampe f pincer n, pup n
Klemmleiste f terminal board, terminal strip, terminal block
Klemmpotential n clamping voltage, clamp voltage
Klemmschaltung f clamping circuit, clamp n
Klemmung f (mech.) jamming n
Klimaanlage f air-conditioning plant
Klimatechnik f air-conditioning n
Klimatechniker m air-conditioning engineer
Klimatisierung f air-conditioning n
Klingneigung f microphony n
Klinke f jack n
Klinkenfeld n jack panel
Klirrdämpfung f harmonic distortion attenuation
Klirrfaktor (K) m harmonic distortion factor; **gradzahliger ~** even-order harmonic distortion; **kubischer ~** third-order harmonic distortion; **quadratischer ~** second-order harmonic distortion; **ungradzahliger ~** odd-order harmonic distortion
Klirrfaktormesser m harmonic distortion meter
Klischee n cliché n
Klystron n Klystron n
Knacken n click n
Knacklaut m crackling sound
knallig adj (Farbe) loud adj

Knattern n motor-boating n, sizzle n, crackling n
Knick m angle n, bend n, crack n, kink n, knee n
knicken v bend v, crack v, kink v, buckle v, split v
knistern v crackle v, rustle v, sizzle v
knochig adj (Bild) too contrasty, soot and whitewash
Knopf m control knob, knob n
Knopflochmikrofon n lapel microphone
Knotenpunkt m junction point
Knotenpunktverstärker m bridging amplifier, junction amplifier
Knotenpunktwiderstand m junction resistance
Knüller m (fam.) (Progr.) hit n, audience-puller n (coll.)
Koaxialkabel n coaxial cable, coaxial line, coax n (coll.)
Koaxkabel n s. Koaxialkabel
Koder m coder n, encoder n
Koder-Kennimpuls m PAL-ident pulse, colour-ident sync pulse
Kode-Umwandlung f (EDV) code conversion
kodieren v code v, encode v
Kodiermatrix f (EDV) coder network
Kodierung f coding n
Koerzitivkraft f coercitivity n
Koffer m box n, bag n, case n
Kofferapparatur f portable equipment
Koffereinheit f portable unit
Koffergerät n portable set
Kofferradio n portable radio, portable n (coll.)
Kohlemikrofon n carbon microphone
Kohlenbogen m carbon arc
Kohlenbürste f carbon brush
Kohlenelektrode f carbon electrode
Kohlenlampe f arc lamp n, carbon lamp, carbon arc lamp
Kohlenlampennachschub m arc

Kohlenlampennachschub 88

feeding
Koinzidenzgatter *n* (EDV) logical
AND circuit, AND element, AND
gate, AND circuit, coincidence
circuit, coincidence gate
Koinzidenzgleichrichter *m*
coincidence detector
Koinzidenzimpuls *m* coincidence
pulse
Koinzidenzschaltung *f* coincidence
circuit
Kollektor *m* collector *n*,
~ commutator *n*
Kollektorgrundschaltung *f* ground-
collector circuit
Kollektorschaltung *f s.*
Kollektorgrundschaltung
Kollektorstrom *m* collector current
Kombikopf *m* (fam.) record/replay
head, combined
recording/reproducing head
Kombinationsantenne *f* combined
aerial, combination aerial
Kombinationssignal *n* uni-pulse
signal
Kombinationston *m* combination
tone
Komiker *m* comedian *n*
Kommando *n* cue *n*; **abgehendes ~**
outgoing cue; **ankommendes ~**
incoming cue
Kommandoanlage *f* talkback
arrangement, talkback system
Kommandoempfänger, drahtloser
radio control receiver, ear-plug *n*,
deaf-aid *n* (coll.)
Kommandolautsprecher *m*
talkback speaker
Kommandoleitung *f* cue line,
cueing circuit
Kommandomikrofon *n* talkback
microphone
Kommando-Ringnetz *n* omnibus
cue circuit
Kommandospur *f* cue track
Kommandotaste *f* cue button
Kommandozeichen *n* cue *n*
Kommandozentrale *f* operations

centre
Kommentar *m* comment *n*,
commentary *n*, news analysis;
~ am Monitor off-tube
commentary
Kommentarleitung *f* commentary
circuit, commentary line
Kommentarton *m* commentary
sound
Kommentator *m* commentator *n*,
news analyst
Kommentatoreinheit *f*
commentator unit
Kommentatorplatz *m*
commentator's position
Kommentatorstelle *f*
commentator's position
kommentieren *v* comment *v*,
comment on *v*
kommerziell *adj* (TV) commercial
adj; **~** *adj* (Bauteil) industrial *adj*
Kommunikation *f* communication
n
Kommunikationsforschung *f*
communication research
Kommunikationsmittel *n pl* media
n pl
Kommunikationssatellit *m*
communications satellite
Kommuniqué *n* communiqué *n*,
official statement
Komödie *f* comedy *n*, comedy play
Komparse *m* extra *n*,
supernumerary *n*, walk-on *n*,
super *n*
Komparsengage *f* walk-on fee,
extra's fee
Komparserie *f* extras *n pl*, crowd *n*,
supers *n pl*
kompatibel *adj* compatible *adj*
Kompatibilität *f* compatibility *n*
Kompendium *n* matte box,
compendium *n*, effects box
Kompensationsmikrofon *n*
balancing microphone,
differential microphone
Kompilierer *m* (EDV) compiling
programme, compiler *n*

Komplementärdarstellung f (EDV) complement representation
Komplementärfarbe f complementary colour
Komplementgatter n (EDV) complement gate
Komplex m (Gebäude) centre n
komponieren v compose v
Komponist m composer n
Komposition f composition n
Kompositionsauftrag m commission n
Kompression f compression n
Kompressor m compressor n
Kondensator m capacitor n, condenser n
Kondensatormikrofon n condenser microphone, electrostatic microphone
Kondensor m condenser n, condenser lens, condensing lens
Konfektionierung f (F) finishing n
Konferenzleitung f conference circuit
Konferenzleitungsnetz n conference network
Konferenzschaltung f conference circuit, multiplex n, hook-up n
Konferenzsendung f multiplex transmission
Konjunktion f (EDV) conjunction n, logical product
Konserve f (fam.) can n (coll.)
Konsole f (EDV) console n, control panel, operator's console
Konsonantenverständlichkeit f consonant articulation
Konstanthalter m stabiliser n
Konstanz f constancy n, stability n
Kontakt m contact n; **verschmorter** ~ scorched contact
Kontaktabzug m contact print
Kontaktbahn f contact track
Kontaktbelastung f contact loading
Kontaktfeder f contact spring
Kontaktfedersatz m contact assembly
Kontaktkopie f contact print, direct print
kontaktkopieren v to make a contact print
Kontaktkopieren n contact printing
Kontaktkopiermaschine f contact printer
Kontaktnase f cam n
Kontaktstecker m contact plug, plug n
Kontaktstift m contact stud, contact pin
Kontaktverfahren n contact process, contact printing method, contact printing
Kontinuität f continuity n
Kontrast m contrast n
kontrastarm adj (Bild) flat adj, low-contrast adj
Kontrastbereich m contrast range
Kontrasteffekt m contrast effect
Kontrastfilter m contrast filter
Kontrastgleichgewicht n contrast balance
kontrastlos adj lacking contrast
Kontrastlosigkeit f lack of contrast
Kontrastregelung f contrast control
Kontrastregler m contrast control knob
kontrastreich adj (Bild) contrasty adj, high-contrast adj; **zu** ~ too contrasty, soot and whitewash
Kontrastübertragungsfunktion (KÜF) f transmission gamma
Kontrastumfang m contrast ratio, contrast range, acceptable contrast ratio (ACR)
Kontrastverhältnis n contrast ratio
Kontrollausgang m monitoring output
Kontrollautsprecher m monitoring loudspeaker, control loudspeaker
Kontrolleitung f control line, control circuit
Kontrollendbild n final-check picture
Kontrollgestell n monitoring bay
Kontrollicht n indicator light; ~ n (Studio) cue light

Kontrollmonitor *m* picture monitor
Kontrollpult *n* control desk
Kontrollraum *m* monitoring area, control room; ~ *m* (R) cubicle *n*
Kontrollschiene *f* monitoring line, preview line
Kontrollschirm *m* monitor screen
Kontrollspur *f* control track, guide track
Kontrollspurkopf *m* control-track head
Kontur *f* contour *n*, outline *n*, border *n*
Konturendeckung *f* contour convergence
Konturentzerrung *f* contour correction
Konturschärfe *f* contour sharpness, edge sharpness
Konturverstärkung *f* contour accentuation, crispening *n*
Konvergenz *f* convergence *n*
Konvergenzeinheit *f* convergence assembly
Konvergenzmagnet *m* convergence magnet
Konvergenzplatine *f* convergence circuit, convergence panel
Konvergenztestbild *n* convergence test pattern, grille *n*
Konversationszimmer *n* green-room *n*
Konversionsfilter *m* conversion filter
Konverter *m* converter *n*
konzentrisch *adj* concentric *adj*, coaxial *adj*
Konzert *n* concert *n*
Konzertmeister *m* leader *n*, first violin
Koordinationsleitung *f* coordination circuit
Koordinationszentrale *f* coordination centre
Koordinator *m* coordinator *n*
Koordinierung *f* coordination *n*
Koordinierungsentfernung *f* (Sat.) coordination distance

Kopenhagener Wellenplan Copenhagen plan
Kopfabrieb *m* head wear
Kopfansage *f* (Einleitung) introductory presentation
Kopfeindringtiefe *f* tip engagement, tip penetration
Kopfeinmessen *n* alignment of heads
Kopfgeschirr *n* headset *n*
Kopfhörer *m* headphone *n*, earphones *n pl*, cans *n pl* (coll.)
Kopfhörsprechgarnitur *f* headset *n*
Kopfrad *n* head wheel
Kopfradaggregat *n* video head assembly
Kopfradeinheit *f s.* Kopfradaggregat
Kopfradgeschwindigkeit *f* head-wheel rotating speed
Kopfschuh *m* vacuum guide
Kopfspalt *m* magnetic gap, head gap
Kopfspaltbreite *f* gap width
Kopfspaltlänge *f* physical gap length; **magnetische** ~ effective gap length
Kopfspalttiefe *f* gap depth
Kopfspaltverlust *m* gap loss
Kopfspur *f* head track
Kopfstrom *m* (fam.) recording current
Kopfträger *m* head-support assembly
Kopfvorsprung *m* tip projection
Kopfvorstand *m s.* Kopfvorsprung
Kopfwicklung *f* head winding
Kopfzuschmieren *n* head-clogging *n*
Kopfzusetzen *n s.* Kopfzuschmieren
Kopie *f* print *n*, copy *n*, reproduction *n*, duplicate *n*; ~ *f* (Band) copy *n*, dubbing *n*, duplicate *n*, re-recording *n*, dub *n*, reproduction *n*; ~ **mit Untertiteln** subtitled print; ~ **putzen** to clean a print; ~ **regenerieren** to regenerate a print; ~ **ziehen** print

v, to strike a print, to make a print; **erste** ~ (F) rush print, answer print; **erste** ~ (Band) first generation; **frische** ~ fresh copy; **kombinierte** ~ married print, combined print; **lichtbestimmte** ~ graded print; **verregnete** ~ scratched print

Kopierabteilung *f* printing department, processing laboratory

Kopieranlage *f* printer *n*

Kopieranstalt *f* printing laboratory, film laboratory

Kopieranstaltsarbeiten *f pl* laboratory work

Kopierdämpfung *f* printer-light dimming

Kopiereffekt *m* (F) accidental printing, spurious printing; ~ *m* (Band) magnetic transfer

kopieren *v* copy *v*; ~ *v* (Band) dub *v*; ~ *v* (F) print *v*

Kopieren *n* (F) printing *n*; **optisches** ~ optical printing

Kopierer (K) *m* shot to be printed, footage for printing

kopierfähig *adj* printable *adj*, suitable for printing

Kopierfehler *m* printing fault

Kopierfilm *m* printer stock, printing stock

Kopierfussel *m* hair in printer gate

Kopiergerät *n* printing apparatus

Kopierkontrast *m* printing contrast

Kopierlänge *f* printing length

Kopierlicht *n* printer light

Kopierlichtschaltung *f* printer-light setting

Kopiermaschine *f* printing machine, printer *n*; **additive** ~ additive printer; **optische** ~ optical printer; **subtraktive** ~ subtractive printer

Kopiermeister *m* film grader

Kopierung *f* (F) printing *n*; ~ *f* (Band) copying *n*, dubbing *n*, duplicating *n*

Kopierverfahren *n* printing process

Kopierwerk *n* printing laboratory, film-processing laboratory, film laboratory

Kopierwerkchemiker *m* laboratory chemist

Kopierwerktechniker *m* laboratory technician

Kopierwert *m* printer-light value, printer-light strength

Koppelschleife *f* coupling loop

Koppelweiche *f* coupling diplexer, combining unit

Koppelzeichen *n* change-over cues *n pl*, cue dots *n pl*

Kopplung *f* coupling *n*; ~ **der Kreise** hook-up *n*

Kopplungskondensator *m* coupling capacitor, blocking capacitor

Kopplungsübertrager *m* coupling transformer

Kopplungswiderstand *m* transfer impedance

Koproduktion *f* co-production *n*

Korn *n* (F) grain *n*; ~ *n* (TV) granule *n*

Körnigkeit *f* granulation *n*, granularity *n*, graininess *n*, grain *n*

Körper, schwarzer black body

Körperfarbe *f* body colour

Körperschall *m* structure-borne vibration

Korrektur *f* correction *n*

Korrekturfilter *m* correction filter, trimming filter

Korrekturkopie *f* first release print

Korrektursignal *n* correction signal **sägezahnförmiges** ~ saw-tooth signal

Korrepetitor *m* repetiteur *n*

Korrespondent *m* correspondent *n*, stringer *n*

Korrespondentennetz *n* corps of correspondents

korrigieren *v* correct *v*

korrosionsfest *adj* corrosion-resistant *adj*

Kosinus- s. Cosinus
Kosmovision f cosmovision n
Kostenbefreiung f licence
  exemption
Kostenerstattung f reimbursement
  n
Kostenteilung f cost-sharing n
Kostenvoranschlag m budget
  breakdown, estimate n
Kostüm n costume n
Kostümausstattung f costume
  design
Kostümberater m costume adviser
Kostümbildner m costume designer
Kostümbildnerei f costumes* n pl,
  costume design unit
Kostümentwurf m costume design
Kostümfilm m period picture
Kostümfundus m costume store
Kostümgestalter m costume
  designer
Kostümliste f costume plot,
  costume list
Kostümschneider m dressmaker n
Kostümverleih m costume hire
Kostümverleiher m costumier n
Kostümwerkstatt f costume
  workroom, costume workshop
Kotflügelantenne f wing aerial
Kraftfahrzeugwerkstatt f vehicle
  workshop
Kraftnetz n (dreiphasig) three-
  phase mains supply
Kraftstecker m power plug
Kraftsteckkupplung f power-plug
  adapter
Kraftstrom m power current,
  electric power
Kraftzentrale f power plant
Kran m (F) crane n, boom n
Kratzer m (Platte) scratch n; ~ m
  (Geräusch) scratching noise
Kreis m (elek.) circuit n
Kreisblende f iris diaphragm
Kreiselantrieb m gyroscopic drive
Kreiselblende f clog wipe
Kreiselkopf m gyroscopic head
Kreiselstativ n gyro-tripod n

Kreisfahrt f track-round n
Kreuzdipol m crossed dipole,
  turnstile aerial
Kreuzgelenk n (Beleuchtung) cross-
  bar n
Kreuzglied n lattice section
Kreuzlicht n crossed spots n pl,
  cross-light n
Kreuzlinientestbild n cross-line
  test pattern
Kreuzmodulation f cross
  modulation
Kreuzschiene f matrix n, cross-bar
  n
Kreuzschienensteckfeld n matrix
  jackfield
Kreuzschienenverteiler m matrix
  distribution panel
Kreuzschienenwähler m matrix
  selector
Kreuzverschraubung f
  (Beleuchtung) cross-joint n
Krimi m (fam.) s. Kriminalfilm
Kriminalfilm m detective film,
  thriller n (coll.)
Kriminalspiel n mystery play
Kristallmikrofon n crystal
  microphone, piezo-electric
  microphone
Kristalloszillator m crystal
  oscillator
Kristalltonabnehmer m crystal pick-
  up
Kritik f notice n, review n, criticism
  n
Kritiker m critic n, reviewer n
Krokodilklammer f alligator clip
Krokodilklemme f s.
  Krokodilklammer
Krümmung f curvature n, bend n
Kufe f (Proj.) gate runner; ~ f
  (Kamera) gate pressure plate
Kufendruck m (Proj.) gate runner
  pressure; ~ m (Kamera) gate
  pressure
Kugel f (fam.) omnidirectional
  microphone
Kugelgelenk n ball-and-socket

joint

Kugellager *n* ball-bearing *n*
Kugelmikrofon *n* omnidirectional
microphone
Kühlgebläse *n* cooling blower
Kühlgefäß *n* cooling vessel
Kühlkörper *m* heat sink
Kühlküvette *f* cooling tank
Kühlluft *f* cooling air
Kühlturm *m* cooling tower
Kühlung *f* cooling *n*, refrigeration *n*
Kühlwasser *n* cooling water
Kühlwasserpumpe *f* cooling-water
pump
Kükendraht *m* chicken-wire *n*
Kulisse *f* wing *n*; **musikalische ~**
background music
Kulissenfundus *m* scenery store
Kulissenhalle *f* scenery store
Kulissenklammer *f* cleat *n*, flat
clamp
Kulissenwand *f* flat *n*
Kultur* *f* cultural affairs *n pl*, arts
features* *n pl*
Kultur und Wissenschaft* science
and arts features
Kulturbericht *m* arts feature, arts
item
kulturelles Wort*
cultural affairs *n pl*
Kulturfilm *m* cultural film, cultural
documentary
Kulturkritik *f* arts review
Kulturkritiker *m* art and literary
critic
Kulturredakteur *m* arts features
editor, cultural affairs editor
Kundendienst *m* after-sales service
Kunstharzlack *m* synthetic resin
varnish
Künstler *m* artist *n*, performer *n*;
ausübender ~ performing artist,
professional artist
Künstlerfoyer *n* artists' foyer, green-
room *n*
Künstlergarderobe *f* artist's
dressing-room
künstlerisch *adj* artistic *adj*
Künstlerzimmer *n* artists' foyer,

green-room *n*
künstlich *adj* artificial *adj*,
synthetic *adj*, dummy *adj*
Kunstlicht *n* artificial light,
tungsten light
Kunstlichtemulsion *f* emulsion for
artificial light
Kunstlichtfilter *m* artificial light
filter
Kunstmaler *m* scenic artist,
background painter
Kupferverluste *m pl* copper loss
Kuppler *m* coupler *n*
Kupplersubstanz, farbige dye
coupler
Kupplung *f* coupling *n*; ~ *f* (mech.)
clutch *n*; ~ *f* (elek.) flexible
connector
Kupplungsbuchse *f* coupling sleeve
Kupplungsdose *f* connector socket
Kupplungsstecker *m* connector
plug
Kurbel *f* crank *n*
kurbeln *v* (fam.) (F) film *v*
Kurbelstativ *n* wind-up stand
Kursprogramm *n* educational
course, course *n*
Kurve *f* diagram *n*, chart *n*, curve *n*,
graph *n*; **sensitometrische ~**
sensitometric curve
Kurvenform *f* waveform *n*
Kurvenleser *m* (EDV) curve
follower, curve tracer
Kurvenschar *f* family of curves
Kurvenschreiber *m* curve-plotter *n*;
~ *m* (EDV) plotter *n*, plotting table,
plotting board, graph plotter,
graphic display unit, graphic
output unit
Kurvenzeichner *m s.*
Kurvenschreiber
Kurzbeitrag *m* insert *n*, inject *n*
kürzen *v* edit down *v*, cut *v*, trim *v*
Kurzfassung *f* abstract *n*, abridged
version, short version
Kurzfilm *m* short film, short *n*
kurzfristig *adj* short-notice *adj*,
short-term *adj*
Kurzkommentar *m* brief analysis

Kurznachricht *f* news flash
Kurznachrichten *f pl* news
summary, news headlines
kurzschließen *v* short-circuit *v*
Kurzschluß *m* short-circuit *n*
Kurzschlußbrücke *f* shorting bridge
Kurzschlußempfangsverfahren *n*
closed-circuit system, closed
circuit
Kurzschlußfestigkeit *f* resistance to
short-circuiting
Kurzschlußflux *m* short-circuit flux
Kurzschlußoszillogramm *n* short-
circuit oscillogram
Kurzschlußstecker *m* short-
circuiting plug
Kurzschlußstrom *m* short-circuit
current
Kurzschlußübertragungsverfahren
n short-circuit transmission
system
Kurzschlußverfahren *n* closed-
circuit system, closed circuit
Kurzspielfilm *m* short feature film
Kurzstopp *m* (Tonband) pause *n*,
temporary stop
Kurzwelle (KW) *f* short wave
Kurzwellensender *m* short-wave
transmitter, high-frequency
transmitter
Küvette *f* (Kopierwerk) tank *n*; ~ *f*
(Blende) fluid iris
Kybernetik *f* cybernetics *n*

L

Labor *n* laboratory *n*, lab *n* (coll.),
labs *n pl* (coll.)
Laborant *m* laboratory assistant
Laboratorium *n* laboratory *n*, lab *n*
(coll.), labs *n pl* (coll.)
Laboringenieur *m* laboratory
engineer
Labortechniker *m* laboratory
technician
Lackieren *n* varnishing *n*,

lacquering *n*, doping *n*
Ladebefehl *m* (EDV) load
instruction
Ladekassette *f* loader *n*, portable
charger
Ladekondensator *m* charging
capacitor, charging condenser
laden *v* charge *v*
Ladestrom *m* charging current
Ladewiderstand *m* charging
resistor
Ladung *f* charge *n*, electric charge
Ladungsbild *n* charge image,
charge pattern
Ladungsspeicher *m* (EDV)
electrostatic store
Ladungszustand *m* state of charge
Lageplan *m* site plan, layout plan
Lager *n* depot *n*, store *n*
~ *n* (tech.) bearing *n*
Lager* *n* stores* *n pl*
Lagergehäuse *n* bearing casing
Lagergehäuse *n* bearing casing
Lagerist *m* store-keeper *n*
lagern *v* store *v*
Lagerung *f* storage *n*
Lagerverwalter *m* stores manager
Laienschauspieler *m* amateur actor
Laminierband *n* magnetic stripe
Lampe *f* lamp *n*; **verspiegelte ~**
reflector lamp
Lampenfassung *f* lamp holder, lamp
socket
Lampenfieber *n* stage-fright *n*
Lampengalgen *m* lamp gallows
arm, lamp offset arm
Lampenhalter *m* lamp fixture
Lampenhaus *n* lamp housing
Lampenkabel *n* lamp cable
Lampenschere *f* lamp cut-out
Lampenschwärzung *f* lamp
blackening
Lampensockel *m* lamp socket
Lampenwendel *f* lamp filament
Landesrundfunkanstalt *f* regional
broadcasting station
Landesrundfunkgesetz *n* regional
broadcasting act

Landesstudio *n* (Verwaltung)
regional station; ~ *n* (Studio)
regional studio
Landfunk* *m* agricultural
programmes* *n pl*
**Landfunk, öffentlicher beweglicher
~ (ÖBL)** land mobile service
Landfunksendung *f* farmers'
programme
Länge *f* length *n*; ~ *f* (F) footage *n*
Längenmarkierung *f* footage mark
langfristig *adj* long-term *adj*, at
long notice
Längsmagnetisierung *f* longitudinal
magnetisation
Langspielband *n* long-playing tape
(LP tape)
Langspielplatte (LP) *f* long-playing
record (LP record), long-playing
disc
Längsschriftaufzeichnung *f*
longitudinal recording
Längstwellenfrequenz *f* very low
frequency (VLF)
Längswelle *f* longitudinal wave
Langwelle (LW) *f* long wave (LW),
kilometric waves *n pl*, low
frequency (LF)
Langwellenbereich *m* long-wave
band, low-frequency band
Langwellensender *m* long-wave
transmitter, low-frequency
transmitter
Langzeitstabilität *f* long-term
stability
Larseneffekt *m* Larsen effect,
microphony *n*
Laser *m* laser *n*
Lassoband *n* adhesive tape, camera
tape
Lastwiderstand, künstlicher dummy
load
Lasurfarbe *f* clear varnish,
transparent colour, transparent
ink
Latte *f* lath *n*, batten *n*, strip
board
Lauf *m* running *n*, run *n*, motion *n*,
operation *n*, travel *n*

Läufer *m* (Motor) rotor *n*
Laufgeschwindigkeit *f* operation
speed, running speed
Laufkatze *f* trolley *n*
Laufkran *m* overhead crane, mobile
hoist
Laufrichtung *f* direction of travel
Laufrolle *f* guide roller, idler *n*
Laufschiene *f* guide rail, track *n*
läuft! (fam.) running!
Laufwerk *n* transport mechanism,
drive mechanism
Laufwerkplatte *f* motor board, tape
deck
Laufzeit *f* (F) screen time, running
time; ~ *f* (Länge) length *n*,
duration *n*, timing *n*; ~ *f* (Signal)
delay time, phase delay; ~ *f*
(Verstärker) transit time
Laufzeitdemodulation *f* delay
demodulation
Laufzeitdemodulator *m* delay-line
detector
Laufzeitdifferenz *f* delay-time
difference
Laufzeiteffekt *m* group delay
distortion
Laufzeitfehler *m* phase-delay error
Laufzeitglied *n* delay line
Laufzeitkette *f* delay line, delay
network
Laufzeitleitung *f* delay line
Laufzeitröhre *f* velocity-modulated
tube
Laufzeitspeicher *m* (EDV) delay-
line memory, delay-line store
Laufzeitverzerrung *f* transit-time
distortion, phase-delay distortion,
delay distortion, phase distortion
Laufzettel *m* inter-office slip
Laut *m* sound *n*, tone *n*
Lautarchiv *n* sound archives *n pl*,
sound library
Lautbank *f* sound bank
Lautheit *f* loudness *n*
Lautheitmesser *m* loudness meter
Lautsprecher *m* loudspeaker *n*,
speaker *n*; **elektrodynamischer ~**
electrodynamic loudspeaker, coil-

Lautsprecher 96

driven loudspeaker, moving-coil loudspeaker; **elektrostatischer ~** electrostatic loudspeaker
Lautsprecheranordnung f loudspeaker layout
Lautsprecherbox f loudspeaker case
Lautsprecherchassis n loudspeaker chassis
Lautsprecherkonus m speaker cone
Lautsprecherschallwand f loudspeaker baffle
Lautsprecherschrank m loudspeaker case
Lautsprechersystem n loudspeaker system
Lautsprecherübertragung f relay by loudspeaker
Lautsprecherübertragungsanlage f public address system (PA system)
Lautstärke f sound volume, sound intensity, volume n
Lautstärkemesser m volume indicator, loudness level meter, sound level meter
Lautstärkepegel m sound level, volume level, loudness level
Lautstärkeregelung f volume control; **automatische ~ (ALR)** automatic volume control (AVC)
Lautstärkeregler (LR) m volume control
Lautstärkeumfang m volume range, dynamic range, loudness range
Lavalliermikrofon n lavalier microphone, lanyard microphone
Lavendel n duping print, lavender n
Lavendelkopie f lavender print
Lavendelmaterial n fine-grain stock for duping
LC-Glied n LC circuit
Lecherleitung f Lecher wire
Leckstrom m leakage current
Leerband n blank tape, clean tape
Leerbandteil n yellow n
Leerlauf m idling n; **~ m** (elek.) open circuit, no-load operation; **~ m** (Prod.) dead time

Leerlaufspannung f open-circuit voltage, no-load voltage
Leerlaufstrom m no-load current
Leerspule f empty spool, empty reel
Lehrfernsehen n educational television (ETV)
Lehrfilm m training film, instructional film
Lehrlingsausbilder m instructor n
Lehrmittel n pl teaching aids
Lehrplan m curriculum n, syllabus n
Lehrsendung f educational broadcast
Leichenmappe f (fam.) obituaries n pl, obits n pl (coll.)
Leihgebühr f hire fee
Leihmiete f rental fee, hire charge
Leinwand f screen n
Leiste f (Programmzeit) strand n, band n
Leistung f (elek.) power n, wattage n; **~ f** (Hilfeleistung) service n, facility n
Leistungsaufnahme f power consumption
Leistungsfähigkeit f (elek.) capacity n
Leistungsschalter m circuit-breaker n
Leistungsschutzrecht n neighbouring rights n pl
Leistungsverstärker m power amplifier
Leitartikel m leading article, leader n, editorial n
leitartikeln v (fam.) editorialise v
Leitartikler m leader-writer n, editorialist n (US), editorial-writer n (US)
Leiter m manager n, chief n, head n **~ m** (elek.) conductor n; **~ der Disposition** planning manager; **~ vom Dienst** (LvD) duty officer
Leiterplatte f printed circuit board (PCB)
Leitfähigkeit f conductivity n
Leitung f (Organisation)

management *n*; ~ *f* (elek.) circuit *n*,
wire *n*, lead *n*; ~ *f* (Übertragung)
cable *n*, line *n*; ~ **einrichten** to set
up a circuit; ~ **ist tot!** line's dead!,
circuit down!; ~ **steht!** circuit up!;
abgehende ~ outgoing circuit,
outgoing line, outgoing channel;
abgeschlossene ~ terminated line,
closed line; **ankommende** ~
incoming circuit, incoming line,
incoming channel; **bespulte** ~
Pupin line, coil-loaded circuit;
gerichtete ~ one-way circuit,
unidirectional circuit; **homogene**
~ homogeneous line, uniform line;
in der ~ **haben** to have on the line
in der ~ **sein** to be on the line;
nachgebildete ~ simulated line,
pad *n*; **offene** ~ open-ended line;
stehende ~ permanent circuit;
über ~ **aufnehmen** to record over
a circuit, to record down the line;
über ~ **aufzeichnen** to record over
a circuit, to record down the line
Leitungsabschluß *m* line
termination, circuit termination
Leitungsabschnitt *m* circuit section,
section of line
Leitungsanpaßtransformator *m* line
matching transformer
Leitungsausgang *m* line output
Leitungsbestellung *f* line booking
Leitungsbrumm *m* line hum
Leitungsbüro *n* line bookings
section, circuit allocation unit
Leitungsdämpfung *f* line
attenuation, line loss
Leitungseingang *m* line input
Leitungsendpunkt *m* terminal
point, terminal *n*, line terminal
Leitungsentzerrer *m* line equaliser
Leitungsfehler *m* line fault
Leitungsnachbildung *f* line balance
Leitungsnetz *n* distributing
network, network *n*, distribution
network; **vermaschtes** ~
interconnected network
Leitungsprüfung *f* line check,

proving circuit
Leitungsüberspielung *f* line feed
Leitungsübertrager *m* line
transformer
Leitungsunterbrechung *f*
disconnection *n*
Leitungsverlust *m* line loss
Leitungsverstärker *m* line amplifier
Leitweg *m* route *n*
Leitwert *m* (Gleichstrom)
conductance *n*; ~ *m*
(Wechselstrom) susceptance *n*;
komplexer ~ admittance *n*
Lektor *m* script-reader *n*
Lektorat *n* script unit
Lesebefehl *m* (EDV) read statement
Lesekopf *m* (EDV) read head,
reading head
Leseprobe *f* first reading, read-
through *n*
Lesung *f* reading *n*
Leuchtdichte *f* luminous density,
luminance *n*, brightness *n*
**Leuchtdichte/Chrominanz-
Übersprechen** *n* cross-colour *n*
Leuchtdichtemesser *m* lumen
meter, brightness meter
Leuchtdichtepegel *m* luminance
level
Leuchtdichtesignal *n* luminance
signal
Leuchtdichtestruktur *f* luminous
texture
Leuchtdichteumfang *m* range of
luminance, contrast range
Leuchtdrucktaste *f* luminous push
button
Leuchte *f* lamp *n*
Leuchtfeld *n* indicator panel, light
display panel
Leuchtfleck *m* bright spot, hot spot
Leuchtphosphor *m* (Bildröhre)
phosphor *n*
Leuchtschicht *f* luminous coating
Leuchtschirm *m* luminescent
screen, fluorescent screen,
phosphor cathode-ray screen
Leuchtstift *m* (EDV) light pen

Leuchtstoff *m* luminescent material, phosphorescent material, fluorescent material

Leuchtstofflampe *f* fluorescent lamp

Leuchtstoffröhre *f* discharged lamp

Leuchtstoffschirm *m* luminescent screen, fluorescent screen, phosphor cathode-ray screen

Leuchtzeichen *n* light indicator, cue light

Leuchtzifferanzeige *f* luminous digital indicator

Libelle *f* spirit level

Licht *n* light *n*; ~ **abblenden** to dim the light, to take down the light, to reduce lighting level, to fade down the light; ~ **abstufen** to step down the light; ~ **aufblenden** to increase lighting level, to fade up the light; ~ **aus!** lights out!, kill the lights!; ~ **bestimmen** (Kopierwerk) grade *v*; ~ **bestimmen** (Beleuchtung) to set the light level; ~ **ein!** lights!, lights on!; ~ **einrichten** to set the lights; ~ **setzen** to set the lights; **alles ~ !** lights up!; **diffuses ~** diffuse light, diffused light, scattered light; **einfallendes ~** incident light; **flaches ~** flat light; **gedämpftes ~** dimmed light, subdued light; **gerichtetes ~** parallel light rays; **hartes ~** hard light; **reflektiertes ~** reflected light; **steiles ~** steep light; **ultraviolettes ~** ultraviolet light; **weiches ~** soft light, diffuse light

Lichtanzeige *f* light indication, light reading

Lichtausbeute *f* light output, light yield

Lichtausgleichfilter *m* light correction filter

Lichtband *n* light-control tape

Lichtbauzeit *f* lighting rigging time

Lichtbestimmer *m* timer *n*, grader *n*

Lichtbestimmung *f* grading *n*, timing *n*

Lichtbestimmungskopie *f* grading copy, grading print

Lichtbestimmungsplan *m* grading chart

Lichtbestimmungstisch *m* grading bench

Lichtbild *n* photo *n*, still *n*; ~ *n* (Dia) transparency *n*, slide *n*

Lichtbildreihe *f* slide sequence *n*

Lichtblende *f* barndoor *n*, flag *n*, gobo *n*, nigger *n*, frenchman *n*

Lichtbogen *m* electric arc, arc *n*

Lichtbogenlampe *f* arc lamp

lichtdicht *adj* light-tight *adj*

Lichtdoubel *n* lighting stand-in

Lichtdurchlässigkeit *f* permeability to light

Lichteffekt *m* lighting effect

Lichtempfänger *m* light cell, photocell *n*

lichtempfindlich *adj* light-sensitive *adj*, photosensitive *adj*

Lichtempfindlichkeit *f* light sensitivity, photosensitivity *n*

Lichter *n pl* (Bild) highlights *n pl*, lights *n pl*

Lichterschwärzung *f* lamp blackening

Lichtfarbe *f* colour of light

Lichtfarbmeßgerät *n* Kelvin meter, colour temperature meter

Lichtfeld *n* light box, spotting box

Lichtfleck *m* light spot

Lichtflußkompensation *f* light flux compensation

Lichtführung *f* direction of lighting, light direction

Lichtgestalter *m* lighting cameraman, director of photography, lighting director

Lichtgestaltung *f* direction of lighting, light direction

Lichtgitter *n* lighting grid

Lichthof *m* halation *n*, halo *n*

lichthoffrei *adj* anti-halation *adj*, anti-halo *adj*, non-halating *adj*

Lichthofschutz *m* anti-halation *n*
Lichthofschutzschicht *f* anti-halation layer, anti-halation backing, film backing
Lichtingenieur *m* lighting supervisor
Lichtintensität *f* light intensity
Lichtkasten *m* light box, spotting box
Lichtkegel *m* cone of light
Lichtleiste *f* lighting rail; **senkrechte** ~ top lighting; **waagerechte** ~ side lighting
Lichtleistung *f* light output, luminous efficiency
Lichtlinie, quasioptische line-of-sight path
Lichtmarke *f* light spot
Lichtmaschine *f* generator *n*; **fahrbare** ~ mobile generator
Lichtmeßgerät *n* light meter, photometer *n*
Lichtmessung *f* photometry *n*
Lichtmodell *n* mimic diagram
Lichtmodulation *f* light modulation
Lichtnetz *n* lighting power circuit, mains lighting supply, single-phase mains supply
Lichtorgel *f* lighting console
Lichtplan *m* lighting plot
Lichtpunkt *m* light spot; **abtastender** ~ scanning spot
Lichtpunktabtaster *m* flying-spot scanner
Lichtpunktabtastung *f* flying-spot scanning
Lichtpunkthelligkeit *f* spot brightness
Lichtquelle *f* light source, luminous source
Lichtrampe *f* footlights *n pl*
Lichtregelanlage *f* lighting-control console, lighting-control equipment, lighting console
Lichtregeleinheit *f* lighting rectifier unit, lighting-control unit
Lichtregie *f* lighting control
Lichtregler *m* dimmer *n*

Lichtrichtung *f* direction of light
Lichtschleier *m* light fog, light fogging
Lichtschleuse *f* light trap
Lichtschranke *f* light barrier
Lichtschreibgerät *n* light pen
Lichtsetzung *f* lighting setting, lighting set-up
Lichtspalt *m* light gap, light slit
Lichtspieltheater *n* cinema *n*, picture house, pictures *n pl* (coll.), movie theater (US)
Lichtsprung *m* sudden light change
Lichtstärke *f* luminous intensity, light intensity, candle-power *n*; ~ *f* (Objektiv) lens speed; ~ *f* (Scheinwerfer) light intensity; ~ **eines Suchers** viewfinder brightness
Lichtstellanlage *f* lighting-control console, lighting-control equipment, lighting console
Lichtsteuerband *n* light-control tape
Lichtsteuerpult *n* lighting-control desk, lighting-control panel
Lichtsteuerraum *m* lighting control room
Lichtsteuerung *f* lighting control
Lichtstrahl *m* light beam, light ray; **gebündelter** ~ focused beam; **gestreuter** ~ scattered beam
Lichtstrahlschreiber *m* light pen
Lichtstrahlung *f* light radiation
Lichtstrom *m* light flux, luminous flux, lamp current
Lichtstrommessung *f* luminous-flux measurement
Lichtton *m* optical sound; **kombinierter** ~ **(COMOPT)** combined optical sound (COMOPT); **separater** ~ **(SEPOPT)** separate optical sound (SEPOPT)
Lichttonabtaster *m* optical-sound head
Lichttonkamera *f* optical-sound recorder
Lichttonkopie *f* optical-sound print

Lichttonlampe *f* optical-sound lamp, exciter lamp

Lichttonnegativ *n* optical-sound negative

Lichttonspur *f* optical-sound track

Lichttonumspielung *f* optical-sound transfer

Lichttonwobbelfilm *m* buzz-track film

Lichtübergang *m* light cross-over

lichtundurchlässig *adj* light-proof *adj*, light-tight *adj*, opaque *adj*

Lichtverlust *m* light loss

Lichtverteilung *f* light distribution

Lichtverteilungskurve *f* light distribution curve

Lichtvorhang *m* light curtain

Lichtwagen *m* (Außen) lighting truck, lighting vehicle, lighting van; ~ *m* (Studio) lighting trolley

Lichtwanne *f* lighting float, broad source, broad *n*, lighting trough

Lichtwert *m* (Beleuchtung) light-value level; ~ *m* (Kopierwerk) exposure value, light value

Lichtwertregler *m* (Beleuchtung) intensity control; ~ *m* (Kopierwerk) light-change control

Lichtwertzahl *f* (Beleuchtung) light-value number; ~ *f* (Kopierwerk) light-change point, printer point

Lichtwurflampe *f* projector lamp

Lichtzeichen *n* light signal, cue light

Lichtzeiger im Bildfeld indication on picture

Lichtzeigeranzeige *f* visual display

Lichtzeile *f* lighting rail, row of lights

Lichtzerlegung *f* dispersion of light

Lichtzettel *m* (Beleuchtung) luminance chart; ~ *m* (Kopierwerk) grading chart

Lichtzwischenschaltung *f* (Kopierwerk) printed-light control

Liegenschaften* *f pl* planning and building maintenance*

Liliput *m* baby spot

Linearität *f* linearity *n*; ~ **der Ablenkung** sweep linearity, scan linearity

Linearitätsfehler *m* linearity error, linearity defect

Linearitätsspektrum *n* line spectrum

Linearitätstestbild *n* linearity test pattern

Liniengitter *n* line grating

Linkssignal (L-Signal) *n* left signal

Linkstrecke *f* link coupling, link line

Linse *f* lens *n*, objective *n*; ~ **fahren** zoom *v*; **akustische** ~ acoustic lens **elektromagnetische** ~ electromagnetic lens; **elektronische** ~ electronic lens; **elektrostatische** ~ electrostatic lens, focusing electrode; **Fresnelsche** ~ Fresnel lens; **gehämmerte** ~ hammered lens; **gekittete** ~ cemented lens; **klare** ~ clear lens; **matte** ~ matt lens; **Stärke einer** ~ lens strength

Linsenantenne *f* lens aerial

Linsendurchmesser *m* lens diameter

Linseneffekt *m* lens flare

Linsenfehler *m* lens error, flaw *n*, lens impairment, lens aberration

Linsensatz *m* set of lenses

Linsenschutzglas *n* safety glass

Lippenmikrofon *n* lip microphone

lippensynchron *adj* lip-sync *adj*

Litze *f* litz wire

live *adv* live *adv*; ~ **senden** to broadcast live

Livebeitrag *m* live insert, live inject

Liveproduktion *f* live production, live show

Liveprogramm *n* live programme

Livereportage *f* live commentary, live relay

Livesendung *f* live transmission, live broadcast; **zeitversetzte** ~ deferred relay

Livestudio *n* live studio

Liveübertragung f live transmission, live relay
Lizenz f licence n
Lizenzabteilung f licensing department
Lizenzbetrag m licence fee
Lizenzdauer f licence period
Lizenzgeber m licenser n, licensing authority
Lizenzgebühr f licence fee, royalty n, royalties n pl
Lizenzinhaber m licensee n
Lizenznehmer m licensee n
lochen v (EDV) perforate v, punch v
Locher m (Person) perforator n, puncher n; ~ m (Gerät) punch n
Lochfilter m (elek.) notch filter
Lochkarte f (EDV) punch card, punched card
Lochkartenspalte f (EDV) card column
Lochkartenzeile f (EDV) row n
Lochkombination f (EDV) punch combination
Lochmaske f (Bildröhre) shadow mask
Lochstanze f punching machine
Lochstreifen m (EDV) punched tape, paper tape, perforated tape
Lochstreifencode m (EDV) paper tape code
Lochstreifengerät n (EDV) paper tape unit, paper tape device
Lochstreifenkarte f (EDV) tape card
Lochstreifenleser m (EDV) punched tape reader, paper tape reader
Lochstreifenlocher m (EDV) paper tape punch, tape perforator
Lochstreifenstanzer m (EDV) tape punch, perforator n
locken v (Oszillator) lock in v
Logik, interne (EDV) internal logic
Logik-Baustein m (EDV) logic unit
Logikschaltbild n (EDV) logic diagram, functional diagram
Lohn m pay n, wages n pl
Lohnempfänger m pl weekly-paid staff

Lokalelement n electrolysis junction
Lokalnachrichten f pl local news
Lokaltermin m recce n (coll.)
Lokomotive f (fam.) audience-puller n (coll.)
Longe f picketing cable
Longitudinalwelle f longitudinal wave
Löschdämpfung f attenuation of erasure
Löschdrossel f bulk eraser
löschen v erase v, wipe v
Löschfrequenz f erase frequency
Löschgenerator m erase oscillator
Löschgerät n (Band) bulk eraser
Löschkopf m erasing head, erase head, wiping head
Löschspannung f erase voltage
Löschsperre f erase cut-out key
Löschstrom m erasing current, erase current
Löschung f (Band) erasing n, erasion n, erasure n, wiping n; ~ f (Licht) extinction n
Lösung f (chem.) solution n
Lösungsmittel n solvent n
lötbar adj solderable adj
Lötdurchführung f soldering bushing
Lötigel m soldered tag block, main distribution frame (MDF)
Lötkolben m soldering iron
Lötkolbenspitze f copper bit
Lötöse f soldering lug, soldering tag
Lötösenstreifen m soldering-lug strip, soldering-tag strip
Lötpin m soldering pin
Lötpistole f soldering gun
Lötstelle f soldered joint, soldered seam; **fehlerhafte** ~ dry joint; **kalte** ~ dry joint
Lötstift m soldering pin
Low-band n low band
Low-band-Norm f low-band standards n pl
Low-key n low key
Luft f air n; ~ **geben** (Dreh) widen

Luft 102

out *v*, pull out *v*; **zuviel** ~ (Bild) too
wide, too loose; **zuviel** ~ (Text)
underscripted *adj*; **zuwenig** ~
(Bild) too tight, too close; **zuwenig**
~ (Text) overscripted *adj*
Luftansauger *m* air intake
Luftaufnahme *f* aerial photograph
Luftbild *n* (opt.) virtual image
Luftbildebene *f* virtual image plane
Luftfilter *m* air filter
Luftleitung *f* open-wire line,
overhead line
Luftperspektive *f* bird's-eye view
Luftspalt *m* head gap, magnetic gap
Lufttrimmer *m* air trimmer
Luftumwälzung *f* air circulation
Lüftung *f* ventilation *n*
Luftverbindung *f* airborne link
Luminanz *f* luminance *n*
Luminanzsignal *n* luminance signal
Luminanzspektrum *n* luminance
range, luminance spectrum
Lumineszenz *f* luminescence *n*
Lupe *f* magnifying glass,
magnifying lens, magnifier *n*
Lüsterklemme *f* porcelain insulator,
chocolate block (coll.)
Lustspielfilm *m* comedy film
Luxmeter *n* luxmeter *n*,
illumination photometer

M

Madenschraube *f* grub screw,
headless screw
Magazin *n* (Lager) depot *n*, store *n*;
~ *n* (Kassette) magazine *n*,
cassette *n*,
cartridge *n*; ~ *n* (Programmform)
magazine *n*; ~ *n* (Zeitschrift)
periodical *n*, magazine *n*;
aktuelles ~ topical magazine;
literarisches ~ literary magazine,
cultural magazine, book
programme
Magazinsendung *f* magazine

programme
Magnesiumfackel *f* magnesium
flare
Magnetaufzeichnung *f* magnetic
recording
Magnetausgleichsspur *f* magnetic
balance track, balancing magnetic
stripe, balancing stripe
Magnetband *n* magnetic tape;
beschichtetes ~ coated tape
Magnetbandgerät *n* (EDV) magnetic
tape unit
Magnetbandkassette *f* (EDV)
magnetic tape cartridge
Magnetbandlaufwerk *n* (EDV)
magnetic tape drive
Magnetbandspeicher *m* (EDV)
magnetic tape store
Magnetbandverformung *f* tape
curling, tape deformation
Magnetbezugsband *n* standard
magnetic tape, reference tape,
test tape, calibration tape
Magnetbild *n* magnetic picture,
magnetically recorded image
Magnetbildaufzeichnung (MAZ) *f*
video tape recording (VTR)
**Magnetbildaufzeichnungs- und
Wiedergabeanlage** *f* video
recorder/reproducer
**Magnetbildaufzeichnungsanlage,
MAZ** *f* (fam.) video tape recorder
(VTR), television tape recorder,
ampex *n* (coll.)
Magnetbildwiedergabeanlage *f*
video tape reproducer
Magnetdraht *m* magnetic wire
Magnetfeld *n* magnetic field
Magnetfilm *m* magnetic sound film
Magnetfilmlaufwerk *n* magnetic
film mechanism
Magnetfilmverformung *f* magnetic
film deformation
Magnetfluß *m* magnetic flux;
remanenter ~ residual magnetic
flux, remanent magnetic flux
magnetisch *adj* magnetic *adj*
magnetische Aufzeichnungsanlage

103 Manteltarifvertrag

magnetic recorder;
~ **Bildaufzeichnung (MAZ)** video
tape recording (VTR)
Magnetisierung f magnetisation n
Magnetismus m magnetism n;
remanenter ~ residual
magnetism, remanent magnetism,
remanence n
Magnetkarte f (EDV) magnetic card
Magnetkern m (EDV) magnetic core
Magnetkopf m magnetic head;
kombinierter ~
recording/reproducing magnetic
head
Magnetkopfrad n head wheel
Magnetmittenspur f magnetic
centre track
Magnetofon n magnetic recorder,
tape recorder, magnetic tape
recorder
Magnetofongerät n magnetic
recorder, tape recorder, magnetic
tape recorder
Magnetofonraum m recording
channel
Magnetperfoband n perforated
magnetic tape, perforated
magnetic film, magnetic film
Magnetplatte f magnetic disc
Magnetplattenspeicher m (EDV)
magnetic disc store
Magnetrandbeschichten n magnetic
striping, magnetic lamination
Magnetrandbespuren n magnetic
striping, magnetic lamination
Magnetrandspur f magnetic track
Magnetschichtträger m tape base
Magnetschriftträger m magnetic
recording medium
Magnetschutzschalter m magnetic
circuit-breaker
Magnetsplitfilm m perforated
magnetic tape, perforated
magnetic film, magnetic film
Magnetspule f magnetic coil, field
coil
Magnetspur f magnetic track
Magnettaste f magnetic button

Magnetton m magnetic sound;
kombinierter ~ (COMMAG)
combined magnetic sound
(COMMAG); **separater ~
(SEPMAG)** separate magnetic
sound (SEPMAG); **separater ~ auf
zwei Spuren (SEPDUMAG)** two
separate magnetic sound tracks
(SEPDUMAG)
Magnettonaufnahme f magnetic
sound recording
Magnettonband n magnetic sound
tape, magnetic tape
Magnettondraht m magnetic wire,
recording wire
Magnettongerät n magnetic
recorder, tape recorder, magnetic
tape recorder
Magnettonkopf m magnetic sound
head, magnetic head
Magnettonmaterial n magnetic
recording medium
Magnettonwiedergabe f magnetic
sound reproduction
Magnettrommelspeicher m (EDV)
magnetic drum store
Magnetverstärker m magnetic
amplifier
Magoptical-Kopie f magoptical
print, magoptical copy, combined
print
Makroaufnahme f extreme close-up
(ECU), macro shot
Makroaufruf m (EDV) macro
instruction
Makrodefinition f (EDV) macro
definition
Makrokilar m pack-shot lens
Maler m painter n
Malteserkreuz n maltese cross,
Geneva cross
Malteserkreuzgetriebe n maltese
cross assembly, Geneva
movement
Malteserkreuzwelle f maltese cross
transmission
Manganin n manganin n
Manteltarifvertrag m skeleton

Manteltarifvertrag   104

agreement
manuell *adj* manual *adj*
Manuskript (MS) *n* manuscript
  (MS) *n*, script *n*, scenario *n*
Marionettenspieler *m* marionette
  player, puppeteer *n*
Marke *f* mark *n*, marker *n*, sign *n*,
  pip *n*, cue *n*
Markenwerbung *f* brand
  advertising
Markierung *f* cue *n*, mark *n*,
  marker *n*, marking *n*; **akustische**
  ~ acoustic cue
Markierungsleser *m* (EDV) optical
  mark reader
Markiervorrichtung *f* marking
  device, marker *n*; **automatische** ~
  automatic scene marking;
  drahtlose ~ radio scene marking
Marron *n* red master
Marronkopie *f* fine-grain print
Maschinenbefehl *m* (EDV)
  computer instruction, machine
  instruction
Maschinenbuchhalter *m*
  accounting-machine operator
Maschinenbuchhaltung *f*
  mechanised book-keeping
Maschineninstruktion *f* (EDV)
  computer instruction, machine
  instruction
Maschinensprache *f* (EDV)
  machine language
Maske *f* mask *n*, make-up *n*; ~ *f*
  (Kamera) mask *n*, matte *n*,
  vignette *n*, border *n*; ~ *f* (Person)
  (fam.) make-up artist; ~ *f* (Raum)
  (fam.) make-up room; ~ **machen**
  make up *v*; **mit** ~ **kopieren**
  (Kopierwerk) to print with matte
  effect
Maskenbildner *m* make-up artist
Maskenbildnerei *f* make-up
  department
Maskenbildnerwerkstatt *f* make-up
  room
Maskenröhre *f* shadow mask tube
Maskenvorlage *f* make-up

reference
maskieren *v* (Kopierwerk) mask *v*
Maß *n* scale *n*, measure *n*,
  dimension *n*, measurement *n*; ~ *n*
  (Kostüm) measure *n*, size *n*
Masse *f* (elek.) ground *n*
Masseband *n* (Erdung) earthing
  strap, earthing braid
Massekern *m* dust core
Massenkommunikationsmittel *n*
  instrument of mass
  communication
Massenkomparserie *f* crowd extras
  n pl, crowd supers *n pl* (US)
Massenmedien *n pl* mass media
Massenszene *f* crowd scene
Mast *m* mast *n*, pylon *n*
Mastbefeuerung *f* mast warning
  lights *n pl*
Mastdurchführung *f* (Ant.) mast
  lead-through
Masthöhe *f* mast height
Mastneigungsmesser *m* mast
  inclinometer
Mastverstärker *m* mast-head
  amplifier
Mastweiche *f* (Ant.) mast diplexer
Material *n* material *n*;
  aufgezeichnetes ~ recorded
  material
Materialassistent *m* film material
  assistant
Materialbericht *m* (F) film material
  report
Matrix *f* matrix *n*; **lineare** ~ linear
  matrix
Matrixdrucker *m* (EDV) matrix
  printer, mosaic printer, wire
  printer, stylus printer
Matrixschaltung *f* matrix circuit
Matrixstufe *f* matrix stage
Matrize *f* matrix *n*; ~ *f* (Platte)
  stamper *n*
matrizieren *v* matrix *v*
matt *adj* matt *adj*, dull *adj*
Mattscheibe *f* ground-glass screen,
  ground-glass plate; ~ *f* (fam.)
  television receiver, television set,

television *n* (coll.)

Mäusezähnchen *n pl* jitters *n pl*, mouse's teeth, serrations *n pl*

Maximalamplitude *f* maximum amplitude

Maximalbildfeld *n* maximum field of view

Maximalfeldwinkel *m* maximum field angle

Maximalsignalpegel *m* peak signal level

MAZ *f* (fam.) *s.* magnetische Bildaufzeichnung, Magnetbildaufzeichnung; ~ **ab!** roll VTR!; ~ **aufzeichnen** VTR *v*, VT *v*, tape *v*

MAZ-Bericht, zusammenfassender VTR summary

MAZ-Cutter *m* VT editor

MAZ-Disposition *f* VTR allocation

mazen *v* (fam.) VTR *v*, VT *v*, tape *v* (fam.)

MAZ-Kontrolle *f* VT control, VTR control

MAZ-Material *n* (Beitrag) VT recording

MAZ-Raum *m* VT area, VT room, VT cubicle

MAZ-Schneideeinrichtung *f* VT editing system; **elektronische** ~ electronic editing system, editec *n*

MAZ-Schneideimpuls *m* VT edit pulse

MAZ-Schnitt *m* VT editing

MAZ-Techniker *m* VT operator, VT engineer/editor

MAZ-Wagen *m* mobile video tape recorder (MVTR)

mechanisch *adj* mechanical *adj*

Medienverbund *m* joint media *n pl*

Medienverbundsystem *n* multi-media system

Mehrbereich- (in Zus.) multi-range *adj*

Mehrbereichantenne *f* multi-channel aerial

Mehrbereichladegerät *n* multi-range battery-charger

Mehrbereichverstärker *m* wide-band amplifier, multi-band amplifier

Mehrbereichverteiler *m* wide-band distributor

Mehrebenen- (in Zus.) multi-level *adj*

Mehrfachbandspieler *m* multi-track tape recorder

Mehrfachbuchse *f* multiple socket

Mehrfachecho *n* multiple echo, flutter echo (US)

Mehrfachgegensprechanlage *f* multiple talkback system

Mehrfachkabel *n* multiple cable

Mehrfachkontaktleiste *f* multi-contact strip, multi-socket strip

Mehrfachkontur *f* multiple ghosting

Mehrfachmeßgerät *n* multimeter *n*

Mehrfachmodulation *f* multi-channel modulation, multiplex modulation

Mehrfachmodulationssystem *n* multi-modulation system

Mehrfachmodulationsweg *m* multi-channel modulation link

Mehrfachstecker *m* multi-point connection

Mehrfachsteckvorrichtung *f* socket-outlet adapter

Mehrfachsucher *m* zoomfinder *n*, auxiliary finder

Mehrfarbenverfahren *n* polychromatic process, polychrome system

mehrfarbig *adj* polychromatic *adj*, polychrome *adj*, multi-coloured *adj*

Mehrgitterröhre *f* multi-grid valve, multi-grid tube

Mehrkanal- (in Zus.) multi-channel *adj*

Mehrkanalverstärker *m* multi-channel amplifier

mehrpolig *adj* multipolar *adj*, multiple-pole *adj*

Mehrschichtenfarbfilm *m* multi-

Mehrschichtenfarbfilm 106

layer colour film
Mehrsignalaufzeichnung *f*
synchronous recording
Mehrspur- (in Zus.) multi-track *adj*
Mehrspurbandmaschine *f* multi-track tape recorder
Mehrzackenschrift *f* multilateral sound track
Meldeleitung *f* control circuit, control line
Meldeleitungsnetz *n* control-circuit network
Meldung *f* message *n*; ~ *f* (Nachrichten) news item, news story, news report, item *n*; **letzte** ~ stop press
Meldungsanfall *m* news intake
Membran *f* membrane *n*, diaphragm *n*
Merkspur *f* cue track, control track
Meß- und Empfangsstation *f* receiving and measuring station
Meßadapter *m* matching unit, measuring adapter
Meßanzeige *f* meter reading, reading *n*
Meßausgang *m* measurement output, test output
Meßbereich *m* measurement range
Meßbereichserweiterung *f* measurement-range extension
Meßbrücke *f* measuring bridge
Meßbuchse *f* test socket, test jack
Meßdemodulator *m* test demodulator, measuring demodulator
Meßdienst *m* maintenance service
Meßdienst* *m* measurements* *n pl*
Meßempfindlichkeit *f* measuring sensitivity
Meßergebnis *n* test result
Messerkontakt *m* knife-edge contact
Messerleiste *f* test contact strip
Messerschmitt *m* (fam.) (Beleuchtung) flat clamp
Meßfilm *m* calibration film, test

film
Meßfühler *m* detecting element, primary element
Meßgenerator *m* signal generator
Meßgerät *n* measuring instrument, measuring apparatus
Meßgestell *n* test bay, test equipment bay
Meßingenieur *m* test engineer, maintenance engineer
Meßkopf *m* measuring head
Meßleitung *f* measuring line
Meßmischer *m* precision modulator, precision demodulator
Meßobjekt *n* test object
Meßpegel *m* test level
Meßplatz *m* test assembly, measuring desk, test set-up, measuring position, test rig
Meßprotokoll *n* test certificate
Meßpunkt *m* test point, check point
Meßraum *m* maintenance room
Meßschalter *m* test switch
Meßschaltung *f* measuring circuit, test circuit
Meßsender *m* signal generator, test oscillator
Meßsendereinkopplungspunkt *m* test point
Meßsignal *n* test signal
Meßspannung *f* test voltage, measuring voltage
Meßstation *f* measuring station
Meßstelle *f* (EDV) measuring point
Meßstellenschalter *m* check switch
Meßtechnik *f* measurement techniques *n pl*, test methods *n pl*
Meßtechnik* *f* measurements* *n pl*
Meßtechniker *m* maintenance technician
Meßton *m* line-up tone; ~ **aufschalten** to send reference tone, to send tone
Messung *f* measuring *n*, measurement *n*, testing *n*, test *n*; **densitometrische** ~ densitometric measurement

Meßverstärker *m* measuring amplifier
Meßwandler *m* measuring transformer
Meßwertaufbereitung *f* (EDV) signal conditioning
Meßwertgeber *m* (EDV) sensor *n*
Metallfolie *f* metal foil
Metallgerüst *n* metal rack, metal framework, metal scaffolding
Metallschlauch *m* flexible conduit
Meterlänge *f* footage *n*, length *n*
Meterskala *f* distance scale
Meterzähler *m* footage counter, film-footage counter
mieten *v* to take on lease, hire *v*, rent *v*
Mieten *n* hire *n*
Mietleitung *f* leased circuit, leased line
Mikro *n* (fam.) *s.* Mikrofon
Mikro- (in Zus.) micro- (compp.)
Mikrobefehl *m* (EDV) microinstruction *n*
Mikrofilm *m* microfilm *n*
Mikrofon *n* microphone *n*, mike *n* (coll.); **~ mit Achtercharakteristik** bidirectional microphone; **am ~ kleben** to hog the mike (coll.); **drahtloses ~** radio microphone; **dynamisches ~** dynamic microphone; **einseitig gerichtetes ~** unidirectional microphone; **gerichtetes ~** directional microphone; **ins ~ kriechen** (fam.) to fondle the mike, to hug the mike; **richtungsunempfindliches ~** omnidirectional microphone; **stark gebündeltes ~** beam microphone, hyperdirectional microphone; **tragbares ~** portable microphone; **ungerichtetes ~** omnidirectional microphone
Mikrofonangel *f* hand boom
Mikrofonanschlußkasten *m* microphone socket
Mikrofongalgen *m* microphone boom

Mikrofonie *f* microphony *n*
Mikrofonkapsel *f* microphone capsule
Mikrofonprobe *f* voice test
Mikrofonrauschen *n* microphone noise, microphone hiss
Mikrofonspeisung *f* microphone power supply
Mikrofonverstärker *m* microphone pre-amplifier
Mikrofonwart *m* microphone storeman
Mikrofotografie *f* microphotography *n*
mikrogeil sein (fam.) to hog the mike (coll.)
Mikrokinematografie *f* microcinematography *n*, cinemicrography *n*
Mikroprogramm *n* (EDV) microprogramme *n*
Mikroprojektion *f* microscope projection
Mikrorille *f* microgroove *n*, fine groove
Mikroschalter *m* microswitch *n*
Mikrotechnik *f* micro-circuitry *n*
Mikrowellenverstärkerstelle *f* microwave repeater point
Militärsender *m* forces station, forces network
Millimeterwellenbereich (EHF) *m* extra-high frequency (EHF)
Mime *m* (fam.) actor *n*
Minderheitenprogramm *n* minority programme
Miniaturschalter *m* microswitch *n*
Miniaturverstärker *m* midget amplifier
Mischabnahme *f* mixing approval
Mischatelier *n* mixing room, reduction room
Mischband *n* reduction material
Mischbedingungen *f pl* (Flüssigkeit) mixing conditions
Mischdiode *f* mixer diode
mischen *v* (Ton) mix *v*; **~** *v* (Bild) mix *v*, overlap *v*, cross-fade *v*,

mischen 108

blend *v*
Mischer *m* (Person und Gerät)
mixer *n*
Mischfarbe *f* mixed colour
Mischfrequenz *f* beat frequency
Mischkopf *m* mixing head,
superimposing head
Mischkristall *m* mixed crystal
Mischlicht *n* mixed light
Mischplan *m* cuesheet *n*
Mischpult *n* mixing console, mixer
n, mixing desk, control desk;
bewegliches ~ mobile mixer
Mischröhre *f* mixer valve, mixer
tube, converter tube
Mischstrom *m* mixer current,
converter current
Mischstudio *n* mixing suite,
dubbing theatre, mixing studio
Mischstufe *f* mixer stage, converter
stage
Mischtisch *m* mixing desk
Mischtonmeister *m* (F) dubbing
mixer
Mischübertrager *m* mixing
transformer, multiple input
transformer
Mischung *f* mixture *n*, mixing *n*,
mix *n*; ~ *f* (HF) converting *n*
Mischverstärker *m* mixer amplifier
Mitarbeiter *m* collaborator *n*,
colleague *n*, associate *n*; ~ *m*
(Journalist) correspondent *n*,
contributor *n*; **fester freier ~**
stringer *n*; **freier ~** free-lance *n*
Mitautor *m* co-author *n*
Mithörkontrolle *f* control line; ~ *f*
(Produktion) foldback *n*; ~ **der HF-
Modulation** monitoring of
transmitted sound signal; ~ **der
Sendemodulation** monitoring of
outgoing sound signal
Mithörleitung *f* foldback circuit
Mitnahmebereich *m* lock-in range,
pull-in range
Mitnahmesynchronisierung *f* sound
signal direct synchronisation
mitschneiden *v* (ausgestrahlte

Sendung) record *v*, to record off
air
Mitschnitt *m* simultaneous
recording, recording off air;
~ **machen** (ausgestrahlte
Sendung) record *v*, to record off
air
Mitschwenk *m* following shot
mitstoppen *v* time *v*
Mitteilung *f* (Durchsage) message *n*,
announcement *n*; ~ *f* (offiziell)
statement *n*
Mittel *n* means *n*; ~ *n* (chem.) agent
n; ~ *n pl* (Finanzen) funds *n pl*;
audiovisuelle ~ audio-visual
means; **optisches ~** optical
instrument
Mittelachse *f* central axis
Mittelanzapfung *f* centre tap
Mittelbewirtschaftung *f* budgeting
n
Mittelgrund *m* central field of
vision, middle distance
Mittelwelle (MW) *f* medium
frequency (MF), medium wave
Mittelwellenbereich *m* medium-
frequency band (MF band),
medium-wave band
Mittelwellensender *m* medium-
wave transmitter, medium-
frequency transmitter
Mittelwert *m* mean value, average
value
Mittenstellung *f* centre positioning
Mitwirkender *m* (Schauspieler)
member of cast; ~ *m* (Vertrag)
contributor *n*; ~ *m* (Mus.) player *n*
Mitwirkung *f* (Vertrag) contribution
n
mnemotechnisch *adj* mnemonic *adj*
Möbelfundus *m* furniture store,
furnishings store
Möbelrestaurator *m* furniture
restorer
Modell *n* model *n*, type *n*, design *n*,
pattern *n*; ~ *n* (Bühnenbild) model
n, miniature *n*; ~ *n* (Person)
model *n*, sitter *n*; **naturgetreues ~**

mock-up *n*
Modellbauer *m* model-maker *n*
Modellbesprechung *f* scenic model
discussion
Modellschreiner *m* pattern-maker
n, model-maker *n*
Modellsendung *f* pilot broadcast
Moderator *m* presenter *n*, anchor
man, discussion chairman,
moderator *n* (US)
moderieren *v* present *v*
Modul *m* module *n*
Modulation *f* modulation *n*; ~ **mit
doppeltem Seitenband (DSB)**
double-sideband modulation;
~ **mit unterdrücktem Träger**
suppressed-carrier modulation;
unterschwellige ~ subliminal
modulation; **unvollständige** ~
undermodulation *n*
Modulationsanzeiger *m* programme-
volume indicator, modulation
indicator, modulation meter
Modulationsausgang *m* modulation
output
Modulationsaussteuerungsmesser
m programme meter, modulation
level meter
Modulationseigenschaften *f pl*
modulation characteristics
Modulationsfrequenz (MF) *f*
modulation frequency (MF)
Modulationsgestell *n* sound bay
Modulationsgrad *m* modulation
depth, modulation factor,
modulation ratio
Modulationsindex *m* modulation
index
Modulationsklirrfaktor *m*
modulation distortion
Modulationsleitung *f* programme
circuit, programme line,
modulation circuit, music line
Modulationspegelanzeiger *m*
programme-volume indicator,
modulation indicator, modulation
meter
Modulationsrauschen *n* modulation

noise
Modulationsröhre *f* modulation
valve, modulator valve
Modulationssendeleitung *f*
programme circuit, programme
line, modulation circuit, music
line
Modulationssignal *n* programme
signal, modulation signal,
programme *n* (coll.)
Modulationstiefe *f* (opt.) depth of
modulation
**Modulationsübertragungsfunktion
(MÜF)** *f* modulation transfer
curve
Modulationsüberwachung *f*
modulation monitoring
Modulationszubringerleitung *f*
modulation feeder circuit, feeder
circuit, contribution circuit,
modulation input circuit
Modulationszubringung *f*
modulation feed, modulation
input, feed *n* (coll.)
Modulator *m* modulator *n*;
symmetrischer ~ symmetrical
modulator
modulieren *v* modulate *v*
Modultechnik *f* modular system
Moiré *n* moiré *n*, moiré pattern,
watered silks effect
Momentanwert *m* instantaneous
value
monaural *adj* monophonic *adj*,
mono *adj* (coll.)
Monitor *m* monitor *n*; ~ *m* (EDV)
monitor *n*, programme supervisor,
monitor programme
monochromatisch *adj*
monochromatic *adj*, monochrome
adj
Monoempfänger *m* mono receiver
Monopack *n* monopack *n*
monophon *adj* monophonic *adj*,
mono *adj* (coll.)
Monosignal *n* monophonic signal
Monoskop *n* monoscope *n*
Montage *f* montage *n*, cross-

Montage 110

cutting *n* (US)

Montagehalle *f* pre-setting studio

montieren *v* mount *v*, assemble *v*,
set up *v*; ~ *v* (cutten) edit *v*, cut *v*

Morsezeichen *n* Morse signal,
Morse character; **Aufnehmen von**
~ copying of Morse signals

Motiv *n* (Drehort) location *n*; ~ *n*
(Mus.) motif *n*

Motivbesichtigung *f* location
survey, recce *n*

Motivsuche *f* lining-up *n*, location
hunt, recce *n*

Motivsucher *m* viewfinder *n*

Motoranker *m* motor armature

Motorantrieb *m* motor drive

Motorschutzschalter *m* motor
protection switch

Multifokusobjektiv *n* multi-focus
lens, variable focus lens

multilateral *adj* multilateral *adj*

Multimeter *n* multimeter *n*

Multiplexer *m* diplexer *n*, dividing
filter

Multiplexsignal *n* multiplex signal

Multiplier *m* multiplier *n*

Multivibrator *m* multivibrator *n*,
multi *n* (coll.); **astabiler** ~ astable
multivibrator; **bistabiler** ~ bistable
multivibrator, flip-flop circuit,
bistable trigger, bivibrator *n*,
binary *n*;
getriggerter ~ gating
multivibrator; **monostabiler** ~
monostable multivibrator

Mundartsendung *f* dialect
broadcast

Münzfernsehen *n* pay television

Musical *n* musical *n*

Musik *f* music *n*; ~ **anlegen** to dub
with music; ~ **unterlegen** to sync
up with music; **ernste** ~ **(E-Musik)**
serious music; **getragene** ~
solemn music; **leichte** ~ **(U-Musik)**
light music; **sinfonische** ~
symphonic music; **untermalende**
~ background music, incidental
music; **zeitgenössische** ~

contemporary music

Musikarchiv *n* music archives *n pl*

Musikarrangement *n* musical
arrangement

Musikaufnahme *f* music recording;
~ *f* (F) scoring *n*

Musikaufnahmeatelier *n* music
studio, scoring stage

Musikband *n* (TV) music track; ~ *n*
(R) music tape; ~ **für
Gesangssynchronisation** voice
tape

Musikberieselung *f* piped music,
non-stop background music,
muzak *n* (coll.)

Musikbücherei *f* music library

Musikensemble *n* ensemble *n*

Musikkassette *f* music cassette

Musikkritiker *m* music critic

Musiklektorat *n* score-reading
panel

Musikmagazin *n* music magazine

Musikmaterial *n* musical material,
orchestral material

Musikprogramm *n* music
programme

Musiksendung *f* music broadcast

Musikshow *f* show *n*

Musikstudio *n* music studio,
scoring stage

Musikteppich *m* music carpet

Musiktitel *m* musical title; ~ *m* (F)
film title with music

Musiktonmeister *m* (F) music
mixer

Musiktruhe *f* radiogram *n*

Musikverleger *m* music publisher

Muster *n pl* rushes *n pl*, dailies *n pl*
(US); ~ **anlegen** to sync up rushes;
~ **ansehen** to view rushes;
~ **aussuchen** to select shots, to
make selections; ~ **trennen** to
break down rushes;
~ **zusammenstellen** rough cut *v*,
to assemble rushes

Musterkopie *f* rush print, dailies *n
pl* (US)

Musterrolle *f* rushes roll

Mutterband *n* master copy, master tape
Mutterfrequenz *f* master frequency
Muttergenerator *m* master generator
Mutteroszillator *m* master oscillator
Muttersender *m* master transmitter, master station, parent station

N

Nachaufführungstheater *n* (F) second-run theatre
Nachaufnahme *f* retake *n*
nachaufnehmen *v* retake *v*
Nachaustastung *f* post-blanking *n*, final blanking
Nachbarbildträger *m* adjacent vision carrier
Nachbarkanal *m* adjacent channel
Nachbartonfalle *f* adjacent sound channel rejector
Nachbartonträger *m* adjacent sound carrier
Nachbearbeitung *f* aftertreatment *n*
Nachbeschleunigung *f* post-acceleration *n*
Nachbildung *f* (EDV) simulation *n*
nachdrehen *v* to do a retake, reshoot *v*
nacheichen *v* recalibrate *v*
Nacheinstellung *f* retake *n*
Nachentzerrung (NE) *f* de-emphasis (DE) *n*, post-equalisation *n*
Nachführung *f* (Richtfunk) follow-up *n*
Nachführungskreis *m* locking circuit
Nachführungsoszillator *m* lockable oscillator
nachgeschaltet *adj* downstream *adj*
Nachhall *m* reverberation *n*, echo *n*
nachhallen *v* reverberate *v*, echo *v*

Nachhallplatte *f* reverberation plate, echo plate
Nachhallraum *m* reverberation room, echo chamber
Nachhallzeit *f* reverberation time (RT)
nachhängen *v* (Ton) to run late
Nachjustierung *f* readjustment *n*, realignment *n*
Nachkorrektur *f* post-correction *n*
Nachlauf *m* (Ton) hunting *n*; ~ *m* (F) tail leader, run-out *n*
Nachlauflänge *f* run-out length
Nachlaufzeit *f* running-down time, stopping time
Nachleuchtdauer *f* afterglow period, persistence *n*
nachleuchten *v* afterglow *v*; ~ *v* (Lichtgebung) to correct lighting
Nachleuchten *n* afterglow *n*, after-image *n*, persistence *n*
Nachleuchtkompensation *f* afterglow compensation
Nachmittagsprogramm *n* afternoon programme
nachproduzieren *v* retake *v*; ~ *v* (Band) re-record *v*
nachprüfen *v* check *v*
Nachricht *f* news item; ~ *f* (Fernmeldewesen) communication *n*; ~ **anheizen** play up *v*; ~ **hochspielen** play up *v* ~ **kippen** (fam.) to kill a story, to drop a story; ~ **rausbringen** (fam.) put out *v*, run *v*; ~ **sterben lassen** (fam.) to kill a story, to drop a story; ~ **unter den Tisch fallen lassen** (fam.) spike *v* (coll.); **gesprochene** ~ (TV) vision item (coll.)
Nachrichten *f pl* news *n pl*; ~ *f pl* (TV) television news; ~ *f pl* (Fernmeldewesen) communications *n pl*; ~ *f pl* (R) radio news
Nachrichtenabteilung *f* news and current affairs*
Nachrichtenagentur *f* news agency,

Nachrichtenagentur 112

wire service (US)
Nachrichtenangebot *n* news offer
Nachrichtenaustausch *m* news
  exchange
Nachrichtenbeitrag *m* news item,
  item *n*
Nachrichtendienst *m* news service
Nachrichtenfilm *m* newsfilm *n*
Nachrichtengebung *f* news release;
  ~ *f* (R,TV) news broadcasting
Nachrichtenindikativ *n* (TV)
  opening titles *n pl*
Nachrichtenmaterial *n* news
  material
Nachrichtennetz *n* communications
  network
Nachrichtenquelle *f* information
  source, news source
Nachrichtenredakteur *m* sub-editor
  n, newswriter *n* (US); ~ *m* (TV) sub-
  editor/script-writer *n*
Nachrichtenredaktion *f* newsroom
  n
Nachrichtensatellit *m*
  communications satellite
Nachrichtensendung *f* news
  broadcast, news bulletin, news
  programme, news transmission,
  newscast *n*; ~ *f* (TV) news show
  (US)
Nachrichtensperre *f* news blackout
  n, embargo *n*
Nachrichtensprecher *m* newscaster
  n, newsreader *n*; ~ **im On**
  newsreader in vision
Nachrichtenstudio *n* news studio
Nachrichtenübermittlung *f* news
  transmission *f*
Nachrichtenübertragung *f* news
  transmission *f*
Nachrichtenverarbeitung *f* (EDV)
  information processing
Nachrichtenwesen *n*
  communications *n pl*
Nachrufe *m pl* obituaries *n pl*, obits
  n pl (coll.)
nachschneiden *v* tidy up *v* (coll.)
Nachschneiden *n* (Kopierwerk)

negative cutting, chequerboard
  cutting
Nachspann *m* end titles *n pl*, end
  captions *n pl*, end credits *n pl*,
  closing titles *n pl*, closing credits
  n pl, closing captions *n pl*
nachstellen *v* reset *v*, readjust *v*;
  Szene ~ to reconstruct a scene
nachsteuern *v* follow up *v*, correct *v*
Nachsteuerspannung *f* error
  voltage (EV)
Nachsteuerspur *f* control track
Nachsteuerung *f* error correction
Nachstimmbereich *m* frequency
  trimming limits *n pl*
Nachstimmdiode *f* capacitance
  diode, varicap *n*, silicon capacitor
Nachstimmgerät *n* trimming
  apparatus
Nachsynchronisation *f* post-
  synchronisation *n*, post-synching
  n
Nachsynchronisationsstudio *n* post-
  sync studio
nachsynchronisieren *v* post-
  synchronise *v*, post-sync *v*
Nachtaufnahme *f* night shot
Nachtbetrieb *m* (Progr.) overnight
  programme operations
Nachteffektaufnahme *f* day-for-
  night shot
Nachtprogramm *n* night
  programme
Nachtrabant *m* post-equalising
  pulse
Nachtreichweite *f* (Sender) night
  range
Nachtvorstellung *f* late-night
  performance
Nachwickelrolle *f* take-up spool,
  take-up reel
Nachwuchs *m* new talent
Nachwuchsstudio *n* staff training
  school
Nachzensur *f* post-censorship *n*
Nachziehbereich *m* (Quarz) locking
  range
Nachzieheffekt *m* smearing effect,

streaking *n*, transparency effect
nachziehen *v* tighten up *v*
Nachziehen *n* afterglow *n*, after-
image *n*, streaking *n*
Nachziehfahne *f* streaking *n*
Nachziehtestbild *n* streaking test
pattern
Nadelgeräusch *n* surface noise
Nadelimpuls *m* needle pulse
nah (Einstellung) close-up (CU) *adj*;
ganz ~ big close-up (BCU), very
close shot (VCS), big close shot
(BCS)
Nahaufnahme *f* close-up (CU) *n*,
close shot (CS), close-up view (US)
~ *f* (Ton) close-perspective
recording
Nahbereichantenne *f* short-range
aerial
Nahbesprechungsmikrofon *n* close-
talking microphone, lip
microphone, noise-cancelling
microphone
Nahbesprechungsschutz *m* wind
gag
Naheinstellung *f* close-up (CU) *n*,
close shot (CS), close-up view (US)
~ *f* (Ton) close-perspective
recording
Nahempfang *m* short-range
reception
Nahempfangsgebiet *n* primary
service area, ground-wave service
area
Näherin *f* seamstress *n*
Nahkontrast *m* close contrast
Nahpunkt *m* (Sat.) perigee *n*
Nahschwund *m* short-range fading,
local fading
Nahschwundzone *f* (Sender) close-
range fading area
Nahtstelle *f* (EDV) interface *n*
Namensvorspann *m* front credits *n*
pl, opening credits *n* *pl*
NAND-Funktion *f* (EDV) NAND
operation, non-conjunction *n*,
dagger operation
Natriumdampflampe *f* sodium-

vapour lamp
Nebelmaschine *f* fog machine
Nebeltopf *m* smoke pot
Nebenbediengerät *n* extended
control panel
Nebenbedienung *f* extended control
Nebengeräusch *n* ambient noise,
wild noise, atmosphere *n*; **~** *n*
(Telefon) side-tone *n*; **~** *n*
(parasitär) electrical interference,
interference *n*
Nebenlicht *n* spill light, stray light
Nebenregie *f* sub-control room, sub
CR (coll.)
Nebenrolle *f* supporting role, small
part
Nebenschluß *m* shunt *n*, by-pass *n*
Nebenschlußleitung *f* shunt line,
parallel line, parallel circuit
Nebenschlußmotor *m* shunt motor
Nebenschlußstrom *m* bleeder
current, shunt current
Nebenschlußwiderstand *m* shunt
resistance
Nebenstudio *n* studio annex
Negativ *n* negative *n*; **~** *n* (Platte)
master *n*, metal negative;
~ abziehen to cut a negative;
eingelagertes ~ negative stock
Negativabzieher *m* negative-cutter
n
Negativabziehraum *m* negative-
cutting room
Negativabziehtisch *m* negative-
cutting bench, negative
synchroniser
Negativbericht *m* negative report
Negativbild *n* negative picture,
picture negative, negative image
Negativcutter *m* negative-cutter *n*
Negativentwicklung *f* negative
developing, negative development
Negativfarbfilm *m* colour negative,
negative colour film
Negativfilm *m* negative film,
negative stock
Negativfussel *m* dirt in the gate
Negativlichtkasten *m* negative light

Negativlichtkasten   114

box

Negativmaterial *n* negative material, negative *n*, negative stock

Negativ-Positiv-Verfahren *n* negative-positive process

Negativschmutz *m* negative sparkle

Negativschnitt *m* negative cutting

Negativschramme *f* negative scratch

Negativstaub *m* negative dirt

Negativsynchronabziehtisch *m* negative-cutting bench, negative synchroniser

Neger *m* (fam.) (TV-Text) crib card, idiot card (coll.); ~ *m* (fam.) (Beleuchtung) gobo *n*, nigger *n*

Neigekopf *m* tilt head

neigen *v* tilt *v*

Neigungswinkel *m* tilt angle, angle of inclination

Nekrolog *m* obituaries *n pl,* obits *n pl* (coll.)

Nennfrequenz *f* nominal frequency

Nennleistung *f* rated output, rated power, nominal power

Nennspannung *f* rated voltage, nominal voltage

Nest *n* (fam.) (Beleuchtung) lighting nest

Netz *n* (elek.) network *n*, mains supply, mains *n pl*, grid *n*, line *n* (US); **geregeltes** ~ regulated mains supply, stabilised mains *n pl*; **sich an das** ~ **hängen** to join the grid; **ungeregeltes** ~ unregulated mains supply, unstabilised mains *n pl*; **vermaschtes** ~ interconnecting mains *n pl*, network *n*; **vom** ~ **abgehen** to leave the grid

netzabhängig *adj* mains-operated *adj*

Netzanschluß *m* mains circuit connection, mains supply, connection to mains, line connection (US)

Netzanschlußgerät *n* power supply unit, mains power unit, power

pack

Netzausfall *m* mains failure; ~ *m* (EDV) power failure

Netzbetrieb *m* mains operation

Netzbrumm *m* mains hum

Netzeinschub *m* power unit, power supply chassis, mains supply panel

Netzfrequenz *f* mains frequency

Netzgerät *n* mains set; ~ *n* power supply unit, mains power unit, power pack

Netzgeräusch *n* mains noise, power line noise

Netzgleichrichter *m* mains rectifier, power rectifier

Netzkabel *n* power cable, power supply cable

Netzmittel *n* wetting agent

Netzmodell *n* (EDV) network analog

Netzmotor *m* mains motor

Netzplanung *f* network planning

Netzschalter *m* mains switch

Netzschalttafel *f* power panel, power switchboard

Netzschaltung *f* network switching

Netzspannung *f* mains voltage

Netzspannungsgleichhalter *m* alternating current voltage regulator, alternating current voltage stabiliser

Netzspeisung *f* mains supply operation, alternating current supply operation, mains supply

Netzstörung *f* mains failure

Netzstrom *m* mains current

Netzteil *m* power supply unit, mains power unit, power pack

Netztransformator *m* mains transformer, power transformer

netzunabhängig *adj* independent of mains

Netzverdrosselung *f* alternating current supply filter

Netzversorgung *f* power supply, mains supply

Netzverteilergestell *n* power distribution bay

Netzwerk *n* network *n*
Netzzusammenschaltung *f* network hook-up
Neues Werk* contemporary music
Neuproduktion *f* new production; ~ *f* (F) remake *n*
Neutralgraufilter *m* neutral density filter
Neutralisation *f* neutralisation *n*, balancing-out *n*
Neuverfilmung *f* remake *n*
News-Show *f* news show (US)
Nichtkopierer (NK) *m* NG take (coll.), NG *n* (coll.)
Niederfrequenz (NF) *f* low frequency (LF), audio frequency (AF), audible frequency, audio *n*
Niederfrequenzparameter *m* low-frequency parameter
Niederfrequenzpegel *m* audio-frequency level
Niederfrequenzschutzabstand *m* audio-frequency protection ratio
Niederfrequenzsignal *n* audio-frequency signal, audio signal
Niederfrequenzstörabstand *m* audio-frequency signal-to-interference ratio
Niederfrequenztransformator *m* audio-frequency transformer
Niederfrequenzverstärker *m* low-frequency amplifier, audio-frequency amplifier, sound amplifier
Niederführung *f* (Ant.) down lead
Niederschlag *m* (Kopierwerk) chemical veiling
Niederspannung *f* low tension, low voltage
Niederspannungslampe *f* low-voltage lamp, low-tension lamp
Niederspannungsnetz *n* low-voltage mains *n pl*
Niederspannungszentrale *f* low-voltage switchboard
Niedervoltlampe *f* low-voltage lamp, low-tension lamp
Niere *f* (fam.) cardioid microphone

Nierencharakteristik *f* cardioid characteristic, cardioid pattern
Nierenmikrofon *n* cardioid microphone
Nitraphotlampe *f* tungsten lamp
Nitrofilm *m* nitrate film, nitro cellulose film
Nitrolack *m* pyroxylin lacquer
Nivellierplatte *f* levelling plate
n-minus-eins-Schaltung *f* clean feed
Nonius *m* vernier *n*
NOR-Funktion *f* (EDV) NOR-function *n*, Peirce-function *n*
Norm *f* standard *n*, standard specifications *n pl*, norm *n*; ~ *f* (TV) standard *n*; **internationale** ~ international standard
Normalfilm *m* standard-gauge film, standard-gauge stock
Normalfilmformat *n* standard gauge
Normalformat *n* standard format
Normalfrequenz *f* reference frequency, standard frequency
Normalfrequenzfunkdienst mit Satelliten standard frequency satellite service
Normalfrequenzgenerator *m* standard frequency generator
Normalhörkopf *m* ideal reproducing head
Normalmagnetband *n* ideal magnetic medium
Normalwiedergabekette *f* standard replay chain
Normband *n* standard tape, reference tape
Normbauteil *n* standard component ~ *n* (Bühne) solid piece
Normbezugsband *n* standard tape, reference tape
Normblende *f* (Bühne) flat *n*
normen *v* standardise *v*
Normenausschuß *m* standards committee, standardisation committee
Normenwandler *m* standards

Normenwandler 116

converter, standards conversion
equipment
Normenwandlung *f* standards
conversion
Normschrank *m* standard rack
cabinet
Notausgang *m* emergency exit
Notbeleuchtung *f* emergency
lighting
Notdruckknopf *m* emergency
button
Notenarchiv *n* music library
Notenbearbeiter *m* music arranger
Notenblatt *n* sheet of music
Notenkorrektor *m* music proof-
reader
Notenschreiber *m* music copyist
Notreparatur *f* emergency repair
Notstromaggregat *n* emergency
power plant
Notstromgenerator *m* emergency
generator
NTC-Widerstand *m* negative
temperature coefficient resistor
(NTC resistor)
nullen *v* ground *v*
Nullerde *f* neutral *n*
Nullkopie *f* first release
Nullpegel *m* zero level
Nullpunkt *m* zero *n*
Nullpunktunterdrückung *f* offset
zero
Nullpunktverschiebung *f* (EDV) null
drift
Nullrückstellung *f* zero reset
Nullserie *f* pilot series
Nulltastimpuls *m* clamping pulse
Nulltastung *f* zero-level clamping
Nullzeit *f* zero time
Numeriermaschine für Bänder tape-
numbering machine
Nummernprogramm *n* (Mus.)
gramophone programme; ~ *n*
(Artistik) artistic programme
nuscheln *v* (fam.) mumble *v*
Nut *f* (Rille) groove *n*; ~ *f* (Schlitz)
slot *n*; ~ *f* (gekerbt) notch *n*
Nutzbereich *m* useful range,

effective range
Nutzmodulation *f* wanted
modulation
Nutzsender *m* wanted-signal
transmitter
Nutzsignal *n* wanted signal
Nutzungsberechtigter *m* (Recht)
usufructuary *n*
Nutzungsrecht *n* right of usufruct
Nuvistor *m* nuvistor *n*
Nyquistempfänger *m* Nyquist
receiver

O

Oberbeleuchter *m* chief electrician,
charge-hand electrician, head
electrician
Oberflächeninduktion *f* surface
induction
Oberingenieur *m* engineer-in-
charge *n*
Oberleitung *f* (elek.) overhead line;
künstlerische ~ art supervision
Oberlicht *n* top lighting, top light
Oberschwingung *f* harmonic
vibration, harmonic oscillation,
harmonic *n*, overtone *n*
Oberspielleiter *m* senior producer
Oberton *m* harmonic *n*, overtone *n*
Oberwelle *f* harmonic wave,
harmonic *n*
Oberwellenfilter *m* harmonic filter,
harmonic trap
Objektiv *n* objective *n*, lens *n*,
objective lens; ~ **mit**
veränderlicher Brennweite
variable focus lens, zoom lens
Objektivanzeiger *m* lens indicator
Objektivdeckel *m* lens cover, lens
cap
Objektivfassung *f* lens mount,
objective mount, lens barrel
Objektivfassungsring *m* lens-
fastening ring

Objektivfläche, gekittete cemented surface of lens
Objektivhalterung f lens mount
Objektivrevolver m lens turret, cine turret
Objektivring m lens ring, lens adapter, focusing ring
Objektivsatz m lens set
Objektivstütze f lens plate
Objektivverriegelungsgriff m lens locking lever
Objektmessung f reflected light measurement
Objektumfang m (Licht) contrast range of subject, brightness range of object
OB-Leitung f local-battery circuit, local-battery line
OB-Telefon n local-battery telephone (LB telephone)
ODER-Schaltung f (EDV) OR-circuit n, OR-gate n
Off, aus dem ~ sprechen to speak off-screen; **im ~** out of vision (OOV)
öffentlich adj public adj
Öffentlichkeitsarbeit f public relations n pl
öffentlich-rechtlich adj under public law
Off-Kommentar m voice-over n, off-screen narration, out-of-vision commentary
Off-Line-Betrieb m (EDV) off-line mode, off-line operation
Öffnung f (opt.) aperture n; **maximale ~** maximum aperture; **relative ~** aperture ratio, relative aperture
Öffnungsfehler m aperture defect, aperture error
Öffnungsverhältnis n aperture ratio
Öffnungswinkel m aperture angle
Öffnungszahl f aperture number
Öffnungszeit f (opt.) aperture time
Offset n offset n
Offsetbetrieb m offset operation
Off-Sprecher m off-screen narrator, voice-over n

Off-Stimme f off-screen voice (OSV)
Off-Text m off-screen narration script, voice-over script
Ohrfilter m psophometric filter
Ohrhörer m earpiece n, earphone n, deaf-aid n (coll.)
Ohrkurvenfilter m aural sensitivity network (ASN), psophometric filter
Okular n ocular n, eyepiece n
Ölbad n oil bath
Öltransformator m oil-filled transformer
On, im ~ sprechen to speak to camera, to be on-camera
On-Line-Betrieb m (EDV) on-line mode, on-line operation
Oper f opera n
Operand m (EDV) operand n
Operationsteil m (EDV) operation part, operator part, function part
Operette f operetta n
Opernfilm m filmed opera
Optik f optics n; **~** f (Objektiv) optical system, lens system; **vergütete ~** coated optical system
Optimalfarbe f optimum colour
optimieren v optimise v
Optimierung f optimisation n
optisch adj optical adj, visual adj
optisch-akustisch adj audio-visual adj
Oratorium n oratorio n
Orchester n orchestra n, band n
Orchesterbüro n orchestral management office
Orchesterinspektor m orchestral supervisor
Orchestermusiker m orchestral musician
Orchesterwart m orchestra attendant
Organisation f organisation n; **gemeinnützige ~** non-profit-making organisation
Organisationsbefehl m (EDV) executive instruction
Organisationsplan m organisation

Organisationsplan 118

chart
Orgelmusik *f* organ music
Original *n* (F, Band) master *n*
Originalaufzeichnung *f* master tape, original recording
Originalband *n* original tape
Originalbeitrag *m* original commentary, unedited commentary
Originalbildnegativ *n* original picture negative
Originalfassung *f* original version
Originalfernsehspiel *n* original television play, original television drama
Originalfilm *m* location film
Originalhörspiel *n* original radio play, original radio drama
Originalkopie *f* master print
Originalmotiv *n* location *n*; **am ~ drehen** to film on location
Originalmusik *f* original music
Originalnegativ *n* original negative
Originalsendung *f* original broadcast
Originaltext *m* original script
Originalton (O-Ton) *m* original sound
Originaltonnegativ *n* original sound negative
Originalübertragung *f* live transmission, live broadcast
Originalwerk *n* original work
Orthikon *n* orthicon *n*, image-orthicon tube
orthochromatisch *adj* orthochromatic *adj*
Ortsantennenanlage *f* community television (CTV)
Ortsbatterie (OB) *f* local battery (LB)
Ortsbatterieanschluß *m* local-battery connection
Ortsbatterievermittlung *f* local-battery exchange
Ortsleitung *f* local line, local circuit, local end
Ortssender *m* local transmitter, low-power transmitter
Ortszeit *f* local time
Oszillator *m* oscillator *n*, generator *n*; **angestoßener ~** flywheel oscillator, triggered oscillator; **synchronisierter ~** locked oscillator, synchronised oscillator
Oszillograf *m* oscillograph *n*, oscilloscope *n*
Oszillogramm *n* oscillogram *n*
Oxydschicht *f* oxide coating

P

Paarigkeit *f* pairing *n*
Paccoschalter *m* Pacco switch
Padding *n* padding *n*
PAL, Simple simple PAL; **Standard ~** delay-line PAL; **unverkoppeltes ~** recording PAL, PAL record; **verkoppeltes ~** transmission PAL, PAL transmit
PAL-Farbträger *m* PAL colour subcarrier
PAL-Jalousieeffekte *m pl* PAL venetian-blind effect, Hanover bars (coll.)
panchromatisch *adj* panchromatic *adj*
Panglas *n* pan filter
Panlicht *n* tungsten light
Panne *f* failure *n*, breakdown *n*; **eine ~ haben** to break down
Pannenschalter *m* cut-out switch, change-over switch
Panoramabreitwand *f* panoramic screen
Panoramaeffekt *m* panoramic effect
Panoramaempfänger *m* panoramic receiver
Panoramakopf *m* panoramic head, panning head
Panoramaregelung *f* pan control
Panoramaschwenk *m* panning shot, pan shot, panoramic movement

Panscheibe f pan filter
Papierabzug m paper print
Parabolsignal n parabolic signal
Parabolspiegel m parabolic reflector, parabolic mirror
Parabolstrahler m paraboloid n, parabolic radiator
Parallaxe f parallax n
Parallaxenausgleich m parallax compensation, parallax correction
parallaxenfrei adj parallax-free adj, free from parallax
Parallaxensucher m parallax viewfinder
Parallel-Addierwerk n (EDV) parallel adder
Parallelfahrt f crab n; ~ f (Aufnahme) lateral dolly shot
Parallelkreis m parallel circuit
Parallelschaltung f parallel connection, shunt connection
Parallelschwingkreis m parallel-resonant circuit
Parallel-Serien-Umsetzer m (EDV) parallel-serial converter
Paralleltonverfahren n parallel sound system
Parameter m parameter n
Pardune f guy rope, guy wire, stay n
Paritätsfehler m (EDV) parity error
Paritätsprüfung f (EDV) parity check
Paritybit n (EDV) parity bit
Parity-Prüfung f (EDV) parity check
Partialbelichtungsmesser m spot photometer
Partialschwingung f partial oscillation
Partitur f full score, score n, music score
Partner m partner n; ~ m (F) co-star n
Partneranstalt f twin station
Partnerschaft f partnership n; ~ f (Anstalt) twinning n
Pastellfarbe f pastel n
Pastellton m pastel tone, pastel

shade
pauschal adj all-inclusive adj, all-in adj
Pauschale f global sum, retainer n, general retainer, all-in figure, lump sum, flat rate
Pauschalgage f global fee, all-rights fee, all-in fee
Pauschalhonorar n global fee, all-rights fee, all-in fee
pauschalieren v to pay a global fee, to pay a flat rate, to contract at a global fee
Pauschalierung f payment of global fee, payment of all-in fee, flat-rate payment
Pause f (Thea.) interval n, intermission n (US); ~ f (Progr.) interval n, break n; ~ f (Zeichnung) tracing n, traced design, blueprint n
Pausenbild n interval caption, interval slide, interlude slide
Pausenfüller m fill-up n, filler n
Pausenzeichen n station identification signal, interval signal
Pegel m level n
Pegelabfall m decrease n, drop in level, fall-off n; **frequenzabhängiger** ~ roll-off n, reduction n
Pegelabweichung f level deviation
Pegelanzeige f level indication, level reading
Pegelanzeiger m level indicator
Pegelaussteuerung f level control
Pegelband n standard level tape
Pegeldiagramm n level diagram, hypsogram n
Pegeleinbruch m level breakdown
Pegelgeber m level generator, standard level generator
Pegelkontrolle f level check
Pegelkontrollgerät n level-checking set
Pegelmesser m level meter, transmission-measuring set, level-

Pegelmesser 120

measuring set
pegeln v to adjust level, line up v
Pegeln n level adjustment, line-up
n
Pegeltestband n level magnetic tape
Pegelunterschied m level difference
Pegelvektorskop n vectorscope n
Pegelverlust m loss of level
peilen v gauge v, to take bearings
Peilsender m radio beacon
Peilung f bearing n, goniometry n,
taking of bearings, radio direction-
finding, radio bearing
Peilwirkung f directivity n
Peitsche f (Kabelanschluß) splitter
n
Peitschenantenne f whip aerial
Pendelbewegung f pendulum
motion, hunting n
Pendelsäge f pendulum saw
Perfoband n perforated magnetic
film, perforated magnetic tape,
magnetic film
Perfomagnetband n s. Perfoband
Perforation f perforation n,
sprocket holes n pl;
angeschlagene ~ picked
perforation; **ausgezackte** ~
damaged perforation;
eingerissene ~ torn perforation
Perforationsloch n perforation hole,
sprocket hole
Perforationsschramme f
perforation scratch
Perforationsseite f perforated edge
Perforiermaschine f perforating
machine
perforiert adj perforated adj
Perigäum n (Sat.) perigee n
Periode f period n
periphere Einheit (EDV) peripheral
unit
Perlkondensator m bead-type
capacitor
Perlleinwand f beaded screen,
highly reflective screen
Perlwand f pearl screen
Personal n personnel n, staff n;

künstlerisches ~ artistic staff
Personalabteilung f staff
administration*
Persönlichkeitsschutz m protection
against invasion of privacy
Perücke f periwig n, wig n
Perückenfundus m wig store
Perückenmacher m wig-maker n
Perückenwerkstatt f postiche
section
Pferdesportnachrichten f pl racing
news
Pflichtenheft n standard
specifications n pl, specifications
n pl
Pförtner m porter n, door-keeper n,
commissionaire n
Phase f phase n; **aus der** ~ **bringen**
dephase v; **differentielle** ~
differential phase;
komplementäre ~ opposite phase
Phasenänderung f phase change,
phase shift
Phasenausfall m phase failure, loss
of synchronism
Phasenbild n (Trick) animation
phase; ~ n (Video) phase diagram
Phasendemodulation f phase
demodulation
Phasendrehung f phase-angle
rotation, phase shift
Phasendrehvorrichtung f phase
shifter
Phaseneinstellung f phasing n,
phase adjustment
Phasenentzerrung f phase
correction, phase equalisation,
phase compensation
Phasenfehler m phase error;
differentieller ~ differential phase
error, differential phase (coll.)
Phasenfrequenzgang m
phase/frequency characteristic,
phase response
Phasengang m phase/frequency
characteristic, phase response
Phasengangentzerrer m phase
corrector, phase equaliser

Phasenlage *f* phase position, phase relationship
Phasenlaufzeit *f* phase delay
Phasenmesser *m* phase indicator, phasemeter *n*
Phasenmodulation (PM) *f* phase modulation (PM)
Phasennacheilung *f* phase lag
Phasenregelung *f* phase control; **automatische** ~ automatic phase control (APC)
Phasenschieber *m* (elek.) phase advancer; ~ *m* (R) phase shifter
Phasenschwankung *f* phase variations *n pl*
Phasenschwankungsmesser *m* phase variation meter
Phasenselektivität *f* phase selectivity
Phasenspannung *f* phase voltage
phasenstarr *adj* phase-locked *adj*, rigid in phase, in locked-phase relation
Phasensynchronisator *m* phase synchroniser
Phasensynchronisierung *f* phase synchronisation
Phasentrick *m* stop-frame animation
Phasenüberwachung *f* phase monitoring
Phasenumkehrstufe *f* phase inverter, phase splitter, phase inverter stage
Phasenumkehrung *f* phase reversal
Phasenvergleich *m* phase comparison
Phasenvergleichsstufe *f* phase comparator stage
Phasenverhältnis *n* phase relationship
Phasenverkopplung *f* phase coupling
Phasenverschiebung *f* phase shift, phase displacement
Phasenverzerrung *f* phase distortion
Phasenvoreilung *f* phase lead

Phasenvorentzerrung *f* phase pre-correction
Phasenwinkel *m* phase angle
Phasenzeichner *m* animator *n*
Phonogerät *n* record player
Photo *n s.* Foto
Pick-up machen (Dreh) pick up *v*
Piep(s)er *m* (fam.) plop *n*, blip *n*, pip *n*
Pigmentfarbe *f* pigment colour, pigment dye
Filot *m* (fam.) pilot signal, pilot *n* (coll.)
Pilotfilm *m* pilot film
Pilotprogramm *n* pilot programme
Pilotschwingung *f* pilot reference tone, reference oscillation, pilot *n* (coll.)
Pilotsendung *f* pilot broadcast, pilot transmission
Pilotsignal *n* pilot signal, pilot *n* (coll.)
Pilotton *m* pilot tone
Pilottonanschluß *m* pilot terminal
Pilottoneinrichtung *f* pilot-tone equipment
Pilottonfrequenz *f* pilot-tone frequency
Pilottongeber *m* pilot-tone generator
Pilottonsystem *n* pilot-tone system
Pilottonverfahren *n* pilot-tone process
Pinza *f* pincer *n*, pup *n*
Pipifax *m* (fam.) baby spot
Piratensender *m* pirate station
Plakat *n* poster *n*, bill *n*
Plakatanschlag *m* billing *n*
Plakattitel *m* poster title
Planstelle *f* established post
Planung, technische technical planning, technical arrangement
Planungsingenieur *m* planning engineer; ~ *m* (UER) duty planner
Platine mit Bandmaschine tape deck; ~ **mit Plattenmaschine** record-playing deck, turntable *n* (coll.)

Platte *f* (Schallplatte) record *n*, disc
n; ~ *f* (Dekor) rostrum *n*, panel *n*;
~ *f* (Foto) photographic plate, plate
n; **gedruckte** ~ (tech.) printed
circuit board
Plattenarchiv *n* record library,
gramophone library, disc library
Plattenarchivar *m* gramophone
librarian
Plattenaufnahmegerät *n* disc
recorder
Plattendrehzahl *f* rotation speed
Platteneinheit *f* (EDV) disc drive
Plattenkamera *f* plate camera
Plattenkassette *f* (Foto) plate
holder, dark slide; ~ *f*
(Schallplatte) record album
Plattenmaschine *f* record
reproducer, record player, pick-up
n, turntable *n*, gramophone *n*,
phonograph *n* (US)
Plattenschneidegerät *n* disc
recorder
Plattenspeicher *m* (EDV) disc store,
disc memory
Plattenspieler *m* record reproducer,
record player, pick-up *n*,
turntable *n*, gramophone *n*,
phonograph *n* (US)
Plattenspielerchassis *n* record-
playing deck, turntable *n* (coll.)
Plattenspielermotor *m* turntable
motor
Plattenteller *m* record turntable,
turntable *n*, gramophone
turntable
Plattenwechsler *m* record changer;
automatischer ~ automatic record
changer, auto changer
Plausibilitätsprüfung *f* (EDV)
reasonableness check
Playback *n* playback *n*
Plotter *m* (EDV) plotter *n*, plotting
table, plotting board, curve-
plotter *n*, graph plotter, graphic
display unit, graphic output unit
Podest *n* platform *n*, stage *n*
Podiumsdiskussion *f* round-table

discussion, panel discussion
Podiumsgespräch *n s.*
Podiumsdiskussion
Pol *m* pole *n*
Polarbahn *f* polar orbit
Polarisation *f* polarisation *n*
Polarisationsfilter *m* polarising
filter
polarisieren *v* polarise *v*
polarisiert, horizontal horizontally
polarised; **vertikal** ~ vertically
polarised
Polarisierung *f* polarisation *n*
Polarität *f* polarity *n*
Polarkoordinatensystem *n* polar-
coordinate system
Polaroid-Kamera *f* polaroid
camera, polaroid *n*
polieren *v* polish *v*
Polieren *n* polishing *n*
Politik Ausland* (R, TV)
diplomatic desk, diplomatic
unit*; ~ **Inland*** (R, TV) political
desk, parliamentary desk,
parliamentary unit*; ~ **und
Zeitgeschehen*** news and
current affairs* *n pl*
Polschuh *m* pole shoe
Pore *f* pore *n*
porös *adj* porous *adj*
Positionierungszeit *f* (EDV) seek
time
Positiv *n* positive *n*, positive picture
Positivabzug *m* positive print
Positivfarbfilm *m* colour print film,
colour positive film
Positivfilm *m* positive film
Positivfilmmaterial *n* positive stock,
printed material; **flaches** ~ low-
contrast positive stock, low-
contrast positive; **steiles** ~ high-
contrast positive stock, high-
contrast positive
Positivkopie *f* positive print,
positive *n*
Positivmuster *n* positive rush print,
positive work print, test print
Poststelle *f* post room

Pot *m* (fam.) potentiometer *n*, fader *n*, pot *n* (coll.)

Potentiometer *n* potentiometer *n*, fader *n*, pot *n* (coll.); **kratzendes ~** noisy potentiometer, scratching potentiometer

Praktikabel *n* rostrum *n*

Praktikant *m* trainee *n*

Prallanode *f* dynode *n*

Präsenzfilter *m* presence filter

prasseln *v* crackle *v*

Prasseln *n* crackling *n*

Präzision *f* precision *n*

Präzisionsoffset *n* precision offset

Präzisionsquarz *m* high-precision crystal

Preemphasis *f* pre-emphasis *n*

Preisliste *f* (Prod.) rate card

Premiere *f* première *n*, first night

Presse *f* press *n*

Presseabteilung *f* publicity department, information office

Pressechef *m* press and public relations chief, head of publicity (BBC), press officer (US)

Pressedienst *m* newsletter *n*; ~ *m* (Agentur) press agency, press service

Presseempfang *m* press reception

Pressefoto *n* news picture

Pressefotograf *m* press photographer, cameraman *n*

Pressefreiheit *f* freedom of the press

Pressegesetz *n* press law

Pressekonferenz *f* press conference

Presseorgan *n* organ *n*

Pressereferent *m* press and public relations officer

Presseschau *f* press review

Presseschauredakteur *m* press review editor

Pressespiegel *m* press review

Pressestelle *f* publicity department, information office

Pressestenograf *m* press stenographer

Pressestimmen *f pl* press review

Presseverlautbarung *f* press release, statement *n*

Primäranweisung *f* (EDV) source language statement, source statement

Primärfarbauszug *m* primary colour component

Primärfarbe *f* primary colour, primary *n*

Primärschramme *f* negative scratch

Primärspeicher *m* (EDV) computing store, main memory, working store, working memory, general store

Primärstrahler *m* (Farbe) primary radiator; ~ *m* (Beleuchtung) primary ray; ~ *m* (Ant.) radiating element; ~ *m* (Sendeanlage) master station

Primärstrom *m* primary current

Primärton *m* primary tone

Primärträger *m* primary frequency

Primärvalenz *f* primary colour; **virtuelle ~** virtual primary

Prinzipschaltbild *n* basic circuit diagram

Prinzipschaltplan *m* s. Prinzipschaltbild

Prioritätsverarbeitung *f* (EDV) priority processing

Prisma *n* prism *n*

Prismensucher *m* prismatic viewfinder, prism viewfinder

Privatsender *m* commercial station

Probe *f* experiment *n*, trial *n*; ~ *f* (tech.) test *n*, check *n*, sample *n*; ~ *f* (Szene) rehearsal *n*; ~ **in der Dekoration** rehearsal on stage; **heiße ~** (TV) rehearsal with cameras; **heiße ~** (R) trial take; **kalte ~** (TV) test shot; **kalte ~** (R) rehearsal without recording

Probeablauf *m* rehearsal *n*

Probeaufnahme *f* test take, trial shot, test shot; ~ *f* (Schauspieler) screen test

Probedurchlauf *m* run-through *n*, walk-through *n*, dry run

Probefilm *m* test film
Probenhaus *n* rehearsal studios
  n pl
Probenraum *m* rehearsal room
Probenstudio *n* rehearsal studio
Probenzeit *f* rehearsal time
Probesendung *f* test transmission
Probestreifen *m* test strip
Problemstück *n* problem play
Produktdetektor *m* product
  detector, product demodulator,
  synchronous detector
Produktion *f* production *n*
Produktionsablauf *m* flow of
  production
Produktionsablaufplan *m*
  production outline
Produktionsabnahme *f* acceptance
  of production
Produktionsabteilung *f* production
  department
Produktionsanforderung *f*
  producer's estimate
Produktionsanlagen *f pl* production
  facilities
Produktionsanmeldung *f* project
  request
Produktionsart *f* type of production
Produktionsassistent *m* production
  assistant
Produktionsauftrag *m* production
  commitment
Produktionsbeistellung *f*
  production assistance
Produktionsbericht *m* data sheet
Produktionsbesprechung *f*
  production conference, planning
  meeting, production meeting, pre-
  production meeting
Produktionsbetrieb* *m*
  programme servicing department
Produktionsbewilligung *f* approval
  of production budget
Produktionsbüro *n* production
  office, routine office
Produktionschef *m* production
  manager
Produktionsdauer *f* duration of

production, production running
  time
Produktionseinheit *f* production
  unit
Produktionsetat *m* production
  budget
Produktionsfirma *f* production
  company
Produktionsgesellschaft *f s.*
  Produktionsfirma
Produktionshilfe *f* production
  assistance
Produktionsingenieur *m* technical
  operations manager (TOM)
Produktionskapazität *f* productive
  capacity, production capacity
Produktionskomplex *m* production
  centre
Produktionskosten *plt* production
  costs
Produktionsleiter (PL) *m*
  production manager
Produktionsmittel *n pl* production
  resources; **mobile ~** mobile
  equipment; **stationäre ~**
  stationary equipment; **technische**
  ~ production facilities
Produktionsmittelbereitstellung *f*
  allocation of production facilities
Produktionsplan *m* production
  schedule
Produktionssekretärin *f* production
  secretary
Produktionsspiegel *m* production
  chart
Produktionsstab *m* production staff
Produktionsstätte *f* production site
Produktionsstätten *f pl* production
  premises
Produktionsstudio *n* production
  studio
Produktionstag *m* production day
Produktionstermin *m* production
  dates *n pl*
Produktionsüberwachung *f* control
  of production
Produktionsvergabe *f* contracting
  out of production

Produktionsversicherung *f* general production insurance

Produktionszeit *f* production time

Produktionszentrum *n* production centre

Produzent *m* producer *n*; **freier ~** free-lance producer

Profi *m* (fam.) professional *n*

Programm *n* programme *n*; **~** *n* (erstes, zweites, drittes) channel *n*, service *n*; **~ fortsetzen** to return to scheduled programmes, to resume normal schedules; **~ übernehmen** *s.* Programm fortsetzen; **festverdrahtetes ~** (EDV) wired programme; **gemeinsames ~** joint programme; **gespeichertes ~** (EDV) stored programme; **ins ~ einsetzen** schedule *v*, to insert into programme; **kurzfristig angesetztes ~** programme inserted at short notice; **laufendes ~** running programme; **nationales ~** network programme, domestic programme; **symbolisches ~** (EDV) symbolic programme

Programmablauf *m* programme flow; **~** *m* (Plan) running order; **~** *m* (EDV) operation *n*

Programmablaufplan *m* running order; **~** *m* (EDV) programme flow chart, programme flow diagram

Programmabsage *f* back announcement, closing announcement

Programmabschaltung *f* (Sender) opting-out *n*, switching-off of programme

Programmabwicklung* *f* programme operations* *n pl*

Programmacher *m* programme maker, programmer *n*

Programmänderung *f* change of programme; **kurzfristige ~** last-minute programme change

Programmangebot *n* programme offer

Programmankündigung *f* trailer *n*, promotion *n*

Programmansage *f* presentation announcement

Programmanzeige *f* billing *n*

Programmausschuß *m* programme committee

Programmaustausch *m* programme exchange; **Internationaler ~** international programme exchange

Programmauswahl *f* choice of programme

Programmauswertung *f* programme rating

Programmbeirat *m* (ARD) programme advisory council

Programmbeistellung *f* programme supply

Programmbeitrag *m* programme insert, programme item, programme contribution

Programmblock *m* programme sequence, sequence *n*

Programmchef *m* (approx.) controller *n* (BBC)

Programmdirektion *f* programme directorate; **~ Fernsehen** television directorate; **~ Hörfunk** radio directorate

Programmdirektor *m* director of programmes, managing director (BBC); **~ Fernsehen** director of television programmes, managing director of television (BBC); **~ Hörfunk** director of radio programmes, managing director of radio (BBC)

Programmdisposition* *f* programme planning*

Programmdurchlauf *m* (EDV) run *n*

Programmeinblendung *f* programme insert

Programmeinheit *f* (15 Minuten) programme segment (BBC 25 minutes)

Programmeinplanung *f* current

Programmeinplanung 126

planning
Programmfahne *f* programme
schedule, programme sheet
Programmfolge *f* sequence of
programmes
Programmfüller *m* fill-up *n*,
filler *n*
Programmgestalter *m* programme
maker, programmer *n*
Programmgestaltung *f*
programming *n*, programme
policy
programmgesteuert *adj* (EDV)
programme-controlled *adj*
Programmgrundsätze *m pl*
programme standards
Programmhilfe *f* facility *n*, facilities
n pl
Programmhinweis *m* programme
promotion, programme trailer,
programme plug
Programmhinweise *m pl*
programme news, programme
information
programmieren *v* programme *v*
Programmierer *m* (EDV)
programmer *n*
Programmiersprache *f* (EDV)
programming language;
maschinennahe ~
machine-oriented language;
maschinenorientierte ~ machine-
oriented language; **problemnahe ~**
problem-oriented language;
problemorientierte ~ problem-
oriented language;
verfahrensorientierte ~ procedure-
oriented language
programmierte Unterweisung (PU)
(EDV) programmed instruction
(PI)
Programmierung *f* programming *n*
Programmingenieur *m* technical
operations manager (TOM)
Programminhalt *m* programme
content
Programmkommission *f*
programme committee

Programmkonserve *f* canned
programme
Programmkoordination *f*
programme coordination
Programmkoordinationsleitung *f*
programme coordination circuit
Programmkorrektur *f* (EDV)
debugging *n*
Programmkosten *plt* programme
costs
Programmlaufzeit *f* (EDV) object
time
Programmleiste *f* programme
strand, programme band
Programmleistung *f* programme
output
Programmleitung *f* programme
circuit, complete programme
circuit
Programmlücke *f* programme gap
Programmpersonal *n* programme
staff
Programmplan *m* programme
schedules *n pl*
Programmplanung *f* programming
n, planning *n*; **laufende ~** current
planning
Programmpool *m* programme pool
Programmproduktion *f* programme
production
Programmregie *f* presentation *n*
Programmrichtlinien *f pl*
programme standards
Programmrückspielleitung *f* return
programme circuit
Programmschema *n* programme
pattern
Programmsparte *f* programme
sector, programme field, type of
programme
Programmspeicher *m* (EDV)
programme store
Programmspeicherung *f*
programme storage; **~** *f*
(Aufnahme) programme recording
Programmstruktur *f* programme
structure
Programmtafel *f* programmes

preview, menu caption (coll.)

Programmton *m* complete sound

Programmübernahme *f* programme relay

Programmübertragung *f* programme transmission

Programmüberwachung *f* quality check

Programmunterbrechung *f* (ungewollt) break in programme; ~ *f* (gewollt) break in programmes; ~ *f* (EDV) interrupt *n*; ~ (durch Prozeß) (EDV) process interrupt

Programmusik *f* programme music

Programmverantwortung *f* editorial responsibility

Programmverbindung *f* (Überleitung) programme link, programme transition

Programmversorgung *f* programme supply

Programmvorschau *f* programme preview

Programmwahlanlage (PWA) *f* programme selector

Programmwechsel *m* change of programme

Programmzeit *f* programme period

Programmzeitschrift *f* programme journal

Programmzulieferung *f* programme supply

Projektanmeldung *f* project request

Projektauftrag *m* assignment sheet

Projektion *f* projection *n*

Projektionsapparat *m* projector *n*

Projektionsempfänger *m* projection receiver

Projektionsentfernung *f* projection distance, throw *n*

Projektionslampe *f* projector lamp

Projektionsoptik *f* projection optics, projecting lens

Projektionswinkel *m* projection angle

Projektleiter *m* project manager

Projektor *m* projector *n*

Projektorbildfenster *n* projection

gate, projection opening

Projektorfenster *n* s. Projektorbildfenster

projizieren *v* project *v*

Prospekt *m* brochure *n*; ~ *m* (Bühne) backcloth *n*; **gemalter** ~ painted backcloth

Prospektmaler *m* scenic artist

Protokoll *n* (EDV) printout *n*

Prozeßautomatisierung *f* (EDV) process automation

Prozeßbericht *m* court report

Prozeßdaten-Übertragungssystem *n* (EDV) process communication system

Prozeßdatenverarbeitungssystem *n* (EDV) process control system

Prozeßleitsystem *n* (EDV) process guiding system

Prozessor *m* (EDV) central processing unit (CPU), processing unit, processor *n*

Prozeßrechner *m* (EDV) process control computer

Prozeßsteuersystem *n* (EDV) process control system

Prozeßsteuerung *f* (EDV) process control

Prüfadapter *m* test adapter

Prüfbericht *m* check list, test report

Prüfbild *n* test chart, test card, test pattern

Prüf-Bit *n* (EDV) check bit

Prüfbuchse *f* test socket

Prüffeld *n* test department

Prüffeldingenieur *m* test engineer

Prüffilm *m* test film

Prüffrequenz *f* standard frequency, test frequency

Prüffrequenz- und Meßverfahren test and measurements *n pl*

Prüfprojektor *m* diascope *n*

Prüfsignal *n* test signal, insertion signal

Prüfsignalgeber *m* test signal generator

Prüftaste *f* test key, test signal key

Prüfton *m* test tone

Prüfung 128

Prüfung *f* test *n*, testing *n*, check *n*,
checking *n*, inspection *n*,
examination *n*
Prüfzeichen *n* (EDV) check
character
Prüfzeile *f* insertion test signal, test
line (coll.); ~ **für Kamera** camera
test; ~ **für Sendestraße** national
insertion test signal, network
insertion test signal
Prüfzeileneinmischer *m* test line
inserter
Prüfzeilengenerator *m* insertion
signal generator
Psophometer *n* psophometer *n*
PTC-Widerstand *m* PTC resistor
Publikum *n* public *n*, audience *n*
Publikumslautsprecher *m pl* public
address system (PAS)
Publizistik *f* journalism *n*
Puffer *m* (EDV) buffer store
Pufferbatterie *f* buffer battery,
balancing battery, floating battery
Pufferbetrieb *m* buffer battery
operation, buffer operation
Pufferdrossel *f* buffer choke,
isolating choke
Pult *n* desk *n*, console *n*
pumpen *v* pump *v*
Pumpen *n* bouncing *n*, breathing *n*
Pumpstativ *n* hydraulic stand
Punktgitter *n* dot grating
Punkthelligkeit *f* spot brightness
Punktlichtabtaster *m* flying-spot
scanner
Punktlichtabtastung *f* flying-spot
scanning
Punktlichtmesser *m* spotlight
meter
Punktschärfe *f* spot focus
punktsequent *adj* dot-sequential
adj
Punktsteuerung *f* (EDV) coordinate-
setting *n*
Puppenfilm *m* puppet film
Puppentrick *m* puppet animation
Puppentrickfilm *m* animated
puppet film

Pyrotechniker *m* pyrotechnician *n*,
special effects man

Q

Quadraturfehler *m* (MAZ)
quadrature error; ~ *m*
(Modulation) quadrature fault
Quadraturmodulation *f* quadrature
modulation
Quarz *m* crystal *n*
Quarzgenerator *m* crystal oscillator
Quarzlampe *f* quartz lamp
Quarzoszillator *m* crystal oscillator
Quarzscheinwiderstand *m* crystal
reactance
Quarzsteuerung *f* crystal control
Quecksilberdampflampe *f* mercury
vapour lamp
Quelle *f* (Information) source *n*; ~ *f*
(tech.) source *n*, origin *n*
Quellpunkt *m* source *n*
Quellwiderstand *m* source
impedance
Querbild *n* horizontal image,
horizontal picture
Querglied *n* (Vierpol) parallel
element
Quermagnetisierung *f* transverse
magnetisation, perpendicular
magnetisation
Quer-Paritykontrolle *f* (EDV)
vertical parity check
Querschramme *f* horizontal scratch
Querschriftaufzeichnung *f*
transverse recording, transverse
scan
Querspuraufzeichnung *f* transverse
recording, transverse scan
Querverbindung *f* interconnection
n, cross connection
Querwelle *f* transverse wave
Quittungssignal *n* (Sat.)
acknowledgement signal
Quiz *n* quiz *n*

Quizsendung *f* quiz programme

R

Rädern *n* (F) sprocket marking
Radio *n* (s. a. Rundfunk, Hörfunk, Funk) radio receiver, wireless set, radio set, radio *n*, wireless *n*, set *n*; ~ **hören** listen in *v*
radiofonisch *adj* radiophonic *adj*
Radiofrequenz (RF) *f* radio frequency (RF)
raffen *v* (Text) edit down *v*, tighten up *v*
Rahmenantenne *f* frame aerial, loop aerial
Rahmeneinblender *m* safe-area generator mixer
Rahmengeber *m* mask generator
Rahmengestell *n* frame *n*, rack *n*, bay *n*
Rahmenprogramm *n* backing programme; ~ *n* (Werbung) framework programme for commercials
Rahmenträger *m* bay support, bay *n*
Rahmenträgeruntergestell *n* rack base, base of a bay, rack footing
Rampenbegrenzungslicht *n* border light
Rampenbeleuchtung *f* foot lighting
Rampenlicht *n* footlight *n*
Randaufhellung *f* edge lighting, rim lighting
Randbelichtungsfenster *n* film-edge marker light aperture
randbespuren *v* stripe *v*
Randeffekt *m* edge fringing, fringe effect
Rändelknopf *m* milled knob, knurled knob
Rändelscheibe *f* knurled wheel, milled wheel
Randmarkierung *f* edge marking

randnumerieren *v* edge-number *v*, rubber-number *v*
Randnumerierung *f* edge numbering, rubber numbering
Random-Access-Programmierung *f* (EDV) random-access programming
Randschärfe *f* (Bild) marginal definition
Randschleier *m* edge fog
Randspur *f* edge track
Randspurbelichtung *f* exposure of optical track
Randunschärfe *f* blurred edges *n pl*, soft edges *n pl*
Randzonensender *m* peripheral station
Rangierfeld *n* distribution panel, cross-connection field
Rangierkabel *n* plug cord
Rangierleitung *f* tie line, solid twin-connection wire
Rangierverteiler *m* distribution frame
Rasseln *n* sizzle *n*
Raster *m* raster *n*; ~ *m* (F) screen *n*
Rasterauflösung *f* raster definition
Rasterbild *n* scanning-pattern image
Rastermaß *n* size of picture element
Rasterplatine *f* screen plate
Rasterschärfe *f* raster definition
Rasterwechselfrequenz *f* field frequency
Rasterwechselverfahren *n* field-sequential system
Ratespiel *n* quiz *n*
Ratiodetektor *m* ratio detector
Rauchbüchse *f* smoke pot
Rauchkasten *m* smoke box
Raum *m* room *n*, space *n*, area *n*, chamber *n*; **elektromagnetisch toter** ~ screened room; **schalltoter** ~ dead room, free-field chamber
Raumakustik *f* room acoustics *n pl*, acoustics *n pl*
Raumbeleuchtung *f* ambient

Raumbeleuchtung 130

lighting
Raumeffekt *m* (Ton) stereo effect
Raumhelligkeit *f* acoustic brilliance
Raumklang *m* acoustic *n*, acoustics
n pl, room acoustics *n pl*
Raumkulisse *f* room acoustics *n pl*,
acoustic coloration, ambience *n*
Raumladung *f* (Röhre) space charge
Raumladungsgitter *n* space-
charged grid
Raumsatellit *m* space satellite
Raumstatik *f* tape noise, bulk-erase
noise
Raumtemperatur *f* room
temperature, ambient
temperature
Raumton *m* (Atmo) effects sound; ~
m (Stereo) stereo sound
Raumvorstellung des Hörers stereo
layout, sound stage, stereo picture
(coll.)
Raumwelle *f* sky wave, indirect
wave, ionospheric wave
Raumwirkung *f* sound perspective,
stereophonic effect, spatial effect
Rauschabstand *m* signal-to-noise
ratio (S/N ratio)
rauscharm *adj* low-noise *adj*
Rauschbegrenzer *m* noise limiter
Rauschbegrenzung *f* noise limiting
rauschen *v* to be noisy
Rauschen *n* noise *n*, atmospherics
n pl; **farbiges** ~ pink noise;
impulsförmiges ~ impulsive noise;
kontinuierliches ~ continuous
noise; **periodisches** ~ periodic
noise; **statisches** ~ static noise,
static *n*; **weißes** ~ white noise
Rauschmaß *n* noise figure
Rauschpegel *m* noise level
Rauschspannung *f* noise voltage,
noise potential
Rauschspitzen *f pl* noise peaks
Rauschspur *f* noise track
Rauschstrom *m* noise current
Rauschton *m* noise *n*, background
noise
Rauschwiderstand *m* noise

resistance
Rauschzahl *f* noise factor, noise
figure
Räuspertaste *f* microphone cut key,
cut button, cough key
RBW-Verfahren *n* RBW system
RC-Glied *n* RC network, RC section
RC-Kopplung *f* RC coupling
Reaktanzröhre *f* reactance valve
Realisator *m* producer *n*, director *n*;
~ *m* (Journalist) reporter *n*
Realzeit- (in Zus.) (EDV) real-time *aa*
Realzeitbetrieb *m* (EDV) real-time
operation, real-time working
Realzeitsteuerung *f* (EDV) real-time
control
Realzeituhr *f* (EDV) real-time clock
Rechen- und Leitwerk *n* (EDV)
arithmetic and logical unit (ALU)
Rechenanlage *f* (EDV) data
processing system, computer *n*
Rechengeschwindigkeit *f* (EDV)
computing speed
Rechenwerk *n* (EDV) arithmetic unit
Recherche *f* news research,
background research
Rechercheur *m* research specialist,
research assistant
Rechnungsprüfer *m* auditor *n*
Rechnungswesen *n* accounting *n*
Rechnungswesen* *n* finance* *n*
Recht auf Gegendarstellung right
of reply; **von dem** ~ **auf
Gegendarstellung Gebrauch
machen** to exercise right of reply
Rechte *n pl* rights *n pl*; ~ **abtreten**
to surrender rights, to give up
rights; **ausschließliche** ~ exclusive
rights; **beschränkte** ~ limited
rights, restricted rights; **einfache**
~ single rights; **große** ~ grand
rights; **kleine** ~ petits droits, small
rights; **sämtliche** ~ full rights,
total rights, inclusive rights, all
rights; **verwandte** ~ neighbouring
rights, related rights;
frei von ~ **n** licence-free *adj,*
exempt from royalties

Rechteckimpuls *m* rectangular pulse, square pulse
Rechteckimpulsfolge *f* rectangular pulse train
Rechtecksignal *n* square wave signal; **H-frequentes ~** line-frequency square wave; **V-frequentes ~** field-frequency square wave
Rechteerwerb *m* acquisition of rights
Rechteübertragung *f* transfer of rights
Rechtsabteilung *f* legal department
Rechtssignal (R-Signal) *n* right-hand signal
Recorder *m* recorder *n*
Redakteur *m* editor *n*; **~** *m* (Nachrichten) sub-editor *n*; **~** *m* (TV, R) producer *n*, specialist correspondent; **~ vom Dienst** duty editor, senior duty editor; **diensthabender ~** duty editor, senior duty editor; **leitender ~** (Nachrichten) assistant editor; **stoffführender ~** script editor
Redakteursausschuß *m* editorial staff committee
Redaktion *f* (Abfassung) editing *n*, sub-editing *n*; **~** *f* (Büro) editorial desk; **~** *f* (Büro, Nachrichten) newsroom *n*, news desk; **~** *f* (Stab) editorial staff
Redaktionsassistent *m* editorial assistant; **~** *m* (Meldungseingang) copy-taster *n*
Redaktionsbesprechung *f* editorial conference
Redaktionskonferenz *f* editorial conference
Redaktionsleiter *m* senior editor, head of desk
Redaktionsraum *m* editorial desk; **~** *m* (Nachrichten) newsroom *n*, news desk
Redaktionsschluß *m* deadline *n*; **~ machen** to put to bed (coll.)
redigieren *v* edit *v*; **~** *v*

(Nachrichten) sub-edit *v*
Reduktion *f* reduction *n*
Redundanz *f* redundancy *n*
Referat *n* (Vortrag) oral report; **~** *n* (Abteilung) department *n*, section *n*
Referent, persönlicher personal assistant (PA)
Reflektor *m* reflector *n*
Reflektorspiegel *m* reflector mirror
Reflexbeleuchtung *f* reflected lighting
Reflexion *f* reflection *n*
Reflexionsgrad *m* reflection factor, reflection coefficient
Reflexionskoeffizient *m* s. Reflexionsgrad
Reflexionsverlust *m* reflection loss, loss by reflection
Reflexionsvermögen *n* reflecting power
Reflexionswand *f* reflector screen
Reflexkamera *f* reflex camera
Reflexsucher *m* reflex viewfinder, reflex finder
Refrainsänger *m* backing singer
Regeleinheit *f* control unit
Regelglied *n* (EDV) final control element
Regelgröße *f* (EDV) controlled condition
Regelkreis *m* automatic control system; **offener ~** (EDV) open loop
Regelkurve *f* control characteristic
regeln *v* regulate *v*, control *v*, adjust *v*
Regelschaltung *f* control circuit
Regelung *f* regulation *n*, adjustment *n*, control *n*, setting *n*; **getastete ~** clamped control
Regelwiderstand *m* variable resistance, variable resistor, rheostat *n*
Regenbogengenerator *m* rainbow test pattern generator
Regenbogentestbild *n* rainbow test pattern
Regeneration *f* regeneration *n*

Regenerationsgerät *n* regenerating equipment

Regenerator *m* regenerator *n*, sync-pulse regenerator

regenerieren *v* regenerate *v*

Regenerierflüssigkeit *f* replenisher *n*

Regenerierung *f* regeneration *n*, reactivation *n*

Regenerierverstärker *m* processing amplifier

Regenschutz *m* rain shield

Regie *f* direction *n*, production *n*; ~ *f* (Thea.) staging *n*; ~ *f* (Titel) directed by ...; ~ *f* (Raum, R) cubicle *n*, control cubicle, production cubicle; ~ *f* (Raum, TV) control room, production control room, gallery *n* (coll.); ~ **führen** direct *v*, produce *v*

Regieanweisung *f* stage direction

Regieassistent *m* assistant director (AD)

Regiebesprechung *f* pre-production meeting

Regie-Kameramann *m* director-cameraman *n*

Regiekanzel *f* (TV) control room, gallery *n* (coll.)

Regiekonzeption *f* director's conception

Regieleitung *f* talkback circuit

Regiepult *n* control desk, mixing desk, console *n*, panel *n*

Regieraum *m* (TV) production control room, control room, gallery *n* (coll.); ~ *m* (R) control cubicle, production cubicle

Regierungssprecher *m* government spokesman

Regiestab *m* director's staff

Regiestuhl *m* director's seat

Regietisch *m* control desk, mixing desk, console *n*, panel *n*

Regie-Tonträger *m* recording channel

Regiewagen *m* mobile control room (MCR)

Regiezentrale *f* master control room

Regionalanstalt *f* regional centre, local station (US)

Regionalfernsehen *n* regional television programmes *n pl*, local television (US)

Regionalnachrichten *f pl* regional news, local news (US), area news (US)

Regionalprogramm *n* regional programme, local broadcasting (US)

Regionalsendung *f* regional broadcast, local program (US), local broadcast (US)

Regionalstudio *n* regional centre

Regisseur *m* producer *n*, director *n*

Regisseur-Kameramann *m* director-cameraman *n*

Register *n* (EDV) register *n*

Registrator *m* filing clerk

Registratur *f* registry *n*

Regler *m* regulator *n*, stabiliser *n*, governor *n*; ~ *m* (fam.) control *n*, fader *n*

regulieren *v* regulate *v*, govern *v*, adjust *v*, control *v*

Reichweite *f* transmission range, range *n*, coverage *n*

Reihe *f* series *n*

Reihenkreis *m* series circuit

Reisebericht *m* travelogue *n*

Reiseempfänger *m* portable receiver, portable *n*

Reisefilm *m* travelogue *n*

Reisekosten *plt* travel expenses

Reisekostenabrechnung *f* travel expenses claim

Reisekostenantrag *m* application for travel allowances

Reisekostenstelle *f* travel allowances clerk

Reisekostenvergütung *f* reimbursement of expenses

Reisekostenvorschuß *m* advance of travel expenses

Reisespesen *plt* travel allowances

Reisetagebuch *n* travel diary
Reisetonbandgerät *n* portable tape recorder
Reißschwenk *m* whip pan, zip pan, swish pan
Reizschwelle *f* threshold of sensation, threshold of stimulation
Reklame *f* advertisement *n*, advertising *n*, ad *n* (coll.), publicity *n*
Rekompatibilität *f* reverse compatibility
Relais *n* relay *n*; **ausfallverzögertes** ~ slugged relay; **gepoltes** ~ polarised relay; **polarisiertes** ~ polarised relay
Relaiskreuzschaltfeld *n* relay matrix
Relaisoptik *f* relay optics, relay lens
Relaisschiene *f* relay spring
Relaisschrank *m* relay frame, relay box
Relaissender *m* relay station, relay transmitter, rebroadcast transmitter
Relaisstation *f* relay station
Remake *n* remake *n*
Remission *f* re-emission *n*, re-radiation *n*, reflectance *n*
Remissionsumfang *m* re-emissive power, spectral re-emission, reflecting power
Remissionsverhältnis *n* coefficient of re-emission, coefficient of reflectance
remittieren *v* remit *v*
Reparatur *f* (tech.) repair *n*, maintenance *n*
Reparaturwerkstatt *f* repair shop
reparieren *v* repair *v*, mend *v*
Repertoire *n* repertoire *n*, repertory *n*
Reportage *f* news report, running commentary, commentary *n*, news coverage, eye-witness report, reportage *n*, story *n* (coll.)
Reportagefahrzeug *n* recording van, recording car

Reportagefilm *m* newsreel *n*
Reportagesendung *f* eye-witness programme
Reportagewagen *m* recording van, recording car
Reporter *m* reporter *n*, newsman *n* (US)
Reprise *f* re-issue *n*, re-run *n*
Reproduktion *f* reproduction *n*, rendering *n*, copying work
Requisit *n* property *n*, prop *n* (coll.)
Requisite *f* (fam.) property room, prop room (coll.)
Requisiten *n pl* properties *n pl*, props *n pl* (coll.), set dressings
Requisitenfundus *m* property store
Requisitenkammer *f* s. Requisitenfundus
Requisitenliste *f* property list, property plot
Requisitenmeister *m* stock-keeper *n*
Requisitenraum *m* property room, prop room (coll.)
Requisiteur *m* property master, property man, propsman *n* (coll.)
Reserve *f* (Progr.) stand-by *n*
Reserveaufnahme *f* hold take
Reservebeitrag *m* substitute item
Reservebetrieb *m* stand-by service, reserve service
Reservegerät *n* spare apparatus
Reserveleitung *f* reserve circuit, spare circuit
Reserveprogramm *n* stand-by programme
Resonanz *f* resonance *n*, echo *n*
Resonanzanzeige *f* resonance indication
Resonanzkreis *m* resonant circuit
Resonanzkurve *f* resonant curve
Resonanzspannung *f* resonant voltage
Resonanzspitze *f* resonance peak
Resonanzverstärker *m* tuned amplifier
Resonanzwiderstand *m* resonant

Resonanzwiderstand 134

impedance

Ressort n department n, area n,
province n, sphere of
responsibility, desk n, field n
(US), beat n (US)

Ressortchef m head of desk

Ressortleiter m head of desk

Restseitenband n vestigial sideband

Restseitenbandübertragung f
vestigial sideband transmission

Restspannung f residual voltage

Reststörspannung f residual
interference voltage

Reststrom m leakage current,
residual current

Restwelligkeit f residual ripple,
ripple n

Retake n retake n

retuschieren v touch up v, retouch
v

Revision f audit n

Revision* f internal auditor*
(BBC)

Revisor m auditor n

Revolvergriff m pistol grip

Revolverkopf m lens turret

Revolverkopfdrehung f turret
rotation

rewriten v rewrite v

RGB-Monitor m RGB monitor

RGB-Pegel n pl RGB levels

RGB-Prinzip n RGB system

RGB-Verfahren n RGB system

RGB+Y-Verfahren n RGB with
separate luminance

R-Gespräch n reversed-charge call

Rhythmus m rhythm n

Rhythmusträger m rhythm tape,
rhythm carrier

Richtantenne f directional aerial,
beam aerial

Richtcharakteristik f directional
pattern, polar diagram, radiation
pattern

Richtdiagramm n directional
pattern, polar diagram, radiation
pattern

richten v adjust v, set v

richten auf direct v, beam v, point v

Richten n adjusting n, setting n

Richtfunk (RiFu) m microwave link
system, point-to-point radio
system, radio-link system

Richtfunkantenne f beam aerial,
directional aerial

Richtfunkempfänger m microwave
receiver, relay receiver, link
receiver

Richtfunknetz n microwave
network, radio-link network,
radio-relay network

Richtfunksender m microwave
transmitter, point-to-point
transmitter, link transmitter

Richtfunkstelle f microwave radio
station, point-to-point radio
station

Richtfunkstrahl m radio beam

Richtfunkstrecke f microwave link,
radio link, directional link

Richtfunkübertragungsdienst* m
microwave transmission
service*, radio-relay
transmission service*

Richtfunkverbindung f microwave
link, radio link, directional link

Richtfunkzubringerlinie f
microwave contribution circuit

Richtigstellung f correction n,
rectification n

Richtkeulenöffnungswinkel m
aerial beam width

Richtkoppler m directional coupler

Richtleiter m crystal diode

**Richtlinien zum Einmessen von
Schallträgern** standards for
measurement of magnetic tapes

Richtmikrofon n unidirectional
microphone, highly directional
microphone

Richtspannung f rectified voltage

Richtstrahlantenne f beam aerial,
directional aerial

Richtstrom m rectified current

Richtungsinformation f directional
information; ~ f (Stereo)

directional information, positional information, stereo information (coll.)

Richtwirkung *f* directional effect, directivity *n*

Riffelmuster *n* moiré *n*, moiré pattern, watered silks effect

Rille *f* (Beleuchtung) grid slot; ~ *f* (Schallplatte) groove *n*

Rillendecke *f* slotted grid

Rillenwinkel *m* groove angle

Ringkern *m* (EDV) toroidal core

Ringleitung *f* ring circuit, ring main

Ringmagnet *m* ring magnet, annular magnet

Ringmodulator *m* ring modulator, double-balanced modulator

Ringmutter *f* annular nut

Ringsendung *f* multiplex broadcast, relay *n*

Ringstart *m* (F) simultaneous release

Ringteiler *m* ring counter

Ringübertrager *m* toroidal transformer, ring transformer

Ringzähler *m* ring counter

Riß *m* (F) break *n*, tear *n*

Rohdrehbuch *n* draft script, preliminary shooting script, draft screenplay

Rohfassung *f* working script, unpolished script

Rohfilm *m* raw stock, stock *n*, raw film

Rohfilmhersteller *m* raw stock manufacturer, film manufacturer

Rohfilmherstellung *f* raw stock manufacture, film manufacture

Rohfilmkern *m* raw stock bobbin, raw stock centre, raw stock core

Rohfilmlager *n* raw stock store

Rohfilmmaß *n* raw stock dimension

Rohfilmmaterial *n* raw stock, stock *n*, raw film

Röhre *f* valve *n*, tube *n*; **implosionsgeschützte** ~ implosion-proof tube; **taube** ~ deaf valve

Röhrenempfänger *m* valve receiver, valve set, tube receiver

Röhrenkolben *m* bulb *n*

Röhrensockel *m* valve socket, valve base, tube holder

Röhrenvoltmeter *n* valve voltmeter, vacuum-tube voltmeter (VTVM) (US)

Rohrgerüst *n* tubular scaffolding

Rohrklammer *f* (Scheinwerfer) scaffold clamp

Rohrkondensator *m* tubular capacitor

Rohrmast *m* tubular mast, tube pole

Rohschnitt *m* rough cut, assembly *n*

Rohschnittabnahme *f* approval of rough cut

Rohschnittvorführung *f* screening of rough cut

Rohübersetzung *f* rough translation

Rolle *f* roll *n*, reel *n*, spool *n*; ~ *f* (mech.) pulley *n*, castor *n*; ~ *f* (Darsteller) part *n*, character *n*, role *n*; **freilaufende** ~ idler *n*; **kleine** ~ bit part, small part

rollen *v* (F) curl *v*

Rollenbesetzung *f* cast *n*, casting *n*

Rollenfach *n* character type

Rollstativ *n* rolling tripod

Rolltitel *m* roller caption, roll titles *n pl*

Rolltitelgerät *n* roller caption equipment

Rolltitelmaschine *f* s. Rolltitelgerät

Rosette *f* rosette *n*

Rost *m* (Gitter) grating *n*, grid *n*

rotationssymmetrisch *adj* dynamically balanced

Rotlicht *n* red light, warning light

Rückblende *f* flashback *n*

Rückfahrt *f* (Kamera) tracking back, tracking out, back-track *n*

Rückflanke *f* trailing edge

Rückflußdämpfung *f* return loss, structural return loss

rückgewinnen *v* recover *v*

Rückgewinnung *f* recovery *n*, reclamation *n*; ~ *f* (elek.)

Rückgewinnung 136

recuperation *n*

rückkoppeln *v* (akust.) feed back *v*, howl round *v*; ~ *v* (elek.) feed back *v*, regenerate *v*

Rückkopplung *f* (akust.) feedback *n*, howl-round *n*, howling *n* (coll.); ~ *f* (elek.) feedback *n*, regeneration *n*, regenerative feedback; **optische** ~ vision howl-round

Rückkopplungsneigung *f* feedback tendency, tendency to regenerate

Rückkühlanlage *f* re-cooling plant

Rücklauf *m* reverse motion, return *n*, return movement, flyback *n*, rewind *n*; **schneller** ~ fast rewind; **synchroner** ~ synchronous rewind

Rücklaufaustastung *f* flyback suppression, blanking *n*

Rücklaufsignal *n* (Abtastung) flyback signal, blanking signal

Rücklaufstrahl *m* flyback beam

Rücklauftrick *m* reverse-motion effect, reverse-running effect

Rückleitung *f* return circuit, flyback circuit (US)

Rückmeldung *f* back indication, operation-completed indication; ~ *f* feedback *n*

Rückpro *f* (fam.) *s.* Rückprojektion

Rückprojektion *f* back projection (BP), rear projection (RP)

Rückprojektor *m* back projector

Rückproschirm *m* back projection screen, rear projection screen, translucent screen

Rückrufrecht *n* right of withdrawal, right to revoke; ~ **wegen Nichtausübung** right of withdrawal because of non-exercise

Rückrufzeichen *n* call-back signal, recall signal

Rucksack *m* (fam.) pack *n*

Rückschicht *f* backing *n*

Rückschlagimpuls *m* kick-back pulse

Rücksetzer *m* backing *n*, set-in *n*

Rückspielleitung *f* playback circuit

Rücksprechleitung *f* talkback circuit

Rückspulung *f* rewinding *n*, rewind *n*

Rückstellung *f* reset *n*

Rückwand *f* back face, back wall, back panel, rear panel, back *n*, rear wall

Rückwärtsgang *m* reverse action, return movement, reverse motion, reverse *n*

Rückwärtsregelung *f* backward-acting regulation, pre-detector volume control

Rückwirkung *f* feedback *n*, reaction *n*

Rufanlage *f* bleeper *n*

Ruffrequenz *f* ringing frequency

Rufsignal *n* calling signal; ~ *n* (akust.) audible calling signal; ~ *n* (Fernschreiber) ringing signal

Ruftaste *f* ringing key

Ruhe *f* silence *n*; ~ **bitte!** quiet, please!

Ruhekontakt *m* back contact, break contact

Ruhestrom *m* closed-circuit current

Rührwerk *n* (Kopierwerk) agitator *n*, stirring device

Rumpeln *n* (Platte) rumble *n*

Rundempfangsantenne *f* omnidirectional aerial

Rundfunk *m* (s. a. Funk, Hörfunk, Radio) radio *n*, broadcasting *n*; **durch** ~ **übertragen** broadcast *v*, to put on the air

Rundfunkanstalt *f* broadcasting station, broadcasting organisation ~ *f* (Hörfunk) radio station

Rundfunkapparat *m* radio receiver, radio *n*, radio set, wireless set, wireless *n*, set *n*

Rundfunkarchiv *n* broadcasting archives *n pl*

Rundfunkchor *m* radio choir, radio chorus

Rundfunkdienst *m* radio service; ~ **mit Satelliten** broadcasting-satellite service

Rundfunkdurchsage *f* special announcement

Rundfunkempfänger *m* radio receiver, radio *n*, radio set, wireless set, wireless *n*, set *n*

Rundfunkempfängerweiche *f* receiving diplexer

Rundfunkgebühr *f* receiver licence fee

Rundfunkgerät *n* radio receiver, radio *n*, radio set, wireless set, wireless *n*, set *n*

Rundfunkgeschichte *f* history of broadcasting

Rundfunkgesellschaft *f* broadcasting company, broadcasting corporation, radio corporation (US)

Rundfunkgesetz *n* broadcasting act

Rundfunkhaus *n* broadcasting house

Rundfunkhörer *m* listener *n*

Rundfunkjournalist *m* radio journalist

Rundfunkkanal *m* radio channel

Rundfunkkomplex *m* broadcasting centre

Rundfunkleute *plt* broadcasters *n pl*

Rundfunkorchester *n* radio orchestra

Rundfunkorganisation *f* broadcasting organisation

Rundfunkrat *m* broadcasting council

Rundfunksatellit *m* broadcasting satellite

Rundfunkschaffender *m* broadcaster *n*

Rundfunksendegesellschaft *f* broadcasting company, radio corporation (US)

Rundfunksender *m* radio transmitter, broadcasting transmitter

Rundfunksendung *f* broadcast *n*, transmission *n*, radio programme

Rundfunksprecher *m* announcer *n*, speaker *n*

Rundfunkstation *f* radio station, broadcasting station

Rundfunkstatut *n* broadcasting charter

Rundfunkstereofonie *f* radio stereophony, stereo radio (coll.)

Rundfunktechnik *f* radio engineering

Rundfunktechniker *m* broadcasting engineer, radio engineer

Rundfunkteilnehmer *m* licence-holder *n*

Rundfunkträger *m* broadcasting organisation

Rundfunkübertragung *f* radio broadcast, radio transmission, radio relay

Rundfunk- und Fernsehstation *f* television and radio station

Rundfunkvermittlung *f* (Post) radio relay exchange

Rundfunkversorgung *f* broadcasting service

Rundgang *m* (Studio) studio gallery

Rundhorizont *m* cyclorama (cyc) *n*; ~ **mit Voute** cyclorama with merging curve

rundlaufen *v* rotate *v*, revolve *v*

Rundschau *f* round-up *n*, review *n*

Rundschwenk *m* pan-round *n*, full-circle panoramic shot

Rundstrahlantenne *f* omnidirectional aerial

Rundstrahlung *f* circular radiation, omnidirectional radiation

Rundumstrahlung *f s.* Rundstrahlung

Rüstwagen *m* rigging tender

Rüttelsicherheit *f* immunity to vibration

Saalgeräusch

S

Saalgeräusch *n* auditorium noise, hall noise, room noise
Sachgebiet *n* subject *n*, special field, speciality *n*
Sachleistung *f* facility *n*
Sachtrick *m* live animation
Sachverständiger *m* expert *n*, specialist *n*
Saft *m* (fam.) current *n*, juice *n* (coll.)
Sägezahn *m* saw-tooth *n*; ~ **mit HF-Mittelwert** saw-tooth with HF mean value
Sägezahngenerator *m* saw-tooth generator, relaxation oscillator
Sägezahnkorrektur *f* saw-tooth correction
Sägezahnsignal mit Farbträger saw-tooth signal with colour carrier
Salat *m* (fam.) pile-up *n* (coll.), rip-up *n* (coll.)
Salatschalter *m* (fam.) cut-out switch
Sammelelektrode *f* collector electrode, collector *n*
Sammellinse *f* collecting lens, condenser lens, convergent lens, converging lens
Samtkufe *f* velvet pad
Sänger *m* singer *n*
Satellit *m* satellite *n*, bird *n* (US); ~ **für direkte Rundfunkübertragung** direct broadcast satellite; ~ **für vielfachen Zugang** satellite with multiple access; **aktiver** ~ active satellite; **geostationärer** ~ geostationary satellite; **geosynchroner** ~ geosynchronous satellite; **künstlicher** ~ artificial satellite, man-made satellite;

passiver ~ passive satellite; **rückläufiger** ~ retrograde satellite **stationärer** ~ stationary satellite
Satellitenantenne *f* satellite aerial
Satellitenbahn *f* orbit *n*
Satellitenerdverbindung *f* satellite-earth link
Satellitenfenster *n* window *n*
Satellitenfernsehen *n* satellite television
Satellitenfernsehprogramm *n* satellite television programme
Satellitenfunk *m* transmission via satellite
Satellitenfunkstrecke *f* satellite link
Satellitenleitung *f* satellite circuit, satellite link
Satellitennetz *n* satellite network
Satellitenrundfunk *m* broadcasting by satellite
Satellitensender *m* satellite transmitter
Satellitenstrecke *f* satellite circuit, satellite link
Satellitenübertragung *f* satellite transmission; **direkte** ~ direct broadcast by satellite, live relay by satellite
Satellitenverbindung *f* satellite circuit, satellite link; ~ **mit mehreren Satelliten** multi-satellite link
Satellitenverkehr *m* traffic by satellite
sättigen *v* saturate *v*
Sättigung *f* saturation *n*
Satz *m* (Reihe) set *n*, assembly *n*, batch *n*
Saugkreis *m* (Filter) acceptor circuit
Saum *m* fringe *n*
säurefest *adj* acid-proof *adj*, acid-resisting *adj*
Säuregrad *m* degree of acidity, acidity *n*
Scatterrichtfunkstrecke *f* scatter radio-relay circuit, scatter link
Scatterverbindung *f* scatter

communication

Schabemesser *n* scraper *n*, scraping tool, retouching knife

Schablone *f* matte *n*, cliché *n*

Schablonenblende *f* vignette *n*, cutout diaphragm, camera matte, effects matte

Schabloneneinblendung *f* overlay insertion

Schablonenmuster für Scheinwerfer projection cut-out

Schablonentrick *m* overlay *n*

Schachmustertestbild *n* chequerboard test pattern

Schaden *m* damage *n*, defect *n*, injury *n*, prejudice *n*

Schall *m* sound *n*

Schall- (in Zus.) sound (compp.), sonic *adj*

schallabsorbierend *adj* sound-absorbing *adj*

Schallabsorption *f* sound absorption

Schallabstrahlung *f* sound radiation, sound projection

Schallarchiv *n* sound archives *n pl*

Schallarchivar *m* sound librarian

Schallaufnahme *f* sound recording

Schallaufnahmeverfahren *n* sound recording system; ~ **mit mehreren Tonspuren** multi-track recording system

Schallaufzeichnung *f* sound recording

Schallaufzeichnungsraum *m* sound studio, sound recording studio, recording channel

Schalldämmung *f* sound insulation

schalldämpfend *adj* sound-damping *adj*, sound-deadening *adj*, sound-absorbing *adj*

Schalldämpfung *f* sound damping, sound absorption, sound deadening

schalldicht *adj* sound-proof *adj*

Schalldichtung *f* sound insulation

Schalldruck *m* sound pressure, acoustic pressure

Schalleffekt *m* sound effect

Schalleistung *f* acoustic output

Schallempfänger *m* sound pick-up

Schallenergie *f* sound energy, acoustic energy

Schallfeld *n* sound field

Schallintensität *f* sound intensity

schallisolieren *v* to insulate for sound

Schallkörper *m* sound box

Schallplatte *f* (s. a. Platte) disc *n*, record *n*, gramophone record, phonograph record (US); **ungepreßte** ~ unprocessed disc; **vertraglich festgelegte Sendezeit für ~n** needle time

Schallplattenabtaster *m* pick-up *n*

Schallplattenarchiv *n* record library, gramophone library

Schallplattenaufnahme *f* phonographic recording

Schallplattenindustrie *f* phonographic industry, gramophone industry

Schallplattenmusik *f* grams *n pl* (coll.)

Schallplattenprogramm *n* disc programme, record programme

Schallplattenteller *m* record turntable, turntable *n*, gramophone turntable

Schallplattenumschnitt *m* dubbing from disc

Schallplattenverstärker *m* pick-up amplifier, gramophone amplifier, phonograph amplifier (US)

Schallquelle *f* sound source, sound generator

Schallrille *f* groove of record, groove *n*

Schallrückwandlung *f* sound transduction

Schallsäule *f* column loudspeaker

Schallschirm *m* acoustic screen

Schallschleuse *f* sound lock

Schallschluckgrad *m* sound absorption coefficient

Schallschluckung *f* sound

Schallschluckung 140

absorption
Schallschutzhaube *f* sound-proof casing, blimp *n*
Schallschwingung *f* acoustic oscillation, acoustic vibration
Schallspeicher *m* sound recording medium
Schallstärke *f* sound intensity
Schallstrahl *m* sound beam
Schallstrahler *m* acoustic radiator
Schallstrahlung *f* sound radiation
schalltot *adj* acoustically dead, dead *adj*, anechoic *adj*, non-reverberant *adj*
Schallträger *m* sound recording medium
Schalltrichter *m* acoustic horn
Schallumwandler *m* sound transducer
Schallvolumen *n* volume *n*
Schallwand *f* baffle *n*, baffle board, acoustic baffle, sounding board
Schallwelle *f* sound wave
Schallwiedergabe *f* sound reproduction
Schallzeile *f* line of loudspeakers
Schaltalgebra *f* (EDV) switching algebra
Schaltanfang *m* start of switching sequence
Schaltbild *n* wiring diagram, circuit diagram
Schaltbrett *n* switchboard *n*, distribution board, control panel, switch panel
Schaltbuchse *f* switch jack
Schaltdiode *f* switching diode
Schaltebene *f* switching level
schalten *v* switch *v*, connect *v*; ~ *v* (verdrahten) wire *v*; ~ *v* (Kreis) to switch into circuit, to connect into circuit; ~ *v* (bedienen) operate *v*; ~ **auf** switch *v* (to)
Schaltende *n* end of switching sequence
Schalter *m* switch *n*
Schalterautomatik *f* automatic switching gear, automatic

switching
Schaltfehler *m* switching error
Schaltfeld *n* switching panel, switch panel
Schaltfrequenz *f* sampling frequency, switching frequency
Schaltgerät *n* switchgear *n*
Schalthäufigkeit *f* number of switching operations in given period
Schaltkapazität *f* circuit capacitance
Schaltkasten *m* switch box, switch enclosure
Schaltkerbe *f* cam *n*
Schaltkonferenz *f* circuit conference, hook-up *n*
Schaltkreis *m* circuit *n*; **gedruckter** ~ printed circuit; **integrierter** ~ integrated circuit (IC)
Schaltplan *m* circuit diagram, wiring diagram
Schaltplanmappe *f* file of circuit diagrams
Schaltplatte *f* circuit board; **gedruckte** ~ printed circuit board
Schaltpult *n* control desk, switch desk, switchboard *n*
Schaltraum *m* switching room, control room, switching area
Schaltrolle *f* sprocket wheel
Schaltschema *n* circuit diagram, wiring diagram
Schaltstelle *f* switching position; **~ mit Kreuzschiene** matrix switching point
Schaltstörung *f* switching break, interference caused by switching
Schalttafel *f* switchboard *n*, distribution board, control panel, switch panel
Schaltung *f* (Steuerung) control *n*; ~ *f* (Verdrahtung) wiring *n*; ~ *f* (Kreis) circuit *n*, connection *n*; ~ *f* (Schaltbild) circuitry *n*, circuit diagram, schematic *n* (US); **aktive** ~ (EDV) active circuit; **gedruckte** ~ printed circuit; **integrierte** ~

integrated circuit (IC)
Schaltungskapazität f circuit
  capacity, wiring capacity
Schaltungstechnik f switching n
Schaltvermögen n breaking
  capacity
Schaltverzögerung f time delay
Schaltwart m switchboard
  attendant
Schaltzeit f switching time
Schaltzentrale f switching centre
scharf adj sharp adj, well-focused
  adj, in focus; ~ **einstellen** focus v,
  to bring into focus
Scharfabstimmung f fine tuning,
  frequency control, frequency
  correction; **automatische** ~
  automatic frequency control
  (AFC), automatic tuning
Schärfe f (Ton) sharpness n; ~ f
  (Bild) definition n; ~ f (Linse)
  clearness n, acuity n; ~ **des**
  Abtastsystems scanning-system
  definition; ~ **des Bildwandlers**
  image-converter resolution;
  ~ **einstellen** focus v, to bring into
  focus; ~ **wobbeln** spot-wobble v;
  ~ **ziehen** focus v, to bring into
  focus
Schärfeassistent m focus puller,
  focus operator, second
  cameraman
Schärfegrad m degree of sharpness
Scharfeinstellung f (opt.) focusing n,
  focus n, adjustment for definition
Schärfenband n focus calibration
  tape
Schärfenring m focus ring
Schärfentiefe f depth of focus,
  depth of field
Schärferad n focus handle, focus
  knob
Schärfezieher m focus puller, focus
  operator, second cameraman
Scharfzeichnung f definition n,
  sharpness n
Scharnier n hinge n, frame joint
Schatten m shadow n,
  shade n; ~ m (im Bild)

shadow areas n pl,
  shadow effect; ~ m (Schwärzung)
  black-crushing n; ~ m (Schminke)
  shadow n, shading n; **reiner** ~
  even shadow
Schattendichte f shade density
Schattenmaskenröhre f shadow
  mask tube
Schattenraster m vignette n, gate n
Schattenschwärzung f black-
  crushing n
Schattenzone f shadow area,
  shadow zone
schattieren v shade v
Schattierung f shade n, shading n
Schaubild n diagram n, chart n,
  graph n, visual aid
Schauplatz m scene of action, scene
  n, theatre n, location n, venue n;
  ~ **sein von ...** to be the scene of ...
Schauspiel n play n, drama n
Schauspiel* n drama* n
Schauspieler m actor n, player n
Schautafel f diagram n, chart n,
  graph n, visual aid
Scheibenkondensator m disc
  capacitor
Scheibentrimmer m disc trimmer,
  disc-type trimmer
Scheinleistung f apparent power
Scheinleitwert m admittance n
Scheinwerfer m lamp n, spotlight n,
  reflector n
Scheinwerferaufhängung f lamp
  suspension
Scheinwerferbestückung f lamp
  complement
Scheinwerferdichte f frequency of
  lights
Scheinwerfergalgen m gallows arm
Scheinwerfergerüst n scaffold
  suspension
Scheinwerfergestänge n lighting
  barrels n pl
Scheinwerferlampe f spotlight
  lamp, reflector lamp, projector
  lamp
Scheinwerferlinse f spotlight lens
Scheinwerfernase f snoot n

Scheinwerferschwenk *m* lamp trunnion
Scheinwerferstand *m* lamp stand
Scheinwerferstativ *n* lamp stand
Scheinwervignette *f* vignette *n*
Scheinwiderstand *m* impedance *n*
Scheinwiderstandsmeßbrücke *f* impedance measuring bridge
Scheitel *m* peak *n*
Scheitelblende *f* scissors shutter
Scheitelfaktor *m* peak factor, crest factor
Scheitelhänger *m* gobo arm
Scheitelpegel *m* peak level; ~ **für Weiß** peak white level
Scheitelspannung *f* peak voltage, crest voltage
Scheitelwert *m* peak value, crest value
Scherenarm *m* pantograph *n*, lazyboy *n*
Scheuklappe *f* (fam.) (Scheinwerfer) barndoor *n*
Scheunentor *n* (fam.) (Scheinwerfer) barndoor *n*
Schicht *f* layer *n*, stratum *n*; ~ *f* (F) emulsion *n*, coating *n*, layer *n*; ~ *f* (Betriebszeit) shift *n*, gang *n*; **empfindliche** ~ sensitive layer, sensitive emulsion; **lichtempfindliche** ~ photosensitive coating, light-sensitive layer
Schichtablösung *f* oxide-shedding *n*, peeling-off *n*
Schichtband *n* ferrous coated tape, coated tape
Schichthärtung *f* hardening of emulsion
Schichtlackierung *f* lacquering of emulsion
Schichtlage *f* emulsion side
Schichtleiter *m* shift leader
Schichtschramme *f* emulsion scratch
Schichtseite *f* emulsion side, sensitised side
Schichtträger *m* tape base, film

base, base *n*, base material, emulsion support, support *n*, emulsion carrier
Schichtträgerseite *f* base side, celluloid side, cell side (coll.)
Schichtwiderstand *m* metallised resistor, carbon resistor
Schiebeblende *f* sliding diaphragm; ~ *f* (Trick) push-over wipe
Schiebemagnet *m* sliding magnet
Schieber *m* fader *n*, control knob, control *n*; ~ *m* (fam.) (Licht) dimmer *n*
Schieberegister *n* (EDV) shift register, shifting register
Schiebeschalter *m* slide switch
Schiebetrick *m* mechanical animation
Schiene *f* rail *n*; ~ *f* (Starkstrom) bus bar, code bar; **gebogene** ~ bent rail, curved rail; **gerade** ~ straight rail
Schienenwagen *m* track dolly
Schirm *m* screen *n*, shield *n*
Schirmbild *n* screen picture, screen image
Schirmbildröhre *f* display tube
Schirmgitter *n* screen grid, screen *n*
Schirmgitterspannung *f* screen-grid voltage, screen voltage
Schirmgitterstrom *m* screen-grid current, screen current
Schirmhelligkeit *f* screen brightness
Schirmröhre *f* display tube
Schirmwanne *f* (Bildröhre) screen connection
Schlager *m* hit song, hit tune, hit *n* (coll.), box-office hit
Schlagermusik *f* pop music
Schlagerparade *f* hit parade
Schlagersendung *f* pop programme
Schlagertexter *m* songwriter *n*
Schlagerwettbewerb *m* song contest
Schlagschatten *m* heavy shadow, hard shadow, cast shadow
Schlagzeile *f* headline *n*, catchline *n*

Schleichwerbung *f* incidental advertising, plug *n* (coll.)
Schleier *m* (TV) fog *n*; ~ *m* (Foto) fog *n*, veiling *n*
Schleife *f* loop *n*; ~ **fahren** to run a loop; **geschlossene** ~ (EDV) closed loop
schleifen *v* (Leitung) loop *v*
Schleifendurchziehkasten *m* loop cabinet
Schleifenfahrstuhl *m* paternoster *n*
Schleifenkasten *m* loop cabinet
Schleifenrahmen *m* loop frame
Schleifenschwund *m* shrinkage *n*, loss of loops
Schleifenständer *m* loop stand
Schleifer *m* wiper *n*, slider *n*
Schleifmittel *n* (Kopierwerk) abrasive *n*
Schleifringläufer *m* slipping rotor
Schleuse *f* (Schall, Licht) lock *n*
Schliere *f* (F) streak *n*
Schlitzantenne *f* slot aerial
Schlitzverschluß *m* slit-type shutter, focal-plane shutter
Schlosser *m* locksmith *n*, mechanic *n*, fitter *n*
Schlupf *m* slip *n*; ~ *m* (Platte, Band) drift *n*
Schlußablauf *m* terminal procedure, closing procedure
Schlußklappe (SK) *f* end board (EB)
Schlußszene *f* closing scene, final scene
Schlußtitel *m* end titles *n pl*, closing titles *n pl*
Schmalband *n* narrow tape; ~ *n* (Frequenz) narrow band
Schmalfilm *m* narrow-gauge film, substandard film
Schmalfilmformat *n* narrow gauge, substandard size
Schmalfilmspule *f* narrow-gauge spool, substandard film spool
Schmalzbohrer *m* (fam.) earphone *n*, earpiece *n*, deaf-aid *n* (coll.)
Schmerzschwelle *f* threshold of pain

schmieren *v* (Schauspieler) ham up *v*; ~ *v* (Bild) smear *v*
Schmierenkomödiant *m* ham actor (coll.)
Schmierung *f* lubrication *n*
Schminke *f* make-up *n*, grease paint
schminken *v* make up *v*
Schminken *n* make-up treatment
Schminkmaterial *n* make-up materials *n pl*
Schminkmeister *m* make-up supervisor, make-up artist
Schminkmittel *n pl* cosmetics *n pl*, make-up media
Schminkraum *m* make-up room
Schminktisch *m* make-up table
Schminkvorlage *f* make-up chart, make-up example
Schminkzettel *m s.* Schminkvorlage
Schnappschuß *m* snapshot *n*
Schnarre *f* buzzer *n*
Schnecke *f* endless screw, worm *n*, helix *n*
Schneckengang *m* (Bewegung) worm drive reduction ratio
Schneckengetriebe *n* worm drive gear
Schnee *m* (Bild) snow *n*, picture noise
Schneideimpuls *m* (MAZ) edit pulse
Schneidelehre *f* joiner *n*, jointer *n*, splicer *n*, splicing press
schneiden *v* (F) cut *v*, edit *v*; ~ *v* (Kamera) cut *v*, switch *v*; **auf Musik** ~ to cut to music
Schneider *m* dressmaker *n*
Schneideraum *m* cutting room, editing room
Schneiderei *f* tailoring *n*, dressmaking *n*
Schneiderin *f* dressmaker *n*
Schneidetermin *m* editing date
Schneidetisch *m* cutting table, editing table, cutting bench
Schneidezeit *f* editing period
Schnelldrucker *m* (EDV) high-speed printer

Schnellreportagewagen *m* (R)
recording car
Schnellschaltwerk *n* pneumatic fast-
pulldown mechanism
Schnellstopp *m* (Tonband) rapid
stop
Schnellstopptaste *f* rapid stop key
Schnellstopschalter *m* fast-break
switch
Schnellwechselkassette *f* quick
change magazine
Schnipex *m* (fam.) baby spot
Schnitt *m* (Vorgang) cutting *n*,
editing *n*; ~ *m* (Ergebnis) cut *n*; ~
m (auf Filmtitel) film editor; **~ in
der Bewegung** cut on move, cut
on action; **elektronischer ~**
electronic editing, electronic cut;
harter ~ auf cut on; **harter ~ zu**
cut to; **mechanischer ~** physical
editing, manual editing; **rollender
~** rolling cut; **rollender ~** (Trick)
horizontal wipe
Schnittabnahme *f* editing
acceptance, final viewing of
cutting copy
Schnittaste *f* cut button, cut key
Schnittbearbeitung *f* editing *n*,
cutting *n*; **elektronische ~**
electronic editing; **mechanische ~**
manual editing
Schnittbildentfernungsmesser *m*
split-field range-finder, split-
image range-finder
Schnittbilder *n pl* sectional view,
cut-in *n*
Schnittbildfolge *f* cut-in order; ~ *f*
(Aufstellung) list of cut-ins
Schnittfolge *f* cutting order
Schnittimpuls *m* (MAZ) edit pulse
Schnittkontrolle *f* editing check
Schnittkopie *f* (F) cutting copy,
work print; ~ *f* (Kopierwerk)
answer print; **erste ~** first answer
print; **zweite ~** second answer
print
Schnittliste *f* editing list, cutting-
room log, continuity list,

logbook *n*
Schnittmarke *f* (TV) edit pulse, edit
cue, frame pulse, cue pulse, cue *n*;
~ *f* (F) cutting point
Schnittmaterial *n* (R) tape for
editing, uncut tape; ~ *n* (F) trims *n*
pl, offcuts *n pl*
Schnittmeister *m* (F) film editor; ~
m (MAZ) tape editor
Schnittmuster anfertigen to make
dress patterns
Schnittreste *m pl* out-takes *n pl*
Schnittrolle *f* assembly *n*
Schnittstabilität *f* (F) cutting
precision; ~ *f* (MAZ) editing
stability, editing accuracy
Schnittstelle *f* (EDV) interface *n*
Schnittvorführung *f* screening of
cutting copy
Schnittwechsel *m* cutting pace
Schnittweite *f* width of cut
Schnittzeit *f* cutting time, editing
time
Schnur *f* (elek.) flexible cord, flex *n*,
cord *n* (coll.), cable *n*
Schnürboden *m* grid *n*
Schnürbodentechniker *m* flyman *n*
Schnürsenkel *m* (fam.) quarter-inch
tape
Schnurverteilung *f* flexible cord
distribution, jackfield distribution
Schrägblende *f* diagonal wipe
Schrägmagnetisierung *f* oblique
magnetisation
Schrägschramme *f* diagonal scratch
Schrägschriftaufzeichnung *f* helical
scan, helical recording
Schramme *f* (Platte) disc scratch,
surface noise; ~ *f* (Band) tape
scratch; ~ *f* (opt.) optical scratch; ~
f (F) shadow scratch, scar *n*
Schreibbefehl *m* (EDV) write
instruction
Schreibbüro *n* typing pool
Schreibdichte *f* (EDV) bit density
Schreiber *m* (Gerät) recorder *n*,
recording apparatus
Schreibkopf *m* (EDV) write head,

recording head
Schreiblocher *m* (EDV) printing card punch
Schreibsperre *f* (EDV) write lockout
Schreibtitel *m* lettered title
Schriftaustastung *f* caption positioning
Schriftbild *n* type face
Schrifteinblender *m* caption mixer
Schrifteinblendung *f* caption insertion, caption superimposition
Schriftgrafiker *m* lettering artist, captions artist
Schriftsetzer *m* caption mixer
Schrifttafel *f* (TV) television programmes preview
Schrittkopiermaschine *f* step printer, intermittent printer
Schrittlauf *m* step-by-step motion, stepping motion
Schrittmotor *m* stepping motor
Schrittschaltwerk *n* step-by-step switch, incremental switch, intermittent movement
Schrotrauschen *n* shot noise, shot effect
Schrumpfausgleich *m* (F) shrinkage compensation
Schrumpfung *f* (F) shrinkage *n*, shrinking *n*
Schukokupplung *f* Schuko-type coupling piece, safety coupling
Schukosteckdose *f* safety socket, earthed socket
Schukostecker *m* safety plug, earthed plug
Schulfernsehen *n* school television, educational television (ETV)
Schulfernsehsendung *f* schools television programme
Schulfilm *m* educational film
Schulfunk *m* school radio, school broadcasting
Schulfunksendung *f* school broadcast, school programme
Schulterstativ *n* shoulder pod, shoulder tripod

Schultertragriemen *m* shoulder harness; ~ *m* (Kamera) camera harness
Schürze *f* (Thea.) apron *n*
Schuß *m* shot *n*; ~ **von oben** top shot, high-angle shot; ~ **von unten** low-angle shot
Schußfeld *n* (Kamera) field of vision, picture area
Schuß-Gegenschuß *m* shot/reaction shot, ping-pong shot (coll.)
Schütz *n* contactor *n*, control-gate *n*, relay *n*, cut-out *n*, circuit-breaker *n*; ~ **mit Schaltverzögerung** time-delayed circuit-breaker
Schutzdeckel *m* protective cover, cover *n*, dust cover
Schutzerde *f* protective earth, protective ground, non-fused earth
Schutzgeländer *n* guard-rail *n*, safety rail, hand-rail *n*
Schutzgitter *n* screen grid, protection screen, grid *n*, guard grid
Schutzgrill *m* wire-lattice guard, guard *n*
Schutzhülle *f* protective envelope
Schutzkanal *m* (Übertragung) reserve channel
Schutzkappe *f* (Kamera) lens cap, lens cover, lens guard; ~ *f* (Scheinwerfer) safety mesh
Schutzkleidung *f* protective clothing
Schutzkontakt *m* protective contact
Schützraum *m* relay room
Schutzschalter *m* cut-out switch, protective circuit-breaker, protected switchgear; ~ **mit Magnetauslösung** magnetic cut-out switch; **magnetothermischer** ~ thermic cut-out switch
Schutzschicht *f* protective coating
Schutzstecker *m* safety plug
Schutzverhältnis *n* protection ratio
Schwachstrom *m* weak current, low-voltage current

Schwachstromanlage *f* low-current installation

Schwachstromwerkstatt *f* low-current workshop

Schwalbenschwanz *m* dovetail *n*

Schwanenhals *m* swan neck, goose neck (US)

Schwanenhalsmikrofon *n* swan-neck microphone

Schwank *m* farce *n*

Schwankung *f* (tech.) fluctuation *n*, variation *n*, oscillation *n*

Schwankungsfrequenz *f* variation frequency

schwarz *adj* black *adj*

Schwarz *n* black *n*

Schwarz ziehen black out *v*, to fade to black, to fade down to black; **gesättigtes ~** clear black; **reines ~** pure black, absolute black

Schwarzabhebung *f* pedestal *n*, set-up *n*, set-up interval

Schwarzabsetzung *f* s. Schwarzabhebung

Schwarzblende *f* fade to black, black-out *n*; **~ ziehen** to fade to black; **~ ziehen** (kurze Unterbrechung) to go to black, black flashing

Schwarzdehnung *f* black stretch

schwärzen *v* blacken *v*, darken *v*

Schwarzfilm *m* black leader, blacking *n*, black spacing

Schwarzhörer *m* pirate listener, unlicensed listener

Schwarzhörerfahndung *f* pirate-listener detection

Schwarzkrümmung *f* black non-linearity

Schwarzpegel *m* black level; **~ absetzen** to set up black level; **~ aufsetzen** to set down black level

Schwarzschulter *f* porch *n*; **hintere ~** back porch; **vordere ~** front porch

Schwarzschulterklemmung *f* black-level clamping, clamping on

front/back porch

Schwarzseher *m* pirate viewer, unlicensed viewer

Schwarzseherfahndung *f* pirate-viewer detection

Schwarzsender *m* pirate transmitter

Schwarztastung *f* blanking *n*

Schwärzung *f* density *n*, blackening *n*; **~** *f* (Foto) optical transmission density, photographic transmission density; **diffuse ~** diffuse density; **gleichbleibende ~** fixed density; **maximale ~** maximum density; **veränderliche ~** variable density

Schwärzungsbereich *m* density range

Schwärzungskurve *f* transfer characteristic curve, Hurter and Driffield curve (H a. D curve)

Schwärzungsstufe *f* density step, density value

Schwärzungsumfang *m* density latitude, density range, density scale

schwarzweiß *adj* black-and-white *adj* (B/W), monochrome *adj*

Schwarzweißabzug *m* black-and-white print

Schwarzweißempfänger *m* black-and-white receiver

Schwarzweißfernsehen *n* black-and-white television

Schwarzweißfilm *m* black-and-white film; **~** *m* (Material) black-and-white stock

Schwarzweißnegativfilm *m* black-and-white negative film; **~** *m* (Material) black-and-white negative stock

Schwarzweißpositivfilm *m* black-and-white positive film; **~** *m* (Material) black-and-white positive stock

Schwarzweißproduktion *f* black-and-white production, monochrome production

Schwarzweißraster *m* chequerboard pattern

Schwarzweißsender *m* monochrome transmitter

Schwarzweißsprung *m* black-to-white transition, black-to-white step

Schwarzweißumkehrfilm *m* black-and-white reversal film; ~ *m* (Material) black-and-white stock

Schwarzwert *m* black level; ~ **absetzen** to set up black level; ~ **aufsetzen** to set down black level; ~ **begrenzen** to clip black level; ~ **stauchen** to crush the blacks

Schwarzwertdiode *f* direct current restoration diode, clamping diode

Schwarzwertfesthaltung *f s.* Schwarzwerthaltung

Schwarzwerthaltung *f* direct current restoration, black-level clamping

Schwarzwertregler *m* (fam.) black-level control

Schwarzwertstauchung *f* black-crushing *n*

Schwarzwertsteller *m* black-level control

Schwarzwertsteuerung *f* black-level adjustment

Schwarzwertwiedergabe *f* direct current restoration

Schwarzwertwiederherstellung *f* re-adjustment of black level

Schwebung *f* beat *n*

Schwebungsfrequenz *f* beat frequency

Schwebungsnull *f* zero-beat frequency

Schwelle *f* threshold *n*, gate *n*

Schwellwert *m* threshold value, threshold level

Schwenk *m* pan *n*, panning *n*, panning shot; ~ *m* (Kran) craning *n*, booming *n*; **seitlicher** ~ (Kran) lateral craning, slewing *n*, jibbing *n*; **senkrechter** ~ tilt *n*, tilting *n*;

senkrechter ~ **nach oben** (Kran) craning-up *n*, booming-up *n*; **senkrechter** ~ **nach unten** (Kran) craning-down *n*, booming-down *n*

Schwenkarm *m* swivel arm, panning handle, pan-and-tilt arm

schwenkbar *adj* swivelling *adj*, swivel-mounted *adj*

Schwenkbereich *m* jib swing

schwenken *v* pan *v*, swivel *v*; **senkrecht** ~ tilt *v*

Schwenker *m* camera operator

Schwenkgriff *m* grip *n*

Schwenkkopf *m* panning head, pan head; ~ **mit Feinantrieb** pan head with vernier control; ~ **mit Kreiselantrieb** gyroscopic mounting, pan head with gyroscopic drive; ~ **mit Schwenkarm** pan head with panning handle; ~ **mit Schwerpunktausgleich** pan head with counterbalance weights

Schwenkstativ *n* camera tripod

Schwenk- und Neigekopf *m* pan-and-tilt head

schwingen *v* oscillate *v*

schwingfest *adj* immune to vibration

Schwingkreis *m* (R) resonant circuit, tuned circuit; ~ *m* (Oszillator) tank circuit, oscillating circuit

Schwingneigung *f* tendency to oscillate, inherent instability; ~ *f* (Rückkopplung) feedback tendency

Schwingspule *f* moving coil; ~ *f* (Lautsprecher) voice coil

Schwingung *f* oscillation *n*, vibration *n*, deflection *n*; **freilaufende** ~ free oscillation; **selbsterregte** ~ self-oscillation *n*

Schwingungszahl *f* vibration frequency, oscillation frequency

Schwingungszug *m* cycle *n*

Schwund *m* fading *n*; ~ *m* (mech.) shrinkage *n*; **selektiver** ~ selective

Schwund   148

fading
Schwungmasse *f* flywheel mass,
  gyrating mass
Schwungrad *n* flywheel *n*
Schwungradkreis *m* flywheel
  circuit
Schwungradoszillator *m* flywheel
  oscillator
Schwungradsynchronisation *f*
  flywheel synchronisation
Schwungscheibe *f* flywheel *n*
Science-Fiction-Film *m* science-
  fiction film
Scoop *m* scoop *n*
Scratch *m* scratch *n*
Script *n* script *n*, scenario *n*;
  ~ *f* continuity girl, script-girl *n*
Scriptgirl *n* continuity girl, script-
  girl *n*
sedezimal *adj* (EDV) sedecimal *adj*,
  hexadecimal *adj*, sexadecimal *adj*
Sedezimalzahl *f* (EDV) sedecimal
  number, hexadecimal number,
  sexadecimal number
Seegersicherung *f* Seeger circlip
Sehbeteiligung *f* viewing figure
Seher *m* (fam.) viewer *n*
Sehfunk *m* television (TV) *n*
Sehschärfe *f* sharpness of vision
Seide *f* silk *n*
Seidenblende *f* silk scrim
Seilzug *m* tackle-line *n*
Seite, erste (Zeitung) front page
Seitenantenne *f* side aerial
Seitenband *n* sideband *n*;
  unterdrücktes ~ suppressed
  sideband
Seitenbänder, unabhängige
  independent sidebands
Seitenbeleuchtung *f* side lighting
Seitenlicht *n* side light, edge light
Seitenschneider *m* side-cutting
  pliers *n pl*, side-cutters *n pl*,
  diagonal-cutting pliers *n pl*
seitenverkehrt *adj* side-inverted *adj*
Sektorenblende *f* rotary disc
  shutter
Sektorenverschluß *m* segment

shutter
Sekundärelektronenvervielfacher
  m electron multiplier
Sekundärstrahler *m* parasitic
  element, secondary radiator
Selbstaufschaukelung *f* self-
  excitation *n*, self-oscillation *n*
Selbstauslöser *m* automatic release,
  auto release
Selbsteinfädelung *f* (Proj.)
  automatic lacing, self-lacing *n*
Selbsterregung *f* self-excitation *n*,
  self-oscillation *n*
Selbsthaltekontakt *m* holding
  contact, locking contact
Selbsthaltetaste *f* self-locking push
  button, self-locking key
Selbstinduktion *f* self-induction *n*
selbstklebend *adj* self-adhesive *adj*,
  self-sealing *adj*
Selbstkontrolle *f* self-censorship *n*;
  freiwillige ~ voluntary self-
  censorship
Selbstkosten *plt* net cost
Selbstleuchter *m* fluorescent
  substance
selbstprüfend *adj* (EDV) self-
  checking *adj*
Selbstregelmotor *m* self-regulating
  motor, self-adjusting motor
selbstreinigend *adj* self-wiping *adj*
Selbstreinigung *f* self-wiping *n*
selbststrahlend *adj* phosphorescent
  adj
Selbstversorgung *f* (elek.) local
  supply
Selektion *f* (EDV) selection *n*
Selektivfilter *m* selective filter
Selektivruf *m* selective calling
Selektivschaltung *f* selective
  switching
Selengleichrichter *m* selenium
  rectifier
Selenzelle *f* selenium cell
Semidokumentation *f* drama
  documentary, dramatised
  documentary
Sendeablaufplan *m* presentation

schedule, transmission schedule

Sendeablaufprotokoll *n* presentation log

Sendeabwicklung *f* broadcasting operations *n pl*

Sendeanlage *f* transmitting station, transmitting installation

Sendeanstalt *f* broadcasting station, broadcasting organisation

Sendeantenne *f* transmitting aerial; **~ mit sehr ausgeprägter Strahlungskeule** highly directional transmitting aerial

Sendeband *n* transmission tape; **~** *n* (Frequenz) transmitting frequency range

Sendebeginn *m* start of transmission

Sendebereich *m* broadcasting area, service area, transmission range, service range, coverage area, area covered, transmission area, area served

Sendebereitschaft *f* staff on call

Sendebetrieb *m* radio and television operations *n pl*

Sendebetriebstechnik *f* radio and television engineering

Sendebild *n* outgoing picture

Sendebüro *n* presentation suite

Sendedauer *f* duration of transmission

Sendeempfangsgerät *n* transceiver *n*

sendefertig *adj* ready for transmission

Sendeform *f* type of broadcast, format *n*

Sendefrequenz *f* transmitting frequency, output frequency

Sendegebiet *n* broadcasting area, service area, transmission range, service range, coverage area, area covered, transmission area, area served

Sendegesellschaft *f* broadcasting company, broadcasting corporation

Sendehilfe *f* facility *n*

Sendehonorar *n* broadcast fee

Sendeingenieur *m* technical operations manager (TOM)

Sendekomplex *m* broadcasting centre

Sendekontrolle *f* continuity *n*

Sendekopie *f* transmission copy, transmission print, transmission tape

Sendeleistung *f* transmitting power, effective radiated power (ERP)

Sendeleiter *m* head of presentation; **diensthabender ~** (R) duty presentation officer; **diensthabender ~** (TV) duty presentation editor

Sendeleitung* *f* presentation* *n*

Sendeleitung *f* (tech.) outgoing circuit, outgoing channel, distribution circuit

Sendemast *m* transmitter mast

Sendemikrofon *n* transmitting microphone

Sendemodulation *f* transmitted modulation

senden *v* transmit *v*, broadcast *v*; **~** *v* (Funk) radio *v*, send *v*; **~** *v* (TV) televise *v*, telecast *v* (US); **~** *v* (Fernschreiber) run *v*; **zu ~ aufhören** to go off the air, sign off *v* (coll.); **zu ~ beginnen** to go on the air

Sendenachweis *m* presentation editor's log

Sendenetz *n* broadcasting network

Sendepaß *m* transmission label

Sendepegel *m* sending level

Sendeplan *m* transmission schedule

Sendeprotokoll *n* technical log

Sender *m* transmitter *n*, station *n*, sender *n*; **~** *m* (Anstalt) broadcasting station, broadcasting organisation; **~ bekommen** to receive a transmitter, to pick up a station; **~ einfangen** to receive a

Sender 150

transmitter, to pick up a station;
~ einstellen to tune in to a station
aus Versehen über den ~ gehen
to go out by mistake; **beweglicher
~** mobile transmitter, mobile
station; **fahrbarer ~** mobile
transmitter, mobile station;
tragbarer ~ portable transmitter;
über den ~ gehen go out *v*
Senderabstimmung *f* transmitter
tuning
Senderanlage *f* transmitting
station, transmitter complex
Senderaum *m* broadcasting studio,
studio *n*
Senderausgang *m* transmitter
output
Senderausrüstung *f* transmitter
equipment
Senderbetrieb *m* transmitter
operations *n pl*
Senderbetriebstechnik *f*
transmitter engineering
Senderbetriebszentrale *f*
transmitter control room
Senderdia *n* station identification
slide
Senderechte *n pl* transmission
rights, broadcasting rights
Senderegie *f* (R) continuity suite,
presentation suite
Senderegiebild *n* vision master
control
Senderegieton *m* sound master
control
Sendereihe *f* broadcast series,
series of broadcasts
Sendergruppe *f* transmitter
network
Senderingenieur *m* transmitter
engineer
Senderkette *f* transmitter chain
Senderkomplex *m* transmitting
station, transmitter complex
Senderleistung *f* transmitter power,
transmitter output power
Sendernetz *n* transmitter network
Senderseite *f* transmitting end,

sending end
Senderstandort *m* transmitter site
Sendertechnik *f* transmitter
engineering
Sendertechniker *m* transmitter
engineer
Senderturm *m* transmission tower
Senderverstärker *m* transmitter
amplifier
Senderwahl *f* tuning *n*, transmitter
selection
Senderweiche *f* combining unit
Sendesaal *m* audience studio,
concert hall, large studio
Sendeschalter *m* transmission
switch
Sendeschiene *f* transmitter
distribution network
Sendeschluß *m* close of
transmission, close-down *n*
Sendesparte *f* broadcasting sector
Sendestation *f* transmitting station,
radio station, broadcasting
station, sending station
Sendestraße *f* transmission circuit,
sending circuit
Sendestudio *n* broadcasting studio
Sendetechnik *f* radio and television
engineering
Sendetechniker *m* transmitter
technician
Sendeton *m* programme sound
Sendetonband *n* transmission tape
Sendeturm *m* radio tower
Sendeverfahren *n* transmitting
system, transmission process
Sendeverstärker *m* sending
amplifier
Sendeweg *m* transmission circuit,
sending circuit
Sendezeit *f* time of transmission,
broadcasting time, transmission
time, programme length, air time,
spot *n* (coll.), slot *n*;
~ überschreiten overrun *v*;
~ überziehen overrun *v*;
~ unterschreiten underrun *v*
Sendezentrale *f* master control

room
Sendezentrum *n* broadcasting
centre
Sendung *f* (Progr.) broadcast *n*,
programme *n*; ~ *f* (tech.)
transmission *n*; ~ **fahren** to run a
transmission; ~ **läuft!** programme
on the air!; ~ **machen** produce *v*;
aktuelle ~ topical programme,
current affairs broadcast; **auf** ~
bleiben to stay on the air; **auf** ~
gehen to go on the air, to come
on the air; **auf** ~ **schalten** to go on
the air, to come on the air; **auf** ~
sein to be on the air;
aufgezeichnete ~ recorded
programme; **aufgezeichnete** ~
(Übernahme) transcribed
programme; **durch die** ~ **führen** to
present the programme;
gespeicherte ~ recorded
programme; **gesponsorte** ~
sponsored broadcast, sponsored
programme; **kommerzielle** ~
commercial programme,
commercial *n*; **multilaterale** ~
multilateral *n*; **unilaterale** ~
unilateral *n*; **vorproduzierte** ~ pre-
produced programme, pre-
recorded programme;
zeitversetzte ~ deferred broadcast
zur ~ checked for transmission,
ready for broadcasting
Sendungen für das Ausland*
external broadcasting*
Senkrechtschwenk *m* tilt *n*, tilting
n; ~ **nach oben** (Kran) craning-up
n, booming-up *n*; ~ **nach unten**
(Kran) craning-down *n*, booming-
down *n*
Sensationsdarsteller *m* stuntman *n*
sensibilisieren *v* sensitise *v*
Sensibilisierung *f* sensitisation *n*
Sensitometer *n* sensitometer *n*
Sensitometerstreifen *m*
sensitometric test strip
Sensitometrie *f* sensitometry *n*
sensitometrisch *adj* sensitometric

adj
Separator *m* sync separator
sequentiell *adj* sequential *adj*
Sequenz *f* (F, Band) sequence *n*
Sequenzsystem *n* sequential system
Sequenzverfahren *n* sequential
process
Serie *f* series *n*
seriell *adj* (EDV) serial *adj*
Serienkopie *f* release print
Serien-Parallel-Umsetzer *m* (EDV)
serial-parallel converter
Serienresonanz *f* series resonance
Serienresonanzkreis *m* series-
resonant circuit, series-tuned
circuit
Serienschaltung *f* series
connection, connection in series
Serienspeisung *f* series supply,
series feed
Service *m* (Kundendienst) after-
sales service
Servicegenerator *m* signal
generator
Servicegerät *n* item of test
equipment
Servomotor *m* servo motor
Servosteuerung *f* servo control
Servosystem *n* servo system
Setzimpuls *m* (EDV) set pulse
Setzmaschine *f* (Video) caption
generator
Shotlist *f* shot list
Show *f* show *n*
Sicherheitsband *n* (Frequenz) guard
band
Sicherheitsbeauftragter *m* security
officer
Sicherheitsfaktor *m* safety factor
Sicherheitsfilm *m* safety film,
safety stock, non-flam film
Sicherheitsgurt *m* safety belt,
safety harness
Sicherheitskette *f* safety chain
Sicherheitskontakt *m* safety
contact
Sicherheitskopie *f* safety copy
Sicherheitsspur *f* (F) guard band,

guard track, safety track
Sicherheitsvorschriften *f pl* safety regulations
Sicherung *f* fuse *n*; **flinke ~** rapid fuse; **träge ~** slow fuse
Sicherungsautomat *m* automatic cut-out, automatic interrupter, circuit-breaker *n*
Sicherungshalter *m* fuse holder
Sicherungsleine *f* bond *n*, safety cord
Sicherungsschalter *m* fuse switch
sichtbar machen visualise *v*
Sichtbarkeit *f* visibility *n*
Sichtbarkeitszone *f* (Sat.) illumination zone, coverage zone
Sichtgerät *n* visual indicator, visual monitor; **~** *n* (EDV) display unit, video display, CRT display unit
Sichtprüfung *f* visual check
Sichtröhre *f* pattern tube
Sichtspeicherröhre *f* viewing storage tube
Sichtverbindung *f* visual communication, visual contact
Sichtzeichen *n* visual signal, marker *n*
Siebfaktor *m* smoothing factor, hum-reduction factor
Siebglied *n* filter section
Siebkondensator *m* smoothing capacitor
Siebung *f* filtering *n*
Signal *n* signal *n*; **analoges ~** (EDV) analog signal; **kodiertes ~** coded signal; **wiedergegebenes ~** reproduced signal, replayed signal
Signalamplitude *f* signal amplitude
Signalaufbauimpulse *m pl* basic signals
Signalaufbereitung *f* signal regenerating, signal shaping, signal processing
Signalausfall *m* loss of signal
Signalbildmonitor *m* picture monitor
Signaleinspeisung *f* signal input,

signal injection
Signalelektrode *f* signal electrode
Signalerzeugung *f* signal generation
Signalflanke *f* signal edge, wavefront *n*
Signalformierung *f* signal shaping
Signalgemisch *n* composite signal
Signalhöchstwert *m* maximum value of signal
Signalhub *m* signal deviation
Signalisationsstrom *m* signalling current
Signalisierung *f* signalling *n*
Signallampe *f* signalling lamp, indicator lamp, cue light, tally light
Signalmischer *m* signal mixer, signal combiner
Signalpegel *m* signal level
Signalschriftträger *m* recording medium
Signalspannung *f* signal voltage; **~ für Szenenschwarz** black-level signal voltage
Signalstärke *f* signal strength
Signalstrom *m* signal current
Signalstruktur *f* structure of signal
Signalverzögerungssystem *n* delay system
Signalweg *m* signal path, channel *n*
Silberbild *n* silver image
Silberblende *f* silvered reflector
Silbersalz *n* silver halide
Silberschirm *m* silver screen
simultan *adj* simultaneous *adj*
Simultanaufnahme *f* combination shot
Simultansystem *n* simultaneous system
Simultanübertragung *f* simultaneous broadcast, simultaneous transmission, simultaneous relay
Sinfonieorchester *n* symphony orchestra
Sinusgenerator *m* sine-wave generator

Sinusquadratimpuls *m* sine-squared pulse
Sinussignal *n* sinusoidal signal
Sinuswelle *f* sine wave, sinusoidal wave
Skala *f* scale *n*, graduation *n*; ~ *f* (Empfänger) dial *n*
Sketch *m* sketch *n*
Skineffekt *m* skin effect
Skineffektwiderstand *m* rf-resistance *n*
Skizze *f* sketch *n*, drawing *n*
Skypan *m* skypan *n*
Slowmotion-Maschine (SMM) *f* slow-motion machine
Sockel *m* pedestal *n*, base *n*
Sockelbelegung *f* socket connections *n pl*, valve base connections *n pl*
Soffitte *f* border *n*
Soffittenleuchte *f* tubular lamp, strip light
Sofortverarbeitung *f* (EDV) real-time processing
Sofortzugriff *m* (EDV) immediate access
soften *v* (F) soften *v*; ~ *v* (opt.) diffuse *v*
Softlinse *f* soft lens, diffusing lens
Softscheibe *f* diffuser *n*; ~ *f* (opt.) soft focus filter, romanticiser *n*; ~ *f* (Beleuchtung) net *n*, scrim *n*
Software *f* software *n*
Solarisation *f* solarisation *n*, image reversal
Solist *m* soloist *n*
Sollfrequenz *f* nominal frequency
Sollgeschwindigkeit *f* nominal speed
Sollwert *m* nominal value; ~ *m* (EDV) set point
Solovortrag *m* solo performance
Sonde *f* probe *n*
Sonderbericht *m* special report, special *n*
Sonderberichterstatter *m* special correspondent
Sonderleitung *f* special circuit

Sondermeldung *f* special announcement
Sondersendung *f* (TV) special *n*
Sonnenblende *f* lens shade, lens hood, sun visor, sunshield *n*, sunshade *n*; ~ *f* (Aufhellung) reflection screen
Sonnenschutz *m* sunshield *n*, sunshade *n*
Sonnentubus *m* (Kamera) lens hood, sunshade *n*
Sonnenzelle *f* solar cell
sortieren *v* sort *v*
soßig *adj* milky *adj*, low-contrast *adj*, low-gamma *adj*
Sozialpolitik* *f* social affairs* *n pl*
Sozialwerk* *n* welfare* *n*
Spalt *m* gap *n*; ~ *m* (opt.) slit *n*
Spaltbreite *f* gap length; ~ *f* (opt.) slit width
Spaltdämpfung *f* gap loss; ~ **infolge Schiefstellung** azimuth loss
Spalte *f* (Presse) column *n*
Spalteinstellung *f* gap adjustment, gap setting
Spaltfilm *m* split film
Spaltoptik *f* light valve
Spannrolle *f* jockey roller, tension roller
Spannung *f* tension *n*, voltage *n*; ~ **geben** power *v*; **bewertete** ~ weighted voltage; **verkettete** ~ voltage between lines
Spannungsabfall *m* voltage drop
Spannungsabfrage *f* (EDV) level sense
Spannungsausfall *m* loss of voltage
Spannungsausfallrelais *n* no-volt release relay
Spannungsbauch *m* voltage maximum, voltage loop, antinode *n*
Spannungseichung *f* voltage calibration
Spannungsfestigkeit *f* voltage rating
Spannungsfühler *m* voltage probe

Spannungsgegenkopplung *f* voltage
negative feedback
Spannungsknoten *m* voltage node,
voltage minimum
Spannungskonstanthalter *m*
voltage stabiliser, automatic
voltage regulator (AVR)
spannungslos *adj* without voltage,
dead *adj*, isolated *adj*
Spannungsmesser *m* voltmeter *n*
Spannungsprüfer *m* voltage tester,
neon tester
Spannungsregler *m* (fam.) *s.*
Spannungssteller
Spannungssteller *m* voltage control,
voltage regulator
Spannungsteiler *m* voltage divider
Spannungsüberschlag *m* flash-over
n
Spannungsumschalter *m* voltage
selector switch, voltage change-
over switch
Spannungsvergleich *m* voltage
comparison
Spannungsversorgung *f* power
supply
Spannungsverstärker *m* voltage
amplifier
Spannungsverstärkung *f* voltage
amplification, voltage gain
Spannungsvervielfacher *m* voltage
multiplier
Spannungswähler *m* voltage
selector
Spannungswandler *m* voltage
transformer
Spannungswert *m* voltage level,
voltage *n*
Sparte *f* sector *n*, area *n*
Spartransformator *m*
autotransformer *n*
Spätausgabe *f* (TV) late-night
edition, late news *n pl*
Special *n* (Sonderbericht) special *n*
Specknudel *f* (fam.) earpiece *n*,
earphone *n*, deaf-aid *n* (coll.)
Speicher *m* store *n*; ~ *m* (EDV) store
n, memory *n*; ~ **mit direktem**

Zugriff (EDV) random-access
memory, random-access store;
~ **mit schnellem Zugriff** (EDV)
zero-access store, fast memory,
fast store, high-speed memory,
high-speed store, rapid memory,
rapid store; ~ **mit sequentiellem
Zugriff** (EDV) sequential-access
store; ~ **mit wahlfreiem Zugriff**
(EDV) random-access memory,
random-access store; **externer** ~
(EDV) external memory, external
store; **geschützter** ~ (EDV)
protected storage area; **interner** ~
(EDV) internal store; **langsamer** ~
(EDV) slow-access store, slow
store; **permanenter** ~ (EDV)
permanent store, permanent
memory, non-volatile store
Speicheradresse *f* (EDV) storage
address, memory address
Speicherausdruck *m* (EDV) core
storage dump, core storage printout
speicherfähig *adj* capable of being
stored
Speicherkapazität *f* (EDV) memory
size, memory capacity, storage
capacity
Speicherplatte *f* storage plate,
storage target
Speicherplatz *m* (EDV) store
location, memory location
Speicherrelais *n* storage relay
Speicherröhre *f* storage-type
camera tube, storage camera
tube, long-persistence tube
Speicherschutz *m* (EDV) storage
protection
Speichersystem *n* storage system,
recording system, memory
system
Speicherung *f* recording *n*, storage
n
Speicherzeit *f* storage time,
retention time
Speicherzelle *f* (EDV) storage unit,
storage element, storage cell

Speicherzyklus *m* (EDV) storage cycle, memory cycle
Speisegerät *n* supply unit
speisen *v* (elek.) feed *v*, supply *v*, charge *v*, energise *v*
Speisung *f* (elek.) power supply, supply *n*, feeding *n*, feed *n*
Spektralanteil *m* spectral component
Spektralbereich *m* spectral region
Spektralempfindlichkeit *f* spectral sensitivity
Spektralfarbe *f* spectral colour
Spektralfarbenzug *m* chromaticity diagram
Spektralkomponente *f* spectral component
Spektralkurvenzug *m* spectral curve
Spektrallinie *f* spectrum line, spectral line
Spektralverteilungskurve *f* spectral curve
Spektralzerlegung *f* spectral analysis
Spektrogramm *n* spectrogram *n*
Spektroskop *n* spectroscope *n*
Spektrum *n* spectrum *n*; **kontinuierliches** ~ continuous spectrum; **sichtbares** ~ visible spectrum, luminous spectrum
Sperrdrossel *f* choke *n*
Sperrfilter *m* rejection filter
Sperrfrist *f* embargo *n*; ~ **bis** ... embargoed till ...
Sperrfristmeldung *f* embargoed news item
Sperrgreifer *m* register pin
Sperrholz *n* plywood *n*
Sperriegel *m* bolt *n*, locking bar, ratchet pawl
Sperrkreis *m* rejector circuit, wave trap
Sperrschaltung *f* rejection circuit
Sperrschicht *f* blocking layer, barrier layer, insulating layer
Sperrschichtzelle *f* barrier-layer cell, barrier-layer photocell

Sperrschwinger *m* blocking oscillator
Sperrsignal *n* blocking signal; ~ *n* (EDV) inhibiting signal, disabling signal
Sperrspannung *f* cut-off voltage
Sperrstift *m* pin *n*, locking pin
Sperrung *f* blocking *n*
Spesen *plt* expenses *n pl*, allowances *n pl*
Spezialeffekt *m* special effects *n pl*
Spiegel *m* mirror *n*, reflector *n*; **dichroitischer** ~ dichroic mirror; **farbzerlegender** ~ dichroic mirror; **halbdurchlässiger** ~ semi-silvered mirror, semi-reflecting mirror
Spiegelblende *f* mirror shutter
Spiegelfassung *f* reflector mount
Spiegelfrequenz *f* image frequency, second frequency
Spiegellampe *f* mirror lamp
Spiegellinse *f* mirror lens
Spiegelreflexblende *f* reflex mirror shutter
Spiegelreflexkamera *f* mirror reflex camera, reflex camera
Spiegelreflexsystem *n* reflex system, mirror reflex system
Spiegelselektion *f* image frequency rejection
Spiegelung *f* reflection *n*
Spiegelzylinder *m* mirror drum
Spiel *n* (Darsteller) acting *n*, performance *n*
spielen *v* (Darsteller) act *v*, perform *v*, play *v*
Spielfilm *m* feature film, full-length film
Spielleiter *m* director *n*, producer *n*; ~ *m* (R) radio producer; ~ *m* (Hörspiel) drama producer; ~ *m* (Quiz) quizmaster *n*; ~ *m* (Conférencier) compère *n*
Spielleitung *f* direction *n*, production *n*
Spielplan *m* schedule *n*, programme *n*, repertoire *n*; **auf dem** ~ **bleiben** to remain running, to be kept in

Spielplan 156

the schedule; **auf dem ~ stehen** to
be billed, to be scheduled
Spielraum *m* tolerance *n*, latitude *n*,
free space, clearance *n*, play *n*
Spielrequisit *n* property *n*, prop *n*
(coll.)
Spinne *f* (Lautsprecher) spider *n*
Spinnwebmaschine *f* cobweb gun
Spinstabilisierung *f* (Sat.)
stabilisation of spin
Spiralkabel *n* helix cable
Spitze *f* point *n*, peak *n*; ~ *f* (Licht)
highlight *n*, hair light
Spitzen setzen to set a highlight
Spitzenaussteuerungsmesser *m*
peak programme meter (PPM)
Spitzengleichrichter *m* peak
rectifier
Spitzengleichrichtung *f* peak
rectification
Spitzenhelligkeit *f* highlight
brightness
Spitzenhub *m* peak deviation
Spitzenleistung *f* peak power
Spitzenlicht *n* highlight *n*, hair light
Spitzenmesser *m* peak indicator,
peak meter
Spitzenpegelfesthaltung *f* peak
level clamping
Spitzenspannung *f* peak voltage
Spitzenspannungsmesser *m* peak
voltmeter
Spitzenstrom *m* peak current
Spitzenwert *m* peak value, peak
level
Spitzenwertmesser *m* peak
indicator, peak meter
Spitze-Spitze-Spannung *f* peak-to-
peak voltage
Split *m* (17,5 Cord) perforated
magnetic film, magnetic film,
perforated magnetic tape
Sponsorsendung *f* sponsored
broadcast, sponsored programme
Sport *m* sport *n*, sports reporting,
sportcast *n* (US)
Sport* *m* (R) sports news
programmes* *n pl*; ~ *m* (TV)

sports and events*
Sportfilm *m* sports film
Sportfunk *m* sports news
programmes* *n pl*
Sportkommentator *m* sports
commentator
Sportredakteur *m* sports editor,
sports journalist
Sportreporter *m* sports reporter
Sportschau *f* television sports news
n pl
Sportsendung *f* sports broadcast,
sportcast *n* (US)
Sportübertragung *f* transmission of
sports event
Sportveranstaltung *f* sports event,
sporting event
Spot *m* (Werbung) commercial spot,
commercial *n*, spot *n*; ~ *m* (fam.)
s. Spotlicht
Spotlicht *n* spotlight *n*, spot *n*
Spotmeter *n* spot photometer
Spotvorsatz *m* cone *n*
Sprachaufnahme *f* voice recording,
speech recording
Sprachband *n* speech band
Sprachfernsehen *n* foreign-
language courses by television
Sprachfrequenzbereich *m* voice
frequency range, speech
frequency range
Sprachkursus *m* language course
Sprachunterricht *m* language
tuition
Spratzer *m* sputter *n*, splash *n*
Sprechanlage *f* intercommunication
system, intercom *n* (coll.)
sprechen *v* speak *v*; ~ *v* (FS-
Nachrichten, R) read *v*
Sprecher *m* speaker *n*; ~ *m*
(Ansager) announcer *n*; ~ *m*
(Nachrichten) newsreader *n*,
newscaster *n*; ~ *m* (F) narrator *n*,
commentator *n*; ~ *m* (Behörde)
spokesman *n*
Sprecherkabine *f* commentator's
booth
Sprechermikrofon *n* commentator's

microphone
Sprecherplatz *m* commentator's
position
Sprecherstelle *f* commentator's
position
Sprecherstudio *n* continuity studio,
presentation studio
Sprechertext *m* commentary *n*,
narration *n*, script *n*
Sprechfrequenz *f* voice frequency,
speech frequency
Sprechfunk *m* radiotelephony (RT)
n
Sprechfunkgerät *n* radio telephone;
tragbares ~ walkie-talkie *n*
Sprechfunkverkehr *m* radio-
telephone traffic
Sprechgeschirr *n* headset *n*
Sprechkontakt *m* voice contact
Sprechkopf *m* sound head
Sprechleitung *f* speech line, speech
circuit, control line
Sprechprobe *f* voice test
Sprechstrom *m* speech current,
voice current
Sprechverbindung *f* speech
communication, voice connection;
gerichtete ~ point-to-point voice
connection, one-way speech
channel; **multiplexe** ~ multiplex
speech connection, multiplex
speech channel
Sprechverkehr, wechselseitiger
intercommunication *n*, intercom
n (coll.)
Springblende *f* automatic
diaphragm, semi-automatic
diaphragm
Spritzarbeit *f* paint spraying
Spritzlackierer *m* spray painter
Spritzpistole *f* spray gun
spritzwasserdicht *adj* splash-proof
adj
spröde *adj* brittle *adj*
Sprödigkeit *f* brittleness *n*
Sprossenschrift *f* variable-density
sound recording, variable-density
track

Sprühentwicklung *f* spray
development
Sprühentwicklungsmaschine *f*
spray processor
Sprühwässerung *f* spray watering
Sprung *m* (Schnitt) jump cut; **auf** ~
kleben jump-cut *v*
Sprungbefehl *m* (EDV) branching
instruction, branch instruction,
control transfer instruction, jump
instruction
Sprungfrequenz *f* transition
frequency
Sprungfunktion *f* step function
Sprungkennlinie *f* step function
response, transient response
Sprungschramme *f* intermittent
scratch
Sprungsignal *n* step function signal
Sprungwand *f* camera trap
Spule *f* bobbin *n*, spool *n*, reel *n*; ~ *f*
(elek.) coil *n*, inductor *n*; ~ **mit**
Seitenflanschen spool with side
plates
spulen *v* spool *v*, reel *v*, wind *v*; ~ *v*
(elek.) coil *v*
Spulenkörper *m* bobbin *n*; ~ *m*
(elek.) coil form
Spulenstrom *m* coil current
Spulentrommel *f* coil turret
Spur *f* (Band) track *n*; ~ *f* (Röhre)
trace *n*
Spurbreite *f* trackwidth *n*
Spurhaltung *f* tape guidance
Spurlage *f* track placement, track
position
Spurnormen *f pl* track
configuration
S-Separator *m* line-sync separator
Staatsrundfunk *m* state
broadcasting authority
Stab *m* staff *n*, team *n*
Stabantenne *f* rod aerial
Stabilisierung *f* stabilisation *n*
Stabilisierverstärker *m* stabilising
amplifier
Stabliste *f* (F) production list
Stadtnetz *n* town mains *n pl*

Staffelei *f* easel *n*
Stahlakkumulator *m* nickel-iron-
alkaline accumulator, Ni-Fe
accumulator
Stammdatei *f* (EDV) master file
Stammleitung *f* trunk line; ~ *f* (Ant.)
main distribution cable
Stammleitungsverteilung *f* trunk
line distribution
Standardausrüstung *f* standard
equipment
Standardkopie *f* standard print
Standarte *f* (Filmkamera) lens
mount; ~ *f* (Fotoapparat) lens
carrier, lens standard
Standbild *n* still *n*, slide *n*, still
frame, still picture, frozen picture
~ **fahren** to freeze the action
Standbildverlängerung *f* stop
frame, hold frame, freeze frame,
still copy, frozen picture,
suspended animation
Ständer *m* stand *n*, support *n*
Standfoto *n* still *n*, still picture
Standfotograf *m* stills photographer,
stills cameraman, stills man,
studio photographer
Standgerät *n* set on a stand
Standkopie *f* stop frame, hold
frame, freeze frame, still copy,
frozen picture, suspended
animation
Standkopieren *n* stop framing,
freeze framing, hold framing
Standmikrofon *n* static microphone
Standort *m* site *n*, location *n*
Standtitel *m* static caption
Stange *f* bar *n*, rod *n*; ~ *f*
(Scheinwerfer) lighting pole,
barrel *n*
Stanze *f* punching machine, punch
n, stamp *n*, die *n*; ~ *f* (Zeichen)
change-over cue
Stanztrick *m* chroma key, blue
screen
Stanzzange *f* perforator *n*
Stapelfernverarbeitung *f* (EDV)
remote batch processing

Stapelverarbeitung *f* (EDV) batch
processing
Star *m* star *n*
Starkstrom *m* heavy current
Starkstromanlage *f* power plant
Starkstromelektriker *m* electrician
n
Starkstromfreileitung *f* overhead
power line
Starkstromingenieur *m* electrical
power engineer
Starkstromnetz *n* power supply
system, mains *n pl*
Starkstromwerkstatt *f* electrical
power workshop
Start *m* start *n*; **asynchroner** ~ non-
sync start; **fliegender** ~ flying
start, pre-start *n*
Startauslösezeichen *n* start pulse,
starting mark, starting signal,
start release signal
Startband *n* head leader, start
leader, leader *n*; ~ **für Cord**
magnetic film leader, mag leader
(coll.); ~ **kleben** (nach
Bandgeschwindigkeit) to splice
leader sticker; ~ **kleben 19 cm**
(blau) to splice 7 1/2"/sec (blue);
~ **kleben 38 cm** (rot) to splice
15"/sec (red); ~ **kleben 76 cm**
(weiß) to splice 30"/sec (white);
~ **kleben 4,75 cm** (grau) to splice 1
7/8"/sec (grey); ~ **kleben 9,5 cm**
(grün) to splice 3 3/4"/sec (green);
~ **mit Bildstrich** leader with
frame bars
Startimpuls *m* sync mark, sync plop
Startkreuz *n* sync cross
Startmarke *f* start mark
Startmarkierung *f* start mark; **auf** ~
einlegen to lace up to start mark
Startmarkierungen anbringen to
make start marks
Startvorlaufzeit *f* run-up time, roll-
in time, pre-roll time, count-down
n
Startvorspann *m* head leader, start
leader, leader *n*

Startzeichen *n* start mark
Startzeit *f s.* Startvorlaufzeit
Statement *n* statement *n*; ~ *n* (journalistisch) straight piece
Station *f* station *n*; **bemannte** ~ attended station; **ferngeschaltete** ~ remote-switched station; **kommerzielle** ~ commercial station; **nicht ständig besetzte** ~ semi-attended station; **unbemannte** ~ unattended station
Stationsabsage *f* closing announcement
Stationsansage *f* station announcement
Stationsdia *n* station caption, station identification slide
Stationskennung *f* (Ton) station identification, identification signal
Stationskennzeichen *n* (Bild) station caption
Statist *m* extra *n*, supernumerary *n*, walk-on *n*, super *n*
Statisterie *f* crowd *n*, extras *n pl*, supers *n pl* (US)
Stativ *n* stand *n*, tripod *n*, support *n* **ausziehbares** ~ telescopic tripod
Stativfahrwagen *m* tripod dolly
Stativkopf *m* tripod head
Stativspinne *f* tripod base, spider *n*
Stativverlängerung *f* tripod extension
stauchen *v* (schwarz) crush *v*
Stauchung *f* (schwarz) crushing *n*
steckbar *adj* plug-in *adj*
Steckdose *f* plug socket, socket *n*; **gespeiste** ~ live socket; **schaltbare** ~ switched socket, switched plug socket
Stecker *m* plug *n*
Steckerleiste *f* multi-contact strip, multi-socket strip
Steckerstift *m* plug pin
Steckfeld *n* patching panel, jackfield *n*, jumper panel (US)
Steckkarte *f* plug-in card
Steckkassette *f* plug-in cassette

Steckkasten *m* socket box
Steckkontakt *m* plug contact, plug *n*
Steckkreuzfeld *n* plug-in matrix
Steckleiterplatte *f* printed circuit
Steckspule *f* plug-in coil
Steckverbindung *f* plug connection
Steckvorrichtung *f* plug and socket; **drehbare** ~ coupler *n*
Stehleiter *f* step-ladder *n*
Stehwelle *f* standing wave
Stehwellenmeßgerät *n* stationary wave test set
Steigleitung *f* riser *n*, rising main
Steilheit *f* (Filmmaterial) gamma *n*, contrast *n*, hardness *n*; ~ *f* (Röhre) mutual conductance, transconductance *n*, slope of valve characteristics; ~ *f* (Kennlinie) slope *n*
Steller *m* fader *n*, control knob, control *n*; ~ *m* (Licht) dimmer *n*; **linearer** ~ linear control, linear fader; **logarithmischer** ~ logarithmic control, logarithmic fader
Stellglied *n* (EDV) final control element
Stellmotor *m* servo motor
Stellprobe *f* first rehearsal
Stellpult *n* control desk, fader desk
Stelltransformator *m* continuously variable transformer
stellvertretend *adj* deputy *adj*, assistant *adj*, acting *adj*
Stellwerk *n* (Licht) lighting-control console
Stellwiderstand *m* rheostat *n*, variable resistor
Stereo *n* stereo *n*, stereophony *n*
stereo *adj* stereophonic *adj*, stereo *adj*
Stereoaufnahmeverfahren AB AB stereophonic recording process; ~ **XY und MS** XY and MS stereophonic recording process
Stereoaufzeichnung *f* stereo recording

Stereoballempfänger 160

Stereoballempfänger *m* stereo rebroadcast receiver
Stereodekoder *m* stereo decoder
Stereoempfänger *m* stereo receiver,
stereo tuner
stereofon *adj* stereophonic *adj*,
stereo *adj*
Stereofonie *f* stereophony *n*, stereo
sound, stereo *n*
stereofonisch *adj* stereophonic *adj*,
stereo *adj*
Stereoprogramm *n* stereo
programme
Stereosendebetrieb *m* stereo
transmitter operation, stereo
operation
Stereosendung *f* stereo
transmission, stereo broadcast
Stereosignal *n* stereo signal
Stereoskop *n* stereoscope *n*
Stereostudio *n* stereo studio
stereotüchtig *adj* stereo-capable *adj*
Stereoumsetzer *m* stereo
transposer, stereo rebroadcast
transmitter, stereo relay
transmitter
Stereowiedergabe *f* stereo
reproduction
Stern-Dreieck *n* star-delta *n*
Sternpunkt *m* television switching
network centre
Sternspannung *f* voltage to neutral
Sternsystem *n* star system, star
connection
Sternverteilungssystem *n* star
distributing system, three-phase
distribution system
Steueranweisung *f* (EDV) control
statement
Steuereinheit *f* (EDV) control unit
Steuerfeld *n* control panel
Steuerfunktion *f* (EDV) control
function
Steuergenerator *m* pilot frequency
generator
Steuergerät *n* control gear
Steuergitter *n* control grid
Steuerhebel *m* operating lever,

control lever, steering lever
Steuerknopf *m* control knob
Steuerleistung *f* grid-driving power,
driving power
Steuerleitung *f* control line
steuern *v* control *v*, regulate *v*, drive
v
Steueroszillator *m* master oscillator
(MO)
Steuerpult *n* control desk, control
console
Steuerquarz *m* oscillator crystal,
frequency-control crystal
Steuerring *m* control ring
Steuersender *m* master oscillator,
control transmitter
Steuersignal *n* drive signal, control
signal
Steuerspur *f* control track
Steuerstromkreis *m* control circuit
Steuerung *f* control *n*; ~ *f*
(Verstärker) drive *n*;
verzögerungsfreie ~ undelayed
control; **zentralisierte** ~ central
control
Steuerwerk *n* (EDV) control unit
Stich *m* (Farbe) cast *n*
Stichel *m* (Platte) cutter *n*
Stichelwinkel *m* (Platte) groove
angle
Stichleitung *f* stub line, stub cable,
stub *n*
Stichleitungsabzweigung *f*
bifurcation stub
Stichleitungsverteilung *f*
distribution stub
Stichwort *n* cue *n*, sound cue, word
cue
Stiftleiste *f* plug strip
Stillstand *m* standstill *n*, stop *n*
Stillstandvorrichtung *f* stopping
device
Stimmdoubel *n* dubbing voice
Stimme *f* voice *n*; **mehr** ~ **geben** to
give more voice
Stimmgabel *f* tuning fork
Stimmprobe *f* voice test
Stimmungsmusik *f* mood music

Stockholmer Wellenplan
Stockholm plan
Stoff *m* subject *n*, subject matter,
material *n*, story *n*
Stoffzulassung *f* acceptance of story
Stopp! (Unterbrechung) stop!; ~
(Ende einer Aufnahme) cut!, hold
it!
Stoppbad *n* (F) stop bath
Stoppbefehl *m* (EDV) breakpoint
instruction, stop instruction, halt
instruction
stoppen *v* (Zeit) time *v*
Stopptrick *m* stop-camera effect,
freeze effect, freeze-frame effect
Stoppuhr *f* stopwatch *n*
Stöpsel *m* plug *n*, stopper *n*; ~ *m*
(zweipolig) two-pole plug
stöpseln *v* plug in *v*, plug up *v*
Störabstand *m* signal-to-noise ratio
(S/N ratio), signal-to-interference
ratio; ~ **ohne Modulation**
unmodulated signal-to-noise ratio
Störanfälligkeit *f* susceptibility to
trouble, susceptibility to
interference
Störaufzeichnung *f* signal-to-noise
ratio recording
Störaustastung *f* noise blanking
Störbegrenzer *m* noise limiter
Störbegrenzung *f* noise limiting;
automatische ~ automatic noise-
limiting (ANL)
stören *v* (ungewollt) interfere *v*; ~ *v*
(gewollt) jam *v*
störfrei *adj* interference-free *adj*,
immune from interference
Störgeräusch *n* (ungewollt) noise
interference; ~ *n* (gewollt)
jamming *n*, jamming noise
Störimpuls *m* interference pulse
Störkompensation *f* interference
compensation
Störlicht *n* light interference
Störmeldung *f* (Anzeige) fault
report
Störmodulation *f* unwanted
modulation

Störmodulationsverhältnis *n*
modulation-to-interference ratio
Störmuster *n* interference pattern;
jalousieartiges ~ venetian-blind
pattern
Störpegel *m* noise level
Störquelle *f* noise source
Störschutzfilter *m* radio
interference filter
Störsignal *n* spurious signal,
interference signal, interfering
signal, break-through *n*, edge
flare
Störsignalkompensation *f* spurious
signal compensation
Störspannung *f* noise voltage,
interference voltage, disturbing
voltage
Störspannungsmesser *m* noise
meter
Störspannungsquelle *f* source of
interference
Störspitze *f* interference peak,
impulse interference
Störstrahlung *f* radio interference,
spurious radiation, stray
radiation
Störtrupp *m* exchange fault gang
Störüberlagerung *f* superimposed
interference; ~ *f* (Pfeifton)
heterodyne interference
Störung *f* breakdown *n*, fault *n*; ~ *f*
(ungewollt) interference *n*; ~ *f*
(gewollt) jamming *n*; ~ *f* (Bild)
pattern interference, jitter *n*,
vision breakdown; ~ **beheben** to
clear a fault; ~ **beseitigen** to clear
a fault; **atmosphärische** ~
atmospherics *n pl*; **technische** ~
technical fault
Störungsannahme* *f* (R,TV) radio
interference group
Störungsbeseitigung *f* fault
clearance, trouble-shooting *n*
Störungsdia *n* fault caption
Story *f* story *n*
Storyboard *n* story-board *n*
stottern *v* (ins Mikro) fluff *v*

Strahl *m* ray *n*, beam *n*
Strahlablenkung *f* beam deflection
Strahlauftreffpunkt *m* irradiated point
Strahlausrichtung *f* beam alignment
Strahlbreite *f* beamwidth *n*
Strahldeckung *f* beam convergence
Strahlengang *m* ray path
Strahlenteiler *m* beam splitter; **optischer** ~ optical beam splitter
Strahlenteilung *f* beam splitting
Strahler *m* radiator *n*; ~ *m* (Ant.) aerial *n*, antenna *n* (US); ~ *m* (Ton) loudspeaker *n*
Strahlrücklauf *m* flyback *n*
Strahlschärfe *f* beam focus
Strahlstrom *m* beam current; ~ **IK fein** fine control of beam current; ~ **IK grob** coarse control of beam current
Strahlstromaustastung *f* beam-current blanking
Strahlstrombegrenzung *f* beam-current limiting
Strahlstrombündelung *f* beam-current focusing, electron focusing
Strahlstromjustierung *f* beam-current adjustment
Strahlstromrauschen *n* beam-current noise
Strahlstromsperre *f* beam gate
Strahlstromsteller *m* beam-current control
Strahlung *f* radiation *n*, emission *n*; **farbige** ~ coloured radiation
Strahlungscharakteristik *f* radiation pattern, radiation characteristic, radiation diagram
Strahlungsdiagramm *n s.* Strahlungscharakteristik
Strahlungsempfänger *m* radiation-sensitive pick-up, radiation-responsive pick-up
Strahlungsenergie *f* radiated energy, radiant energy; ~ *f* (Sender) transmitted energy

Strahlungsleistung *f* radiated power **effektive** ~ **(ERP)** effective radiated power (ERP)
Strahlungsrichtung *f* beam direction
Strahlungsverteilung, spektrale spectral distribution of radiation
Strahlungswiderstand *m* radiation resistance
Strahlunterdrückung *f* beam gate
Strahlwobbeln *n* beam wobble
Straßenzustandsbericht *m* information on road conditions, road news *n pl*
Strecke *f* (fam.) cable *n*, line *n*; **Aufzeichnung über** ~ recording from line
Streifen *m* (Negativ) streak *n*; ~ *m* (Video) striation *n*; ~ *m* (F) film strip, film *n*
Streiflicht *n* glancing light, rim light
Streulicht *n* stray light, diffused light, spill light
Streulichtfaktor *m* diffusion factor
Streulichtscheinwerfer *m* broadside *n*
Streulichtschirm *m* diffusing screen
Streupunkt *m* dispersion point; **maximaler** ~ main dispersion point
Streuschirm *m* diffusing screen
Streuung *f* (opt.) aberration *n*, dispersion *n*, diffusion *n*; ~ *f* (TV) scattering *n*
Streuwinkel *m* (Abtastwinkel) angle of scatter, angle of divergence, angle of spread; ~ *m* (Scheinwerfer) angle of dispersion, diffusion angle; **maximaler** ~ maximum angle of dispersion
Strichrastertestbild *n* bar test pattern, bar pattern
Strippe *f* (fam.) line *n*
Stroboskop *n* stroboscope *n*
Strom *m* current *n*, juice *n* (coll.)

stromabwärts *adj* downstream *adj*
Stromaggregat *n* generating unit, generating plant
Stromaufnahme *f* current consumption, current input, charging rate, power consumption
stromaufwärts *adj* upstream *adj*
Stromausfallrelais *n* power failure relay, no-current relay
Strombauch *m* current loop, current antinode
Stromdichte *f* current density
Stromgegenkopplung *f* negative current feedback
Stromknotenpunkt *m* current intersection, current junction
Stromkreis *m* circuit *n*, electric circuit; **geschlossener ~** closed circuit; **offener ~** open circuit
Stromlaufplan *m* circuit diagram
stromlos *adj* currentless *adj*, dead *adj*, out of circuit
Strommesser *m* ammeter *n*
Stromquelle *f* power source
Stromspitze *f* peak current
Stromstärke *f* current intensity
Stromunterbrechung *f* power failure, break of current
Stromverdrängungseffekt *m* skin effect
Stromverdrängungsmotor *m* hysteresis motor
Stromversorgung *f* power supply
Stromversorgungsschwankung *f* power-supply variation
Stromverstärkung *f* current amplification
Stromwandler *m* current transformer
Stromzange *f* clip-on probe, current probe
Strudelbewegung *f* turbulence *n*; ~ *f* (Luft) Clear Air Turbulence (CAT)
Stück *n* (Thea.) play *n*, piece *n* (coll.) ~ *n* (fam.) (Beitrag) item *n*, piece *n* (coll.); **ein ~ herausbringen** to

produce a play
Stückeschreiber *m* (fam.) playwright *n*
Studienfernsehen *n* adult education television programme
Studienplan *m* curriculum *n*, syllabus *n*
Studio *n* studio *n*; **~ klar?** studio ready?, ready to start?; **~ mit Nachhall** live studio, studio with reverberation; **aktuelles ~** current affairs studio; **fahrbares ~** mobile studio; **nachhallfreies ~** dead studio; **schalltotes ~** dead studio
Studioanlage *f* studio layout
Studioausgangsbild *n* outgoing signal
Studioausgangsmodulation *f* outgoing modulation
Studioausgangston *m* outgoing sound
Studioauskleidung *f* studio treatment, studio lining
Studioausrüstung *f* studio equipment
Studiobelegschaft *f* studio staff
Studiobelegung *f* studio usage
Studiobelegungsplan *m* studio allocations schedule, studio bookings *n pl*
Studiobeleuchtung *f* studio lighting
Studiodisposition *f* studio allocation, studio bookings *n pl*
Studioebene *f* floor level, studio flat
Studioempfänger *m* studio monitor
Studiogrundriß *m* floor plan, studio plan
Studiohilfe *f* studio hand
Studiokomplex *m* production centre
Studioleiter *m* station manager
Studiolicht *n* house light
Studiomaschine *f* professional machine
Studiomeister *m* scene supervisor
Studioplanung* *f* studio planning*
Studioproduktion *f* studio production

Studioredakteur *m* presenting editor, anchor man
Studioregisseur *m* studio director
Studiosendung *f* studio broadcast
Studiotechnik *f* studio engineering
Studiotonmeister *m* (F) floor mixer, production mixer
Studiowart *m* studio attendant
Stufe *f* step *n*, degree *n*, grade *n*; ~ *f* (Verstärker) stage *n*
Stufenkeil *m* (opt.) stepped photometric absorption wedge, step wedge
Stufenlinse *f* Fresnel lens
Stufenlinsenscheinwerfer *m* Fresnel lens spotlight
Stufenschalter *m* step switch, sequence switch
Stukkateur *m* plasterer *n*
stumm *adj* silent *adj*, mute *adj*
Stummfilm *m* silent film
Stumpfklebelade *f* butt joiner
Stumpfklebepresse *f* s. Stumpfklebelade
Stundenbericht *m* log *n*
Stundenzähler *m* hour-counter *n*
Stuntman *m* stuntman *n*
Stützmikrofon *n* stand microphone
Stützpunkt, keramischer ceramic support
Substitutionsmessung *f* measurement by substitution
Sucher *m* viewfinder *n*; **elektronischer** ~ electronic viewfinder; **lichtstarker** ~ bright viewfinder; **optischer** ~ optical viewfinder
Sucherfenster *n* viewfinder window
Sucherkasch *m* viewfinder frame
Sucherlupe *f* viewing magnifier
Sucherobjektiv *n* viewfinder lens, viewing lens
Sucherokular *n* viewfinder eyepiece
Sucherrahmen *m* viewfinder frame
summen *v* buzz *v*, hum *v*
Summenbedienpult *n* vision control desk
Summenregler *m* (fam.) group fader

Summensignal *n* composite signal, mixed signal
Summensteller *m* group fader
Summenverstärker *m* group amplifier, master amplifier
Summer *m* buzzer *n*
Super-Ikonoskop *n* supericonoscope *n*, image iconoscope
Superkontrastmaterial *n* very high-contrast film stock
Super-Orthikon *n* image orthicon, superorthicon *n*
Symbolsprache *f* (EDV) symbolic language, symbolic programming language
Symmetrieachse *f* symmetry axis
symmetrieren *v* symmetrise *v*, balance *v*
Symmetrierglied *n* balanced-to-unbalanced transformer, balun *n*
Symmetrieübertrager *m* balanced transformer
symmetrisch *adj* symmetrical *adj*
synchron *adj* synchronous *adj*, in sync (coll.); ~ *adj* (tech.) in synchronism, sync *adj* (coll.), locked *adj*
Synchronabziehtisch *m* synchroniser *n*
Synchronatelier *n* dubbing studio
Synchronbahn *f* (Sat.) synchronous orbit
Synchronbetrieb *m* (Sender) common-wave operation
Synchronbild *n* synchronous picture
Synchrondemodulator *m* synchronous demodulator
Synchronfirma *f* dubbing company
Synchrongeräusch *n* dubbed effect
Synchronimpuls *m* synchronisation pulse, sync pulse
Synchronimpulsamplitude *f* sync amplitude
Synchronisation *f* synchronisation *n*; ~ *f* (F) dubbing *n*
Synchronisationssignal *n* sync

signal

Synchronisationsstörung, horizontale horizontal jitter; **vertikale ~** run-through *n*

Synchronisator *m* synchronising unit, synchroniser *n*

Synchronisierbereich *m* locking range, hold range

synchronisieren *v* (F) dub *v*; *~ v* (tech.) synchronise *v*, to bring into step, lock *v*; *~* **nach Textband** to dub to visual tape; *~* **nach Vorlage** to dub to script

Synchronisieren *n* (F) dubbing *n*; *~ n* (tech.) synchronising *n*, locking *n*

Synchronisierleitung *f* locking circuit

synchronisiert *adj* (F) dubbed *adj*; *~ adj* (tech.) synchronised *adj*, locked *adj*

Synchronisierung *f* synchronisation *n*; *~ f* (F) dubbing *n*

Synchronität *f* synchronism *n*

Synchronklappe *f* clapper board, clapper *n*

Synchronlauf *m* synchronous running

Synchronliste *f* dubbing cue sheet

Synchronmarke *f* synchronising mark, sync mark

Synchronmotor *m* synchronous motor

Synchronnetz *n* synchronised network

Synchronregisseur *m* dubbing director

Synchronrolle *f* dubbing part

Synchronsatellit *m* synchronous satellite

Synchronschleife *f* dubbing loop, post-sync loop

Synchronsignal (S-Signal) *n* synchronisation signal

Synchronsignalgemisch *n* mixed sync signals *n pl*, mixed syncs *n pl* (coll.)

Synchronsignalwert *m* sync

amplitude

Synchronsprecher *m* dubbing speaker, dubbing actor

Synchronstart *m* sync start

Synchronstimme *f* dubbing voice

Synchronstudio *n* dubbing theatre

Synchronton *m* synchronous sound

Synchronumrichter *m* synchronous converter

Synchronumroller *m* synchroniser *n*

Synchronwert *m* synchronising level, sync level

Synchronzeichen *n* synchronising mark, synchronising cue, sync mark

Synchronzeichengenerator *m* blip generator

Synopsis *f* synopsis *n*

System *n* system *n*, method *n*; **punktfrequentes ~** point-sequential system; **rasterfrequentes ~** field-sequential system; **trägerfrequentes ~ (TF-System)** carrier-frequency system; **zeilenfrequentes ~** line-sequential system

Systemanalyse *f* (EDV) system analysis

Szenarium *n* scenario *n*

Szene *f* scene *n*, set *n*; *~ f* (F) shot *n*; *~* **durchstellen** to run through a shot; *~* **einrichten** to set up a shot; *~* **nachstellen** to reconstruct a scene

Szenenausleuchtung *f* scenery illumination, set lighting

Szenenausschnitt *m* scene excerpt

Szenenbauplan *m* studio plan

Szenenbeleuchtung *f* scene lighting, general scene lighting

Szenenbeleuchtungsumfang *m* scene lighting level, lit area

Szenenbild *n* set *n*, setting *n*, decor *n*, scenery *n*

Szenenbildner *m* designer *n*, set designer, scenery designer, scenic

Szenenbildner 166

designer, art director
Szenentester *m* (Kopierwerk) scene
tester
Szenenübergang *m* inter-scene
transition
Szenenwechsel *m* change of
scenery

T

Tachoimpulsrad *n* (MAZ) tone
wheel, tachometer disc
Tachometer *m oder n* speedometer
n; ~ (F) tachometer *n*, film speed
indicator
Tafel *f* chart *n*
Tagbetrieb *m* day working
Tagegeld *n* subsistence allowance,
daily allowance
Tagesbericht *m* (Dreh) daily report,
continuity sheet
Tagesgage *f* daily fee, daily rate
Tagesgeschehen *n* (ZDF) daily TV
news and current affairs
transmission
Tageskommentar *m* daily
commentary
Tageslicht *n* daylight *n*
Tageslichtemulsion *f* daylight
emulsion
Tageslichtspule *f* daylight loading
spool
Tagesreichweite *f* (Sender) daytime
service range, day range, diurnal
range
Tagesschau *f* (ARD) daily TV news
transmission
Take *m* take *n*, sequence *n*
taken *v* take *v*
Takenummer *f* take number
Takt *m* cadence *n*, rhythm *n*, beat *n*,
time *n*, tact *n*, rate *n*; ~ *m*
(elektron.) pulse *n*
Taktfrequenz *f* (EDV) clock
frequency, clock rate

Taktgeber *m* metronome *n*; ~ *m*
(Impuls) pulse generator; ~ *m*
(EDV) clock *n*, clock generator;
synchronisierter ~ synchronised
pulse generator (SPG),
synchronised generator, sync-
pulse generator
Takthaushalt *m* pulse generation
and distribution system, sync
pulse system
Taktimpuls *m* (EDV) clock pulse,
clock signal, timing pulse
Taktspur *f* (EDV) clock marker
track, clock track
Taktsynchronisierung *f* pulse
synchronisation
Taktverkopplung, wechselseitige
intersynchronisation *n*
Tandempotentiometer *n* tandem
potentiometer
Tank *m* tank *n*
Tankentleerung *f* tank draining
Tannenbaum *m* cue lights *n pl*
Tantieme *f* royalty *n*
Tanzmusik *f* dance music
Tanzorchester *n* dance orchestra
Target *n* target *n*
Taschenempfänger *m* pocket
transistor
Tastatur *f* keyboard *n*, keys *n pl*
Taste *f* push button, button *n*, key *n*
Tastimpuls *m* keying pulse, keying
impulse
Tastkopf *m* probe *n*
Taströhre *f* keying valve, keying
tube
Tastsignal *n* keying signal
Tastung *f* (Signal) keying *n*
Tastverhältnis *n* duty cycle, pulse
duty factor, keying ratio
Tatsachenbericht *m* documentary *n*
Tauchlöten *n* dip soldering
Tauchspule *f* (Mikro) moving coil
Taumeln *n* (Sat.) tumbling *n*
Team *n* team *n*, crew *n*
Technik *f* engineering *n*
Techniker *m* technician *n*, engineer
n, operator *n*

Technikkoordinationsleitung *f* technical coordination circuit

Teil, bildwichtiger centre of interest

Teilbelichtung *f* partial exposure

Teilbild *n* field *n*, split picture, partial image; **kongruentes ~** coincident image, partial coincident picture

Teilbilddauer *f* field duration, field rate

Teilbildfolgezahl *f* interlace sequence

Teilbildzahl *f* interlace sequence

Teilhabervertrag *m* partnership contract

Teilnehmer *m* participant *n*; ~ *m* (Telefon) subscriber *n*

Teilnehmerbetrieb *m* (EDV) time-sharing mode

Teilnehmermessung *f* audience rating

Teilung *f* (Skala) graduation *n*, scale *n*; **logarithmische ~** logarithmic calibration

Telefonanschluß *m* line *n*, installation *n*, telephone connection

Telefonbeantworter *m* answering machine

Telefonbuchse *f* telephone jack

Telefonfreileitung *f* overhead line

Telefonhörer *m* telephone receiver

Telefoniebetrieb *m* telephony *n*

Telefoniekanal *m* telephone channel

Telefoninterview *n* interview by telephone, telephoned interview

Telefonist *m* switchboard operator, operator *n*, PBX operator

Telefonrufbeantworter *m* answering machine

Telefonsammelnummer *f* collective telephone number

Telefonselbstwählanlage *f* subscriber trunk dialling installation (STD)

Telefonsprechverkehr *m* telephone traffic

Telefonverbindung *f* telephone connection

Telefonwartung* *f* telephone maintenance crew

Telefonzentrale *f* telephone switchboard, private branch exchange (PBX)

Telefoto *n* wire picture

Telefotostelle *f* wire picture office

telegen *adj* telegenic *adj*

Telegrafie, drahtlose wireless telegraphy (WT)

Teleobjektiv *n* telephoto lens

Telephon *n s.* Telefon

Teleprompter *m* teleprompter *n*, prompter *n*

Teleskop *n* telescope *n*

Teleskopantenne *f* telescopic aerial

Teleskoparm *m* telescopic arm

Teleskopmast *m* telescopic mast

Teleskopsäule *f* telescopic column; ~ *f* (Kamera) hydraulic tripod

Teller *m* (Platte) turntable *n*; ~ *m* (Magnetofon) disc *n*, plate *n*

Temperaturabhängigkeit *f* temperature dependence

Temperaturänderung *f* temperature change

Temperaturaustauscher *m* heat exchanger

Temperaturbereich *m* temperature range

Temperaturdrift *f* temperature drift

Temperaturfestigkeit *f* temperature stability

Temperaturgang *m* temperature response

Temperaturkonstante *f* temperature constant

Temperaturschwankung *f* temperature variation

Ten-light *n* ten-light *n*

Termin *m* (Progr.) slot *n*, outlet *n*

terminieren *v* (einsetzen) bill *v*, place *v*

terrestrisch *adj* terrestrial *adj*

Test *m* test *n*

Testband *n* test tape, standard tape

Testbetrieb *m* (EDV) test mode
Testbild *n* test chart, test card, test pattern; ~ **aufschalten** to put out test card
Testbildgeber *m* test pattern generator
Testfarbe *f* test colour
Testfilm *m* test film, test strip
Testkopie *f* (Kopierwerk) grading copy, first trial print; ~ *f* (F) rush print
Testsendung *f* (Progr.) pilot programme, pilot *n*, trial programme; ~ *f* (tech.) test transmission
Testsignal *n* test signal
Tetrode *f* tetrode *n*
Text *m* text *n*; ~ *m* (Nachrichten) script *n*; ~ *m* (verbindende Worte) continuity script; ~ **breitwalzen** to pad a script, to stretch a script; ~ **einstreichen** to edit down a script, to cut down a script, to sub down a script; ~ **kürzen** to edit down a script, to cut down a script, to sub down a script; ~ **überziehen** overscript *v*
Textausschnitt *m* excerpt *n*; ~ *m* (Band) cut *n*
Textband *n* visual tape, written band
Textbandprojektor *m* visual tape projector, written-band projector
Textbandverfahren *n* dubbing with visual tape
Textbuch *n* (Thea.) book *n*; ~ *n* (Oper) libretto *n*
texten *v* script *v*; **auf Bild** ~ to script to film; **gegen das Bild** ~ to write against the picture
Texter *m* script-writer *n*, scripter *n*; ~ *m* (Nachrichten) sub-editor/script-writer *n*
Textprobe *f* level check
Theater *n* theatre *n*
Theateraufzeichnung *f* theatre recording
Theaterkopie *f* (F) release print

Theaterleiter *m* (F) cinema manager
Theaterring *m* (F) cinema circuit
Theaterübertragung *f* direct broadcast from theatre, theatre live transmission
Thema *n* topic *n*, subject *n*
Themamusik *f* theme music
Themenliste *f* (Nachrichten) news prospects *n pl*
Thermistor *m* thermistor *n*
Thermokreuz *n* thermocouple *n*
thermomagnetisch *adj* thermomagnetic *adj*
Thermoschutzschalter *m* thermal circuit-breaker
Thermostat *m* thermostat *n*
Thernewid *m* thermistor *n*
Thomsonfilter *m* Thomson filter
Ticker *m* (fam.) ticker *n* (coll.); **über den** ~ **laufen lassen** teleprint *v*, to put on telex
Tiefen *f pl* (Ton) bass *n*, bass notes, low frequencies, low-pitched notes; ~ *f pl* (Bild) dark-picture areas
Tiefenabschwächung *f* bass cut, bass roll-off
Tiefenanhebung *f* bass boost, bass lift
Tiefenschärfe *f* depth of field, depth of focus
Tiefenschärfebereich *m* zone of sharpness, field of focus
Tiefenschärfentabelle *f* depth of field chart
Tiefensperre *f* low-frequency rejection filter, bass cut
Tiefpaß *m* low-pass filter
Tiefpaßfilter *m* low-pass filter
Tiefton *m* low frequency, bass *n*
Tieftongenerator *m* low-frequency generator
Tieftonlautsprecher *m* (Empfänger) woofer *n*, bass loudspeaker
Tiefziehpresse *f* thermoplastic machine
timen *v* time *v*

Timing *n* timing *n*
Tip *m* tip *n*, tip-off *n*, lead *n*, pointer *n*
Tischgerät *n* table set, table model
Tischler *m* carpenter *n*, joiner *n*
Tischlerei *f* carpenter's shop, joiner's shop
Tischmikrofon *n* desk microphone, table microphone
Titel *m* title *n*, heading *n*; ~ *m* (TV,F) caption *n*; ~ *m* (Mitarbeiter) credit title, credits *n pl*; ~ *m* (Mus.) number *n*; ~ **aufziehen** (Bild) to run captions; ~ **aufziehen** (Grafik) to mount titles; **einkopierter ~** superimposed title, overlay title; **negativer ~** white-on-black caption; **positiver ~** black-on-white caption; **rollender ~** roller titles *n pl*, roller caption; **unbeweglicher ~** static caption; **vorläufiger ~** working title; **wandernder ~** moving title
Titelanfertiger *m* caption artist, titling artist
Titelaufnahme *f* caption shooting, titling-bench work
Titelband *n* title strip
Titelbank *f* titling bench, rostrum *n*
Titelgerät *n* titler *n*, title printer
Titelinsert *n* caption *n*
Titelkarton *m* art board, fashion board
Titelkonferenz *f* titles planning meeting
Titelliste *f* list of credits, title sequence
Titelmaschine *f* titler *n*, title printer
Titelmusik *f* title music; ~ **aufziehen** to fade in title music
titeln *v* title *v*
Titelnegativ *n* title negative
Titelpositiv *n* title positive
Titelregister *n* register of titles
Titelrolle *f* title roll; ~ *f* (Darsteller) title role, lead role, name part
Titelschreiber *m* Ancor machine
Titelschrift *f* title lettering, caption lettering
Titelständer *m* caption stand, titles easel
Titeluntergrund *m* title background
Titelvorlage *f* title card
Titelvorspann *m* opening titles *n pl*, opening credits *n pl*
Titelzeichner *m* caption artist, titling artist
Tochterband *n* tape copy
Toleranz *f* tolerance *n*; ~ *f* (mech.) clearance *n*
Toleranzbereich *m* range of tolerance, permissible variation
Toleranzfeld *n* tolerance zone
Ton *m* sound *n*, note *n*, tone *n*
Ton- (in Zus.) sound (compp.)
Ton ab! turn over sound!; ~ **anlegen** to put sound to picture, to lay the sound track; ~ **aus!** take out sound!, cut sound!; ~ **einpegeln** to adjust sound levels; ~ **im Bild** sound on vision, microphony *n*; ~ **in Ordnung** o.k. for sound; ~ **klar!** o.k. for sound!; ~ **läuft!** sound running!; ~ **läuft weg** sound is out of sync, runaway *n*; ~ **rotzt** (fam.) sound is grotty (coll.); ~ **unterlegen** to dub sound, to lay the sound; **internationaler ~ (IT)** international sound; **internationaler ~** (Übertragung) local sound; **nur ~** sound only; **reiner ~** pure sound
Tonabnehmer *m* sound pick-up, sound head, head assembly; ~ *m* (Gerät) pick-up *n*; **akustischer ~** acoustic pick-up
Tonabtastdose *f* pick-up cartridge, pick-up head
Tonabtasteinrichtung *f* sound head, sound pick-up device, sound scanning device
Tonabtaster *m* sound pick-up, sound head, head assembly
Tonabtastkopf *m* pick-up head, playback head, sound scanning head

Tonabtastung *f* playback *n*, sound scanning, sound pick-up, sound gate

Tonabzweigverstärker *m* sound branching amplifier

Tonangel *f* boom arm

Tonangler *m* boom operator

Tonarchiv *n* sound library, sound archives *n pl*

Tonarm *m* pick-up arm

Tonarmlift *m* pick-up arm lowering device, cueing device

Tonassistent *m* sound man

Tonatelier *n* sound studio, recording studio, sound recording studio

Tonaufnahme *f* sound recording, transcription *n*

Tonaufnahme- und Wiedergabegerät *n* sound recording and reproducing equipment

Tonaufnahmegerät *n* sound recording equipment, sound recorder

Tonaufnahmemaschine *f s.* Tonaufnahmegerät

Tonaufnahmepult *n* sound control desk, sound mixing desk

Tonaufnahmeraum *m* recording channel

Tonaufnahmestudio *n* sound recording studio, sound studio

Tonaufnahmetechnik *f* sound recording

Tonaufnahmewagen *m* recording car, recording van

Tonaufzeichnung *f* sound recording

Tonaufzeichnungsanlage *f* sound recording equipment

Tonaufzeichnungsraum *m* recording channel

Tonaufzeichnungsverfahren *n* sound recording system

Tonausblendung *f* sound fade

Tonausfall *m* loss of sound, sound breakdown

Tonband *n* sound tape, audio tape, sound track; **internationales ~ (IT-Band)** international sound track, music and effects track (M and E track), international sound (coll.)

Tonbandamateur *m* tape recording enthusiast

Tonbandaufnahme *f* sound tape recording

Tonbandbreite *f* sound tape width

Tonbandfreund *m* tape recording enthusiast

Tonbandgerät *n* tape recorder

Tonbandkassette *f* tape cassette

Tonbandlauf *m* tape travel

Tonbandmaschine *f* tape recorder

Tonbandtransport *m* tape transport

Tonbericht *m* sound report

Tonbezugsband *n* reference audio tape

Tonbezugspegel *m* reference audio level

Ton-Bild-Versatz *m* (gewollt) sound track advance, sound advance, sync advance; **~** *m* (ungewollt) slippage of sound to picture

Tonblende *f* sound fade, sound fader; **~** *f* (Frequenz) variable correction unit (VCU)

Tonblitz *m* sound flash, plop *n*, blip *n*, noisy join

Tonblubbern *n* bubbling *n*, motor-boating *n*

Tondauerleitungsnetz *n* permanent sound network

Tondokument *n* sound document

Tondose *f* (Platte) pick-up head, pick-up cartridge

Toneffekt *m* sound effect

Toneffektraum *m* sound effects studio

Toneinblendung *f* fade-up *n*

Tonendkontrolle *f* sound master control

Tonfalle *f* sound trap

Tonfarbe *f* (Musikinstrument) colour of tone, timbre *n*

Tonfassung *f* sound version

Tonfehlschaltung *f* sound switching

Tonsäule

error
Tonfilm *m* sound film, sound
motion picture, talkie *n* (coll.)
Tonfolge *f* frequency run
Tonfolie *f* cellulose disc
Tonfrequenz *f* audio frequency (AF),
sound frequency, voice frequency;
hohe ~en top frequencies, trebles
n pl
Tonfrequenzschwankungsfaktor *m*
audio-frequency variation factor
Tonfrequenzspitzenbegrenzer *m*
audio-frequency peak limiter
Tonfunk *m* sound radio
Tongalgen *m* microphone boom
Tongemisch *n* composite sound,
complete effects without speaker;
ausgewogenes ~ well-balanced
sound mix
Tongenerator *m* audio-frequency
signal generator, audio oscillator
Tonhöhe *f* pitch *n*
Tonhöhenschwankung *f* pitch
variation; **langsame ~en** wow *n*;
schnelle ~en flutter *n*
Toninformation *f* audio information
Toningenieur *m* sound engineer,
sound control engineer, audio
engineer
Tonjäger *m* amateur sound
recordist
Tonkamera *f* sound camera
Tonkanal *m* sound channel
Tonklebestelle *f* sound join, sound
splice; **fehlerhafte ~** bad sound
join
Tonkomponente *f* sound component
Tonkopf *m* sound head
Tonkopie *f* sound print, sound copy
Tonlampe *f* sound exciter lamp
Tonlampengehäuse *n* exciter lamp
housing, exciter lamp assembly
Tonlaufwerk *n* sound-film traction
Tonleitung *f* audio circuit, sound
circuit; **internationale ~ (IT-
Leitung)** international sound
circuit, effects circuit
Tonleitungsdauernetz *n* permanent

sound network
Tonleitungsnetz *n* sound network;
internationales ~ international
sound network
Tonmeister *m* recording engineer; ~
m (F) sound recordist
Tonmeßtechnik *f* sound
maintenance
Tonmischpult *n* sound mixer, sound
mixing console, sound mixing
desk, mixing console
Tonmischung *f* sound mixing; ~ *f*
(F) sound dubbing
Tonmischverstärker *m* sound
mixing amplifier
Tonmotor *m* capstan motor
Tonnegativ *n* sound negative, sound
track negative
Tonnegativbericht *m* sound
negative report
tonnenförmig *adj* barrel-shaped *adj*,
cylindrical *adj*
Tonpegel *m* sound level
Tonpegeländerung *f* change in
sound level
Tonpegelkontrolle *f* sound level
check
Tonpegelschwankung *f* variation in
sound level
Tonpegelsprung *m* jump in sound
level
Tonplatte *f* audio disc, audio record
Tonpopel *m* blooping patch
Tonpositiv *n* sound positive
Tonprobe *f* sound level check
Tonprojektor *m* sound projector
Tonprojektorlampe *f* exciter lamp
Tonqualität *f* sound quality, tone
quality
Tonraum *m* sound booth
Tonregie *f* sound control room
Tonregler *m* sound control, sound
fader
Tonrelief *n* sound picture
Tonreportage *f* radio OB
Tonrundfunk *m* sound
broadcasting, radio *n*
Tonsäule *f* sound column, column

Tonsäule   172

loudspeaker

Tonschaltraum *m* sound switching
area

Tonschleuse *f* sound gate

Tonschnitt *m* sound editing

Tonschramme *f* sound scratch

Tonschwingung *f* sound vibration

Tonscript *n* sound script

Tonsender *m* sound transmitter

Tonsignal *n* sound signal

Tonsignalübermittlung *f* sound
signal transmission

Tonspalt *m* headgap *n*

Tonsperre *f* sound trap

Tonspur *f* sound track; ~ *f* (Platte)
groove *n*

Tonstärke *f* sound volume, sound
intensity, loudness *n*

Tonstartmarke *f* sound start mark

Tonsteller *m* sound control, sound
fader

Tonstern *m s.* Tonsternpunkt

Tonsternpunkt *m* radio switching
centre

Tonsteuersender *m* sound driver

Tonstörung *f* audio interference

Tonstrom *m* sound current, signal
current

Tonstudio *n* sound studio, sound
channel

Tonstudiobetrieb *m* (kommerziell)
commercial sound studio

Tonsystem *n* sound system

Tontechnik *f* sound engineering,
audio engineering

Tontechniker *m* sound man, sound
operator, sound recordist, sound
mixer, desk operator, programme
operations assistant (POA)

Tonteil *m* sound section

Tonträger *m* (Material) base *n*,
sound track support; ~ *m* (Funk)
sound carrier; ~ *m* (Raum)
recording channel; ~ *m* (Recht)
phonogram *n*

Tonträgerraum *m* recording
channel

Tonüberblendung *f* sound mixing,

sound fading

Tonüberblendungsstanze *f* sound
change-over dot

Tonübersprechen *n* crosstalk *n*

Ton- und Bildübertragung *f* sound
and vision transmission

Tonung *f* tone *n*, tonality *n*

Tonunterkleber *m* perforated
scotch tape

Tonverfremdung *f* coloration *n*

Tonverteilerverstärker *m* sound
distribution amplifier

Tonverzerrung *f* sound distortion

Tonvolumen *n* sound volume

Tonwagen *m* (fam.) recording car,
recording van

Tonwanne *f* line source unit, line
source loudspeaker

Tonwiedergabe *f* sound
reproduction, playback *n*

Tonwiedergabegerät *n* sound
reproducer

Tonzeile *f* row of loudspeakers

Tonzuspielung *f* sound feed

Topfkreis *m* cavity resonator

Tor *n* (Scheinwerfer) barndoor *n*

Torblende *f* (Scheinwerfer)
barndoor *n*

Tornistergerät *n* back-type set

Torschalter *m* gate circuit switch

Torschaltung *f* gate circuit, gate *n*

Totale *f* long shot (LS)

totschweigen *v* (Nachricht) suppress
v

Trabant *m* satellite *n*; ~ *m* (Impuls)
equalising pulse

Trafo *m* (fam.) transformer *n*

tragbar *adj* portable *adj*

tragbare Fernsehkamera hand-held
TV camera, creepie-peepie *n* (US)

Träger *m* (Bühne) beam *n*, joist *n*,
bracket *n*; ~ *m* (F, Band) tape
base, film base, base *n*, substrate
n, support *n*; ~ *m* (HF) carrier *n*,
carrier wave (CW); **unterdrückter**
~ suppressed carrier

Trägerenergie *f* carrier energy

trägerfrequent *adj* carrier-

frequency *adj*
trägerfrequentes System (TF-System) carrier-frequency system
Trägerfrequenz (TF) *f* carrier frequency
Trägerfrequenzanlage *f* carrier-frequency equipment
Trägerfrequenzstrecke *f* carrier-frequency line, carrier circuit
Trägerimpuls *m* carrier pulse
Trägerseite *f* (F) base side
Trägerspannung *f* carrier voltage
Trägerwelle *f* carrier wave (CW)
Tragödie *f* tragedy *n*
Tragöse *f* buckle *n*
Tragriemen *m* carrying strap, shoulder strap, neck strap
Trailer *m* trailer *n*
Transduktor *m* transducer *n*, magnetic amplifier
Transfokator *m* zoom lens
Transformator *m* transformer *n*; **rotierender ~** rotary transformer
Transformatorstation *f* transformer station
Transformatorwagen *m* transformer truck, transformer trailer
Transistor *m* transistor *n*
transistorbestückt *adj* transistorised *adj*, solid-state *adj* (US)
Transistorempfänger *m* transistorised receiver
Transistorfassung *f* transistor socket
transistorisieren *v* transistorise *v*
transistorisiert *adj* transistorised *adj*, solid-state *adj* (US)
Transistorisierung *f* transistorisation *n*
Transitleitung *f* transit circuit
Transkoder *m* transcoder *n*
Transkodierung *f* transcoding *n*
Transkriptionsdienst *m* transcription service
Transmittanz *f* transmittance *n*
Transparenz *f* transparency *n*

Transparenzschirm *m* transparent screen
Transponder *m* transponder *n*
Transportgreifer *m* feeding claw
Transportkoffer *m* packing case
Transportrolle *f* film roller, transport roller
Transversalaufzeichnung *f* transverse recording
Transversalkopf *m* transverse head
Transversalmagnetisierung *f* transverse magnetisation
Transversalwelle *f* transverse signal
Trapezverzerrung *f* trapezium distortion, keystone distortion
Travelling-Matte-Verfahren *n* travelling matte process
Traverse *f* (Stativ) cross arm
Treatment *n* draft script, treatment *n*
Treiberstufe *f* driver stage, driver *n*
Treibertransformator *m* driver transformer
Trennklinke *f* break jack
Trennschalter *m* circuit-breaker *n*, cut-out *n*, isolating switch, isolator *n*
Trennschaltung *f* isolation network
Trennschärfe *f* selectivity *n*
Trennschleife *f* separation filter, isolating section, isolating loop
Trenntaste *f* cut key
Trenntransformator *m* isolating transformer
Trennungsentschädigung *f* separation allowance
Trennverstärker *m* isolation amplifier, trap-valve amplifier, trap amplifier, buffer amplifier
Trennweiche *f* diplexer *n*
Triac *m* (elek.) triac *n*
Tribüne *f* platform *n*, rostrum *n*
Trichtergrammofon *n* horn gramophone, acoustic gramophone
Trichterlautsprecher *m* horn loudspeaker

Trick   174

Trick *m* special effect, special
effects *n pl*, animation *n*;
figürlicher ~ cartoon animation;
mechanischer ~ mechanical
animation; **optischer** ~ optical
effect, optical *n*
Trickabteilung *f* special effects
section, animation department
Trickaufnahme *f* rostrum shot,
animation picture
Trickbank *f* rostrum bench, cartoon
camera bench, animation board,
animation stand, stop-frame
rostrum
Trickblende *f* wipe *n*, optical *n*
Trickeffekt *m* special effect, stunt
effect, cartoon effect
Trickeinblendung *f* (F) animated
intercut; ~ *f* (elektron.) electronic
inlay, superimposition *n*
Trickfilm *m* rostrum film,
animation *n*, special effects film,
animated film
Trickgrafik *f* animated caption
Trickkamera *f* rostrum camera,
bench camera
Trickkameramann *m* rostrum
camera operator, animation
cameraman
Trickkopiermaschine *f* optical
effects printer, aerial-image
printer
Trickmischeinrichtung *f* electronic
switch unit
Trickmischer *m* (Person) animation
mixer; ~ *m* (Gerät) special effects
mixer, special effects generator,
animation mixer
Trickmodell *n* model for model
shot, scale model, animation
model
Trickpult *n* special effects desk,
vision mixer's desk, animation
desk
Trickstudio *n* animation studio,
effects room
Tricktaste *f* trick button, animation
camera trigger

Tricktisch *m* rostrum bench,
cartoon camera bench, animation
board, animation stand, stop-
frame rostrum
Tricktitel *m* animated title,
animated caption
Tricktitelaufnahme *f* rostrum
caption shot
Tricküberblendung *f* animation
superimposition
Trickzeichner *m* animator *n*,
cartoonist *n*, cartoon-film artist
Trigger *m* trigger *n*
triggern *v* trigger *v*
Trimmer *m* trimmer *n*
Trimmpotentiometer *n* trimming
potentiometer
Trimmwiderstand *m* trimming
resistor
Tripel *n* triplet *n*, triple *n*
Trittschall *m* impact sound
Trittschallfilter *m* impact-sound
filter
Trockenbatterie *f* dry cell battery
Trockeneis *n* dry ice
Trockenhaube *f* drying hood
Trockenschrank *m* drying cabinet,
drying chamber, dry box
trocknen *v* dry *v*
Trocknen *n* drying-out *n*
Trocknung *f* drying *n*
Trog *m* trough *n*, vat *n*, tray *n*, tank
n
Trommel *f* drum *n*, cylinder *n*
Trommelblende *f* barrel shutter,
drum shutter, drum diaphragm
Trübung *f* (Entwicklung) milkiness
n, turbidity *n*
Truca *f* optical printer
Trucaaufnahme *f* process shot
Trucaverfahren *n* process-shot
system
Truhe *f* (Gerät) console *n*, cabinet *n*
Tubus *m* snoot *n*, extension tube
Tuchel *m* (fam.) Tuchel-type plug
Tüll *m* tulle *n*
Tuner *m* tuner *n*
Tunneldiode *f* tunnel diode

Türken bauen to fake a scene
Türkontakt *m* (Sicherheit) door
contact
Tute *f* (fam.) snoot *n*, extension tube
Tüte *f* (fam.) microphone *n*, mike *n*
(coll.); ~ *f* (fam.) (Objektiv)
telephoto lens

U

... **über alles** ... over all
über alles (Aufnahme u.
Wiedergabe)
recording/reproducing
überarbeiten *v* revise *v*, rewrite *v*,
trim *v*
überbelichten *v* overexpose *v*
Überbelichtung *f* overexposure *n*
Überbestimmtheit, informative
redundancy *n*
überblenden *v* (Ton) mix in *v*, fade
v, blend in *v*, add *v*; ~ *v* (Bild) fade
v, change over *v*, dissolve *v*,
superimpose *v*, mix *v*, overlay *v*,
inlay *v*, lap-fade *v*, cross-fade *v*
überblenden, hart cut *v*; **weich ~**
fade over *v*
Überblenden *n* dissolve *n*, mix *n*,
fading *n*, cross-fade *n*, fade-over
n, lap dissolve; ~ *n* (Einkopierung)
superimposition *n*, inlay *n*,
overlay *n*; ~ *n* (Durchblendung)
superposition *n*; ~ *n* (Proj.) change-
over *n*
Überblender *m* fader *n*; ~ *m* (Proj.)
change-over *n*
Überblendregler *m* fader *n*
Überblendung *f* dissolve *n*, mix *n*,
fading *n*, cross-fade *n*, fade-over
n, lap dissolve; ~ *f* (Einkopierung)
superimposition *n*, inlay *n*,
overlay *n*; ~ *f* (Durchblendung)
superposition *n*; ~ *f* (Proj.) change-
over *n*; **harte ~** cut *n*; **seitliche ~**

(Trick) push-over wipe; **weiche ~**
fade-over *n*
Überblendvorrichtung *f* fader *n*
Überblendzeichen *n* change-over
cue, change-over mark, change-
over signal, cue dot
Überblendzeichenstanze *f* change-
over cue punching machine
Überblick *m* general view, survey *n*,
summary *n*; **kurzer ~** round-up *n*
Überdeckungseffekt *m* excessive
level of effects, excessive
effects *n pl*
überdrehen *v* (F) to shoot slow-
motion; ~ *v* (mech.) overwind *v*
Übereinstimmung *f* synchronism *n*,
harmony *n*, consistency *n*
überentwickelt *adj* overdeveloped
adj
Überentwicklung *f*
overdevelopment *n*,
overdeveloping *n*
Übergabepunkt *m* handover point
Übergang *m* transition *n*, change *n*;
~ *m* (Anschluß) change-over *n*,
junction *n*; ~ *m* (Progr.) continuity
n
Übergangselement *n* electrolysis
junction
Übergangsfrequenz *f* transition
frequency, turn-over frequency,
cross-over frequency
Übergangsszene *f* transition *n*,
transition scene
Übergangswiderstand *m* transition
resistance, contact resistance,
transfer resistance
übergeben *v* (an) hand over *v* (to)
überhängen *v* (Ton, Bild) hang over
v
überholen *v* (tech.) overhaul *v*,
recondition *v*
überholt *adj* (Nachricht) out of date,
old *adj* (fam.)
Überholung *f* (tech.) overhauling *n*,
reconditioning *n*
Überkompensation *f*
overcompensation *n*

überkompensieren *v*
overcompensate *v*
Überkompensierung *f*
overcompensation *n*
Überlagerer *m* beat frequency
oscillator, beat oscillator
Überlagerung *f* superimposition *n*; ~
f (Frequenz) heterodyning *n*,
beating *n*; ~ *f* (EDV) overlay *n*
Überlagerungsempfänger *m*
superheterodyne receiver,
superhet *n* (fam.)
Überlandleitung *f* land line
Überlänge *f* (Schnitt) overlength *n*,
excessive duration; ~ *f*
(Aufnahme) excessive footage
überlappen *v* overlap *v*
Überlappung *f* overlapping *n*,
overlap *n*
Überlappungsbereich *m*
overlapping area, overlapping
region
übermitteln *v* transmit *v*, convey *v*
Übermittlung *f* transmission *n*,
conveyance *n*
Übermittlungsdauer *f* transmission
time
übermodulieren *v* overmodulate *v*
Übermodulierung *f* overmodulation
n
Übernachtungskosten *plt* overnight
expenses
Übernahme *f* relay *n*, rebroadcast *n*
~ **von** ... relay of ..., rebroadcast
of ...
übernehmen *v* (Progr.) relay *v*
Überreichweite *f* propagation
beyond horizon, anomalous
propagation
Überschlag *m* flash-over *n*, arc-over
n
Überschlagspannung *f* breakdown
voltage, flash-over voltage
überschneiden *v* overlap *v*, cut
across *v*; ~ *v* (Ton) cut *v* (from...to)
überschreiben *v* (Video) overseam *v*
Überschwingamplitude *f* overshoot
amplitude

überschwingen *v* overshoot *v*, ring *v*
Überschwingen *n* overshoot *n*,
ringing *n*
Überschwinger *m* overshoot *n*
Überschwingfrequenz *f* ringing
frequency
Überschwingung *f* overshoot *n*,
ringing *n*
Übersensibilisierung *f*
hypersensitisation *n*
übersetzen *v* (mech.) gear *v*,
transmit *v*
Übersetzung *f* (mech.) gearing *n*,
transmission *n*
Übersetzungsverhältnis *n* gear
ratio, transmission ratio, speed
ratio, transformation ratio
Übersicht *f* general view, survey *n*,
summary *n*
Überspannung *f* overvoltage *n*,
excessive voltage
Überspannungslampe *f* overvoltage
lamp
Überspannungsrelais *n* overload
voltage relay, overvoltage relay,
maximum-voltage relay
Überspannungsschutz *m* surge
arrester, overvoltage protection
Überspannungssicherung *f* excess
voltage cut-out, lightning arrester
überspielen *v* re-record *v*, transfer
v, transcribe *v*; ~ *v* (Leitung) to
transmit over closed circuit
Überspielleitung *f* closed circuit
Überspielung *f* re-recording *n*,
transfer *n*, transcription *n*; ~ *f*
(Leitung) closed-circuit
transmission; ~ **von Licht- auf**
Magnetton magnetic transfer;
~ **von Magnet- auf Lichtton**
optical transfer
Übersprechdämpfung *f* crosstalk
attenuation, crosstalk
transmission equivalent
übersprechen *v* crosstalk *v*
Übersprechen *n* (Ton) crosstalk *n*; ~
n (Bild) crossview *n*
übersteuern *v* overmodulate *v*,

overdrive *v*, overload *v*
Übersteuerung *f* overmodulation *n*,
overdriving *n*, overloading *n*; ~ *f*
(Mikro) blasting *n*
überstrahlen *v* irradiate *v*
Überstrahlung *f* irradiation *n*,
halation *n*, halo *n*, dazzle *n*, flare
n, bloom *n*, overshoot distortion,
overthrow distortion, lens flare
Überstrom *m* overcurrent *n*, excess
current
Überstromrelais *n* overcurrent
relay
Überstromsicherung *f* overcurrent
protection
Überstunden *f pl* overtime *n*
übertragen *v* broadcast *v*, transmit
v, relay *v*; ~ **aus** ... relayed from ...;
über Satelliten ~ satellite-
transmitted *adj*
Übertrager *m* repeating coil,
transformer *n*; ~ *m* (NF) audio-
frequency transformer;
rotierender ~ rotary transformer
Übertragung *f* transmission *n*,
broadcast *n*, relay *n*; ~ *f* (außen)
outside broadcast (OB); **drahtlose**
~ radio transmission; **sequentielle**
~ sequential transmission;
zeitversetzte ~ deferred relay
Übertragungsanlage *f* public
address system (PAS); **stereofone**
~ stereo transmission system
Übertragungsdauer *f* duration of
transmission
Übertragungsdienst (Ü-Dienst) *m*
outside broadcast operations (OB
operations) *n pl*; ~ **Bild** television
OB operations *n pl*; ~ **Ton** sound
OB operations *n pl*
Übertragungsfehler *m* transmission
fault
Übertragungsfunktion *f* transfer
function
Übertragungskabel *n* programme
line, programme cable
Übertragungskanal *m* transmission
channel, channel *n*

Übertragungskapazität *f*
transmission capacity
Übertragungskette *f* transmission
chain; ~ *f* (TV) television chain
Übertragungskoeffizient *m*
transmission coefficient
Übertragungskonstante *f*
transmission constant, transfer
constant
Übertragungskosten *plt*
transmission costs
Übertragungsleistungsverstärkung
f transduced gain
Übertragungsleitung *f* transmission
line, transmission circuit, OB line
Übertragungsnorm *f* transmission
standard
Übertragungsort *m* OB point
Übertragungspegel *m* transmission
level
Übertragungsprimärvalenzen *f pl*
transmission primaries
Übertragungsrechte *n pl*
transmission rights
Übertragungssatellit *m*
transmission satellite
Übertragungssystem *n* transmission
system; **akustisches** ~ acoustic
transmission system
Übertragungstechnik *f* outside
broadcasting
Übertragungstechnik* *f* outside
broadcasts* *n pl*
Übertragungsverfahren *n*
transmission system,
transmission method
Übertragungsverlust *m*
transmission loss
Übertragungsverzerrung *f*
transmission distortion
Übertragungswagen *m* OB vehicle,
OB van; ~ *m* (Ton) sound OB van,
radio OB van
Übertragungsweg *m* transmission
path, transmission channel,
transmission medium
Übertragungszeit *f* transmission
time, duration of transmission,

Übertragungszeit 178

duration of propagation
Übertragungszug *m* mobile OB unit
überwachen *v* control *v*, monitor *v*,
supervise *v*, watch *v*, inspect *v*
Überwachung *f* control *n*,
supervision *n*, monitoring *n*,
inspection *n*
Überwachungsempfänger *m*
monitoring receiver
Überwachungsleitung *f* monitoring
line
Überwachungspult *n* control desk,
monitoring desk
Überwachungsraum *m* control
room
überziehen *v* (Zeit) overrun *v*
Überziehen *n* (Zeit) overrun *n*
Überzug *m* coat *n*, coating *n*, layer
n
UHF-Fernsehsender *m* UHF
television transmitter
Uhrzeigersinn, gegen den anti-
clockwise *adj and adv*; **im ~**
clockwise *adj and adv*
Uhrzeitgeber *m* (EDV) real-time
clock
ultrahart *adj* ultra-hard *adj*
ultrahohe Frequenz ultra-high
frequency (UHF)
Ultrakurzwelle (UKW) *f* very high
frequency (VHF), ultra-high
frequency (UHF)
Ultrakurzwellenbereich *m* very-
high-frequency band (VHF band)
Ultralinearschaltung *f* ultra-linear
circuit
Ultraschall *m* ultrasonics *n*, ultra-
sound *n*
Ultraschall- (in Zus.) ultrasonic *adj*
Ultraschalleitung *f* ultrasonic delay
line
ultraschwarz *adj* blacker than black
Ultraviolettfilter *m* ultra-violet
filter
ultraweiß *adj* whiter than white
Umbesetzung *f* (Darsteller)
recasting *n*, change of cast
Umfang *m* (Bereich) range *n*

Umfeld *n* ambient field, outer field
Umfeldbild *n* cut-off area, out-of-
frame area
Umfeldhelligkeit *f* ambient
brightness
Umformer *m* rotary converter,
converter *n*, dynamotor *n*
Umhängemikrofon *n* necklace
microphone
umkabeln *v* re-cable *v*
Umkehr *f* (Kopierwerk) reversal *n*
Umkehrbad *n* reversing bath
Umkehrduplikat *n* reversal
duplicate
Umkehremulsion *f* reversal
emulsion
umkehren *v* (Kopierwerk) reverse *v*
Umkehrentwicklung *f* reversal
development, reversal processing
Umkehrfarbfilm *m* reversal-type
colour film
Umkehrfilm *m* reversal film
Umkehrprisma *n* inverting prism,
erecting prism, reversing prism,
image erecting prism
Umkehrsucher *m* prismatic
viewfinder
Umkehrung *f* reversal *n*, crush *n*,
crushing *n*
Umkehrverfahren *n* reversal
process
Umkodierer *m* transcoder *n*
Umkodierung *f* transcoding *n*
umkopieren *v* (Bild) print *v*; ~ *v*
(Ton) re-record *v*
Umlaufbahn *f* (Sat.) orbit *n*
Umlaufblende *f* rotary disc shutter,
rotary shutter; **hintere ~** rear
rotary shutter
Umlaufmenge *f* total circulating
capacity
Umlaufschmierung *f* circulation-
system lubrication, constant-
circulation lubrication
Umlenkprisma *n* deviating prism,
deviation wedge
Umlenkrolle *f* idler *n*, guide roller
Umlenkspiegel *m* deviation mirror

Umlicht *n* ambient light
umpolen *v* to reverse polarity
Umpoler *m* pole-changer *n*
Umpolung *f* polarity reversal
Umrechnungskoeffizient *m* conversion factor
Umriß *m* outline *n*
Umrißbild *n* outline picture
umrollen *v* rewind *v*, respool *v*
Umroller *m* rewinder *n*;
 elektrischer ~ power rewinder;
 fahrbarer ~ mobile rewinder
Umrolltisch *m* rewind bench
Umrüstbuchse *f* adapter socket
Umrüstteil *n* conversion unit, adapter *n*
Umschaltautomatik *f* switching matrix
umschaltbar *adj* switchable *adj*; ~ *adj* (Motor) reversible *adj*
umschalten *v* switch over *v*, change over *v*; ~ *v* (nach) (Sendung) go over *v* (to); ~ *v* (auf) cut *v* (to)
Umschalter *m* change-over switch, selector switch
Umschaltfrequenz *f* switching frequency, commutating frequency
Umschaltgerät *n* change-over switch, selector switch
Umschaltkennung *f* change-over identification
Umschaltkontakt *m* change-over contact
Umschaltpause *f* (Sender) switching period; ~ *f* (Progr.) break in transmission
Umschaltung *f* switching *n*, switch-over *n*, change-over *n*, commutation *n*
Umschaltzeit *f* switching time; ~ *f* (Dauer) duration of change-over, change-over time, time for reversal
Umschau *f* (Progr.) current affairs magazine, topical magazine
umschneiden *v* (Bildwechsel) cut *v*, switch *v*; ~ *v* (umspielen) re-

record *v*, transfer *v*; ~ *v* (Schnittkorrektur) re-edit *v*, change around *v*; **in der Länge** ~ edit down *v*
Umschneiden *n* re-recording *n*, transfer *n*, copying *n*
Umschneideraum *m* processing channel
Umschnitt *m* edit down *v*
umschreiben *v* rewrite *v*
umsetzen *v* convert *v*, transform *v*, transpose *v*
Umsetzer *m* (Sender) translator *n*; ~ *m* (Wandler) converter *n*
Umsetzung *f* conversion *n*, transformation *n*, translation *n*
Umspielanlage *f* copying equipment
umspielen *v* re-record *v*, transfer *v*, dub *v*, copy *v*
Umspielmaschine *f* copying equipment
Umspielraum *m* processing channel
Umspielung *f* re-recording *n*, transfer *n*
umspulen *v* respool *v*, rewind *v*
Umspuler *m* rewinding machine, rewinder *n*
Umtastfrequenz *f* keying frequency
Umtastung *f* inversion *n*, shift *n*
U-Musik *f s.* Unterhaltungsmusik
Umwälzung *f* rotation *n*, revolution *n*
umwandeln *v* convert *v*, transform *v*
Umwandlung *f* conversion *n*, transformation *n*
Umwandlungswirkungsgrad *m* conversion efficiency
unbegrenzt *adj* unlimited *adj*
unbelichtet *adj* unexposed *adj*
unbeschichtet *adj* uncoated *adj*
unbeschränkt *adj* unlimited *adj*
unbewertet *adj* ungraded *adj*, unweighted *adj*
unbrauchbar *adj* unusable *adj*
unbunt *adj* achromatic *adj*
Unbuntbereich *m* achromatic region, achromatic locus
UND-Gatter *n* (EDV) logical AND

UND-Gatter 180

circuit, AND element, AND gate, AND circuit, coincidence circuit, coincidence gate

undurchsichtig *adj* opaque *adj*, non-transparent *adj*

UND-Verknüpfung *f* (EDV) AND operation

Unendlicheinstellung *f* infinity focusing, infinity adjustment, infinity focus

ungedämpft *adj* undamped *adj*, sustained *adj*

ungeerdet *adj* ungrounded *adj*

ungefärbt *adj* uncoloured *adj*

ungekürzt *adj* unabridged *adj*

ungeschnitten *adj* unedited *adj*, uncut *adj*

ungetastet *adj* unclamped *adj*

unhörbar *adj* inaudible *adj*

Unikat *n* only existing print

unilateral *adj* unilateral *adj*

Universalgetriebe *n* universal drive

Universaltestbildgeber *m* general-purpose test signal generator, electronic test pattern generator

Univibrator *m* univibrator *n*

unlinear *adj* non-linear *adj*

Unlinearität *f* non-linearity *n*

unmaskiert *adj* (Negativ) unmasked *adj*

unmoduliert *adj* unmodulated *adj*

unredigiert *adj* (Nachricht) unedited *adj*

unscharf *adj* unsharp *adj*, hazy *adj*, blurred *adj*, out of focus

Unschärfe *f* lack of definition, unsharpness *n*, blurring *n*, lack of focus, fuzziness *n*; **Bild aus der ~ ziehen** refocus *v*, focus up *v*; **Bild in die ~ ziehen** defocus *v*

Unschärfeblende *f* mix on focus pull

unsensibilisiert *adj* desensitised *adj*

unterbelichten *v* underexpose *v*

Unterbelichtung *f* underexposure *n*

unterbrechen *v* interrupt *v*, break into *v*

Unterbrecher *m* interrupter *n*, cut-

out *n*, breaker *n*

Unterbrechung *f* interruption *n*, break *n*; ~ *f* (EDV) device request interrupt; **beabsichtigte kurze ~** (Sendung) break *n*; **kurzzeitige ~** momentary break; **unbeabsichtigte kurze ~** (Sendung) temporary fault

Unterbrechungsbad *n* stop bath

unterbringen *v* (Progr.) place *v*

unterdrehen *v* to shoot with low speed, to shoot for time lapse effect

unterdrücken *v* (Nachricht) suppress *v*

Unterentwicklung *f* underdevelopment *n*

Untergestell *n* base *n*, underframe *n*, stand *n*

Unterhaltung *f* entertainment *n*; **leichte ~** light entertainment

Unterhaltungsfilm *m* light entertainment film

Unterhaltungskünstler *m* variety artist

Unterhaltungsmusik *f* (U-Musik) light music

Unterhaltungsorchester *n* light orchestra

Unterhaltungsprogramm *n* light entertainment programme, show *n*; ~ *n* (TV) television show

Unterhaltungssendung *f* light entertainment programme, show *n*; ~ *f* (TV) television show

Unterhaltungsstudio *n* audience studio

unterirdisch *adj* underground *adj*, subterranean *adj*

Unterkleber *m* (F) joiner tape, splicing patch

Unterlänge *f* (Aufnahme) insufficient footage; ~ *f* (Schnitt) underlength *n*, insufficient duration

unterlegen, Geräusch to dub sound effects; **Musik ~** to dub music

Unterlegscheibe *f* washer *n*

untermalen *v* to dub music
Untermalung *f* (Mus.) background
music, incidental music;
akustische ~ background
atmosphere
untermodulieren *v* undermodulate
v
Untermodulierung *f*
undermodulation *n*
Unterprogramm *n* (EDV) subroutine
n
Unterputzdose *f* concealed socket
Unterrichtsfernsehen *n* educational
television (ETV)
Unterrichtsfilm *m* educational film
Untersatz, fahrbarer mobile
mounting unit, mobile chassis
Unterscheidungsschwelle *f*
threshold of discrimination
Unterscheidungsvermögen *n* power
of selection
unterschneiden *v* (Ton) intercut *v*,
overlay *v*, underlay *v*
Unterschnitt *m* cut-in *n*, overlay *n*,
underlay *n*; ~ *m* (live) film insert,
film inject
unterschwingen *v* overdamp *v*
Unterschwingung *f* sub-harmonic
oscillation
Unterseekabel *n* submarine cable
untersetzen *v* reduce *v*, gear down *v*
Untersetzung *f* gear reduction,
reduction *n*
Unterspannung *f* undervoltage *n*,
underrunning voltage
Unterspannungsrelais *n*
undervoltage relay, underload
relay
Unterstromrelais *n* undercurrent
relay
Unterteilung *f* subdivision *n*,
partitioning *n*
Untertitel *m* subtitle *n*, caption *n*
untertiteln *v* subtitle *v*
Untertiteln *n* subtitling *n*
Unterwasseraufnahme *f*
underwater shot, underwater
filming

unverkoppelt *adj* free-running *adj*
unverzögert *adj* instantaneously-
operating *adj*, undelayed *adj*
unzerbrechlich *adj* unbreakable *adj*
Uraufführung *f* première *n*, first
night, first performance; ~ *f* (F)
first run
Urheber *m* author *n*, originator *n*
Urheberpersönlichkeitsrecht *n*
copyright in dramatic character
Urheberrecht *n* copyright *n*
Urheberrechtsgesetz *n* copyright
law
Urheberrechtsschutz *m* copyright
protection
Ursendung *f* first broadcast
Ursprungsdienst *m* (Anstalt)
originating station
Ursprungsland *n* country of origin
Ursprungspunkt *m* point of origin,
origin *n*
Urteilsindex *m* reaction index
Ü-Wagen *m* OB vehicle, OB van; ~
m (Ton) sound OB van, radio OB
van; **drahtloser ~** radio car

V

Vakuum *n* vacuum *n*
Vakuumführungsschuh *m* vacuum
guide
Vakuumlampe *f* vacuum lamp,
incandescent lamp
Valenzelektron *n* valency electron
Variometer *n* variometer *n*
Variometerabstimmung *f*
variometer tuning
Vario-Objektiv *n* zoom lens
Varioptik *f* zoom lens
Varistor *m* varistor *n*
VDR-Widerstand *m* voltage-
dependent resistor (VDR), varistor
n
Vektor *m* vector *n*, vector quantity
Vektordiagramm *n* vector diagram

Vektoroszilloskop 182

Vektoroszilloskop *n* vectorscope *n*
Vektorskop *n* vectorscope *n*
Vektorventil *n* valve *n*
verankern *v* anchor *v*, stay *v*, guy *v*
Veranstaltung *f* function *n*, event *n*, show *n*
Veranstaltungsbüro *n* ticket office
Verarbeitung *f* processing *n*, treatment *n*
verbessern *v* improve *v*; ~ *v* (richtigstellen) put right *v*, correct *v*
verbinden *v* (schalten) connect *v*, link *v*; ~ *v* (mit) (Telefon) put through *v* (to)
Verbindung *f* (Telefon) connection *n*, communication *n*; ~ *f* (Leitung) link *n*, junction *n*, connection *n*, circuit *n*; ~ *f* (chem.) compound *n*; **chemische** ~ chemical compound; **fliegende** ~ physical connection; **galvanische** ~ electrical connection; **gerichtete** ~ unidirectional link; **internationale** ~ international junction; **rangierbare** ~ shunt connection, parallel connection; **richtungsumschaltbare** ~ reversible link
Verbindungskabel *n* junction cable, connecting cable, trunk line
Verbindungsleiste *f* connecting bar, bus bar
Verbindungsleitung *f* junction circuit
Verbindungsmann *m* liaison officer, go-between *n* (coll.)
Verbindungspunkt *m* connection point, junction point
Verbindungsreferat *n* liaison office
Verbindungsstelle *f* liaison office; ~ *f* (elek.) junction *n*, point of connection, cable joint
Verblitzung *f* dendriform exposure of film
Verbreitungsgebiet *n* coverage area, broadcasting area, service area
Verbreitungsrecht *n* distribution

right
Verdampfungskühlung *f* vapour cooling
Verdoppler *m* doubler *n*
verdrahten *v* wire *v*; **lötlos** ~ wrap *v*
Verdrahtung *f* wiring *n*; **lötlose** ~ wrapped jointing
Verdrahtungsplan *m* wiring diagram
Verdrahtungsseite *f* wiring side
verdrillen *v* twist *v*
Verdunkler *m* dimmer *n*, dimming switch
verdünnen *v* dilute *v*
Verdünner *m* diluting agent
Verdünnung *f* dilution *n*
Verfahren *n* process *n*, system *n*, method *n*, procedure *n*, technique *n*; **additives** ~ additive process; **subtraktives** ~ subtractive process
Verfasser *m* writer *n*, author *n*
verfilmen *v* film *v*, to make a screen version of
Verfilmung *f* film version, screen adaptation
Verfilmungsrechte *n pl* screen rights *n pl*
Verfolger *m* (fam.) *s.* Verfolgerscheinwerfer
Verfolgerscheinwerfer *m* follower *n*, follow spot, follow spotlight
Verfolgerspot *m s.* Verfolgerscheinwerfer
Verfolgungsaufnahme *f* follow shot, follow focus shot
vergagen *v* jazz up *v*, gag up *v* (US)
Vergleichsimpuls *m* comparison pulse, reference pulse
Vergleichsmessung *f* comparison measurement
Vergleichsphase *f* reference phase
Vergleichsspannung *f* reference voltage, comparison voltage
Vergleichstest *m* comparison test
Vergleichsverstärker *m* comparison amplifier
Vergnügungssteuer *f* entertainment tax, admission tax (US)

vergrößern v (Bild) enlarge v, blow up v; ~ v (Brennweite) increase v; ~ v (Maßstab) magnify v

Vergrößerung f blow-up n, enlargement n

Vergrößerungsapparat m enlarger n

Vergrößerungskopie f enlargement n, blow-up n

Vergrößerungsmaßstab m degree of enlargement

Vergütung f (Geld) remuneration n; ~ f (entspiegeln) lens correction, coating of lens

Vergütungsanspruch m claim for remuneration

Vergütungsordnung f pay scale, salary scale

verhallen v fade away v

Verhältnisgleichrichter m ratio detector

Verhältnisregelung f (EDV) ratio control

Verhältnissteuerung f (EDV) ratio control

verhaspeln v (sich) to get muddled, fluff v

Verkabelung f cabling n, wiring n

Verkabelungsplan m wiring diagram

Verkehrshinweise m pl traffic news

verkleinern v reduce v, diminish v

Verkleinerung f reduction n, decrease n, diminution n

Verkleinerungskopie f reduction print

Verkleinerungsmaschine f reduction printer

Verknüpfung f (EDV) linkage n

verkoppeln v couple v, join v

Verkopplung f coupling n

Verkürzungsfaktor m shortening factor, velocity factor

Verlagsrechte n pl copyright n

Verlängerung f (Zeit) prolongation n, extension n; ~ f (tech.) lengthening n, extension n, elongation n

Verlängerungsfaktor m extension factor, prolongation factor

Verlängerungskabel n extension cable, pad n

Verlängerungsleitung f extension circuit

Verlaufblende f graduated filter, gradual filter

Verlauffilter m graduated filter, gradual filter

Verlautbarung f announcement n, statement n, press release

Verlegung f (fam.) (Kabel) laying n (coll.)

Verleih m hire service; ~ m (F) distribution n; ~ m (Gesellschaft) distributors n pl

Verleihanteil m distributor's share

Verleiher m distributor n

Verleihfiliale f branch distributors n pl

Verleihfilm m distributor's film

Verleihfirma f distributing agency, distributor n

Verleihkopie f distribution print

Verleihorganisation f distributing organisation

Verleihrechte n pl distribution rights

Verleihvertrag m distribution agreement

Verleihvertreter m film salesman

Verlustfaktor m loss factor

Verlustleistung f power dissipation, power loss

Verlustwärme f dissipated heat

Verlustwiderstand m equivalent resistance, loss resistance, non-reactive resistance, ohmic resistance

Vermaschung f interconnection n

Vermietung f (Leitung) lease n

Vermischtes n miscellaneous news n pl; ~ n (R,TV) news round-up, rest of the news

Vermittlung f s. Vermittlungsstelle

Vermittlungsstelle f (Post) exchange n

Vernichtungswiderstand *m* dummy load

Veröffentlichung *f* publication *n*; **nicht zur ~** not for publication; **zur ~** for publication

Veröffentlichungsrechte *n pl* publishing rights

verpflichten *v* engage *v*, cast *v*, sign up *v*, to put under contract

verrauschen *v* to be degraded by high noise level

verrauscht *adj* noisy *adj*

Verriegelung *f* (mech.) locking mechanism, locking *n*; **~** *f* (elek.) interlocking circuit

Verriegelungsautomatik *f* automatic locking

Verriegelungsgriff *m* locking lever

Verriegelungsimpuls *m* locking pulse

Verriegelungslasche *f* clamping strip

Verriegelungsring *m* locking ring

Versandabteilung *f* shipping office, shipping* *n*

Versatzstück *n* special *n*

Verschachtelung *f* (Farbträger) interleaving *n*

verschieben *v* (mech.) displace *v*, shift *v*; **~** *v* (Zeit) postpone *v*, defer *v*

Verschiebung *f* (mech.) displacement *n*, shift *n*; **~** *f* (Zeit) postponement *n*, deferment *n*; **axiale ~** axial displacement; **gradlinige ~** displacement in straight line

verschleiern *v* fog *v*, screen *v*, veil *v*

verschlucken *v* (Silben) slur *v*, swallow *v*

Verschluß *m* (Kamera) shutter *n*

Verschlüsselung *f* encoding *n*

Verschlußgeschwindigkeit *f* shutter speed

Verschlußzeit *f* shutter time

Verschnitt *m* waste *n*

verschwärzlichen *v* blacken *v*; **~** *v* (Farbe) to back off one colour

Verschwärzlichung *f* blackening *n*

Versenkvorrichtung *f* trapdoor *n*

versorgen *v* feed *v*

Versorgung *f* supply *n*; **~** *f* (Sender) coverage *n*, service *n*

Versorgungsbereich *m* (Sender) coverage area, service area

Versorgungsgebiet *n* s. Versorgungsbereich

verspannen *v* guy *v*, stay *v*

versprechen *v* (sich) fluff *v*

Versprecher *m* fluff *n*

Verständigung *f* audibility *n*, reception quality, readability *n*

Verständigungsanlage *f* communication system

Verständigungsprobe *f* communication check, level check

Verständlichkeit *f* intelligibility *n*, readability *n*

verstärken *v* (Licht) intensify *v*; **~** *v* (elek.) amplify *v*; **~** *v* (Kopierwerk) reinforce *v*

Verstärker *m* (elek.) amplifier *n*, repeater *n*; **~** *m* (Kopierwerk) intensifier *n*; **gegengekoppelter ~** feedback amplifier, negative-feedback amplifier; **parametrischer ~** parametric amplifier; **rückgekoppelter ~** feedback amplifier, amplifier with regeneration; **trägerfrequenter ~** carrier-frequency amplifier

Verstärkeramt *n* (Post) repeater station

Verstärkerdaten *n pl* amplifier data

Verstärkergestell *n* amplifier bay, repeater bay

Verstärkerröhre *f* amplifier valve, amplifier tube

Verstärkerzentrale *f* amplifier room

Verstärkerzug *m* amplifier chain

Verstärkung *f* amplification *n*, gain *n*; **~** *f* (Foto) intensification *n*; **differentielle ~** differential gain; **fotografische ~** redevelopment *n*, photographic intensification; **selektive ~** selective amplification

veränderliche ~ variable gain, variable intensification

Verstärkungsänderung *f* gain variation

Verstärkungsfaktor *m* amplification factor; **differentieller ~** differential gain distortion

Verstärkungsregelung *f* gain control; **automatische ~** automatic gain control (AGC)

Verstärkungsregler *m* (fam.) *s.* Verstärkungssteller

Verstärkungssteller *m* gain control

Verstärkungsstufe *f* amplification stage

verstellen *v* (justieren) adjust *v*, set *v*; **~** *v* (Kamera) to bring out of focus; **~** *v* (Bildstrich) frame *v*

verstümmelt *adj* (Text) garbled *adj*

Versuchsprogramm *n* experimental programme

Versuchssendung *f* (Progr.) pilot programme

Versuchsstreifen *m* test strip

Versuchsstudio *n* (R) training studio

Verteiler *m* distributor *n*, distribution frame, distribution board, manifold *n*

Verteilerkasten *m* distribution box, junction box, terminal box

Verteilerkreis *m* distribution circuit

Verteilerleitung *f* distribution conduit, distribution circuit, distribution line, induction manifold

Verteilersatellit *m* distribution satellite

Verteilerschrank *m* distribution switchboard

Verteilertafel *f* distribution panel, distribution frame, distribution board

Verteilerverstärker *m* distribution amplifier

Verteilnetz *n* distribution network, distribution system

Verteilung *f* distribution *n*

Verteilungsnetz *n* distribution network, distribution system; **nationales ~** national distribution network

Vertikalablenkspule (V-Ablenkspule) *f* vertical deflection coil

Vertikalauflösung *f* vertical definition

Vertikalaustastimpuls *m* field blanking pulse, vertical blanking pulse (US)

Vertikalfrequenz (V-Frequenz) *f* field frequency, vertical frequency (US)

Vertikalimpuls (V-Impuls) *m* field pulse, vertical pulse (US)

Vertikalsägezahn *m* vertical saw-tooth

Vertikalsynchronimpuls *m* field synchronising pulse, vertical synchronising pulse (US)

Vertikalumroller *m* vertical rewinder

vertonen *v* (F) to make a sound recording, to add sound to a film; **~** *v* (Mus.) to set to music, score *v*

Vertonung *f* (F) sound recording; **~** *f* (Mus.) setting to music, scoring *n*

Vertrag *m* contract *n*, agreement *n*

Verträglichkeit *f* compatibility *n*, tolerance *n*

Vertragsbedingung *f* condition of contract

Vertragsentwurf *m* draft agreement, draft contract

Vertragsmusiker *m* musician on contract

Vertragspartner *m* contracting party

Vertragszeit *f* life of contract, duration of contract, length of contract

verunreinigen *v* contaminate *v*, pollute *v*

Verunreinigung *f* contamination *n*, pollution *n*

Vervielfacher *m* multiplier *n*

Vervielfältiger *m* (Person) copying-machine operator, clerical operator; ~ *m* (Apparat) duplicator *n*, copying machine, office printing machine

Vervielfältigung *f* duplication *n*, office printing, copying *n*

Vervielfältigungsrecht *n* reproduction right

Vervielfältigungsstelle *f* printing office

verwackeln *v* (Bild) blur *v*

Verwaltung *f* administration *n*; ~ **Fernsehen** television administration; ~ **Hörfunk** radio administration

Verwaltungsrat *m* administrative council

Verwässerung *f* (Farbe) dilution *n*

Verweilzeit *f* dwell time

verweißlichen *v* desaturate *v*

Verweißlichung *f* desaturation *n*

Verwertung *f* utilisation *n*, commercialisation *n*, use *n*, exploitation *n*; **kommerzielle ~** commercial use

Verwertungsanteil *m* distributor's share

Verwertungsgesellschaft *f* distribution company

Verwertungsrecht *n* distribution rights *n pl*

Verwertungsvertrag *m* distribution agreement

Verzeichnung *f* distortion *n*; **optische ~** optical distortion

Verzerrer *m* (Ton) harmonic generator

Verzerrung *f* distortion *n*; **~ durch Ein- und Ausschwingvorgänge** transient distortion, build-up and delay distortion; **geometrische ~** geometric distortion; **harmonische ~** harmonic distortion; **lineare ~** linear distortion; **nichtlineare ~** non-linear distortion

Verzerrungsgebiet *n* distortion range

Verzerrungsmeßgerät *n* distortion measuring set, distortion analyser

Verziehen *n* (Band) buckling *n*

verzögern *v* delay *v*, retard *v*

Verzögerung *f* delay *n*, retardment *n*, time lag

Verzögerungskassette *f* delay unit

Verzögerungsleitung *f* delay line; **akustische ~** (EDV) acoustic delay line, sonic delay line; **einstellbare ~** variable delay line

Verzögerungszeit *f* delay time

Verzweigungsdose *f* bifurcation box

Verzweigungspunkt *m* junction point

Verzweigungssystem *n* bifurcation system

Verzweigungsverstärker *m* branching amplifier

VF-Verstärker *m* video amplifier

VHF-Fernsehsender *m* VHF television transmitter

Vibrationsmesser *m* vibrating reed meter

Vibrator *m* vibrator *n*

Video *n* video *n*

Videoaufzeichnung *f* video recording

Videobandkassette *f* video tape cassette

Videofilterkreuzschiene *f* video matrix

videofrequent *adj* video-frequency *adj*

Videofrequenz (VF) *f* video frequency

Videofrequenztechnik *f* video techniques *n pl*

Videogeräteraum *m* video apparatus room

Videoinformation *f* video information

Videokabel *n* video cable

Videoklebeband *n* (MAZ) splicing tape

Videokontrolle *f* video check

Videokopf *m* video head

Videomagnetband *n* video tape
Videomagnetspule *f* video spool
Videomeßdienst *m* video quality control
Videoplatte *f* video disc
Videoprüfsignalgeber *m* video test signal generator
Videosignal *n* video signal, picture signal
Videospur *f* video track
Videotape *n* video tape
Videotechniker *m* video operator
Video-Überwachungsstelle *f* video monitor point
Videoumschalter *m* video switch
Videoverstärker *m* video amplifier
Videoverteiler *m* video distributor, video matrix
Vidikon *n* vidicon *n*
Vielfachgegenstecker *m* multi-contact socket, multi-way connector
Vielfachkanalfernsprechleitung *f* multi-channel telephone cable
Vielfachmeßgerät *n* multimeter *n*, multitester *n*
Vielfachstecker *m* multi-contact plug, multiple plug
Vielfachzugriff *m* (EDV) multiple access
Vierdrahtleitung *f* four-wire line, four-wire circuit
Vierdrahtmeldeleitung *f* four-wire control circuit
Vierergang *m* four-frame motion
Vierkanttubus *m* square tube
Vierpol *m* quadripole *n*, four-terminal network, two-port network, four-pole network
Vierspur *f* four-track *n*
Vierspurmaschine *f* four-track machine
Viertelspur *f* quarter track
Viertelwelle *f* quarter wave
Vignette *f* vignette *n*, matte *n*, mask *n*
Vignettierung *f* vignetting *n*
Vintenstativ *n* Vinten tripod

Vogelperspektive *f* bird's-eye view
Vokalverständlichkeit *f* clarity of vowels
Vokalwerk *n* vocal work, vocal score
Volksmusik *f* folk music
Volksstück *n* regional play, popular play
volkstümlich *adj* popular *adj*, pop *adj* (coll.)
Vollaussteuerung *f* (Sender) full modulation, full drive; ~ *f* (Ton) maximum level, maximum volume
Vollbild *n* picture *n*, frame *n*
Vollbildfrequenz *f* picture frequency, frame frequency, frame repetition rate
Vollpegel *m* maximum level, full modulation
Vollspur *f* full track
Vollsynchronisation *f* full synchronisation, total dubbing
Volontär *m* trainee *n*
Volumenanzeiger *m* volume indicator
vorabaufnehmen *v* pre-record *v*; ~ *v* (F) pre-film *v*
vorabstimmen *v* pretune *v*, preset *v*
Vorabtext *m* advance script
Voranhebung *f* pre-emphasis *n*
Vorarbeiter *m* foreman *n*
Vorausplanung *f* forward planning
Vorbad *n* pre-bath *n*
Vorbau *m* pre-assembly *n*
Vorbaubühne *f* pre-assembly shop
vorbauen *v* pre-assemble *v*
Vorbauhalle *f* pre-assembly studio, pre-setting studio
Vorbehalt, unter with reservation
vorbelichten *v* pre-expose *v*
Vorbelichtung *f* pre-exposure *n*
Vorbereitungszeit *f* line-up time, preparation time
Vorbesichtigung *f* recce *n*; ~ *f* (tech.) location survey
Vorderflanke *f* leading edge, front face

Vordergrund *m* foreground *n*
Vordergrundprogramm *n* (EDV) foreground programme
Vorderlicht *n* front light
Vorderlichtwagen *m* mobile front light dimmer
voreinstellen *v* preset *v*, set up *v*
vorentzerren *v* pre-emphasise *v*, pre-correct *v*
Vorentzerrung *f* pre-emphasis *n*, pre-equalisation *n*, pre-correction *n*
vorfahren *v* (Kamera) track in *v*
Vorfahrt *f* (Kamera) track-in *n*
Vorführband *n* demonstration tape
Vorführdauer *f* running time, screen time
vorführen *v* screen *v*, project *v*, exhibit *v*, show *v*
Vorführer *m* projectionist *n*, operator *n*
Vorführgenehmigung *f* projection permit, exhibition permit
Vorführkabine *f* projection booth, projection room
Vorführkino *n* viewing theatre, projection theatre
Vorführkopie *f* release print, viewing print
Vorführraum *m* viewing theatre, screening room
Vorführtermin *m* viewing date, preview date
Vorführung *f* showing *n*, performance *n*, exhibition *n*; ~ *f* (F) viewing *n*, screening *n*, projection *n*; **geschlossene ~** private showing; **offene ~** public showing
Vorführungsrechte *n pl* exhibition rights
Vorgabezeit *f* advance time
Vorgang, azyklischer (EDV) acyclic process
vorgeschaltet *adj* upstream *adj*
Vorhangblende *f* curtain shutter, curtain fading shutter, curtain wipe; **horizontale ~** horizontal

curtain shutter; **vertikale ~** vertical curtain shutter
Vorhangschiene *f* curtain track
vorhören *v* pre-hear *v*, pre-listen *v*
Vorhören *n* pre-hearing *n*, pre-listening *n*
Vorlauf *m* forward motion; **schneller ~** fast forward run
Vorlaufband *n* tape leader, leader *n*
Vorlauflänge *f* leader length
Vorlaufzeit *f* leader duration, pre-roll time; ~ *f* (Leitung) test period, line-up time
Vormagnetisierung *f* magnetic biasing, premagnetising *n*
Vormagnetisierungsstrom *m* bias current
Vormischung *f* pre-mixing *n*
Vormittagsprogramm *n* morning programme
Vormontage *f* (Schnitt) assembly *n*
Vornorm *f* tentative standard
Vorpremiere *f* (F) advance showing, preview *n*; ~ *f* (Thea.) try-out *n*
Vorproduktion *f* pre-production *n*
vorproduzieren *v* pre-produce *v*
Vorrang *m* priority *n*
Vorrangmeldung *f* priority item, flash *n*, snap *n*
Vorratsgefäß *n* storage tank
Vorratstrommel *f* delivery spool, feed spool
Vor-Rückverhältnis *n* forward-to-back ratio, front-to-back ratio, front-to-rear ratio
Vorsatzlinse *f* supplementary lens, additional lens, attachment lens; **~ für Nahaufnahme** supplementary close-up lens, portrait attachment
Vorsatzmodell *n* foreground model
Vorsatzrampe *f* ground cove
Vorsatztubus *m* lens tube
Vorschaltzeit *f* (Leitung) test period, line-up time
Vorschau *f* (F) trailer *n*; ~ *f* (Bild) preview *n*
Vorschaubild *n* monitor picture

vorschauen *v* preview *v*
Vorschaumonitor *m* preview monitor
Vorschub *m* feed *n*
Vorschulprogramm *n* pre-school broadcasting
Vorschuß *m* advance *n*
Vorspann *m* (F) leader *n*; ~ *m* (Titel) opening titles *n pl*, opening credits *n pl*; ~ **mit Bildstrich** framed leader, racked blanking, racked spacing
Vorspannband *n* leader tape
Vorspannfilm *m* leader film, head leader
Vorspannschwarzfilm *m* black leader
Vorspanntitel *m* opening titles *n pl*, opening credits *n pl*
vorsprechen *v* (Rolle) audition *v*
Vorsprechen *n* audition *n*, auditioning *n*
Vorstellung *f* performance *n*, show *n*, showing *n*; **geschlossene** ~ private performance
Vorstufe *f* (Treiber) pre-amplifier *n*, driving stage, input stage
Vorsynchronisation *f* pre-dubbing *n*
Vortrabant *m* pre-equalising pulse
Vortragsrecht *n* right of personal access
Vorübertragungsversuch *m* pre-transmission test
Vorverkauf *m* advance sales *n pl*
Vorverstärker *m* pre-amplifier *n*; ~ **mit Tunneldiode** tunnel-diode pre-amplifier
Vorverstärkerstufe *f* pre-amplifier stage
Vorvertrag *m* preliminary contract
Vorverzerrung *f* pre-emphasis *n*, pre-accentuation *n*
Vorwahl *f* preselection *n*
vorwählen *v* preselect *v*
Vorwähler *m* preselector *n*
Vorwahlkreuzschiene *f* preselector matrix
Vorwahlstellung *f* preselector

setting
Vorwärtsgang *m* forward motion
Vorwärtsregelung *f* forward-acting regulator; ~ *f* (EDV) feed-forward control
Vorwärts-Rückwärts-Meßgerät *n* (Ant.) reflectometer *n*
Vorwickelrolle *f* feed sprocket, supply reel
Vorzensur *f* pre-censorship *n*
Voute *f* cove *n*, merging curve
V-Separator *m* vertical pulse separator
VU-Meter *n* volume unit meter, VU-meter *n*, volumeter *n*

W

Wachmann *m* guard *n*, watchman *n*
Wachsaufnahme *f* wax recording
Wachsplatte *f* wax disc
Wackelkontakt *m* loose contact, intermittent contact
Wagen mit drahtloser Kameraanlage roving eye
Wähler *m* (tech.) selector *n*; ~ *m* (Telefon) dial *n*
Wahlschalter *m* selector switch
Wahlschiene *f* code bar
Wahrheitstabelle *f* (EDV) function table, truth table, Boolean operation table
Walkie-Talkie *m* walkie-talkie *n*
Walze *f* roller *n*
Wand *f* wall *n*; ~ *f* (Dekoration) screen *n*, panel *n*, scenic flat; **absorbierende** ~ (Ton) sound-absorbing wall, absorbing wall; **absorbierende** ~ (Licht) baffle *n*; **reflektierende** ~ reflecting screen, reflecting panel, reflecting wall; **schluckende** ~ (Ton) sound-absorbing wall, absorbing wall
Wanderfeldröhre *f* travelling-wave tube (TWT)

Wanderkino *n* touring cinema, road cinema

Wandermaskenverfahren *n* travelling matte process

Wandler *m* transducer *n*, converter *n*

Wandsteckdose *f* wall socket, wall outlet

Wanne *f* (Licht) lighting trough; ~ *f* (Ton) line source unit, line source loudspeaker

Wärmeleitwert *m* thermal conductivity

Wärmeschutzfilter *m* heat filter, heat protection filter

Wärmestrahlen *m pl* heat rays, thermal rays

Warmleiter *m* negative temperature coefficient resistor (NTC resistor)

Warnpfeil *m* warning arrow

Wartebahn *f* (Sat.) parking orbit

warten *v* (Gerät) maintain *v*

Wartezeit *f* delay *n*, waiting time

Wartung *f* maintenance *n*, upkeep servicing

Wartungsdienst *m* maintenance service

Wartungsraum *m* servicing area

Waschanlage *f* (Kopierwerk) washing tank, washing plant

waschen *v* wash *v*

Wasserbad *n* water-bath *n*

Wasserfleck *m* water stain

wasserfrei *adj* anhydrous *adj*, free from water

Wasserkühlung *f* water-cooling *n*

wässern *v* (Foto) rinse *v*

Wasserstandsmeldungen *f pl* water level bulletin

Wässerungsschleier *m* rinse fog

Wasserwaage *f* spirit level

Wattussy *m* (fam.) flag *n*

Wechselkassette *f* changing magazine

Wechselobjektiv *n* interchangeable lens

Wechselrahmen *m* changing frame

Wechselsack *m* changing bag

Wechselschalter *m* change-over switch

Wechselspannung *f* alternating current voltage, alternating voltage

Wechselsprechanlage *f* intercommunication system, intercom *n* (coll.)

Wechselsprechverbindung *f* intercommunication circuit

Wechselstrom *m* alternating current (AC)

Wechselstromleistung *f* alternating current power

Wechselstromlöschkopf *m* alternating current erase head

Wechselstrommotor *m* alternating current motor

Wechselstromvormagnetisierung *f* alternating current magnetic biasing

Wechselstromwiderstand *m* alternating current resistance

wechselweise *adv* alternately *adv*, reciprocally *adv*, in turn

wegnehmen *v* (Ton, Bild) cut *v*; ~ *v* (Pegel) fade *v*

Wehrexperte *m* defence correspondent, military affairs specialist

weich *adj* (Bild) blurred *adj*, soft *adj* ~ *adj* (Negativ) weak *adj*

Weichbildscheibe *f* diffusing disc

Weiche *f* combining unit, selective coupler, diplexer *n*

Weicheiseninstrument *n* soft-iron instrument

Weichstrahler *m* diffuser *n*

Weichzeichner *m* diffuser scrim, soft-focus lens

Weichzeichnung *f* diffusion *n*, soft focus

Weiß *n* white *n*, blank *n*; ~ **übersteuern** to burn out the whites; **gesättigtes** ~ clear white; **reines** ~ pure white

weiß *adj* white *adj*, blank *adj*

weiß, knallig glaring white, burnt-out *adj* (coll.)

Weißabgleich *m* white balance

Weißbalance *f* white balance

Weißband *n* white tape

Weißentzerrung *f* white distortion

Weißfilm *m* white film; ~ *m* (Start) white leader, white spacing, blank film

Weißkrümmung *f* white non-linearity

Weißpegel *m* white level

Weißschwarzsprung *m* white-to-black step

Weißspitze *f* peak white, white spike, specular *n*

Weißspitzensignal *n* peak white signal

Weißton *m* (Ton) white noise

Weißtonregelung *f* adjustment of white balance

Weißwert *m* white level

Weißwertbegrenzer *m* white-level limiter, white-level clipper

Weißwertbegrenzung *f* white-level limiting, white-level clipping

Weißwertregelung *f* adjustment of white level, white-level control

Weißwertstauchung *f* white crushing

Weißwertübersteuerung *f* overmodulation of white level

Weißzeile *f* white line

Weisung *f* directive *n*, instruction *n*, order *n*, direction *n*

Weiteinstellung *f* extreme long shot (ELS), very long shot (VLS)

Weitwinkelbereich *m* wide-angle range

Weitwinkelobjektiv *n* wide-angle lens

Welle *f* wave *n*; **elektrische** ~ synchro-link *n*, selsyn *n*; **elektromagnetische** ~ electromagnetic wave; **fortschreitende** ~ progressive wave, travelling wave; **stehende** ~ standing wave

Wellenangaben *f pl* wavelength

announcement

Wellenausbreitung *f* wave propagation

Wellenband *n* wave range, waveband *n*

Wellenbauch *m* wave loop, antinode *n*

Wellenbereich *m* wave range, waveband *n*

Wellenberg *m* wave crest

Wellenblende *f* wash dissolve

Wellenform *f* waveform *n*

Wellenlänge *f* wavelength *n*; **dominierende** ~ dominant wavelength; **farbtongleiche** ~ dominant wavelength; **kompensative** ~ complementary wavelength

Wellenlängenmesser *m* wavemeter *n*

Wellenlängenskala *f* wavelength scale

Wellenlängenspektrum *n* wavelength spectrum

Wellenplan *m* frequency plan, frequency allocation plan; **Kopenhagener** ~ Copenhagen plan; **Stockholmer** ~ Stockholm plan

Wellenschwund *m* fading *n*

Wellental *n* wave trough

Wellenwiderstand *m* surge impedance, wave impedance, characteristic impedance

Wellenzug *m* wave train

Welligkeit *f* ripple *n*; ~ *f* (MAZ) contour effect

Welturaufführung *f* world première

Weltvertrieb *m* world distribution

Werbeblock *m* advertising block

Werbeeinblendung *f* advertising break, commercial *n*

Werbeeinnahmen *f pl* advertising revenue

Werbefachmann *m* advertising consultant

Werbefernsehen *n* commercial television, sponsored television (US)

Werbefernsehgesellschaft *f* television programme company

Werbefilm *m* publicity film

Werbefunk *m* commercial radio

Werbekampagne *f* advertising campaign, promotion campaign

Werberahmenprogramm *n* framework programme for commercials

Werbesendung *f* sponsored programme

Werbespot *m* commercial spot, commercial *n*

Werbeträger *m* advertising medium

Werbung *f* publicity *n*, advertising *n*, promotion *n*

Werkaufnahme *f* industrial photo, still *n*

Werkmeister *m* foreman *n*

Werkstattmeister *m* workshop manager

Werktitel *m* working title

Werte, elektrische electrical data

Wertetabelle *f* (EDV) function table, truth table, Boolean operation table

wertlos *adj* unusable *adj*; ~ *adj* (Aufnahme) unfit for transmission, NG *adj* (coll.)

Western *m* western *n*, horse opera (US coll.)

Wettbewerbssendung *f* contest programme, competitive-game programme

Wettbewerbsverzerrung *f* unfair comparative advertising

Wetterbericht *m* meteorological report, weather report

Wetterkarte *f* weather chart, weather map

Wettervorhersage *f* weather forecast

Wicklung *f* winding *n*, wrapping *n*, spooling *n*, coiling *n*

Wicklungssinn *m* direction of winding

widerrufen *v* revoke *v*, cancel *v*,

countermand *v*

Widerstand *m* resistance *n*, resistor *n*; **abgerauchter** ~ burnt-out resistor; **angepaßter** ~ matched impedance; **spannungsabhängiger** ~ voltage-dependent resistor (VDR), varistor *n*; **veränderlicher** ~ variable resistor, variable resistance; **verbrannter** ~ burnt-out resistor

Widerstandsanpasser *m* impedance matching network, impedance adapter

Widerstandsmatrix *f* impedance matrix

Widerstandsnetzwerk *n* resistance network

Widerstandsnormal *n* standard resistor

Widerstandstransformator *m* impedance matching transformer

wiederanfeuchten *v* remoisten *v*

Wiederaufnahme *f* (F) retake *n*

Wiederaufrollen *n* rewinding *n*

wiederaufspulen *v* rewind *v*

wiederaufwickeln *v* rewind *v*

wiederaufzeichnen *v* re-record *v*

wiederausstrahlen *v* reradiate *v*

Wiederausstrahlung *f* reradiation *n*

Wiedereinschaltautomatik *f* hold-in circuit

Wiedergabe *f* replay *n*, reproduction *n*, playback *n*, repro *n* (coll.); **naturgetreue** ~ faithful reproduction, good definition, high fidelity reproduction, orthophonic reproduction

Wiedergabecharakteristik *f* playback characteristics *n pl*, reproducing characteristics *n pl*, reproducing frequency response, response characteristic

Wiedergabedaten *n pl* playback data

Wiedergabeentzerrung *f* playback equalisation

Wiedergabegerät *n* playback unit, reproducer *n*, reproduction equipment

Wiedergabegüte *f* quality of reproduction; **hohe ~ (HI-FI)** high fidelity (hi-fi)

Wiedergabekanal *m* reproducing channel

Wiedergabekette *f* reproducing chain, replay chain, playback chain

Wiedergabekopf *m* playback head, reproducing head

Wiedergabekurve *f* frequency response curve, reproduction curve, fidelity curve

Wiedergabepegel *m* playback level, reproduction level; **zulässiger ~** permissible playback level

Wiedergabepult *n* playback desk

Wiedergabequalität *f* quality of reproduction

Wiedergaberecht *n* reproduction right; **mechanische ~e** mechanical reproduction rights

Wiedergaberöhre *f* cathode-ray tube (CRT), picture tube, display tube, kinescope *n* (US)

Wiedergabespalt *m* reproducing gap

Wiedergabetreue *f* fidelity of reproduction, reproduction fidelity

Wiedergabeverluste *m pl* playback loss

Wiedergabeverstärker *m* playback amplifier, reproducing amplifier

Wiedergabevorrichtung *f* playback device

wiedergeben *v* (Ton) reproduce *v*, play back *v*; **~** *v* (F) project *v*

wiederherausgeben *v* (Buch) re-publish *v*, re-issue *v*

wiederholen *v* (Aufnahme) retake *v*; **~** *v* (Sendung) repeat *v*, re-run *v* (US); **~** *v* (Text) repeat *v*, read again *v*; **~** *v* (Fernschreiben) re-run *v*

Wiederholung *f* (Sendung) repeat *n*, rebroadcast *n*, re-run *n* (US); **~** *f*

(Musik) repeat *n*, replay *n*; **~** *f* (Aufnahme) retake *n*

Wiederholungshonorar *n* repeat fee, reproduction fee

Wiederkehrgenauigkeit *f* accuracy of return, repeating accuracy

Wiederverfilmung *f* remake *n*

Wiederverteilung *f* redistribution *n*

Wildwestfilm *m* western *n*, horse opera (US coll.)

Winde *f* winch *n*

Windeständer *m* winch-base *n*

Windlast *f* (Ant.) wind-loading *n*

Windmaschine *f* blower *n*, fan *n*

Windschutz *m* (Mikro) wind shield, wind bag

Windung *f* winding *n*, twist *n*, turn *n*, thread of screw

Wink *m* tip *n*, tip-off *n*, lead *n*, pointer *n*

Winkel *m* angle *n*

Winkelstück *n* angle plate, angle piece; **~** *n* (Rohr) elbow *n*

Wirbelstrom *m* eddy current

Wirbelstromverlust *m* eddy-current loss

Wirkleistung *f* effective power

Wirkleitwert *m* conductance *n*

Wirkwiderstand *m* pure resistance, ohmic resistance

Wirtschaftsredakteur *m* economics correspondent, economics editor

Wirtschaftswerbung *f* commercial advertising

Wischblende *f* soft-edged wipe

Wissenschaft und Technik* science and features*

Wobbelfrequenz *f* sweep frequency, wobble frequency

Wobbelgenerator *m* wobbulator *n*, sweep-frequency signal generator

Wobbelmeßsender *m* wobbulator *n*, sweep-frequency signal generator

wobbeln *v* sweep *v*, wobble *v*, wobbulate *v*

Wobbeln *n* sweeping *n*, wobbling *n*, wobbulation *n*; **~ des Strahlstroms** spot wobble

Wobbelton *m* tone frequency run

Wobbelung *f* sweeping *n*, wobbling *n*, wobbulation *n*

Wobbler *m* wobbulator *n*, sweep-frequency signal generator

Wochenendprogramm *n* weekend programme

Wochenquerschnitt *m* weekly summary, weekly round-up

Wochenrückblick *m* (Nachrichten) weekly news magazine

Wochenschau *f* newsreel *n*

Wolfram *n* tungsten *n*

Wort* *n* (R) spoken word programme

Wortarchiv *n* script library

Wortlänge *f* (EDV) word length

Wortmeldung *f* item with newsreader on camera, item with newsreader in vision, vision story (coll.); ~ *f* (Zitat) straight read

Wortprogramm *n* spoken word programme

Wortsendung *f* spoken word broadcast

X

Xenonlampe *f* xenon lamp

Y

Yagiantenne *f* yagi aerial, yagi *n* (coll.)

Y-Signal *n* luminance signal, y-signal *n*

Z

Zackenschrift *f* variable-area sound track

Zähler *m* counter *n*

Zählerschrank *m* meter cupboard

Zählimpuls *m* counting pulse, meter pulse

Zahnantrieb *m* gear drive

Zahnkranzrolle *f* toothed wheel rim, gear rim, gear ring

Zahnrad *n* gear wheel, toothed wheel, cog wheel

Zahntrommel *f* sprocket *n*, sprocket wheel

Zarge *f* (Lautsprecher) cabinet *n*, enclosure *n*; ~ *f* (Plattenspieler) plinth *n*

ZDF *n* (Zweites Deutsches Fernsehen) German Television ZDF

Zeichen *n* signal *n*, sign *n*, cue *n*, mark *n*; ~ *n* (EDV) character *n*

Zeichenbüro *n* drawing office, drafting office

Zeichendichte *f* (EDV) bit density

Zeichenkarton *m* art board, fashion board

Zeichentrick *m* animation *n*, animated diagram, animated cartoon

Zeichentrickfilm *m* animated cartoon film

Zeichenvorlage *f* drawing pattern

Zeichner *m* animator *n*, designer *n*, draughtsman *n*; **grafischer** ~ *m* graphic artist; **technischer** ~ technical draughtsman

Zeichnung *f* drawing *n*, design *n*, diagram *n*, plan *n*, sketch *n*; ~ *f* (Bildeindruck) contour impression

Zeigeranzeige *f* pointer reading

Zeigerinstrument *n* indicator

instrument
Zeile *f* (TV) line *n*, scanning line
Zeilen schinden (fam.) to pad out a story
Zeilenablenktransformator *m* line output transformer (LOPT)
Zeilenablenkung *f* horizontal deflection, horizontal sweep, line scanning
Zeilenabtastung *f* line scanning, line blanking
Zeilenamplitude *f* line amplitude
Zeilenaustastimpuls *m* line blanking pulse, horizontal blanking pulse (US)
Zeilendauer *f* line duration, line period
Zeilendrucker *m* (EDV) line printer, line-at-a-time printer
Zeilendurchlauf *m* line traversal
Zeileneinschwinger *m* scan rings *n* *pl*
Zeileneinstellung *f* line posting
Zeilenfangregler *m* horizontal hold
zeilenfrei *adj* line-free *adj*, spot-wobbled *adj*
Zeilenfrequenz *f* line frequency, horizontal frequency (US)
Zeilengleichlaufsignal *n* line synchronisation signal
Zeilenhonorar *n* linage *n*
Zeilennorm *f* line standard
Zeilenoffset *n* line offset
Zeilenraster *m* line-scanning pattern
Zeilenrauschen *n* line noise, low-frequency noise
Zeilenreißen *n* line-tearing *n*
Zeilenrücklauf *m* line flyback, horizontal flyback (US)
Zeilenrücklaufzeit *f* line flyback period
zeilensequent *adj* line-sequential *adj*
Zeilenspratzer *m* line jitter
Zeilensprung *m* interlaced scanning, line interlace
zeilensynchron *adj* line-

synchronous *adj*
Zeilensynchronimpuls *m* line synchronising pulse, line pulse, horizontal synchronising pulse
Zeilenversatz *m* line-pulling *n*
Zeilenvorschub *m* (EDV) line feed
Zeilenzahl *f* number of lines
Zeilenzeit *f* line period
Zeit *f* time *n*; **die ~ nehmen** time *v*, clock *v*
Zeitablenkgenerator *m* sweep generator, time-base generator
Zeitablenkung *f* time base, time-base deflection, sweep *n*
Zeitansage *f* (R) time announcement, time check; ~ *f* (Telefon) speaking-clock announcement
Zeitaufnahme *f* time exposure, time shot
Zeitbasis *f* time base; **angestoßene** ~ triggered time base; **getriggerte** ~ triggered time base
Zeitdehner *m* slow motion
Zeitdehneraufnahme *f* high-speed picture, slow-motion picture, high-speed shot
Zeitdehnerkamera *f* high-speed camera, slow-motion camera
Zeitdehnung *f* (Kamera) high-speed effect, high-speed shooting, high-speed camerawork; ~ *f* (Oszilloskop) sweep magnification
Zeiteichung *f* time calibration
Zeitfehlerkorrektur *f* (MAZ) time-base error correction
Zeitfestsetzung *f* timing *n*
Zeitfunk *m* (R) radio talks and current affairs programmes *n pl*
Zeitgeschehen *n* (TV) television current affairs programmes *n pl*
Zeitimpuls *m* timing pulse, clock pulse
zeitkonstant *adj* constant with time
Zeitkonstante *f* time-constant *n*
Zeitkritik *f* current affairs commentary, topical comment
Zeitlupe *f* time-lens *n*, slow-motion

Zeitlupe
196

effect; ~ *f* (Tempo) slow motion

Zeitlupentempo *n* slow motion

Zeitlupenverfahren *n* slow-motion method

Zeitmarke *f* time marker

Zeitmarkengenerator *m* time-marker generator

Zeitmultiplexdekoder *m* time-division multiplex decoder (TDM decoder)

zeitnah *adj* topical *adj*

Zeitplan *m* time-schedule *n*, time-table *n*

Zeitraffer *m* stop motion, quick motion, time lapse, speeded-up action; ~ *m* (Gerät) quick-motion camera, quick-motion apparatus, stop-motion camera, time-lapse equipment, time-lapse motion camera

Zeitrafferaufnahme *f* single-picture taking, stop motion, time-lapse shooting

Zeitraffung *f* quick-motion effect, stop-motion effect

Zeitsprung *m* time leap

Zeitstück *n* period play

Zeitüberschreitung *f* overrun *n*

Zeitung *f* newspaper *n*, paper *n*, journal *n*

Zeitungsarchiv *n* reference library

Zeitungsausschnitt *m* cutting *n*, clipping *n*

Zeitungsleute *plt* journalists *n pl*, pressmen *n pl*, newspapermen *n pl* (US), the press

Zeitunterschreitung *f* underrun *n*

Zeitversatz *m* time lag

Zeitverschiebung *f* time shift

zeitversetzt *adj* deferred *adj*

Zeitvertrag *m* unestablished staff contract

Zeitvertragsinhaber *m* member of unestablished staff

Zeitzähler *m* time recorder

Zeitzeichen *n* time signal, time pips *n pl*

Zelle *f* cell *n*; **fotoelektrische** ~

photoelectric cell (PEC)

Zellhornfilm *m* nitrocellulose stock, celluloid film

Zenerdiode *f* Zener diode

Zenereffekt *m* Zener effect

Zensur *f* censorship *n*

Zensurkarte *f* censor's certificate

Zentralarchiv *n* main reference library

Zentralbatterieanschluß (ZB) *m* common-battery connection (CB)

Zentralbatterievermittlung *f* common-battery exchange

Zentralbedienplatz *m* central operation position

Zentraldisposition (ZD) *f* production planning department

Zentraleinheit *f* (EDV) central processing unit (CPU), processing unit, processor *n*

Zentralgeräteraum *m* central apparatus room (CAR)

Zentralredaktion *f* (aktuell) centre desk

Zentralregistratur *f* central registry

Zerhacker *m* chopper *n*, alternator *n*, interrupter *n*, vibrator *n*

Zerlegung des Spektrums decomposition of spectrum, splitting of spectrum

Zerreißblende *f* dragon's-teeth wipe

Zerreißen *n* tearing *n*; ~ **des Bildes** picture-tearing *n*

zerstreuen *v* (opt.) diffuse *v*, disperse *v*, scatter *v*

Zerstreuung *f* (opt.) diffusion *n*, dispersion *n*, dispersal *n*, scattering *n*

Zerstreuungskreis *m* circle of confusion, coma *n*

Zerstreuungslinse *f* diverging lens, divergent lens, negative lens

Zerstreuungspunkt *m* point of divergence, focus of divergence, centre of dispersion, virtual focus

Ziehbereich *m* pull-in range, lock-in range

ziehen *v* (Kopie) print *v*; ~ *v*

(Blende) focus *v*
Ziehen des Bildes
   frame rolling, picture slip
Ziehkreis *m* pulling-in circuit
Zifferanzeigegerät *n* digital reader
Zimmerantenne *f* indoor aerial,
   room aerial
zischen *v* hiss *v*, whistle *v*
Zischen *n* hissing *n*, frying *n*,
   whistling *n*
Zone *f* zone *n*, area *n*;
   abgeschattete ~ shadow zone,
   shadow area
Zoom *m* zoom lens
zoomen *v* zoom *v*
Zoomen *n* zooming *n*
Zoomfahrt *f* zoom travel
Zubehör *n* accessories *n pl*, fittings
   n pl, attachments *n pl*
Zubehörgerät *n* accessory
   equipment
Zubringer *m* (fam.) *s.*
   Zubringerleitung
Zubringerleitung *f* programme line,
   transmission line, local end
zudecken *v* (Ton) drown out *v*
Zuführung *f* (Leitung) feed line,
   supply line, contribution circuit;
   ~ *f* (Vorgang) supply *n*, feed *n*
Zuführungsleitung *f* feed line,
   supply line, contribution circuit
Zugabe *f* supplement *n*, bonus *n*; ~ *f*
   (Thea.) encore *n*
Zugfilm *m* (Labor) leader film
Zugnummer *f* audience-puller *n*
Zugriff *m* (EDV) access *n*; **direkter** ~
   random access, direct access;
   sequentieller ~ sequential access;
   wahlfreier ~ random access, direct
   access
Zugriffszeit *f* (EDV) access time
Zugseil *n* halyard *n*
Zuhörer *m* listener *n*
Zuhörerschaft *f* audience *n*
zukreisen *v* (Blende) iris in *v*
Zulaufmenge *f* flow rate
Zulieferprogramm *n* supply
   programme
Zuluft *f* air supply, air intake

Zumischung *f* admixture *n*
Zündkreis *m* firing circuit, ignition
   circuit; ~ *m* (TV) unblanking
   circuit
Zunge *f* (Mus.) tongue *n*; ~ *f*
   (Frequenzmesser) reed *n*
Zuordnung *f* allocation *n*; ~ *f*
   (Person) attachment *n*
zurückhalten *v* (tech.) retard *v*; ~ *v*
   (Nachricht) hold back *v*
zurücknehmen *v* (Licht) take down
   v
Zusammenfassung *f* summary *n*; ~ *f*
   (Drehbuch) synopsis *n*
zusammenschalten *v* interconnect *v*
Zusammenschaltung *f*
   interconnection *n*; ~ *f* (Sender)
   grouping *n*, switching to common
   programme, hook-up *n*
zusammenschneiden *v* (F) assemble
   v, join *v*, mount *v*, splice *v*, cut
   together *v*; ~ *v* (Band) splice *v*
zusammenstellen *v* (Text) compile *v*,
   put together *v*
zusammenstreichen *v* edit down *v*,
   trim *v*, tighten up *v*
Zusatz *m* supplement *n*, addition *n*,
   addendum *n*
Zusatzgerät *n* accessory instrument,
   ancillary apparatus, attachment *n*,
   ancillary unit
Zusatzlicht *n* booster light
Zusatzprogramm *n* additional
   programme
zuschalten *v* connect to *v*, switch on
   v, hook up *v*, close *v*, to put in
   circuit; ~ *v* (sich) (Sender) opt in *v*
Zuschalten eines Senders hook-up
   n
Zuschalter *m* routing switch
Zuschaltung *f* putting in circuit,
   insertion *n*
Zuschauer *m* spectator *n*; ~ *m* (TV)
   viewer *n*; ~ *m* (F) cinema-goer *n*,
   moviegoer *n* (US)
Zuschauerauskunft* *f* programme
   inquiries* *n pl*
Zuschauerbefragung *f* television
   audience survey, audience

research survey, audience survey

Zuschauerbefragung* f audience research*

Zuschauerforschung* f audience research*

Zuschauermessung f audience rating

Zuschauerpost* f television programme correspondence*, viewer's letters* n pl

Zuschauerzahl f size of audience

Zuschneider m head dressmaker

Zuspielband n insert tape; ~ n (Mischband) mixing tape

zuspielen v play in v, feed v, insert v, inject v

Zuspielleitung f contribution circuit, reverse programme circuit

Zuspielmaschine f remote replay machine

Zuspielung f remote contribution inject, remote contribution insert

Zustand m state n, condition n; **latenter** ~ latent condition

zutasten v blank v, suppress v

Zutastung f blanking n, suppression n

Zuteilungsblatt n allocation sheet

Zuverlässigkeit f (Mensch) reliability n; ~ f (Gerät) dependability n

zuziehen v (Zoom) fade out v, fade down v

Zweckmeldung f inspired news item

Zweibandabtaster m Sepmag telecine

Zweibandabtastung f Sepmag telecine system

Zweibandkopierung f double-track printing

Zweibandprojektor m Sepmag projector

Zweibandverfahren n Sepmag n

Zweidrahtleitung f two-wire circuit

Zweiebenenantenne f twin-stock aerial, twin stock

Zweiereinstellung f two-shot n

Zweietagenantenne f two-level aerial

Zweiflügelblende f two-blade shutter, two-wing shutter

Zweiformatbildprojektor m dual-standard projector

Zweigleitung f (Ant.) spur feeder

zweikanalig adj two-channel adj, double-channel adj

Zweinormen- (in Zus.) dual-standard adj

Zweiphasennetz n two-phase mains n pl

zweipolig adj bipolar adj, two-pole adj

Zweiraumkassette f double-chamber magazine

Zweiseitenbandempfänger m double-sideband receiver

Zweispur f dual track

Zweispurmaschine f dual-track tape recorder, twin-track tape recorder

Zweistrahl m dual trace, dual beam

Zweistrahloszillograf m double-beam oscilloscope

Zweistreifenverfahren n double-headed system

zweistreifig adj double-headed adj

Zweitbelichtung f double exposure, re-exposure n

Zweitempfänger m secondary receiver, second home set

Zweitentwicklung f secondary development

Zweitsendung f (R) repeat broadcast, repeat n; ~ f (TV) second showing

Zweiweggleichrichter m full-wave rectifier

Zwischenabbildungsobjektiv n intermediate image-forming lens, auxiliary lens

Zwischenansage f intermediate announcement; ~ f (R) cue n

Zwischenbasisschaltung f circuit with combined coupling

Zwischenduplikat n intermediate

dupe
Zwischenfrequenz (ZF) *f*
intermediate frequency (IF)
Zwischenfrequenzumsetzung *f*
intermediate-frequency
transposition
Zwischenfrequenzverfahren *n*
intermediate-frequency method
Zwischenmodulation *f*
intermodulation *n*
Zwischenmusik *f* interval music,
interlude music
Zwischennegativ *n* (Farbe)
internegative *n*, intermediate
negative; ~ *n* (schwarz-weiß)
duplicated negative, duplicate
negative
Zwischenplatte *f* intermediate plate
Zwischenpositiv *n* fine-grain print,
lavender print
Zwischenpunkteinspeisung *f*
intermediate-point feed
Zwischenpunktflimmern *n* interdot
flicker
Zwischenrad *n* idler *n*
Zwischenring *m* adapter ring,
intermediate ring; ~ **für**
Nahaufnahme close-up adapter
Zwischenschaltleistungsverlust *m*
insertion loss
Zwischenschaltleistungsverstärkung
f insertion gain
Zwischenschaltung *f* insertion *n*,
interposition *n*, interconnection *n*,
interpolation *n*
Zwischenschicht *f* intermediate
layer

Zwischenschnitt *m* cut-away *n*,
insert *n*, continuity shot
Zwischenschuß *m* cut-away shot
Zwischenspeicher *m* (EDV)
intermediate store, scratchpad
memory (SPM), temporary store
Zwischensprung *m* (TV) interlace *n*
Zwischentitel *m* title-link *n*, time-
link *n*, information caption
Zwischenträger *m* subcarrier *n*
Zwischenträgerverfahren *n*
intercarrier sound system
Zwischenübertrager *m* matching
transformer
Zwischenverbindung *f* (Progr.)
junction *n*, continuity *n*
Zwischenverstärker *m* repeater *n*,
intermediate amplifier
Zwischenzeile *f* interline *n*,
interlace *n*; **schlechte** ~ line
pairing, bad interlace
Zwischenzeilenabtastung *f*
interlaced scanning
Zwischenzeilenbild *n* interlaced
picture
Zwischenzeilenflimmern *n* interline flicker, wave flicker
Zwischenzeilenverfahren *n*
interlacing *n*, interlaced scanning,
scanning interlace system
Zwitschern *n* chirping *n*, birdies *n*
pl, canaries *n pl*
Zwittersticker *m* sexless connector,
hermaphrodite connector
zyklisch *adj* (EDV) cyclic *adj*
Zyklus *m* (EDV) cycle *n*
Zykluszeit *f* (EDV) cycle time